You-Choose-the-Ending SKiTS For Youth Ministry

by
Stephen Parolini

Group
Loveland, Colorado

DEDICATION

This book is dedicated to the many youth group members I worked with at First Baptist Church of Loveland, Colorado. Thanks for all the great dinner theater productions . . . and your friendship.

Credits
Book Acquisitions Editors: Mike Nappa and Amy Simpson
Editor: Amy Simpson
Managing Editor: Michael D. Warden
Chief Creative Officer: Joani Schultz
Copy Editor: Helen Turnbull
Art Director and Designer: Jean Bruns
Cover Art Director: Helen H. Lannis
Cover Designer: Joel Armstrong
Computer Graphic Artist: Joyce Douglas
Cover Illustrator: Dennas Davis
Production Manager: Gingar Kunkel

Unless otherwise noted, Scriptures quoted from The Youth Bible, New Century Version, copyright © 1991 by Word Publishing, Dallas, Texas 75039. Used by permission.

Library of Congress Cataloging-in-Publication Data
Parolini, Stephen, 1959–
    You-choose-the-ending skits for youth ministry / by Stephen
Parolini.
        p.   cm.
    Includes indexes.
    ISBN 1-55945-627-2
    1. Drama in Christian education.   2. Church group work with youth.
I. Title.
BV1534.4.P37   1997
246'.72--dc21   96-37023
                                                            CIP

10 9 8 7 6 5 4 3   06 05 04 03 02 01 00
Printed in the United States of America.

Visit our Web site: www.grouppublishing.com

CONTENTS

CHOOSE-YOUR-OWN INTRODUCTION

Choose your favorite introduction type from the following list, then read that introduction to this book:

A. . . . Since Sliced Bread
B. To the Seasoned Veteran
C. Minimalism

A. ...SINCE SLICED BREAD

Hey there, skit fans! This is your lucky day. Yes, you now hold in your hands the greatest skit book since . . . well . . . since the last great skit book. But hey, this one's really different. In fact, you've probably never seen a book like this. Sure, it's packed full of great skits for kids to perform and discuss, but there's something just a little different about *You-Choose-the-Ending Skits for Youth Ministry.* You see, each skit has three different endings. That's right! It's like getting fifty-seven skits for the price of nineteen. What a bargain!

So what are you waiting for? Skim the table of contents, the "you can find it here" theme index, or the easy-to-use Scripture index (p. 144), and find a skit your kids can get excited about. Oh, and you might want to skim the "Rest of the Introduction" on the following pages for a few tips on how to use this book. You know it *is* a good book—a *really* good book. I happen to think it's one of my best . . . so call all your friends and have them buy up all the copies . . .

B. TO THE SEASONED VETERAN

Welcome to a whole new frontier in the world of skits. Since you picked up this book to peruse it, you're probably intimately familiar with the skit concept and how it can enhance your youth ministry program. And you're probably looking for another book of creative, insightful, and thought-provoking skits to use with your group. You know, the kind of book that explores issues kids are dealing with today and that helps them see how their faith connects with those issues. Well, congratulations on your wisdom and impeccable taste. This is the book you were looking for.

Since you're the kind of person who really knows skits, you probably don't need to read the rest of the introduction, so . . . Wait! I've misjudged you. Of course you want to read the rest of the introduction. You're thorough and always willing to go the extra mile for your kids. And hey, it's only a few paragraphs. So go ahead; skip to "The Rest of the Introduction" on the following pages. And thanks for choosing *You-Choose-the-Ending Skits for Youth Ministry.* I think you made a great choice.

C. MINIMALISM

These are skits. Use them. You'll like them.

THE REST OF THE INTRODUCTION

As you can tell by this introduction, *You-Choose-the-Ending Skits for Youth Ministry* isn't your typical collection of skits. The first and most unique aspect of this book is that each skit includes three very different endings, each usable on its own to create a complete skit suitable for discussion. (See "Using the Ending Options" below for a lot of interesting ways to use these endings.) That means you're really getting fifty-seven skits rather than nineteen. Second, these skits require minimal blocking (um . . . for you newcomers, that means movement or action on the stage) so they can be used without much (or any) rehearsal. Third, each of the skits requires just a few actors, so even small youth groups can enjoy using them. Fourth, many of the skits are interactive: They creatively involve the audience. And fifth, the dialogue in the skits is real—with drama, suspense, and just the right touch of humor. Instead of puns and parody, you get real life. OK, you may also get just a little bit of wackiness, depending on the skit ending you choose.

Still with me? Good. Skim through the table of contents, the theme index, or the Scripture index (p. 144) to get an idea of what's in this volume. Then grab your Hollywood-bound (or not) youth group students, check out the "Using the Ending Options" section that follows, and get your kids thinking about how faith impacts all aspects of their lives with these *You-Choose-the-Ending Skits for Youth Ministry.*

USING THE ENDING OPTIONS

So how do you use these skits? Well, I'm glad you asked. (You *did* ask, didn't you?) Here's the scoop:

Each skit in this book includes three distinctly different ending options designed to stimulate unique discussion on the themes. Somewhere around the halfway point in each skit, the skit stops and can branch off in any of three specific directions (as indicated by the ending options listed right there at the halfway point). You can use these optional endings in a variety of ways. Here are a few ideas:

● **Choose Your Own Adventure:** Have the actors practice all three endings. Then after they perform the skit up to the "freeze" point, read aloud the three ending option titles, and have the audience vote on which ending they'd like the actors to use.

● **Potluck:** Have the actors practice all three endings, then have someone in the audience pick a number out of a hat (one, two, or three). Have the actors perform the skit ending that corresponds to the number the audience member picked.

● **Surprise, Surprise:** Have the actors practice only the first half of the skit. Then have the actors or the audience choose an ending (based on the title or by choosing a number between one and three), and have the actors finish the skit without knowing how it will end.

● **Classic:** Read through all the ending options, and choose which one you want to use for your discussion time. Then have the actors prepare only this ending along with the first half of the skit. When they perform the skit, have the actors ignore the freeze point and complete the skit as if it had only one ending.

● **Bucket o' Skits:** Have the actors practice all three endings. Have them perform all three, then have the class discuss the questions that are unique for each ending.

● **Improvisational:** Do you have some truly creative actors in your group? Use their skills, and allow them to improvise their own ending after the freeze point in the skit. You'll need to come up with your own questions (although many of the existing ending questions might apply), but the resulting discussion may be worth the extra effort. This ending option often works best after you've already performed one of the prepared endings.

● **The Skit According to . . . :** Add another ending option to all skits simply by asking kids to complete the skit according to the way they think it might *really* end, based on their lives and the people they know at school, at home, and at church. Remind kids to be sensitive to others when performing an ending like this so they don't put down real people with their words or actions.

GENERAL SKIT NOTES

● While the skits will work best with some rehearsal (at least reading through the lines and practicing the actions), they can be used on an impromptu basis, too. This can be a fun way to involve kids who wouldn't normally choose to act in a skit.

● The questions that follow each skit ending include many questions unique to that ending and one or two common questions that apply to all the endings for that skit.

● Since very few props and blocking instructions are needed to make these skits work, your budding actors might want to add more props, set design, and actions to the skits. The more your kids invest in the skits, the more impact the skits will have as discussion starters.

● Use the skits in a variety of settings. You can plan a meeting to address a specific topic and use a related-theme skit to introduce the topic. Or you can make the skit the focus of the meeting. You can use the skits with your whole church, too, to help parents and other adults learn more about your teenagers' world. Or you may want to have your group present the skits (using the ideas in the "Using the Ending Options" section on page 6) to members of another youth group.

Please note that if you use the "Choose Your Own Adventure," "Potluck," "Surprise, Surprise," or "Bucket o' Skits" method, you'll need props for all possible endings, and you may need to add another actor or two for some endings. (The ending options list for each skit tells you if you need any other actors.)

There are probably many other ways to use these skits. Have your kids brainstorm about a few more. Then use this book until it's dog-eared and falling apart. Remember, each skit is like three skits in one. Enjoy them all.

WHAT'S A HEAVEN FOR?

SCRIPTURE:

Matthew 7:21-23;
Matthew 18:2-4;
and John 14:2-3

THEMES:

Disagreement,
friendship, heaven,
sharing faith

THE SETTING:

Three teenagers are coming out of a theater, discussing a movie's interpretation of heaven. As the three characters read their lines, have them walk around the meeting room (as if walking home) rather than stand still onstage.

THE PROPS:

You'll need three chairs (if you use ending option two).

THE CHARACTERS:

Stacy, a teenage girl
Jennifer, a teenage girl
Juan, a teenage guy
Talk Show Host (if you use ending option two), an enthusiastic man or woman
Two Kids (if you use ending option three), who pretend to be a car

THE SCRIPT:

JUAN: Well, what did you think?

STACY: *(Sincerely)* Wow.

JENNIFER: Wow? You thought that movie deserved a "wow"?

STACY: Maybe even a double-wow.

JENNIFER: You're kidding, right?

STACY: No. I really liked that movie.

JUAN: It certainly got *me* thinking.

JENNIFER: *(To Juan)* You mean *you* liked it too?

JUAN: I didn't say that. I said it got me thinking.

STACY: I loved what the movie said about heaven.

JENNIFER: *(Puzzled)* Hello, Stacy? This wasn't a movie about heaven. It was a black comedy about three messed-up kids who kill themselves because they'd done everything they wanted to in life.

STACY:	And your point is . . .
JENNIFER:	My point is that this film didn't have anything to do with heaven.
JUAN:	I wouldn't say that, Jen. What about the ending? You know, when the three characters promised to meet again . . . in the afterlife?
JENNIFER:	What about it?
STACY:	I think the film was saying that no matter what terrible things you've done in life, no matter how many mistakes you've made, there's always room for one more in heaven.
JENNIFER:	*(Surprised)* And you believe that?
STACY:	Sure. Why would God want to hurt people anyway? Juan, you go to church. Didn't you tell me once that God loved everybody the same?
JUAN:	Yes, but . . .
STACY:	Then I rest my case.
JENNIFER:	I still don't see the connection. Nothing was said about heaven. They just said they'd meet again. Ever heard of reincarnation?
STACY:	They weren't talking about reincarnation.
JENNIFER:	Sure they were. It's a well-known fact that reincarnation is in vogue these days. I'm sure the filmmaker wanted to slip his beliefs in there somewhere. And by the way, I tend to believe this reincarnation thing.
JUAN:	Ladies, I think you're missing the point of the film.
STACY:	And that point is . . .
JUAN:	I think what they were saying is that if you choose a reckless lifestyle on earth, you pay for it in the end. There was no hope for those three kids. That was the irony of their final goodbyes.

(Both girls stop and stare at Juan.)

● ● ● ●

Freeze the skit. Then have participants or audience members choose from the following ending options to finish the skit. Choose additional actors if necessary.

1. Charlie Brown (no new characters)

2. Talk Show (new character: Talk Show Host)

3. Accidental Tourist (new characters: two kids who pretend to be a car)

● ● ● ●

1. CHARLIE BROWN

JENNIFER:	Excuse me?
STACY:	No hope?
JENNIFER:	You're not going to turn all "Christian" on us again, are you?
STACY:	Yeah. What's with the sudden evangelizing tone?
JUAN:	I just said . . .
JENNIFER:	*(Interrupting)* It's not what you said. It's what you were about to say.
STACY:	Right. You were just going to climb on your soapbox to tell us that no one gets to heaven unless they go to church . . .
JENNIFER:	*(Finishing Stacy's sentence)* . . . or believe the way you do.
JUAN:	Look, I wasn't going to . . .
STACY:	*(Interrupting)* We know your kind. The only opinions that count are yours. You never have any room for any new ideas.
JUAN:	I was just stating my . . .
JENNIFER:	*(Interrupting)* And we don't have time for your narrowmindedness.
JUAN:	But I was just going to say . . .

(Stacy and Jennifer storm off.)

JUAN:	Why is it that whenever they remember I'm a Christian, I get no respect?

QUESTIONS

- When have you felt the way Juan did?
- Do you ever feel as if people disrespect Christians? Explain.
- Which of the three characters are you most like? Which one are your friends most like?
- What does this skit say about the way people view the afterlife? What do you believe about heaven?

Read Matthew 7:21-23; Matthew 18:2-4; and John 14:2-3.

- What do these verses tell us about heaven?
- What are appropriate ways for Christians to share their beliefs about heaven with non-Christian friends?

2. TALK SHOW

(Talk Show Host enters the scene and pulls Stacy, Jennifer, and Juan over to three chairs and has them sit as if they are panel members on a talk show. The host virtually takes over the skit.)

TALK SHOW HOST:	Yes, it's time for the "Who Do You Think You Are?" show! I'm your host, Pat Prickly. Welcome Jennifer, Stacy, and Juan.

(Jennifer, Stacy, and Juan look around, bewildered.)

JUAN:	Um . . . excuse me. What are we . . .
TALK SHOW HOST:	*(Interrupting)* Our topic today is the afterlife. Stacy, you have some strong opinions on what happens when people die. Share them with our viewers.
STACY:	Mm . . . OK. I believe that everyone will make it to heaven. We all make mistakes, and I believe God is merciful enough to let everyone in.
JUAN:	Wait a minute, Stacy. Did I hear you say the word "everyone"?
STACY:	Sure. Why would the Creator choose to destroy his creations?
TALK SHOW HOST:	Good point, Stacy. What do you think about that, Jennifer?
JENNIFER:	I'm not so sure there *is* a Creator. But I *am* sure that people get plenty of second chances in life. That's what reincarnation is all about.
JUAN:	*(Getting a little upset)* This isn't a discussion about reincarnation. It's about the afterlife. It's about heaven. And believe me, not everyone's gonna make it in, Stacy!

(Stacy glares at Juan.)

TALK SHOW HOST:	Wow! This is getting interesting. Stacy, let him have it!
STACY:	OK, Wise Juan. Tell me this: Am I going to heaven?
JUAN:	I'm not the one who decides, but are you a Christian?
JENNIFER:	Here it comes.
STACY:	I believe in oneness and unity and . . .
TALK SHOW HOST:	*(To Juan)* I believe that's a no, Juan.
JUAN:	Then based on what the Bible says, no. You won't get in.
STACY:	*(Angrily)* You self-righteous snob! Who are you to say who can make it into heaven?

(At this point, all three kids begin arguing with each other while the Talk Show Host wraps things up. Jennifer, Stacy, and Juan can say the lines below simultaneously or improvise as necessary until the end of the skit.)

JENNIFER:	What's the big deal here? There is no such thing as heaven. Everyone gets a second chance when they die, but that's all about

reincarnation, not heaven. The Bible? Who said the Bible is the authority on what happens after you die? Sure it's an interesting book, but that doesn't mean it's right.

JUAN: The Bible clearly states that only those who believe in Christ will make it to heaven. I don't care if you're the nicest person in the whole world. If you don't have Jesus as your Savior, you're out. That's it! Finito!

STACY: I'm a good person, and I deserve heaven as much as the next guy. And as far as this reincarnation thing is concerned, it's all a bunch of baloney. What are you going to be reincarnated as, Jennifer, a rat? a pig? And Juan, I'm beginning to wish everyone *didn't* go to heaven the more I hear *you* talking!

TALK SHOW HOST: Wow! What a show. Once again we've managed to take three good friends and turn them into enemies right before your eyes. That's it for this week's edition of "Who Do You Think You Are?" I'm your host, Pat Prickly, saying good night and good luck.

QUESTIONS ▼ ▼ ▼ ▼ ▼ ▼ ▼ ▼ ▼ ▼ ▼ ▼

● Why do people have such strong opinions about the afterlife and heaven?

● Why did the three teenagers so easily become angry at one another in this skit? When have you been in a similar situation?

● How do you feel when you tell your friends what you believe about heaven? How do your beliefs factor into the way your friends relate to you?

Read Matthew 7:21-23; Matthew 18:2-4; and John 14:2-3.

● What do these verses tell us about heaven?

● What are appropriate ways for Christians to tell their friends what they believe about heaven?

▲ ▲ ▲ ▲ ▲ ▲ ▲ ▲ ▲ ▲ ▲ ▲ ▲ ▲ ▲

3. ACCIDENTAL TOURIST

STACY: So what you're trying to say is . . . none of those kids are getting into heaven? I'm sorry, Juan, but you are way off base here. Jen may be missing the boat with that reincarnation bit, but at least she sees some hope for the people in the movie. Doesn't the Bible say God is merciful? I think a merciful God would let everyone into heaven.

JUAN: Everyone?

STACY: OK, maybe Hitler won't make it. But everyone else should.

(While Stacy is speaking, the two kids who pretend to be a car make a loud screeching sound and run into all three, knocking them—carefully—to the ground. Then Stacy and

Jennifer get up and walk to the front of the room. Juan slips away to the back of the room or offstage.)

JENNIFER:	What was that all about?
STACY:	I'm not sure. *(Looking around)* Where are we?
JENNIFER:	Last thing I remember, we were walking home from a movie with Juan . . .
STACY:	*(Completing Jennifer's thought)* . . . and then we heard that awful screeching sound . . .

(Jennifer and Stacy suddenly look at each other as they realize what just happened.)

JENNIFER AND STACY:	*(Together)* We're dead!
JENNIFER:	Oh no! What are we going to do?
STACY:	My poor mom.
JENNIFER:	What about Juan?
STACY:	*(Looks around the room, searching for Juan.)* Surely he's dead, too? He was standing right next to us.
JENNIFER:	Then where is he?
STACY:	Maybe he's still hanging on to life—you know, the way they do in those emergency-rescue TV shows.
JENNIFER:	Hold that thought, Stace. *(Pauses.)* Look around.

(Stacy looks around.)

JENNIFER:	Are you thinking what I'm thinking?
STACY:	I think so. We're in heaven, aren't we?
JENNIFER:	Heaven? No way. We're in some kind of limbo waiting to be rein-carnated.
STACY:	*(Getting angry with Jennifer)* Hardly. Don't you hear that harp music?
JENNIFER:	*(Angrily)* Harp music? That's not harp music. That's the sound of thousands of souls singing as they await their new lives.
STACY:	You've got to be kidding!
JENNIFER:	What is it with you? Can't you admit when you're wrong?
STACY:	Who says I'm wrong? This sure looks like . . . *(Pauses and then suddenly becomes concerned with her situation.)* Um . . . is it getting hot in here?

JENNIFER:	(Fanning herself) Sure is. Maybe we're being reincarnated somewhere in the Sahara.
STACY:	Or heaven's air conditioning is broken.
JENNIFER:	Look over there. Hey, isn't that . . .
JENNIFER AND STACY:	(Together, horrified) Adolph Hitler!

QUESTIONS ▼ ▼ ▼ ▼ ▼ ▼ ▼ ▼ ▼ ▼ ▼ ▼

● How would you feel if you were Stacy or Jennifer? What truth were they about to discover?

Read Matthew 7:21-23; Matthew 18:2-4; and John 14:2-3.

● What do these verses say about heaven?

● How do you feel, knowing that the Bible says only a select few will end up in heaven?

● How do you respond to friends who believe they're going to heaven just because they're good people?

● Why would God choose to invite only a select few to join him in heaven?

● How would your friends respond to the message of this skit? How would you explain the skit to them?

● How do you feel, knowing that people who love God will get the gift of heaven?

▲ ▲ ▲ ▲ ▲ ▲ ▲ ▲ ▲ ▲ ▲ ▲ ▲ ▲ ▲

SO WHAT IF I'M LATE?

SCRIPTURE:

Luke 6:31 and
Luke 19:12-26

THEMES:

Honesty, parents
and stepparents,
responsibility, trust

THE SETTING:

Two parents are standing inside their living room as they await the
arrival of their teenage son.

THE PROPS:

None

THE CHARACTERS:

Tim, a teenage boy
Dad, Tim's father
Mom, Tim's mother
Tony (if you use ending option two), Tim's friend
Mr. and Mrs. Martin (if you use ending option two), Tony's parents

THE SCRIPT:

DAD: *(Pacing)* What time is it?

MOM: *(Watching Dad pace back and forth)* One minute later than the last time you asked.

DAD: *(Worried)* He should've been home an hour ago.

MOM: What do you think happened?

DAD: I don't want to think about it. He's always been on time before.

MOM: Surely we would've heard if he'd been in an accident?

DAD: *(Suddenly alarmed)* What if he took that turn on 83 too fast? No one would see his car if he slipped down the side of the hill.

MOM: *(Shaking her head)* Don't be so melodramatic. I'm sure he's just running late.

DAD: But he's supposed to call when he's running late.

MOM: Maybe he couldn't get to a phone.

DAD: *(Looks at Mom)* Honey, there's a cell phone in the car.

MOM: Well I'm not going to worry too much about him. He's a big boy.

DAD:	*(Starting to get a little angry)* Obviously not big enough if he doesn't have the decency to call when he's going to be late.
MOM:	*(Trying to calm Dad)* Just don't be too tough on him. You said yourself that he's never done this before. We're all entitled to a few mistakes.
DAD:	I know, but if he didn't call just because he "forgot," then I'm not going to be very happy.
MOM:	*(Running to an imaginary window and peeking out)* Wait! Is that a car I hear?
DAD:	Let's just hope we don't see red and blue flashing lights.

Freeze the skit. Then have participants or audience members choose from the following ending options to finish the skit. Choose additional actors if necessary.

1. Role Reversal (no new characters)

2. Unbelievable? (new characters: Tony and Mr. and Mrs. Martin)

3. Beaver Cleaver (no new characters)

1. Role Reversal

(Mom and Dad peer out an imaginary window as they watch a car drive up. Tim races up to the stage and enters the house.)

TIM:	Mom! Dad! I've been worried sick about you! Where have you been? I've been trying to call you for the last two hours.
DAD:	Um . . . we've been right here. Where have you been?
MOM:	You were supposed to call when you were going to be late.
TIM:	*(Insistent)* I *did* call. I called plenty of times. When you didn't answer, I started to worry, so I called all your friends, trying to track you down. That's why I didn't come home right away. I spent the last two hours trying to find you.
MOM:	But we've been here all along.
TIM:	I even called the hospitals just in case you were in an accident or Dad had a heart attack or something.
DAD:	I'm fine, really.

TIM:	But *I* didn't know that. For all I knew, you could've been shot by burglars. When you didn't answer the phone, I knew something was wrong. You always answer when I call from a friend's house.
MOM:	Honest, Tim, we didn't leave the house once.
TIM:	I'm not sure I believe you. Maybe I should ask the neighbors.
DAD:	*(As if he's hiding something)* No, don't do that. They wouldn't . . . um . . . know if we left . . . because . . . they're not home.
TIM:	Their lights are on. I'm calling. *(Walks over to imaginary phone and picks up receiver.)*
MOM:	*(Goes over and takes the phone from Tim.)* OK . . . you caught us. We did go out.
DAD:	We went over to Chuck and Marcy's for coffee and ice cream.
TIM:	Chuck and Marcy's? Of course! Why didn't you call to tell me? Why did you let me worry so much?
MOM:	*(Meekly)* I guess we got busy talking with our friends and didn't realize what time it was. We're sorry. We just weren't thinking.
DAD:	It won't happen again.
TIM:	You're right it won't. You're grounded.
DAD AND MOM:	What?
TIM:	You heard me. No more late night coffee and ice cream until you've proven yourselves trustworthy again.

(Mom and Dad give Tim a "that's not fair" look and freeze in position.)

QUESTIONS ▼ ▼ ▼ ▼ ▼ ▼ ▼ ▼ ▼ ▼ ▼ ▼

● What surprised you about this ending? How does it compare to real life?

● What implications does this skit have about trustworthiness?

● How would you react if your parents or stepparents weren't home when you expected them to be?

Read Luke 6:31.

● How does this verse apply to the parents in this skit? How does it apply to the way you relate to your parents or stepparents? What does it say about trust?

Read Luke 19:12-26.

● In this story, the person who was trustworthy in a small matter earned the most respect and reward. How does this apply to the way you should relate to your parents or stepparents?

▲ ▲ ▲ ▲ ▲ ▲ ▲ ▲ ▲ ▲ ▲ ▲ ▲ ▲

2. UNBELIEVABLE?

(Tim walks up to the stage and enters the home.)

DAD: Finally! Where have you been?

TIM: Boy, am I glad to see you guys. You're not going to believe what just happened to me.

MOM: Do I smell smoke on your clothes?

(Mom and Dad fold their arms and glare at Tim.)

MOM AND DAD: This better be good.

TIM: OK, but you'd better approach this with an open mind. It's a little unbelievable.

DAD: *(Still glaring)* We're all ears.

TIM: OK. It all started about an hour and a half ago. I was sitting in Tony's living room when we heard this huge explosion.

(Dad looks over at Mom and smirks.)

TIM: No, really! The explosion shook the house, and it seemed to come from the basement. So Tony and I raced down the hall to the basement door just in time to see Mr. Martin coming up the stairs, coughing and wheezing. There was smoke everywhere.

DAD: *(Sarcastically)* This is getting good. Go on.

TIM: I told you it was hard to believe. Anyway, he mumbled something about an experiment gone bad and collapsed to the floor. Tony ran to dial 911 and discovered that the phones were dead. Must've been the explosion or something. Anyway, I ran to the car and got the cell phone so we could call the police. That's when the house burst into flames. Tony dragged his dad out to the front lawn while I raced to get his mom out of the back room. I guess I dropped the phone when I was trying to help her outside.

MOM: *(To Dad)* At least he's got a good imagination.

TIM: Then Tony realized that the dog was still in the house. I raced back in and searched for him until the smoke got too thick. I'm afraid I couldn't get to him in time.

DAD: Tim, that's a very interesting story, but I don't buy it. I'm afraid we're going to have to ground you until you can be trusted again.

(Dad is interrupted by a knock on the door. All eyes turn toward the imaginary front door.)

MOM: *(To Dad)* Honey, are those police lights out there?

DAD: *(Angrily, to Tim)* What did you really do?

(Mom opens the door to see Tony Martin and Mr. and Mrs. Martin standing there, all huddled in blankets.)

TIM: *(To Mom and Dad)* I almost forgot—I invited the Martins to stay here until they can find another place. You always said we should help people in need.

(Mom and Dad are speechless, but they nod anyway as Tony and Mr. and Mrs. Martin enter the house.)

TIM: *(To the audience)* What does it take to get your parents to trust you these days, anyway?

QUESTIONS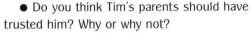

● Do you think Tim's parents should have trusted him? Why or why not?

● Why is it so difficult to build trust with parents and stepparents? What are some practical ways to build trust?

Read Luke 6:31.

● How does this verse apply to the parents in this skit? How does it apply to the way you relate to your parents or stepparents?

Read Luke 19:12-26.

● In this story, the person who was trustworthy in a small matter earned the most respect and reward. How does this apply to the way you can relate to your parents or stepparents? the way your parents or stepparents can relate to you?

3. BEAVER CLEAVER

(Tim races up to the front door of the house and enters, almost knocking over his parents, who are standing in the doorway, tapping their feet as they wait for him.)

TIM: *(Out of breath)* Gee, Mom, Dad, you waited up for me.

DAD: *(Angrily)* You're more than an hour late.

MOM: Why didn't you call?

TIM: Well, Dad, um . . . there's a good explanation for this.

DAD: Let's hear it then.

TIM: I was over at Eddie's house . . .

MOM: We know.

TIM: *(In an excited voice)* Eddie and I decided to go to the malt shop for ice cream. On the way there, the car broke down. So we had to hoof it back to Eddie's house and get his car. But then his car wouldn't start so we had to call a service station to tow the car.

DAD:	But you could've called us to let us know you were OK.
TIM:	Gee, Dad, I know. I did call once, but the line was busy. I guess I was so busy trying to figure out what to do about the car that I didn't think about how you guys might be feeling.
MOM:	We were worried sick about you.
TIM:	I'm sorry.
DAD:	Well, at least you're home safely.
MOM:	How did you get home if the car wouldn't start? Did the tow-truck guy get it working?
TIM:	Wait 'til you get a load of this. It was a tow-truck *girl*, Mom. Isn't that swell? And no, she didn't get the car working. The car is over at Phillip's garage. Golly, I would've called you from there, but some guy was on the phone and wouldn't hang up. I just asked 'em to take me home instead.
DAD:	I guess we should've trusted you.
MOM:	Well, I'm just glad you're OK, Timmy.
TIM:	Gee Mom, Dad, you guys are swell. I won't forget to call next time.
MOM:	Well, we've all learned something today, haven't we?
TIM:	Yeah, I learned never to trust Eddie when he says, "Don't worry about that sound. It's probably just your muffler."

(Mom, Dad, and Tim hug and laugh together.)

QUESTIONS ▼ ▼ ▼ ▼ ▼ ▼ ▼ ▼ ▼ ▼ ▼

● How realistic is this ending?

● How would your parents or stepparents react in a similar situation?

● What could Tim have done to help his parents not worry?

● How might Tim's lack of communication with his parents affect his future choices?

● In this ending, the parents were understanding and trusted that their son was telling the truth. What would happen to their relationship if they found out Tim had actually smashed the car because he was driving recklessly?

Read Luke 6:31.

● How does this verse apply to the parents in this skit? How does it apply to the way you relate to your parents or stepparents? What does it say about trust?

Read Luke 19:12-26.

● In this story, the person who was trustworthy in a small matter earned the most respect and reward. How does this apply to the way you can relate to your parents or stepparents? the way your parents or stepparents can relate to you?

▲ ▲ ▲ ▲ ▲ ▲ ▲ ▲ ▲ ▲ ▲ ▲ ▲ ▲ ▲

SHE DOESN'T PRAY MY WAY

SCRIPTURE:

Matthew 25:31-46;
Romans 14:1-12;
and 15:1-7

THEMES:

Acceptance,
cliques, prayer,
worship

THE SETTING:

A few teenagers are standing around waiting for a youth group meeting to begin.

THE PROPS:

You'll need six chairs.

THE CHARACTERS:

Donna, a youth group member
Michael, a youth group member
LeAnne, a youth group member
Brian, a youth group member
Samantha, the youth group leader
Nikki, a visitor to the youth group
Jesus (if you use ending option three)

THE SCRIPT:

(Donna, Michael, LeAnne, and Brian are milling around the youth group room as they wait for a meeting to start.)

DONNA: *(To Michael)* Have you decided if you're going on the mission trip yet?

MICHAEL: No. I'm still not sure if I can get off work.

BRIAN: Get off work? You still mow lawns for a living. So you let the grass grow a little bit longer.

MICHAEL: I don't "mow lawns." I work for a landscaping company.

LEANNE: *(Smiling)* Yeah. He's a lawn maintenance engineer.

DONNA: I still think you should go. It's worth the effort of finding someone to take over your "lawn maintenance." You wouldn't regret it.

LEANNE: Donna's right. There's nothing like helping people who have nothing and showing them what God's love is all about.

MICHAEL: I'll see what I can do. I *would* like to go.

(Nikki enters the room and stands apart from the others, quietly looking around. She

doesn't engage in conversation with the others.)

BRIAN:	*(Noticing Nikki)* Do you see what I see?

MICHAEL: *(Looks over at Nikki)* That's Nikki something-or-other from physics class, isn't it?

DONNA: Who's Nikki something-or-other?

LEANNE: I know her. She's in my advanced algebra class. Last name is Berwood or Derborg. Something like that.

BRIAN: But what's she doing here?

DONNA: Did any of you guys invite her?

(Brian, LeAnne, and Michael shake their heads "no.")

(Samantha enters the room and sits down in a chair.)

SAMANTHA: Let's get started, everyone. We have lots to go over today.

(Brian, LeAnne, Michael, Donna, and Nikki wander over and sit down in chairs, facing Samantha.)

SAMANTHA: Let's get the announcements and newsy bits out of the way first.

(Brian, Donna, LeAnne, and Michael all sing, "Announcements, announcements, we love to hear announcements" to the tune of "A-Tisket, A-Tasket," as they always do when Samantha mentions the word. Nikki just smiles politely and looks on.)

SAMANTHA: Nicely done, as always. All right. First announce . . .

(Brian, Donna, Michael, and LeAnne interrupt by singing, "Announcements, announcements, we love to hear announcements" again.)

SAMANTHA: Oops! Let's try that again. OK, here's what's going on. I need all your money for the mission trip by next Friday. We need to mail in the forms so we're sure to get our first choice of where we want to go. Is anyone else planning on going who hasn't already talked to me?

MICHAEL: I'll know by Tuesday.

NIKKI: *(Quietly)* I'd like to know more about the trip.

SAMANTHA: Oh, I'm sorry. Everybody, this is Nikki Harwood.

LEANNE: *(Whispers to Donna)* I was close.

SAMANTHA: *(Continuing)* I ran into her last Wednesday when I was visiting you guys at school and invited her to join us. *(To Nikki)* I'll be glad to tell you more about the trip after our meeting.

(Michael, Donna, Brian, and LeAnne smile politely at Nikki.)

SAMANTHA:	OK. That's really the only announc...news for today. Why don't we open with a prayer. Just jump in if you feel like it and I'll close. Michael, would you start?
MICHAEL:	Um...sure.

(All characters bow their heads for prayer.)

MICHAEL:	Dear God, thanks for bringing us here today. And...um...help us learn more about you.
NIKKI:	*(Quietly)* Yes, Lord.

(Pause.)

DONNA:	Dear God, help us as we prepare for our mission trip this summer. I know you want us to reach out to those in need. Help us know what to say and what to do.
NIKKI:	*(Quietly)* Be with us, Lord.

(Pause.)

LEANNE:	Help us as we study today to grow closer to you...
NIKKI:	*(Quietly)* Yes, Lord.
LEANNE:	...and to grow closer to one another.

(Pause.)

NIKKI:	*(Animated)* Father, I thank you, Lord, for this group. And Lord, I thank you that I am able to worship your holy name, Father, here in this place. Lord, please send your Spirit to be with us and guide us. Open our hearts, Lord, to the leading of your Spirit as we share together, Father. In Jesus' wonderful name...

(Awkward pause.)

SAMANTHA:	Hear all our prayers, Lord, spoken and unspoken. Amen.

(LeAnne, Michael, Brian, and Donna look at Nikki, then at each other.)

Freeze the skit. Then have participants or audience members choose from the following ending options to finish the skit. Choose additional actors if necessary.

> **1. Beam Me Up, Scotty** (no new characters)

> **2. Welcome to the Club** (no new characters)

> **3. Look Who's Talking Now** (new character: Jesus)

1. BEAM ME UP, SCOTTY

(Samantha stands up.)

SAMANTHA: I almost forgot. I left the snacks in the car. I'll be right back. *(She leaves the room.)*

(Donna, LeAnne, Michael, and Brian all huddle together.)

DONNA: *(Quietly to LeAnne)* Did you hear the way Nikki prayed?

LEANNE: Must be one of those superspiritual types.

MICHAEL: I don't like it.

BRIAN: Kinda gives me the creeps. Why doesn't she pray like normal people?

(Nikki's smile begins to fade as she hears the others talking about her.)

DONNA: I say we freeze her out of the group.

BRIAN: She doesn't fit in.

MICHAEL: Maybe she can find a different youth group.

(Samantha returns and sees the other kids excluding Nikki.)

SAMANTHA: OK, what's up, guys? Why aren't you including Nikki in your little circle?

DONNA: Um . . . we weren't excluding anyone.

BRIAN: We were just . . .

LEANNE: It's just that she's . . .

MICHAEL: She doesn't pray like we do.

(All characters look at Michael. Nikki looks as if she's about to cry.)

BRIAN: Michael's right. I know this is her first meeting and all, but she's going to have to find a way to fit in.

DONNA: Nothing personal, Nikki.

(Nikki hides her face in her hands and begins to cry.)

NIKKI: *(To no one in particular)* I wish someone could just beam me out of here.

(At this point, freeze the skit and have audience members close their eyes and make a "whirring" noise. While eyes are closed, have Nikki slip offstage and out of the room. Cue the audience to open their eyes and stop the noise. Then continue the skit.)

DONNA: *(Looking over where Nikki was sitting)* Um . . . what just happened here? Where'd Nikki go?

LeAnne: She was sitting right there.

Michael: She disappeared!

Samantha: *(Looking around the room)* I wonder . . .

QUESTIONS

● What do you think happened to Nikki?

● When have you felt the way Nikki did? When have you felt the way the other kids in this skit did?

● Why is it so difficult to accept people who are different from you?

● What is ironic about the kids' prayers? Read Romans 14:1-12 and 15:1-7.

● What do these passages tell us about accepting differences among Christians? Why is it important to focus on the basics of faith instead of the things that separate us?

● How might the teenagers in this skit have better dealt with their discomfort about Nikki's prayer? How might the leader have dealt with the situation?

2. WELCOME TO THE CLUB

Samantha: Thanks for your prayers, everyone. Before we go any further, Nikki, I think you ought to know something about our group . . .

Michael: We don't go for all that weird, superspiritual stuff.

Donna: If you're going to fit in here, you're going to have to learn a few things.

(During the next few lines, LeAnne, Michael, Brian, and Donna begin to disagree on what the group believes. As each person disagrees, have him or her scoot farther away from the rest of the group. While this is going on, Nikki is simply watching and taking it all in, somewhat bemused by the turn of events. By the time the last line is spoken, LeAnne, Michael, Brian, and Donna should be sitting far apart from each other with their arms folded.)

LeAnne: Like . . . we don't believe in dancing.

Brian: *(Puzzled, to LeAnne)* I don't know about *you,* but *I* don't have a problem with dancing. It's R-rated movies we don't agree with.

Michael: *(To Brian)* Excuse me? R-rated movies? I think there are plenty of good movies that just happened to be rated R. *(To Nikki)* What we really don't like, though, are people who believe in all that healing miracle baloney.

Donna: *(To Michael)* We, meaning who? My grandmother was healed by a miracle. Of course we believe in miracles. *(To Nikki)* But if you're planning on speaking in tongues, now that's another story.

Brian: I think you've got it all wrong. *(To Nikki)* We don't really have a problem with speaking in tongues. But you'll probably feel uncomfortable if you like listening to country music. We're all pop fans here.

MICHAEL: *(To Nikki)* He means alternative.

LEANNE: *(To Nikki)* No, he means techno.

DONNA: *(To Nikki)* Rap.

BRIAN: *(To Nikki)* I'm sure it's R-rated movies that we're opposed to.

DONNA: No, it's the tongues thing.

MICHAEL: Miracles!

LEANNE: Dancing!

BRIAN: R-rated movies!

DONNA: Tongues.

(LeAnne, Michael, Brian, and Donna are now sitting far apart from each other with their arms folded.)

SAMANTHA: *(Looks over at Nikki who is completely confused.)* Welcome to our little club.

QUESTIONS

● What nugget of truth is hidden in this skit ending? When have you been in a similar situation?

● Why is it so easy to find things that separate us and so difficult to find things that build acceptance in groups?

Read Romans 14:1-12 and 15:1-7.

● What do these passages tell us about accepting others? Why is it important to focus on the basics of faith instead of the things that separate us?

● For all we know, Nikki might have simply been parroting a prayer she'd heard on television so she would fit in. How would you feel if you were in the group and discovered that she wasn't even a Christian?

● What are some practical ways we can reach out to people who express themselves differently than we do?

3. LOOK WHO'S TALKING NOW

(During this ending, have the Jesus character stand offstage and speak Nikki's lines at the same time she does. Don't let anyone know who this character is. They'll find out soon enough.)

SAMANTHA: I almost forgot. I left the snacks in the car. I'll be right back. *(She stands up and leaves the room.)*

DONNA:	Um . . . Nikki, I think we ought to tell you something about this group.
NIKKI (JESUS):	What's that?

(Donna looks at LeAnne.)

LEANNE:	Well, we don't go for any of that charismatic stuff in this group.
MICHAEL:	Yeah, we're pretty boring.
BRIAN:	Not boring, just normal.
NIKKI (JESUS):	*(Politely, yet firmly)* I'm sorry if it bothers you, but this is the way I pray.
BRIAN:	Not us.
LEANNE:	Brian's right. If you want to really fit in, you'll need to learn how we do things.
MICHAEL:	We're just trying to help you feel comfortable.
NIKKI (JESUS):	I don't think God ever guaranteed that we'd always feel comfortable in our faith.
DONNA:	We don't want to make any waves, but you're just not going to feel welcome here unless you pray like we do.
MICHAEL:	And worship like we do.
BRIAN:	And live like we do.
NIKKI (JESUS):	*(Spoken without anger)* So I can't join this group if I have a different style of worship or if I pray in a different way?

(Brian, LeAnne, Donna, and Michael look at each other.)

LEANNE:	No.

(Freeze the skit and have the audience members close their eyes. Have Nikki slip away and Jesus take her place. Then resume the skit.)

(Michael, Donna, Brian, and LeAnne look up and are surprised to see someone else sitting in Nikki's chair.)

JESUS:	*(Sadly)* Then I guess I'm not welcome here. *(Gets up and sadly begins to walk away, pausing to look at Michael, Donna, Brian, and LeAnne for a moment before leaving.)*
DONNA:	That was weird.
LEANNE:	He was just sitting there in Nikki's chair.
MICHAEL:	How did he get there?

BRIAN: Hey, guys, did you happen to notice his hands?

(Donna, LeAnne, Michael, and Brian look at each other in horror.)

DONNA, LEANNE,
MICHAEL, AND BRIAN: *(Together)* Come back, Jesus!

QUESTIONS

● What was your reaction when you discovered that Jesus was the person sitting in Nikki's chair?

Read Matthew 25:31-46.

● How is this passage appropriate to this skit?

● Why do people exclude others who don't act or speak the way they do? When have you done this to someone? When have you been the target of such an act?

Have kids form two groups. Have one group read Romans 14:1-12 and the other read Romans 15:1-7. Then ask the following questions, and have group members share insight based on what they read.

● What do these passages tell us about accepting others? Why is it important to focus on the basics of faith instead of the things that separate us?

● What do you think God thinks is important about the way people pray? What things aren't so important to God about the way people pray?

SEE YOU LATER

SCRIPTURE:
Philippians 3:12-14
and 1 John 2:15

THEMES:

Friendship, future,
goals, graduation,
success

THE SETTING:

Three teenagers are standing around and talking immediately after high
school graduation.

THE PROPS:

You'll need three graduation hats (if available) and a sign that says, "Ten
years later..."

THE CHARACTERS:

Ben, a high school graduate guy
Traci, a high school graduate girl
Vanessa, a high school graduate girl

THE SCRIPT:

*(The three teenagers have just graduated from high school and are hugging and congratu-
lating each other as the skit opens.)*

BEN:	We did it! We're free!
VANESSA:	No more teachers.
TRACI:	No more books.
BEN:	Well, until college that is.
VANESSA:	Thanks for ruining my party, Ben.
BEN:	Sorry. Forget I ever said it.
VANESSA:	Forget what?
TRACI:	Can you believe this? We're finally out of high school!
VANESSA:	*(Thoughtfully)* It's kind of sad, really.
BEN:	Sad for the new freshman class, maybe.
VANESSA:	I'm serious. I mean, who knows when we'll see each other again. This could be the beginning of the end of our friendship.
BEN:	*(Sarcastically)* Talk about ruining the party.
TRACI:	What do you mean, Vanessa? We've got a whole summer ahead of us.
VANESSA:	But then Ben leaves for the university in September.
BEN:	August, actually.

VANESSA:	And what about you, Traci? Aren't you leaving in the fall for Europe?
TRACI:	Yeah, but that's months away. *(Trying to comfort Ben and Traci)* And besides, it doesn't have to mean the end of our friendship.
BEN:	*(With determination)* Traci's right. Even though we're going to go our separate ways this fall, we don't have to lose touch with each other. I bet we'll still be friends in ten years.
VANESSA:	*(Thoughtfully)* I wonder how we'll change between now and then.
TRACI:	One thing's for sure. I'm going to be a famous supermodel. But don't worry. I'll be sure to pencil you guys into my schedule when I'm in town.
BEN:	Please do. You'll want to hear all about how I single-handedly revolutionized online technology. And of course you'll want to stay at one of my mansions.
TRACI:	Maybe I'll share some beauty secrets with you to help with your receding hairline.
BEN:	Or a few tips on how to make it big in Hollywood. By then I'll be bored with the high-tech world I've created and the millions of dollars I've earned.
TRACI:	Maybe you'll produce my first feature film.
BEN:	Sure. *(Looks over at Vanessa)* What do you think you'll be doing in ten years?
VANESSA:	*(Quietly)* Oh, some variation on what I'm already doing.
TRACI:	And that is . . .
VANESSA:	Listening to you two dream of success.
BEN:	You'll probably win the Nobel Prize for something or another.
TRACI:	Or become the next Billy Graham, with all the time you spend in church.
VANESSA:	I think I'll be pretty much the same person I am today, but hopefully with a better job.
BEN:	I wonder what the future holds.

● ● ● ●

Freeze the skit. Then have participants or audience members choose from the following ending options to finish the skit. Choose additional actors if necessary.

1. **The Future According to Ben and Traci** (no new characters)

2. **Vanessa's Vision** (no new characters)

3. **It Could Happen** (no new characters)

● ● ● ●

1. THE FUTURE ACCORDING TO BEN AND TRACI

(Have someone walk across the stage area, holding up the sign that says, "Ten years later..." Vanessa is working as manager of a local McDonald's restaurant when Ben comes in the front door.)

BEN:	*(Walks up to Vanessa)* I'd like a Big Mac, a large fries, and ...
VANESSA:	*(Interrupting)* Ben? Ben Hobsen? Is that you?
BEN:	*(Can't quite place the face)* Yes ... it's me. *(Stares back at Vanessa, not recognizing her.)*
VANESSA:	Ben, it's me, Vanessa.
BEN:	*(Relieved to discover who this girl is)* Vanessa! It's been so long— what, five years?
VANESSA:	Ten.
BEN:	So what's been happening around here lately? I've been so busy with my company that I haven't had time to keep up with things in this little town.
VANESSA:	Oh, things are pretty much the same as they always were. Unemployment is climbing, crime is on the rise, and church attendance is on the decline.
BEN:	How pleasant.
VANESSA:	So have you heard about Traci?
BEN:	Traci?
VANESSA:	Traci Summers. She was our best friend in high school.
BEN:	Just kidding, Vanessa. Of course I remember Traci. And who hasn't seen her? Her picture's on almost every top magazine there is.
VANESSA:	And a few of the bottom ones, too. Didn't you hear about the pictures?
BEN:	Who hasn't. Pretty bad timing, huh? Who would have thought she'd pose for pictures like that.

VANESSA:	Doesn't seem to be hurting her career much.
BEN:	Not since she started making movies. They love that kind of publicity.
VANESSA:	*(Over her shoulder to an unseen employee of the restaurant)* I'll be right there. *(To Ben)* Looks like the troops need me again. They're just like my youth group kids—always crying out for help. Will I see you at church tomorrow?
BEN:	Sorry. Don't have time. Haven't had time for church for years, you know, with the business taking up so much of my energy. Besides, I'm only here for a day. I'm on my way to D.C. for a conference on telecommuting.
VANESSA:	Next time, maybe.
BEN:	Count on it. *(Awkward pause)* Well, you'd better get back to your crew. You always were a good leader.
VANESSA:	Good luck with your conference.
BEN:	*(Heading out the door)* See ya.

(Vanessa looks sadly at Ben as he leaves, then she turns around to head back to work.)

VANESSA:	Looks like a bus just pulled up. Let's get crackin'.

QUESTIONS ▼ ▼ ▼ ▼ ▼ ▼ ▼ ▼ ▼ ▼ ▼ ▼

● What feelings did you have after this ending? When have you felt these feelings in real life?

● What surprised you most about what happened to the people in the skit?

● Both Ben and Traci seemed to get what they wanted. Based on this ending, do you think they're happy? What did they have to sacrifice to succeed?

● How often do people actually reach their goals and dreams?

Read Philippians 3:12-14 and 1 John 2:15.

● What do these passages tell us about what goals we should have for the future? How does that apply to the goals Ben and Traci had?

● Do you hope to keep in contact with high school friends? How can you accomplish that goal?

● What role does your faith play in your plans for the future?

▲ ▲ ▲ ▲ ▲ ▲ ▲ ▲ ▲ ▲ ▲ ▲ ▲ ▲ ▲

2. VANESSA'S VISION

(Have someone walk across the stage area, holding up the sign that says, "Ten years later..." Vanessa is sitting on the floor, pretending to read a book to some small children. She is serving as a missionary in a third world country.)

VANESSA:	...and then Jesus said to the people, "Let the children come to me." You see, little ones, Jesus loves children.

(Vanessa begins singing "Jesus Loves the Little Children" or "Jesus Loves Me." Not long after she begins, two other voices join hers and Ben and Traci enter from offstage. When Vanessa hears the voices, she turns and sees her friends. She stops singing and races to greet them both with hugs.)

VANESSA: Ben! Traci! I knew you'd come! *(To the imaginary children)* Run along, children. I'll read more stories later.

(Ben, Traci, and Vanessa sit down in a semicircle on the ground. There are few chairs in this community.)

BEN: We had to come.

TRACI: When we heard about how your funding fell through, we knew we had to get here before you were sent home.

VANESSA: *(Beaming)* I'm so glad you came. It's been tough since we learned that there was no money left to support our work, but we keep praying and hoping that something will change so we can stay a few more years. These people really need the hope we bring.

TRACI: *(Looking over at Ben)* Do you want to tell her?

VANESSA: Tell me what?

BEN: *(Smiling)* No, you tell her. It was your idea.

TRACI: Vanessa, you've heard how well my singing career has been going, haven't you?

VANESSA: Yes, and I'm so proud of you. You're reaching so many people through your music.

TRACI: And you've heard about Ben's success?

VANESSA: Of course. *(To Ben)* You write so often. How do you have time with all you're doing with the business dealings and the online ministry and all that other stuff you're doing?

BEN: I make time for *you. (To Traci)* Hurry up and tell her, Traci, or I will.

TRACI: Well, we're going to fund your mission project for the next five years—longer if you need it.

(Vanessa is speechless and on the verge of "happy tears.")

VANESSA: I . . . I don't know what to say.

BEN: Don't say anything. You deserve this and so much more.

TRACI: Ben's right. It was your commitment to reaching others for Christ . . .

BEN:	. . . and the incredible example of your faith . . .
TRACI:	. . . that helped turn our lives around. We owe you everything.
VANESSA:	You owe me nothing. That was all God's work.
BEN:	You're right, as always. *(Thoughtfully)* What an incredible ten years it's been since high school.
VANESSA:	I can't wait for the next ten!

(Vanessa, Ben, and Traci hug.)

QUESTIONS ▼ ▼ ▼ ▼ ▼ ▼ ▼ ▼ ▼ ▼ ▼ ▼

● What did you learn about Vanessa from her vision of the future? What hopes did she have for her two friends?

● What surprised you most about this ending?

● How did Vanessa incorporate Ben and Traci's dreams into her picture of the future?

● How realistic do you think this version of the future is? Explain.

Read Philippians 3:12-14 and 1 John 2:15.

● What do these passages tell us about the goals we should have for the future? How do these verses apply to the goals Ben, Traci, and Vanessa had?

● What are your biggest goals for the future? What plans do you have to keep in touch with high school friends?

● What does it take to keep your faith at the center of your plans for the future?

▲ ▲ ▲ ▲ ▲ ▲ ▲ ▲ ▲ ▲ ▲ ▲ ▲ ▲ ▲

3. IT COULD HAPPEN

(Have someone walk across the stage area, holding up the sign that says, "Ten years later . . ." Vanessa and Traci are standing, looking down at the ground solemnly. Ben is not a character in this ending.)

VANESSA:	Why? Why did it have to happen?
TRACI:	We don't always know the answer to the "why" questions, Vanessa. You taught me that.
VANESSA:	That was a long time ago. Things have changed.
TRACI:	*(Looks over at Vanessa.) You've* changed, Vanessa.
VANESSA:	Yeah. I finally put away childish things. I grew up.
TRACI:	Your faith in God wasn't childish, Vanessa. It was a precious gift. And if it weren't for your persistence, I don't think I would have heard God calling my name. No, Vanessa, faith in God may be childlike, but it's not childish.
VANESSA:	Sorry to disappoint you, Traci, but I don't know why I believed all that stuff for so long. My life didn't get better. God didn't stop the

people I loved from leaving or dying. All I ever got out of Christianity was a lifetime's worth of pain and suffering.

TRACI: I'm sorry to hear you talk like this, Vanessa. You were always the stable one, the voice of reason.

VANESSA: *(Continuing)* And now this! *(She points to the ground.)*

TRACI: It is sad, isn't it?

VANESSA: So maybe he didn't keep in touch like he said he would. At least he could have told *us* what was going on. We were his best friends.

TRACI: Yeah—ten years ago. He chose his own paths, Vanessa. He just made bad decisions. And he paid for them with his life.

VANESSA: I would never have thought in a million years that AIDS would take him from us.

TRACI: *(Looks at the ground again.)* Even though we didn't keep in touch like we'd promised, we'll still miss you, Ben.

VANESSA: Yeah. We'll miss you.

(Traci and Vanessa begin to walk offstage in opposite directions. Both stop to look at each other.)

TRACI: I'll be praying for you, Vanessa.

VANESSA: Um . . . thanks. I hope it works.

QUESTIONS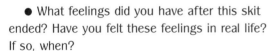

● What feelings did you have after this skit ended? Have you felt these feelings in real life? If so, when?

● How are the surprises in this skit similar to what might happen in real life?

● Are the ways Traci and Vanessa seemed to change like the ways people change in real life? If so, how?

● What aspects of our future are out of our control? What aspects can we control?

Read Philippians 3:12-14 and 1 John 2:15.

● What do these passages tell us about the goals we should have for the future? How do these verses apply to the goals Ben, Vanessa, and Traci had?

● How can faith in God help us survive surprises the future has in store for us?

● What are some practical ways to strengthen our faith so we can better face the future?

YOU CALL THAT FOOD?

SCRIPTURE:

Proverbs 11:1 and Luke 6:31

THEMES:

Generation gap, honesty, parents and stepparents

THE SETTING:

Three teenagers are sitting at a table in the school lunchroom.

THE PROPS:

You'll need a table, three chairs, and food (optional). You'll also need a microphone (real or fake) if you use ending option two, and a toy gun if you use ending option three.

THE CHARACTERS:

Sue, a teenage girl
Tom, a teenage guy
Denise, a teenage girl
Mom, Denise's mother
Announcer, an enthusiastic guy or girl (if you use ending option two)

THE SCRIPT:

SUE: I'm really getting sick of this cafeteria food.

TOM: So why don't you bring food from home or go to Burger World?

SUE: My mom says it's a waste of money to eat out all the time, and we never have anything interesting at home. My mom still thinks I eat peanut butter and jelly sandwiches.

DENISE: Your parents must've been talking to mine. All my dad ever buys is bologna. Can you believe it? It's not like I want steak every day. I just want to choose my own food. It wouldn't hurt to have a turkey croissant sandwich once in a while, would it?

TOM: So why don't you tell your parents how you feel?

SUE: My mom wouldn't listen anyway. She's too busy working to care about the food I eat.

DENISE: My dad's more interested in the newspaper. Ever try to talk to someone through the sports section?

SUE: My mom spends so much time on the phone with her business clients, she ought to have a phone jack surgically implanted into her skull . . .

DENISE:	*(Interrupting as she picks through the food on her tray)* Yuck! Whoever thought it was a good idea to put pickles on a chili dog ought to be shot!
SUE:	That's nothing. Last night my mom fixed eggplant with cheese sauce.
TOM:	So what's so bad about that?
SUE:	The cheese sauce was made from Limburger cheese!
DENISE:	Why do parents do that? It's like they were never teenagers or something.
SUE:	Yeah. It's like some chemical thing kicks in when they're older that wipes out the "Hey, I can still have fun" part of their brain.
DENISE:	Exactly.

(Denise and Sue pause and stare at each other.)

SUE:	I hope that never happens to me.
DENISE:	Me neither. I'm never growing old.
TOM:	*(Pointing across the room)* Say, Denise, isn't that your mom?

(Denise's Mom begins walking across the stage.)

Freeze the skit. Then have participants or audience members choose from the following ending options to finish the skit. Choose additional actors if necessary.

1. Switcheroo (no new characters)

2. Youth-o-Matic (new character: Announcer)

3. Terminator (no new characters)—See note at the beginning of this ending option.

1. SWITCHEROO

DENISE:	*(Suddenly embarrassed)* Um . . . yeah . . .
SUE:	What's she doing here?
TOM:	Looks like she's helping out in the kitchen.

(Denise's mom sees Denise and heads over to the table where she's sitting.)

MOM:	Denise. How nice to see you!

DENISE:	Oh, hi, Mom. What are you doing here?
MOM:	Just helping out in the kitchen. Did you like the pickles on the chili dogs?
SUE:	*(Forcing a polite smile)* Your idea?
MOM:	How'd you guess?
DENISE:	*(Trying to look sincere)* Loved them, Mom. Just loved them.
TOM:	That's not what you told . . .

(Denise elbows Tom.)

DENISE:	*(Interrupting Tom)* I'm glad you're helping out, Mom. You always know what to do with food.

(Sue and Tom look at each other, puzzled.)

MOM:	Thanks, dear. I really enjoy cooking, but you already know that. *(She starts to walk away, then pauses and turns around.)* I almost forgot: We're having your favorite supper tonight—baked beans and sauerkraut. Maybe you'd like to invite your friends?
DENISE:	Sounds yummy, Mom.
SUE:	Um . . . sure. That sounds great. I was going to go out for pizza, but baked beans and sauerkraut? Mmm.
TOM:	No, thanks. I really don't like . . .
DENISE:	*(Finishing Tom's sentence)* . . . missing out on this meal? But you have to go to a doctor's appointment, don't you, Tom?

(Tom tries to speak but is silenced when Denise elbows him again.)

MOM:	Maybe next time. See you two at supper then.
DENISE:	Can't wait! Bye.

(Denise and Sue smile at Denise's mom then turn to each other and act as if they're going to throw up. Tom shakes his head.)

QUESTIONS ▼ ▼ ▼ ▼ ▼ ▼ ▼ ▼ ▼ ▼ ▼ ▼

Read Proverbs 11:1 and Luke 6:31.

● Which character in this skit are you most like? Explain.

● Why do parents and stepparents sometimes seem to have no clue about what teenagers like or dislike?

● Why wouldn't Denise speak up about the food her mother cooks?

● What are the short-term and long-term results of Denise's (or Sue's) decision not to tell her mom how she feels?

● How might these passages apply to →

Denise or Sue? What might you need to change in your relationship with your parents or stepparents to follow the advice of these passages?

● Why is an honest relationship with your parents or stepparents important? What happens to your relationship with your parents or stepparents if you hide the truth often?

▲ ▲ ▲ ▲ ▲ ▲ ▲ ▲ ▲ ▲ ▲ ▲ ▲ ▲ ▲

2. YOUTH-O-MATIC

DENISE: *(Squinting in Mom's direction)* Yes, that's her.

(Denise's mom starts to walk over, but the Announcer, who is holding a microphone, jumps into the scene between the teenagers and Mom. Mom walks slowly offstage during the rest of this skit. The Announcer begins speaking as if he or she is an announcer for an infomercial selling the new "Youth-o-Matic" device.)

ANNOUNCER: Say, are your parents or stepparents out of touch with reality? Do they miss the boat when it comes to meeting your needs as a teenager? Do you find yourself mumbling something like "Get a clue, Mom" more than five times a day? Then what you need is the new Youth-o-Matic from Communico *(holding up and displaying the imaginary device)*.

DENISE: The "Youth-o-Matic"?

ANNOUNCER: That's right!

SUE: What does it do?

ANNOUNCER: *(Demonstrating how to use the imaginary device)* Just punch in the current age of your parents or stepparents, then punch in your current age. Presto, chango! Your parents or stepparents will completely understand you—your favorite foods, your hidden desires, your dreams, and even why you do that thing you do with your hair!

DENISE: Wow!

ANNOUNCER: But wait—that's not all. You can also dial in your favorite responses to questions like "What's for dinner?" "Can I have the car keys?" and "Could you give me two hundred bucks for Beatles Reunion concert tickets?"

SUE: It's the answer to all my problems!

TOM: Excuse me, but what are you doing in our skit?

ANNOUNCER: *(Ignoring Tom)* That's right! With the Youth-o-Matic, you can say goodbye to comments like "What is that you're listening to?" or "Would you please turn that thing down?" and "Hey, we're having baked beans and sauerkraut for dinner."

SUE AND DENISE: How much?

ANNOUNCER: What would you pay for this wonderful device? one hundred dollars? two hundred dollars? *(Somewhat apologetically)* Well . . . um . . . it's actually three hundred dollars.

SUE AND DENISE: *(Sadly)* Aw . . .

ANNOUNCER: *(With enthusiasm)* But you'll get that much and more when you use the free bonus attachment—the "Allowance-o-Matic." Just dial in the amount you want, point it at Mom or Dad, and . . .

SUE: Presto, chango!

DENISE: Sign us up right away!

TOM: *(Clearly frustrated)* I'm outta here.

ANNOUNCER: The Youth-o-Matic—order yours today! *(Quietly)* Offer good while supplies last. Prices slightly higher in Alaska and Hawaii.

QUESTIONS ▼ ▼ ▼ ▼ ▼ ▼ ▼ ▼ ▼ ▼ ▼ ▼

● What is the most significant generation-gap issue in your relationship with your parents or stepparents? What are some ways to bridge that gap?

● If you had the option, would you choose an easy fix (like the Youth-o-Matic) for communication problems you're having with parents or stepparents? Why or why not?

● Would you want your parents or stepparents to be "just like you"? Why or why not?

● Why do you think teenagers and parents don't communicate better? How might your relationships change if you spoke the truth (with love) to your parents or stepparents? Read Proverbs 11:1 and Luke 6:31.

● How might these passages apply to Denise or Sue? What might you need to change in your relationship with your parents or stepparents to follow the advice of these passages?

● Is telling your true feelings worth the risk of hurting your parents or stepparents? Explain. What are some healthy ways you can tell your parents or stepparents your true feelings?

▲ ▲ ▲ ▲ ▲ ▲ ▲ ▲ ▲ ▲ ▲ ▲ ▲ ▲ ▲

3. TERMINATOR

NOTE: Because violence is a way of life for some teenagers, you may want to use caution in considering whether this ending should be an option for your group. This ending uses exaggeration to start discussion about the issue of solving conflicts.

DENISE: *(Looking around in alarm)* My mom? Where?

TOM: *(Pointing to Denise's mom)* Isn't that her, right over there in the kitchen?

SUE:	She's helping out in the kitchen?
DENISE:	Yes. Look, she's putting pickles in the chili dogs.
SUE:	How horrible!
TOM:	OK. I'll take care of this. *(He stands and walks toward Denise's mom.)*

(Sue and Denise look at each other, puzzled.)

TOM:	*(To Denise's mom)* You Denise's mom?
MOM:	Yes.
TOM:	Get a clue, Mom! *(He pulls out a gun and shoots Denise's mom.)*

(Denise's mom crumples to the ground. Denise and Sue gasp in horror and run to Denise's mom. Denise checks her Mom's pulse.)

DENISE:	*(Looks up at Tom.)* Tom! You killed my mom!
TOM:	Looks like the end of your food problems. Glad to help out.
SUE:	Why, Tom? Why did you do it?
TOM:	Just trying to help Denise. *(Pauses.)* Hey, Sue, didn't you say your mom worked too much?
SUE:	*(Hesitantly)* Yeah.
TOM:	Where does she work?
SUE:	First National Bank.

(Tom holds up his gun and begins to head out of the cafeteria.)

SUE:	Wait! Come back here!
TOM:	You'll be able to have whatever you want for dinner tonight!

QUESTIONS ▼ ▼ ▼ ▼ ▼ ▼ ▼ ▼ ▼ ▼ ▼ ▼

● How is the way Tom dealt with the problems similar to the way you try to solve communication problems with parents or stepparents? How is it different?

● Why is violence often chosen as the way to solve a problem? Does violence really solve problems? Why or why not?

● What would be a more appropriate way for Denise and Sue to deal with the problems they're having with their parents? What would be a better way for Tom to help them?

Read Proverbs 11:1 and Luke 6:31.

● How might these passages apply to Denise or Sue? What might you need to change in your relationship with your parents or stepparents to follow the advice of these passages?

● When have you failed to share your true feelings with your parents or stepparents? What are some changes you can make in your patterns of relating to your parents or stepparents?

▲ ▲ ▲ ▲ ▲ ▲ ▲ ▲ ▲ ▲ ▲ ▲ ▲ ▲

SCRAMBLED EGGS

SCRIPTURE:

Leviticus 19:18
and Romans
12:17-21

THEMES:

Conflict, peer
pressure, problem
solving, revenge,
standing up for
beliefs

THE SETTING:

Three friends, Ben, Tony, and Mark, are standing beside Tony's car when Deion enters the scene.

THE PROPS:

You'll need four chairs (to represent a car) and egg cartons. Set up the four chairs at the center of the stage, two in front and two behind as if they are seats in a car.

THE CHARACTERS:

Ben, a teenage guy
Tony, a teenage guy
Mark, a teenage guy
Deion, a teenage guy
Mr. Slaughter, a high school teacher (if you use ending option two)

THE SCRIPT:

(Ben, Tony, and Mark are talking among themselves when Deion arrives on the scene. Ben is holding one or more egg cartons.)

DEION:	Sorry I'm late. I had to help clean up after dinner.
BEN:	You're so domestic, Deion. Maybe we should let you hold the eggs. *(Begins to hand an egg carton to Deion.)*
TONY:	Just don't drop them.
MARK:	Yeah, scrambled eggs won't do us much good tonight . . .
DEION:	*(Receiving the eggs)* What do we need eggs for?
TONY:	Well, it's certainly not omelet night at the movies.
BEN:	We need them for our evening entertainment.
MARK:	Yeah, the payback event of the decade.
DEION:	*(Facetiously)* Let me see if I can piece this together. You've got a bunch of eggs. You've got a car. You're planning on paying someone back. I know! Some old lady loaned you some eggs when you didn't have enough change for breakfast at Benny's. And now you're planning on driving over to her house to replenish her depleted egg supply.
BEN:	Um . . . close. But not quite.

DEION:	*(In mock horror)* You mean you're going to egg someone's house?
TONY:	Yep. It's egg-slinging time!
DEION:	Who's the victim?
MARK:	Slaughter.
DEION:	Mr. Reginald Slaughter? Curator of all knowledge mathematical? Leader of the rebellion against the Math Is for Wimps Coalition? Designer of the "It's mathematically impossible for you to get an A" test?
TONY:	*(To Mark)* What did he just say?
MARK:	Yeah. That's the guy.
DEION:	Why?
BEN:	You saw what he did to Mark and Tony's tests.
TONY:	Yeah, he tore 'em up like yesterday's trash.
DEION:	Well, you *were* looking at each other's papers.
TONY:	*(Angrily)* We *were* just checking our answers. We both knew that stuff.
MARK:	He didn't have to humiliate us . . .
TONY:	. . . in front of the whole class.
BEN:	So now it's payback time. We thought it might be kinda nice to scramble a few eggs over at Slaughter's place.
DEION:	*(Suddenly realizing the guys' plan is real)* You guys are serious, aren't you?
BEN:	What do *you* think?

Freeze the skit. Then have participants or audience members choose from the following ending options to finish the skit. Choose additional actors if necessary.

> **1. Wimpy Lives Here** (no new characters)
>
> **2. Brady Bunch** (new character: Mr. Slaughter)
>
> **3. Voice of Reason** (no new characters)

1. WIMPY LIVES HERE

DEION: What do I think? I think you guys are just a little crazy.

TONY: What are you saying? You don't want to come?

DEION: I didn't say that. It's just that . . .

MARK: Oh, I get it. You're afraid you're going to get caught.

BEN: What's the big deal, Deion? It's not like you have a lot of love for old Slaughterhouse. Didn't he give you an F on your last test for showing up late to class?

DEION: Yeah.

MARK: So you have just as good a reason to get back at him as we do.

BEN: So what are we waiting for?

TONY: Let's go slaughter his house!

DEION: Funny, Tony. Real funny.

(Ben, Tony, and Mark begin to get into the car. Deion hesitates.)

BEN: You coming or are you wimping out?

DEION: Oh, well. I never really did like Slaughter. Let's go teach the teacher a lesson or two.

(Deion gets into the "car" and all characters "zoom" off the stage, dragging their chairs with them.)

QUESTIONS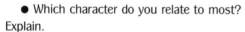

● Which character do you relate to most? Explain.

● Why do you think Deion chose to go along with his friends in this questionable activity? When have you felt similar pressure to go with the crowd?

Read Leviticus 19:18 and Romans 12:17-21.

● What do these passages tell us about "paying back" people we believe have wronged us?

● How can we "live in peace with everyone" when we don't agree with the actions of others?

● This skit deals with two major issues: peer pressure and revenge. Which of these issues would be most difficult for you to deal with in a similar situation? Explain.

● Which would be worse: being rejected because you refuse to follow the crowd in a questionable activity or getting caught seeking revenge against someone? Explain. What might Jesus do if confronted with a similar situation?

2. BRADY BUNCH

DEION: I think you guys don't have to go anywhere.

TONY: What do you mean? Slaughter lives two miles from here.

DEION:	Look over there. *(Points offstage.)*
MARK:	Yeah, so what are we looking at?
BEN:	Of course! Slaughter's car!
MARK:	Are you sure it's his? What's he doing in this neighborhood?
DEION:	His daughter lives across the street.
TONY:	Are you thinking what I'm thinking?
BEN:	It's a sign! We're supposed to egg his car, not his house.
DEION:	What are you guys waiting for?

(Ben, Tony, Mark, and Deion head offstage. Seconds later they return with at least one empty egg carton.)

TONY:	He won't even recognize his car! *(All characters look offstage.)*

(Mr. Slaughter enters the room from the opposite side of the stage and walks up to Mark, Tony, Ben, and Deion.)

MR. SLAUGHTER:	*(Straining to see what everyone is looking at)* What are you gentlemen so interested in?

(Mark, Tony, Ben, and Deion turn and see Mr. Slaughter.)

BEN:	Mr. Slaughter . . . um . . . what are you doing here?
MARK:	Um . . . yeah . . .
MR. SLAUGHTER:	Actually, I just came from Deion's house, and I was heading to your house, Mark. I wanted . . . *(his voice trails off as he sees his car)* . . . to tell you . . .

(Mr. Slaughter looks at the guys, who try to hide the empty egg cartons, then looks back toward the car.)

MR. SLAUGHTER:	*(Surprisingly calm)* You boys wouldn't happen to know what happened to my car, now would you?
MARK:	Your car?
TONY:	You have a car?
BEN:	*(Turns and looks at car.)* Wow! Would you look at that!
DEION:	Well . . . um . . . actually . . . *(Takes a deep breath.)* Yes.

(Ben, Tony, and Mark glare at Deion.)

MR. SLAUGHTER:	Yes, Deion?
DEION:	Well, Mr. Slaughter, we were kind of upset about the way you've been treating us in class, and . . . well . . . we egged your car.

MR. SLAUGHTER:	Hmm. That wasn't very smart of you, now was it?
TONY, BEN, MARK, AND DEION:	*(Together)* No.
BEN:	We didn't mean to.
MARK:	Yeah, we were going to egg your house.
DEION:	All we wanted to do was . . .
TONY:	It was Ben's idea.
MR. SLAUGHTER:	Well, I probably deserved it.

(Mark, Ben, Tony, and Deion look at each other, shocked.)

MR. SLAUGHTER:	I haven't been myself lately. I've been a real ogre in class.
MARK:	*(To himself)* You can say that again.
TONY:	Then you're not gonna bust us?
MR. SLAUGHTER:	*(Thoughtfully)* No.
DEION:	*(After a brief pause)* We're sorry we messed up your car.
MR. SLAUGHTER:	And I'm sorry I've been such a pain in class. I promise I'll do better.
BEN:	We'll clean up your car right away.
MARK:	We will?
TONY:	We will.
MR. SLAUGHTER:	And I'll help. Maybe after it's clean we can all head out to Benny's or something. My treat. *(Pauses.)* Anyone for scrambled eggs?

(All characters laugh and walk offstage.)

QUESTIONS ▼ ▼ ▼ ▼ ▼ ▼ ▼ ▼ ▼ ▼ ▼

● What "lessons" did characters learn in this sitcom style ending?

● How is this ending like the way television shows often solve problems? What is unrealistic about this ending?

● What might have happened in real life when Mr. Slaughter saw the boys standing around with the empty egg cartons?

Read Leviticus 19:18 and Romans 12:17-21.

● What do these passages tell us about "paying back" people we believe have wronged us?

● When have you felt like paying someone back? How did you respond? How did your response affect the situation?

● Does peer pressure really work this way in real life? Explain. How do you deal with pressure to do things you know aren't right?

3. VOICE OF REASON

DEION:	What do I think? I think you guys are going about this all wrong.
TONY:	What do you mean? We don't have enough eggs?
DEION:	No. I think if you have a problem with Slaughter, you should go and talk to him about it.
BEN:	Revenge is so much sweeter.
MARK:	And more fun.
DEION:	But it's not the right answer, and it won't solve your problems with Slaughter. In fact, when he finds out who egged his house, he'll probably make your lives even more miserable in class.
TONY:	Can't get much worse than it already is.
MARK:	Let's get going, guys.
BEN:	Mark's right. We better get going. *(To Deion)* You comin' or not?
DEION:	*(Brief pause)* Not.

(Mark takes the eggs from Deion, then Mark, Ben, and Tony get into the "car." They shuffle offstage with their chairs and the empty chair.)

QUESTIONS ▼ ▼ ▼ ▼ ▼ ▼ ▼ ▼ ▼ ▼ ▼ ▼

Read Leviticus 19:18 and Romans 12:17-21.
• How do these passages support what Deion was saying? How could the guys overcome evil with good in this situation?
• What are the likely consequences of Deion's decision to not join his friends?
• How easy was it for Deion to tell his friends no? How easy is it for you to stand up against something you know is wrong?

• How easy is it for you to disagree with friends when you know they're asking you to do something wrong? What makes it difficult or easy?
• Which would be worse: being rejected because you refuse to follow the crowd in a questionable activity or getting caught seeking revenge against someone? Explain. What might Jesus do if confronted with a similar situation?

▲ ▲ ▲ ▲ ▲ ▲ ▲ ▲ ▲ ▲ ▲ ▲ ▲ ▲ ▲

IS ANYONE LISTENING?

SCRIPTURE:
Psalm 145:18;
Matthew 6:5-15;
and 1 Timothy 2:8

THEMES:
Drinking, prayer,
sex

THE SETTING:
Three high school juniors are sitting in their respective bedrooms, praying. It's the last week of school before summer vacation.

THE PROPS:
You'll need three signs, one that says, "June," one that says, "July," and one that says, "August," if you use ending option two. To add to the illusion that these three teenagers are in separate locations, you might set up three dividers on the stage to represent three different rooms. You'll also need two chairs if you use ending options one and two.

THE CHARACTERS:
Jay, a teenage guy
Leslie, a teenage girl
Tamara, a teenage girl

THE SCRIPT:

(After reading a line, each character must freeze in place until it's time for that person to read another line.)

JAY: *(Obviously uncomfortable with praying)* This prayer thing better work. Here goes nothing: God, if you're really there, could you take a few moments to listen to me? I mean, I'm sure you already know what I'm going to say, but I need to say it anyway.

I'm in trouble. Big trouble. You know the other night when I went over to Jack's house? Well, I didn't really go to Jack's. I went to that party Mom told me not to go to. And boy, did I make some bad decisions there.

LESLIE: *(Confident and in control)* Dear God, there's a lot going on in my life right now, and I need some guidance. There's the school stuff, things about my family, and . . . well, let me just go through my list.

First of all, I need to know what to do about college. I know it's time to start thinking about where to go, and I just don't know if I'm hearing your voice clearly on this issue. You see, I really want to go to a private school, but everyone else seems to want me to go to the state university. I've sent for applications to both, and I know I've got another year to think about this. But I want to know: Whose side are you on? I'd appreciate a clear answer to this one.

TAMARA: *(Sincere and reflective)* Dear God, I'm kinda worried about a friend at school. Jay's been acting real weird lately, but he won't tell me what's wrong. I know he's got lots of questions and uncertainty in his life, since his parents are divorcing and stuff, but I also think he's ready to hear more about you. Help me know how to relate to Jay this week. I really care about him as a friend . . . OK, as a potential boyfriend. *(Pauses.)* Yes, Lord, that's another thing I want to talk to you about. You know I don't want to start dating a guy who doesn't know you.

JAY: First, I decided to drink a little—you know, like everybody else at the party. I never even thought twice about it before, but lately I've been wondering *why* I drink. Tamara tells me it's just because I want to fit in, and she's probably right.

Anyway, I guess I drank a little too much because I don't remember a lot of what happened later. Tom told me I went to the lake with everyone. I can't remember much about it. But that's not why I'm talking to you. It's about that girl. I don't know her name.

LESLIE: OK, that's the first thing. Second item on my prayer list is this: What should I do about my parents? They seem to be fighting a lot more lately, and I'm worried they might do something drastic and get divorced. When I asked Mom about it, she said things were OK, but I don't know if I believe her. Please help them get along better. And help me know what I can do.

OK, the last item on my list is a biggie.

TAMARA: What should I do about that, Lord? How can I be Jay's friend when I feel the way I do about him? I know he's a bit reckless and he's got a not-so-good reputation, but he's a great person inside. I know it.

Please help me know how to reach Jay . . . to help him know you.

JAY: Um . . . you know what happened better than I do, God, but I guess I need to tell you anyway. While we were at the lake, I guess I kinda ended up with this girl, and . . . well, you know what happened. I really don't know why she was there in the first place. She didn't seem to fit in. I guess some other girls dragged her along.

It's not that I'm a prude or anything—far from it. But what my friends said I did . . . it was wrong. I don't think I could even look her in the eye now. I feel like I've ruined her life.

LESLIE: OK, here goes. I got myself into a situation I shouldn't have been in, Lord. Some friends wanted me to go to this party, see, and I tried to tell them that wasn't my kind of thing. But then I thought about how you dined with sinners, and . . . well, I went along. I had some punch—lots, actually. How was I supposed to know it was spiked? You know what happened next. I can't believe it myself; it just doesn't make any sense. But from what my friends say . . . *(suddenly loses her composure and becomes upset)* . . . what if I'm . . . what if I'm pregnant? Lord, please don't let me be pregnant. Please . . . *(Places her head in her hands and begins to cry.)*

TAMARA: Oh, yes, Lord, one more thing. Please help me as I prepare for this summer's mission trip. I'm a little worried about all the violence I've been hearing about on the news. Please prepare the people's hearts before we get there, and keep us safe in our travel. Amen.

JAY: That's all. Amen, I guess.

LESLIE: *(Sobbing)* Amen.

Freeze the skit. Then have participants or audience members choose from the following ending options to finish the skit.

> **1. God Answers Prayer** (no new characters)
>
> **2. Mysterious Ways** (no new characters)
>
> **3. Waiting Room** (no new characters)

1. GOD ANSWERS PRAYER

(Choose three volunteers from the audience. Have each volunteer run across the front of the stage, calling out in chronological order one of the following months: June, July, or August. This will signify the passing of the summer months. Then have Tamara and Jay walk onstage and sit down as if in the lunchroom at school.)

TAMARA: *(Looks at her plate of food.)* Yuck! This cafeteria pizza is always like cardboard. *(Pauses, then looks at Jay.)* Jay, I'm glad you told me about what happened. I worried about you all summer. When I was sitting in that bug-infested hut in South America, I kept wondering what was bothering you so much.

JAY: I'm sorry I made you so worried. I didn't mean to. It's just that I had so much on my mind—so much to think about. I guess I had to work it out by myself... well, not quite by myself.

TAMARA: *(Curiously)* What do you mean, "not quite by myself"?

JAY: Tamara, I finally understand what you've been trying to tell me these past couple of years. It took a lot of soul-searching and more than a few visits with your pastor, but I get it now. I know what it means to give your heart to Christ.

TAMARA: *(Smiling)* Are you saying what I think you're saying?

JAY: It's true. I rededicated my life to Christ. No more running for me.

TAMARA: Oh, I'm so happy for you! You don't know how many nights I've prayed for you.

(Leslie walks up and stands near their table.)

JAY: But I do. Believe me, I do. Without your prayers, I might still be kicking myself for believing what my ex-friends said happened that night.

(Leslie starts to walk away.)

JAY: Leslie, join us, please.

LESLIE: *(Cautiously)* OK, if you don't mind people talking about us behind our backs.

JAY: You and I know that nothing happened that night.

TAMARA: Jay just explained it all to me. It's such a cruel joke to play on someone.

LESLIE: I'm afraid I *let* myself be a target for this kind of thing. I should have guessed the punch would be spiked. And *my* ex-friends had been preaching to me about why sex is such a normal thing and that I must be abnormal or something for wanting to be a virgin. I was the perfect victim in waiting.

JAY: And I was the perfect idiot for drinking myself into oblivion. One thing's for sure: My drinking days are over.

LESLIE: Mine too. *(Smiles.)*

JAY: *(Pauses briefly, then speaks to Tamara.)* Isn't this Sunday the first youth group meeting of the year?

TAMARA: Yeah. The parents are putting on a dinner, and the people who went on the mission trip are telling about it. Can you come?

JAY: Wouldn't miss it. How about you, Leslie?

LESLIE: My church's youth group doesn't start meeting until next week, but I'm going away this weekend with my folks. I'm visiting the state university to see if I want to go there next year.

TAMARA: Sounds like fun.

LESLIE: Yeah, the university is looking better all the time. But I'm mostly excited to spend some time with my parents.

TAMARA: Well, maybe our youth groups can get together sometime.

LESLIE: That would be fun.

JAY: *(Pauses briefly, then speaks.)* Tamara, do you think you'll need a ride to youth group on Sunday? I mean, I'd be happy to pick you up.

TAMARA: *(Trying to be calm)* Yes, I do think I'll need a ride.

QUESTIONS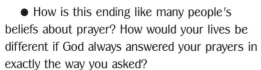

● How is this ending like many people's beliefs about prayer? How would your lives be different if God always answered your prayers in exactly the way you asked?

● When has God answered your prayer in the way you hoped he would? When has he answered your prayer in an unexpected way?

Read Psalm 145:18; Matthew 6:5-15; and 1 Timothy 2:8.

● What do these passages tell us about prayer?

● If God always answered prayers in the ways we wanted him to, how would he respond when two people asked for opposing things? What role should prayer play in our private lives?

● When do you pray? What kinds of things do you pray about?

● Jesus spent a lot of time in prayer, talking to his Father. What kinds of things do you think Jesus prayed about? What can we learn about prayer from the way Jesus prayed?

2. MYSTERIOUS WAYS

(Have a volunteer run across the front of the stage, carrying the "June" sign, the "July" sign, then the "August" sign to signify the passing of the summer months. Then have Leslie and Jay walk onstage and sit down as if in the lunchroom at school.)

JAY: *(Looking at his food)* When are they going to stop serving gruel in the lunchroom? *(Quietly, to Leslie)* What did your mom say?

LESLIE: *(Upset)* I didn't even ask her. Look, Jay, there is no way I'm going to get an abortion. No way. I'm going to have this baby.

JAY: *(Confused and upset)* And what do you expect me to do?

LESLIE: Well, I don't want you to marry me, if that's what you're worried about. I just think you should help out financially with the hospital costs and all that. Mom doesn't have much money these days since Dad left. He hardly ever sends his child-support check. I'm not even sure where he is.

JAY: I don't know how much I can help. I'm already working two part-time jobs to help out with the bills at home.

LESLIE: *(Getting even more upset)* Look, Jay, you really messed up my life, all right? You have to pay for what you did. This is the worst possible thing that could've happened to me. Now I won't be going to college. I may not even finish high school, thanks to you.

JAY: How many times do I have to tell you I'm sorry? It's not been so easy for me, either, you know. You heard about that church group in South America?

LESLIE: *(Puzzled)* So? What does that have to do with you?

JAY: My best friend, Tamara, was on that plane.

LESLIE: *(Pauses before speaking.)* I'm sorry. I didn't know.

JAY: *(Pauses, then speaks.)* What are we going to do now?

LESLIE: I don't know. But whatever you do, don't pray about it.

QUESTIONS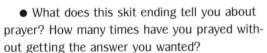

● What does this skit ending tell you about prayer? How many times have you prayed without getting the answer you wanted?

● Respond to the following statement about prayer: If you know what you want in life, don't pray about it.

● Why would God choose to answer prayers in ways we don't like?

Read Psalm 145:18; Matthew 6:5-15; and 1 Timothy 2:8.

● What do these passages tell us about prayer?

● How do these passages apply to what we learned in this skit ending?

● What good could come from the circumstances that these kids found themselves in? What role does responsibility play in this skit?

● How might the phrase "God works in mysterious ways" apply to the people in this skit? to your own life?

3. WAITING ROOM

(Have audience members stand and spin three times in place, repeating the words "June," "July," and "August" with you as they spin, to indicate the passing of the summer months. When audience members sit down, make sure Tamara, Jay, and Leslie are back in their rooms and praying again. Each character continues to freeze in place until it's time for that person to read another line.)

JAY: What's the deal, God? I've been waiting and wondering now for three months about what I'm supposed to do about this mess I got into last May. This girl—I found out her name was Leslie—she won't even look at me at school. It's like the whole world has been put on hold until this thing gets resolved, but I don't know what to do. Do I talk to her? Do I just try to forget it ever happened? Do I . . . *(stops praying and scowls)* . . . Oh, what's the use. This prayer stuff is just a bunch of baloney anyway. I'm just wasting my time. *(Gets up and walks offstage.)*

LESLIE: OK, God. I know I'm not pregnant. You've answered that prayer anyway. But what's up with my parents? I've been asking for your help for months and nothing's changed. How am I supposed to get on with my life with everything in so much turmoil? When are you going to do something about their relationship?

And that curve you threw me about college isn't funny, God. Why do my best friends have to be going to three different schools? We were going to go to the same one. That was the plan all along. Now I don't know what to do. Where are you, God?

TAMARA: Was that mission trip really worth the trouble? It seemed like no one really listened to what we were saying. I know we must have done some good, but we went through so much for what seems like so little in return. Help me see the good we did, please, Lord.

And as always, please be with Jay. I know he's got lots of questions and uncertainty in his life, but I also think he's ready to hear more about you. Help me to know how to relate to Jay . . .

QUESTIONS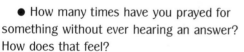

● How many times have you prayed for something without ever hearing an answer? How does that feel?

● Why would God choose to make us wait for answers to prayer? How do you know when you've heard an answer to your prayer?

Read Psalm 145:18; Matthew 6:5-15; and 1 Timothy 2:8.

● What do these passages tell us about prayer? Is it easy for you to trust that God knows what's best for you? Why do we grow impatient when we don't hear an answer we're hoping for right away?

● How might the kids in this skit grow in response to the situations they've faced?

● How have you grown from answers to prayer? What kinds of things might God be telling us when our prayers aren't answered right away?

SPEAK UP

SCRIPTURE:

Matthew 10:16-20,
Matthew 26:69-75,
and John 8:42-47

THEMES:

Politics and religion, sharing faith, standing up for beliefs

THE SETTING:

Five teenagers are sitting in a classroom, discussing current events.

THE PROPS:

You'll need to set up five to ten chairs in a classroom-type arrangement, with kids facing the audience.

THE CHARACTERS:

Ray, a teenage guy
Sheila, a teenage girl
Greg, a teenage guy
Celine, a teenage girl
Tracy, a teenage girl
Mr. Jackson, a high school teacher
A Rooster's Crow (if you use ending option three)

THE SCRIPT:

(Explain to the audience that Greg, Celine, and Tracy are Christians and members of the same church. During the skit, we hear their thoughts as well as their comments in class. If you have plenty of willing actors, you can add to this illusion by having three different people stand behind them and read Greg's, Celine's, and Tracy's thoughts during the skit. Otherwise have Greg, Celine, and Tracy speak their "thought" lines as if to themselves and speak their regular lines more loudly and directed toward the other actors. Mr. Jackson can stand in the audience or wander among the teenagers during the skit. Also, you may want to include more actors by adding more students who sit in the classroom and listen to the dialogue.)

RAY:	OK. I can believe that some of the problems in our society are caused by things out of our control, but if you ask me, religion is our biggest problem.
SHEILA:	Ray's got a point. I mean, look at the abortion issue. It wouldn't even be an issue if the stupid Christians hadn't started messing around where they don't belong.
GREG:	*(To himself)* Oh no, here come the attacks.
CELINE:	*(To herself)* Please don't ask me what I think. Please don't ask me what I think.
TRACY:	*(To herself, clearly upset)* Don't get me started.

RAY:	That's just part of what I mean. Look at politics these days. Every politician is going around saying, "I have the truth" and is quoting some biblical verse to prove he or she is right.
SHEILA:	And not only that—you should see all the religious references that are popping up on television these days. I don't want to be told what to think.
GREG:	*(To himself)* Religious references on television? What channel is she watching?
MR. JACKSON:	But what about the fact that our country was founded on Christian principles?
RAY:	Things change. And besides, I thought that the deal was that we had complete religious freedom. That means freedom to choose any religion you want.
SHEILA:	Or no religion at all.
RAY:	But everywhere you look, Christianity rears its ugly head. Take a look at our money, for example. In God we trust? That's quite an assumption, if you ask me.
GREG:	*(To himself)* What should I say? What should I say?
TRACY:	*(To herself)* I'm going to say something. I have to say something.
CELINE:	*(To herself)* Tracy, Greg, why aren't you saying something?
SHEILA:	And what about our national holidays? Take Christmas, for example. Sure, it's mostly commercial now, but it's still based on a religious event. So is Easter.
MR. JACKSON:	Does anyone else have anything to offer? If Ray and Sheila had their way, our society would be void of any religious content. Class?

● ● ● ●

Freeze the skit. Then have participants or audience members choose from the following ending options to finish the skit. Choose additional actors if necessary.

1. To Boldly Go . . . (no new characters)

2. Miracles Happen (no new characters)

3. Hide and Seek (new character: A Rooster's Crow)

● ● ● ●

1. TO BOLDLY GO...

TRACY: *(To herself)* OK, here goes. Help me out here, Lord.

TRACY: *(Boldly)* I'm afraid I can't sit here and listen to this baloney any longer. Religion isn't the biggest problem with our society. It's lack of religion, or more accurately, a lack of faith in God.

CELINE: *(To herself)* Way to go, Tracy!

MR. JACKSON: Finally a rebuttal. Continue, Tracy.

TRACY: *(Unsure of what to say)* Well...um...

GREG: *(Jumping in to help)* I think what Tracy is saying is that without faith in God, there is no purpose in life. And without purpose, all you've got left is a clueless society.

SHEILA: If you ask me, religion is what makes society clueless.

RAY: Yeah. It tells you what to think instead of encouraging you to think for yourself.

GREG: I disagree. But I think we need to define our terms here. Religion is a term that doesn't really fit what I believe in. To me, Christianity isn't a religion but a way of life. It's a set of guidelines to live by.

TRACY: It's not a list of do's or don'ts as much as it is a lifestyle.

CELINE: *(To herself, hopeful)* It looks like we're finally going to win a round.

MR. JACKSON: Good point, Tracy. But what about Ray's point that people shouldn't be obligated to participate in any particular religion? Should "In God we trust" be removed from our money so we don't hurt anyone's feelings?

SHEILA: *I* think so.

GREG: No. Should we erase all records of the Holocaust just because it was an event tied to religion? I don't think so. Neither should we ignore that our country's roots come from Christianity.

MR. JACKSON: Ray?

RAY: *(Pauses.)* I'd need to think about that one.

TRACY: No one forces you to believe the things Christianity preaches, but no one should force you to keep your faith silent, either.

MR. JACKSON: Celine? You've been awful silent. What do you think?

CELINE: *(Collects all her strength.)* Um...I agree with Tracy and Greg.

SHEILA:	I'm sorry, but I don't see how religion, or whatever you call it, is going to make our world a better place. Besides, if God is so great, why are there so many problems in the first place?
MR. JACKSON:	*(Looks at watch.)* Well, we're not going to solve the world's problems in a day. Besides, it looks like our time is up.

(Celine, Sheila, Tracy, Greg, and Ray stand up to leave the room.)

MR. JACKSON:	Chapter seven tomorrow!

QUESTIONS ▼ ▼ ▼ ▼ ▼ ▼ ▼ ▼ ▼ ▼ ▼ ▼

● How realistic was this discussion? What comments did you relate to most?

● Have you ever spoken up for your faith at school or among your friends? If so, how did those who were listening react?

● What part of Ray and Sheila's comments disturbed you most? How would you respond to people who were saying these things? How comfortable would you feel if you were speaking about your faith in a classroom setting such as this one?

Read Matthew 10:16-20 and John 8:42-47.

● What do these passages imply about how non-Christians will respond to what Christians say about their faith? What is our role in relating to people who disagree with our faith?

● If you were the teacher, and a Christian, would you risk sharing your opinion on this issue if you knew your job could be on the line for what you say? Why or why not?

▲ ▲ ▲ ▲ ▲ ▲ ▲ ▲ ▲ ▲ ▲ ▲ ▲ ▲ ▲

2. MIRACLES HAPPEN

CELINE:	*(To herself)* Dear God, please help Ray and Sheila understand.
TRACY:	OK, I think this class is missing the point. People can abuse religion just as they can abuse anything else. Sure, there are problems in religion. In fact, most of what you hear in the media about religion is the dark side. But that doesn't even come close to giving people a picture of what it really means to have faith in God.
GREG:	*(To himself)* Help me speak the truth.
GREG:	Tracy's right. I know it's not easy to understand, but faith in God is what's really needed in our society. Education can't give us a true purpose in life; politics can't help us find meaning; only the one true God can do that.
CELINE:	*(To Sheila and Ray)* And he can do that for you, too. Christianity isn't a religion, it's a relationship—a connection with our Creator made possible by Jesus' death on the cross.
MR. JACKSON:	Hold on, everyone. This isn't church, it's school.
GREG:	But that's the whole point. Faith in God isn't something that

happens only on Sunday or at Christmas or Easter. It's a way of life.

TRACY: When you accept Christ as your Savior, your whole life is affected. You can finally have hope in a hopeless world. You can finally find peace even when things are going terribly wrong around you. We can't separate our faith from other aspects of our lives because our faith *is* our lives.

(Mr. Jackson, Sheila, and Ray pause to reflect on what the other kids are saying.)

RAY: I could sure use some hope.

SHEILA: So what would someone do if he or she wanted to know more about this God of yours?

(Tracy, Greg, and Celine look at each other and smile.)

CELINE: Talk to us after school.

RAY: You mind if I listen in, too?

GREG: Please. We'd love to have you join us.

MR. JACKSON: *(Looks at watch)* Well, looks like our class time is up. We'll have to get back on track with our subject tomorrow.

(Celine, Greg, Tracy, Ray, and Sheila get up and head out the door.)

MR. JACKSON: *(Stopping Tracy and speaking quietly)* Do you think you guys could tell me more about this stuff, too?

TRACY: Sure.

QUESTIONS ▼ ▼ ▼ ▼ ▼ ▼ ▼ ▼ ▼ ▼ ▼ ▼

● How would you feel if this ending happened to you in real life?

● Have you ever listened to someone else speak up for his or her faith? If so, how did you feel as you were listening?

● How could the curiosity expressed by Sheila, Ray, and the teacher be attributed to a miracle? What other responses might they have in real life?

● Why is it difficult for most people to speak up about their faith in public or among peers? Read Matthew 10:16-20 and John 8:42-47.

● How are we to respond to people who disagree with our beliefs? How will people typically react when you speak up about your faith?

● If you were the teacher, how might you have reacted when the class discussion started turning toward issues of faith? What responsibility do teachers have when it comes to discussing faith in public schools?

▲ ▲ ▲ ▲ ▲ ▲ ▲ ▲ ▲ ▲ ▲ ▲ ▲

3. HIDE AND SEEK

GREG: Um . . . I don't really know what to think about all the religious stuff.

(Tracy and Celine look at Greg with puzzled expressions.)

SHEILA: That's odd. I thought you were one of those churchgoing types.

RAY: Yeah. Didn't you go on some mission trip last summer to Ecuador? My mom read about it in the paper. That was a church thing, wasn't it?

GREG: Um . . . yeah. It was sponsored by a church. But I'm not sure what I believe about all that stuff.

MR. JACKSON: Celine, what do you think?

CELINE: *(Swallows hard.)* Well, my parents make me go to church, so I know a little about this stuff, but I'm no expert. *(Pauses.)* I guess I agree with Ray and Sheila.

SHEILA: You guess?

CELINE: Yeah, I guess.

RAY: How come you haven't said anything yet, Tracy? You're always one of the first people to express an opinion on world issues.

TRACY: I was just . . . um . . . thinking about what you said. Maybe you're right. Maybe people shouldn't be forced to see Christian symbols or hear Christian messages in public forums.

A ROOSTER'S CROW: *(Makes a crowing sound to end the skit.)*

QUESTIONS ▼ ▼ ▼ ▼ ▼ ▼ ▼ ▼ ▼ ▼ ▼ ▼

Read Matthew 26:69-75.

● How are the Christians in this skit like Peter in this Scripture passage? Why is it often easier to deny your faith than to speak up about it?

● How would you have felt if you were another Christian in class and you were watching this discussion?

● Have you ever been in a situation where you had the opportunity to speak up for your faith and didn't do so? If so, why did you decide to keep quiet? What was the result of this experience?

● All three Christians in this story not only didn't speak up for what they believed, but they also caved in to the pressure of others. When have you felt like doing this? How can we build confidence in our faith so we don't give in like the Christians in this skit did?

Read Matthew 10:16-20 and John 8:42-47.

● What do these passages tell us about how we should relate to people who don't agree with our beliefs?

● If you were the teacher, and a Christian, how might you have felt as you heard your fellow Christians "wimp out"? Would you have talked to them after school if you had had the chance? Why or why not?

▲ ▲ ▲ ▲ ▲ ▲ ▲ ▲ ▲ ▲ ▲ ▲ ▲ ▲

RACING LIFE

SCRIPTURE:

Psalm 121;
Romans 8:31-39;
and Hebrews
10:22-23

THEMES:

Angels, depression, guilt, hope,
life is precious,
terminal illness

THE SETTING:

Two teenagers are in a car, driving down a dark country road.

THE PROPS:

You'll need two chairs facing the audience. These represent the car. You'll also need a large sheet of cardboard (with an illustration of the front end of a train engine drawn on one side, if possible) if you use ending option two.

THE CHARACTERS:

Devon, a teenage guy
Brianna, a teenage girl
Denai, Devon's sister (if you use ending option three)
Volunteer, to hold cardboard train (if you use ending option two)

THE SCRIPT:

(Devon and Brianna are driving home from a youth group activity along dark country roads. Devon is driving. Have the people playing Devon and Brianna lean to the left and right as if making sharp turns on the road when the script indicates they should do so.)

DEVON:	That was the biggest waste of time in my life.
BRIANNA:	*(Looking over at Devon)* What are you talking about? I thought it was kind of fun.
DEVON:	*(Looks over at Brianna.)* You think it's fun to sit around with a bunch of kids who could be dead tomorrow? I thought it was completely depressing.
BRIANNA:	*(Looks at the road up ahead.)* Um . . . I think you'd better watch the road.

(Devon looks at the road, then Devon and Brianna both lean to the left.)

BRIANNA:	I think you're being insensitive. That little bit of time we spent with those kids probably made their lives just a little more bearable. I mean, when hope is all but gone, what else is there?
DEVON:	You tell me.
BRIANNA:	Well, there's people. Like you and me. Just being there for those kids has got to make a difference.
DEVON:	Brianna, all we did was spend an hour with them. You think that's

gonna make everything better? Their cancer won't go away because some lame youth group kids came to visit.

(Devon and Brianna lean to the right.)

BRIANNA:	Why are you so angry about all this? All we did was visit some cancer kids and try to brighten up their day.
DEVON:	Cancer kids? Now who's being insensitive?
BRIANNA:	OK. Some "terminally ill" kids. Is that better?
DEVON:	Doesn't matter what you call them. They're all gonna die.
BRIANNA:	*(Upset)* Devon! *(Pauses, then becomes apologetic.)* Oh, I'm sorry, Devon. I forgot. Denai had cancer, didn't she?
DEVON:	*(Nods sadly.)* Yes.
BRIANNA:	Then why did you come tonight? You knew we'd be seeing all those kids.
DEVON:	I . . . I don't know. Maybe I felt guilty about not spending enough time with my sister. Maybe I just like to feel depressed all the time. I don't know.

(Devon and Brianna lean to the right.)

BRIANNA:	You *do* seem depressed a lot. I've been worried about you lately. I mean, I *care* about you. You're my friend. I wish you could enjoy life a little more like you used to.
DEVON:	Enjoy life? I just don't know how to do that anymore. What is there to enjoy? People are dying all over the place. The world's a mess. My life is a mess. Where's the hope in that?
BRIANNA:	I'm sorry if this sounds trite, but you've got to trust God that things are going to turn out OK.
DEVON:	*(Looks over at Brianna.)* I'd like to, Bree, but I don't know how. Sometimes I just . . . I just wonder if there really is a God.
BRIANNA:	*(Looks ahead then suddenly screams in horror.)* Devon! The train—we're going to hit . . .

Freeze the skit. Then have participants or audience members choose from the following ending options to finish the skit. Choose additional actors if necessary.

1. Crossing Guard (no new characters)

2. Last Train (new character: volunteer to hold cardboard)

3. X-Files (new character: Denai, Devon's sister)

● ● ● ●

1. CROSSING GUARD

(Devon and Brianna swerve radically to the left and then fall out of their chairs as if their car has rolled. They sit up slowly and look at each other.)

DEVON:	Wow! Did we just do what I think we did?
BRIANNA:	*(Grimacing in pain)* Um . . . yeah . . . I think so. We did miss the train, didn't we?
DEVON:	*(Looks up)* Yeah. And there it goes. How did we manage to miss that?
BRIANNA:	I guess it wasn't our time yet.
DEVON:	Are you OK?
BRIANNA:	Yeah. I think I have some bruises, but I don't think I'm seriously hurt. How about you?
DEVON:	I'm OK.
DEVON:	*(After a pause)* Do you think God was trying to tell me something?
BRIANNA:	Well, he certainly got *my* attention.
DEVON:	No, really, Bree. I mean, there I was, talking about how life didn't mean much anymore, about how I felt hopeless. Then we almost were killed by a train, but we weren't. We should've been, but we weren't. That must mean something, right?
BRIANNA:	Well, I guess so.
DEVON:	*(Smiling)* I guess I needed a little sense knocked into me.
BRIANNA:	*(Pretending to be upset)* But did you have to bring me along for the ride?
DEVON:	I'm sorry, Bree. I really didn't see that train coming.
BRIANNA:	*(Smiling)* I know, I know. Actually, I'm glad I was with you. Who knows what would have happened if you'd been racing along this road alone.
DEVON:	Let's not think about that.
BRIANNA:	Devon, do you mind if I say a little prayer of thanks?
DEVON:	Sure—after me.

(Brianna and Devon bow their heads.)

DEVON: Thank you, Lord, for reminding me how precious life really is . . .

QUESTIONS ▼ ▼ ▼ ▼ ▼ ▼ ▼ ▼ ▼ ▼ ▼ ▼
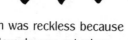

● Do you think Devon was reckless because he was so depressed? How do you act when things seem to be falling apart all around you?

● Do you think God reaches into people's lives the way Devon believes he did? Why or why not?

● What did it take to get Devon to believe that life is truly worth living? Why does it take a near catastrophe or a traumatic experience for some people to start thinking seriously about their faith?

Read Psalm 121 and Romans 8:31-39.

● How might these passages help us see why life is worth living? How can God's love help us when we're feeling depressed or lost?

● What would you have said to Devon if you were his friend and knew he was deeply depressed? How do you comfort your friends?

● How can we help others see the value of life? How can our faith help us see that life is special?

▲ ▲ ▲ ▲ ▲ ▲ ▲ ▲ ▲ ▲ ▲ ▲ ▲ ▲

2. LAST TRAIN

(Tell the audience that as Devon and Brianna race toward the oncoming freight train, time slows down so we can hear their thoughts. Have a volunteer stand at the back of the room, holding the large sheet of cardboard. As the skit progresses, have this person walk slowly toward Devon and Brianna's "car." Make sure this volunteer is able to time the approach so he or she gets to the front of the stage just as the skit ends.)

DEVON   *(To himself, panicked)* Dear God, why is this happening to me? What did I do to deserve this?

BRIANNA   *(To herself, calmly)* Father, please save us from this terrible situation. Please, Lord, keep us alive. Don't let us hit that train.

DEVON   *(To himself, still panicked)* God, at least spare Brianna! She didn't do anything wrong. She loves you so much, and she's a friend to so many people!

BRIANNA: *(Still calm)* Please, Lord, help Devon see how much you love him. Help him reach out to you in this brief moment.

DEVON: *(Calmer)* I'm sorry I didn't reach out to Denai more. I was afraid. I didn't want to lose her, and every time I saw her lying there in that bed, all I could think about was losing her. I'm sorry I was so selfish.

BRIANNA: I love you, Lord. Please help my family cope if we don't pull out of this.

DEVON: Dear God, I'm sorry! I'm sorry I lost faith in you! Please forgive . . .

(At this time, the volunteer should make the cardboard train collide with the front of

Devon and Brianna's car. As the cardboard hits them, Devon and Brianna both scream then slump to the ground, not moving.)

QUESTIONS ▼ ▼ ▼ ▼ ▼ ▼ ▼ ▼ ▼ ▼ ▼ ▼

● What do you think happened to Devon and Brianna?

● Why does it often take a tragic or traumatic experience to help people realize the value of life?

● What do you think would have happened in Devon's life if he hadn't been confronted by a life-and-death situation? How do you act when things seem to be falling apart all around you?

Read Psalm 121 and Romans 8:31-39.

● How might these passages help us see why life is worth living? What role does God's love for you play in your desire to live?

● Do you think Brianna reacted to Devon the way she should have? What else could she have done to help him?

● How can we help others see the value of life?

▲ ▲ ▲ ▲ ▲ ▲ ▲ ▲ ▲ ▲ ▲ ▲ ▲ ▲

3. X-FILES

(Have audience members close their eyes while Denai replaces Brianna in the chair next to Devon. If you have access to a bright light, have the lights go out for a few seconds while they switch places, then have a bright light flash as the regular lights come up, revealing Denai in Brianna's chair.)

DEVON: *(Confused, looking over at Denai)* Denai? But . . . it can't be. You're . . . you're . . .

DENAI: Dead? I know.

DEVON: *(Looking around)* Where's Brianna? Where are we? Wait a minute. We were driving along the road . . . and . . .

DENAI: Devon . . .

DEVON: *(Ignores her)* The train! We were heading straight for the train!

DENAI: Devon, please listen to me.

DEVON: *(Looks over at Denai.)* You aren't here. *(Looks away.)* You can't be here.

DENAI: Devon, please look at me. I am here.

DEVON: *(Looks back at her.)* Denai? Is that really you?

DENAI: Yes. I just wanted to tell you that it's OK.

DEVON: What do you mean? What's OK?

DENAI: It's OK that you didn't come see me every day. I know it was hard for you.

DEVON: I wanted to, Denai. I really wanted to help.

DENAI:	I know.
DEVON:	But I didn't. And now you're gone, and things are so empty at home.
DENAI:	Devon, please don't forget about everyone else. Mom and Dad— they really love you. And Brianna, she's a great friend. There are a lot of people who care. Don't check out of life just because you feel sad about my being gone.
DEVON:	It's just so hard.
DENAI:	God will give you the strength. He can help you if you only ask. Life *is* worth living, Devon. It really is.

(Devon hugs Denai.)

DENAI:	Trust God, Devon. Just trust him. He's giving you a second chance.
DEVON:	Denai . . . Denai . . .

(Have the lights go down again, or ask everyone to close their eyes while Brianna slips back into her seat and Denai slips offstage. Once again, if you have access to a bright light, flash it as the lights come back up.)

(Brianna and Devon turn and look behind them.)

BRIANNA:	*(Relieved)* I can't believe how close we came.
DEVON:	Second chance.
BRIANNA:	*(Looks at Devon.)* What was that?
DEVON:	I think God was giving me a second chance. At life, I mean.
BRIANNA:	What just happened back there, Devon? You seem . . . different.
DEVON:	I'm not sure, Brianna. I think I was just visited by an angel.

QUESTIONS

● What do you think happened to Devon?

● Do you believe that God sometimes sends angels to help us when we're in trouble? Explain.

● How do you think Devon will act now that he's had this unusual experience?

Read Psalm 121 and Romans 8:31-39.

● How does knowing that God loves you help you deal with difficult situations? What do these passages tell us about the value of life?

● Devon felt guilty for not reaching out to his sister. How do you deal with guilt?

Read Hebrews 10:22-23.

● What does this passage tell us about how God deals with our guilt?

ONE MORE VERSE

SCRIPTURE:
Psalms 29, 66, 100, and 150

THEMES:
Generation gap, music, worship

THE SETTING:
Members of a youth group are sitting around a campfire with their youth leader.

THE PROPS:
You'll need a toy drum. If it's possible that you may use ending option one, ask teenagers what kind of music they like to sing in worship services so you can have music or recordings available. If you use ending option two, you'll also need a CD or cassette tape of a popular contemporary Christian song—the more upbeat the better.

THE CHARACTERS:
Brett, a teenage guy
Jamie, a teenage girl
Kurt, a teenage guy
Tori, a teenage girl
Jack, a youth leader

THE SCRIPT:

JACK: All right, everyone, let's worship!

JAMIE: *(To the other teenagers)* Here we go again.

JACK: *(Begins singing in a dull voice.)* It only takes a spark to get a fire going . . .

(After a moment, Jack realizes that no one is singing along with him, and he stops.)

JACK: Maybe you didn't hear me. I said, "It's time to worship!"

(Jack begins singing again. Kurt and Tori join in for a moment and then drop out when they realize no one else is singing along.)

JACK: *(Stops singing again.)* OK, OK. Maybe that song is a little on the old side. I can be contemporary if I have to. *(In a loud, fake, rock 'n' roll voice)* ARE YOU READY TO ROCK?

(Tori and Brett get all excited and are ready to join in this time. Jamie looks interested but skeptical. Kurt rolls his eyes.)

JACK: Count me in, Tori.

TORI: One, two, three, four!

JACK: *(Goes back to his dull singing voice.)* Kumbaya, my Lord. Kumbaya.

(The youth group members frown and slump down on the ground, frustrated with their leader.)

JACK: *(Stops singing again and looks around at the youth group members.)* C'mon, guys. Don't you want to worship?

JAMIE: Sure! That's why we're here.

BRETT: But . . . um . . . those ancient songs don't really do it for me.

KURT: Me neither.

TORI: I prefer songs with a little more of a beat, you know?

JACK: *(Puzzled at first, then smiles as if he understands what Tori has said.)* Oh, sure. I get it. I should've known. *(Gets up, leaves the stage, and comes back with a toy drum and starts banging on the drum and singing loudly.)* Michael, row the boat ashore. Alleluia. Michael, row the boat ashore. Alleluia.

(Tori, Kurt, Brett, and Jamie groan, and Jack stops singing once again.)

TORI: That's . . . um . . . not quite what I meant.

JACK: *(Upset)* Look. It's time to worship and, doggone it, we're going to worship. So stop being party poopers, and let's get to it!

● ● ● ●

Freeze the skit. Then have participants or audience members choose from the following ending options to finish the skit.

1. Interactive (no new characters)

2. Trading Places (no new characters)

3. Hit the Road, Jack (no new characters)

● ● ● ●

1. INTERACTIVE

(Tori, Brett, Jamie, and Kurt look at one another in shock.)

TORI: Jack, I think you're way out of line here.

JAMIE: You can't force someone to worship.

TORI: Especially if that style of worship just doesn't connect.

BRETT: Actually, I worship best when I'm alone in my room at home. I'm not too good at this corporate worship stuff.

JAMIE:	And I love to sing, but not those old songs. I like the new praise stuff we sing at worship services.
KURT:	I prefer quiet worship times.
TORI:	I like singing, but sometimes I just don't feel like worshiping. I mean, it's been a pretty tough week for me.
JACK:	*(Looking hurt but really trying to do things right)* OK, so what you're saying is . . .
KURT:	What we're saying is that we don't all worship the same way.
TORI:	And we can't be forced to worship when we just don't feel like it.
JACK:	All right. Maybe I *am* a little behind the times. *(Pauses.)* How about if you guys lead the worship time?

(Tori, Brett, Kurt, and Jamie look at each other and nod.)

(At this time, have the actors lead the rest of the group in a brief worship time, using their own ideas for worship. They could lead songs, spend time in prayer, share prayer concerns and joys, and add any other components they choose.)

QUESTIONS ▼ ▼ ▼ ▼ ▼ ▼ ▼ ▼ ▼ ▼ ▼ ▼

● What was it like to be led by your peers in worship? Did this style of worship connect with you?

● How do you feel about worshiping when you've had a bad day or things aren't going right in your life? Does God expect us to worship even when things aren't going well? Why?

Have teenagers form four groups, and have each group read one of the following Psalms: 29; 66; 100; and 150.

● What does your passage tell us about worship?

● What roles do age, culture, and tradition play in determining the ways we worship?

● How do you prefer to worship God? What are some ways we can worship God together regardless of age, culture, or tradition?

● If you were in the situation portrayed in this skit, would you be bold enough to tell your leader your feelings about worship? about other aspects of the youth group that don't connect with you? How can clear communication with your leader help make your youth group meetings better?

▲ ▲ ▲ ▲ ▲ ▲ ▲ ▲ ▲ ▲ ▲ ▲ ▲ ▲

2. TRADING PLACES

(Kurt, Tori, Brett, and Jamie look at Jack in shock, then suddenly decide he's right.)

KURT:	But what you're saying is . . . is . . .
TORI:	. . . absolutely right!
BRETT:	We should worship your way.
JAMIE:	Brett's right. Those songs really are great worship tunes . . .

(Jack is surprised at these responses but doesn't know what to say.)

KURT:　　　　　　Hey, everyone, let's worship!

JAMIE:　　　　　　*(Leading the singing)* It only takes a spark . . .

(Kurt, Brett, and Tori all join in happily.)

JAMIE, KURT,
BRETT, TORI:　　　*(Together)* . . . to get a fire going, and soon all those around . . .

JACK:　　　　　　*(Interrupting the song)* Wait! Hold on a second. That song really isn't right for you guys. It's too old.

BRETT:　　　　　　No way! Worship songs are timeless. Besides, I'm really starting to get into this worship time.

TORI:　　　　　　Me too. Hey, let's stop gabbing and get back to worshiping. *(Begins singing.)* Kumbaya, my Lord. Kumbaya . . .

(Jamie, Brett, and Kurt all join in enthusiastically.)

TORI, JAMIE,
BRETT, KURT:　　　Kumbaya, my Lord. Kumbaya . . .

JACK:　　　　　　*(Interrupting again)* Stop! Stop singing. My grandparents sang Kumbaya. What about this? *(Pulls out a CD or cassette player and plays a contemporary Christian song.)*

(Tori, Jamie, Brett, and Kurt groan.)

KURT:　　　　　　I don't know why you older people listen to that stuff.

TORI:　　　　　　It hurts my head.

JAMIE:　　　　　　How can you worship to that noise?

BRETT:　　　　　　*(Walks over and turns off the music.)* Now this is real worship.

(Picks up the drum, starts beating it, then begins leading the group in "Michael, Row the Boat Ashore.")

(Jack throws up his hands and walks offstage.)

QUESTIONS ▼　▼　▼　▼　▼　▼　▼　▼　▼　▼　▼　▼

● What surprised you about this ending?
● Why do adults and teenagers seem to have such different ideas about music and worship?

Have kids form four groups, and have each group read one of the following Psalms: 29; 66; 100; and 150.

● What kinds of worship does your psalm talk about?
● What would happen in our church if people's preferences for worship styles suddenly changed?→

● What methods of worship are you most uncomfortable with? Why do you think some other people are uncomfortable with the worship styles you prefer?

● How can we learn from each other's different styles of worship? What are some ways we can help each other develop a broader acceptance of worship styles?

▲ ▲ ▲ ▲ ▲ ▲ ▲ ▲ ▲ ▲ ▲ ▲ ▲ ▲ ▲

3. HIT THE ROAD, JACK

BRETT: Wait a second. Sing that last song again—the one with the drum.

JACK: Huh?

BRETT: I mean it. Sing it again. *(To others)* Listen to this, everyone.

(Jack hits the drum again and sings "Michael, Row the Boat Ashore.")

KURT: *(Looks at Brett, puzzled.)* Why are you . . .

BRETT: Shh.

(Jack finishes the song or stops after a verse or two.)

BRETT: *(Pretending to be impressed)* Wow. *(To others)* Did you guys hear what I heard?

TORI: *(Catching on to Brett's plan)* Oh, yeah. That was just . . . it was really . . .

JAMIE: *(Smiling)* Unique!

KURT: *(Correcting her)* What Jamie means is we didn't know how great a singer you were.

BRETT: Kurt's right. Do you have any professional singing experience?

JACK: *(Starting to believe what they're saying)* Well, I did sing a solo in the Easter pageant when I was seven.

TORI: I knew it!

JAMIE: And here you are, wasting that talent, leading a little youth group like this.

JACK: I *do* like singing those songs.

TORI: It shows. I think you should find a band and take your singing on the road.

KURT: Yeah. There are lots of young people out there who would really get into those songs.

JAMIE: Maybe you could record a worship album.

JACK: You really think so? Kids really like this stuff?

JAMIE: Sure.

JACK:	*(Proudly)* Would you like to hear them again? *(Starts singing one of the songs.)*
KURT:	*(Stopping him)* Oh, we'd *love* to listen and worship with you, but you're going to need to practice for your big concert tour.
JAMIE:	Yeah, I can't *wait* until you hit the road, Jack.

(Kurt, Tori, and Brett glance at Jamie, who bites her lip.)

JACK:	*(Thoughtfully)* Well, I guess you're right. I'll go call some of my buddies to see if I can get a band together. *(Stands up.)* Thanks, guys. And don't worry. I'll be sure to get you free tickets when Jack's Amazing Worship Band comes to town.

(Jack skips off the stage. Tori, Brett, Jamie, and Kurt look at each other and breathe a sigh of relief.)

KURT:	I'm sorry we had to do that.
JAMIE:	Me too.
BRETT:	*(After a short pause)* OK, who wants to lead the worship time?

QUESTIONS ▼ ▼ ▼ ▼ ▼ ▼ ▼ ▼ ▼ ▼ ▼ ▼

● Have you ever felt about a worship experience the way the teenagers in this skit did? If so, how did you respond? How should you have responded?

● Why do some adults seem so out of touch with the way teenagers like to worship?

● How can you help adults understand the way you like to worship?

● What can you do to help adults connect better with the music and issues you're dealing with? How can you connect better with the worship styles they prefer?

Have kids form groups of four, and have each person in each group look up and read one of the following Psalms: 29; 66; 100; and 150. Have kids discuss the following questions in their groups then share their insight with the rest of the group.

● What new ideas do these passages give you about what worship is?

● How might you "update" these passages to reflect how our church chooses to worship or how you like to worship? How does the time we live in affect our method of worship?

● What is the ultimate goal of worship? How can we reach that goal without "turning off" people because of a style of worship?

● If you were in the situation portrayed in this skit, would you be bold enough to tell your leader your feelings about worship, or would you rather pretend to enjoy his or her worship style?

THERE'S NOTHING WRONG WITH SEX ANYMORE

SCRIPTURE:

Genesis 2:24;
Matthew 5:27-28;
and 1 Corinthians
7:2-3

THEMES:

Dating, friendship,
peer pressure, pre-
marital sex, sex

THE SETTING:

Two couples are sitting and talking in the dark corners of a youth room.

THE PROPS:

You'll need couches or floor cushions for the couples to sit on and a partition (optional). You may want to use pizza as a prop if you use ending
option two. You'll need two telephones if you use ending option three.

THE CHARACTERS:

Scott, Kathy's boyfriend
Kathy, Scott's girlfriend
Mike, Bonnie's boyfriend
Bonnie, Mike's girlfriend
Server (optional), male or female to serve pizza (if you use ending
option two)

THE SCRIPT:

(Two couples, oblivious to each other, are sitting in a youth group room on a couch or on floor cushions, talking about their relationships. You might want to set up a partition that separates Scott and Kathy from Mike and Bonnie to add to the illusion that they're unable to hear each other talk.)

(Scott scoots close to Kathy and puts his arm around her.)

SCOTT:	My parents are going out tonight.
KATHY:	*(After a short pause)* So?
SCOTT:	Sooo . . . we can finally be alone together.
KATHY:	What are you saying, Scott?
SCOTT:	You know, we can finally be *alone together*. *(Nudges her with his elbow.)* Know what I mean? Just you and me. Get it? Comprende?
KATHY:	*(Sarcastically)* Um . . . Scott, do you think you could be a little more romantic about it?

SCOTT:	Sorry. I just don't know how to talk about this particular topic.
KATHY:	We've talked about this before, Scott.
SCOTT:	Yeah, but that was a long time ago. And since we're still together and we really care about each other, I was just thinking . . .

(Scott and Kathy freeze in place while Mike and Bonnie talk.)

BONNIE:	Did you ever think that maybe that advice just wasn't valid anymore? Lots of things have changed since Jesus' day. People are different now.
MIKE:	I don't know. Seems to me some of those things in the Bible are also timeless. I happen to believe that saving sex for marriage is one of them.
BONNIE:	And I really respect you for that. But I think I'm . . . we're ready *now*.
MIKE:	Bonnie, it's not that I don't want to be with you. God knows I spend lots of energy trying to keep those feelings in check. But I don't think that it's a matter of "being ready." I just don't want to discount what the Bible says simply because of the way I feel.
BONNIE:	But we love each other, don't we?
MIKE:	Yeah, I think so. But even that . . . I'm not sure how much we know about love yet.
BONNIE:	Stop acting so mature. Why don't you just loosen up a little?

(Bonnie and Mike freeze in place as Scott and Kathy talk again.)

KATHY:	Thinking what? Maybe we should sleep together?
SCOTT:	Well, I wasn't exactly thinking about sleeping. *(Smiles.)*
KATHY:	Scott . . .
SCOTT:	Uh oh, here it comes.
KATHY:	Hear me out, Scott. I really *do* care for you. And I hope that never changes, but . . .
SCOTT:	But?
KATHY:	But I don't think we're ready to take that step yet.
SCOTT:	*(Pleading)* But we *love* each other. Isn't that what's most important?
KATHY:	I think that if we truly love each other, we can wait until the time is right.
SCOTT:	*(Upset)* And that time would be . . .
KATHY:	I don't know.

SCOTT:	*(Still upset)* Well, I think that time is tonight. *(Stands up.)* When you come to your senses and realize I'm right, come over to my house. I'll be waiting. *(Walks offstage.)*

(Kathy freezes in place while Mike and Bonnie talk again.)

MIKE:	Loosen up? Is that all that sex means to you?
BONNIE:	No, of course not. I *know* it's a big decision. At least we didn't just jump into bed on the first date like so many of our friends.
MIKE:	Yeah, they didn't have the Bible to stop them.
BONNIE:	You mean to make them feel guilty.
MIKE:	No, I meant what I said. Maybe I'm the last remaining male teen-age virgin, but I still think what the Bible teaches about sex is valid today.
BONNIE:	*(Frustrated)* Sometimes I think you love that Bible of yours more than me!

Freeze the skit. Then have participants or audience members choose from the following ending options to finish the skit. Choose additional actors if necessary.

1. Roulette (no new characters)

2. Let's Get Together (no new characters)

3. Backward Glances (optional new character: Server)

1. ROULETTE

(Have audience members close their eyes and pretend to sleep in their chairs as you call out the days of the week three or four times in order to signify a few weeks passing. When the audience members open their eyes, the actors are onstage where they were before, but they are less "clingy" and sitting farther apart from their respective boyfriends/girlfriends.)

KATHY:	*(Upset)* So what are we going to do?
SCOTT:	*I* don't know. Why do you always expect me to have the answers?
KATHY:	You're the one who got us into this mess in the first place.
SCOTT:	Me? *Me?* Who was it who decided to come over to my house while my parents were away?
KATHY:	*(Angry)* I *didn't* come over to sleep with you.

SCOTT:	*(Looking around)* Not so loud.
KATHY:	*(Ignoring him)* I just came over to talk. When you left, you were so angry at me. I didn't want things to end that way.
SCOTT:	Face it, Kathy. You wanted to do it. You certainly didn't try to stop me.
KATHY:	I didn't try, but I wanted to. Scott, what we did was wrong.
SCOTT:	No. It was perfectly natural; perfectly normal. There is nothing wrong with sex between two people who love each other.
KATHY:	But that's just it, Scott. I *don't* love you.
SCOTT:	*(Surprised)* You . . . what?
KATHY:	I don't love you. And I feel like such an idiot that it took such a big mistake for me to realize it.
SCOTT:	What do you mean?
KATHY:	How can I love someone who doesn't respect my beliefs? You took advantage of my one moment of weakness *(starts to cry),* and I'm going to have to live with that the rest of my life.
SCOTT:	But I didn't . . . *(Pauses)* . . . I didn't mean to hurt you.
KATHY:	You did.
SCOTT:	*(Quietly)* I'm sorry.

(Kathy and Scott stare off into space for a moment.)

SCOTT:	So what are we going to do?
KATHY:	I don't know about you, but I'm going to pray for forgiveness—and for the test results to say I'm *not* pregnant. *(After a brief pause, she stands up.)* I'm sorry, Scott. I have to be alone. *(Leaves quickly.)*
SCOTT:	*(After she's gone, in a quiet voice)* Bye. *(Pauses for a long, awkward moment.)* God, do you have a minute? I think I've really messed up.

(Scott freezes in place while Mike and Bonnie talk.)

MIKE:	So how are you doing?
BONNIE:	Um . . . fine. I'm doing OK.
MIKE:	How did your parents react when you talked to them?
BONNIE:	Well, they were upset that I didn't tell them sooner. But you were right. They were very understanding and supportive.
MIKE:	That's got to be tough—telling your parents that some guy took advantage of you.

BONNIE: It was the hardest thing I've ever done.

(Mike nods silently.)

BONNIE: I wanted to thank you.

MIKE: Me? For what?

BONNIE: For being such a good friend during this time.

MIKE: Hey, no problem. Just because we aren't . . . um—I guess "dating" is the best word—doesn't mean I don't care for you.

BONNIE: But it wasn't easy for you to convince me to talk to my parents.

MIKE: Actually, it *was* easy. I've known you for a long time, Bonnie, and it's not like you to hide the truth from your parents. You *had* to talk to them.

BONNIE: Yeah, I did. I'm sorry I yelled at you.

MIKE: Don't worry about it. *(Pauses.)* So did you talk to him?

BONNIE: Yes. He said he was sorry, but I don't believe him. I mean, he practically broadcast it over the school intercom.

MIKE: You're not going to see him again, are you?

BONNIE: No. I'm not planning on doing *any* dating for a while. I just need some time to sort things out.

MIKE: Good for you.

BONNIE: There's something else I'm going to need, too.

MIKE: What's that?

BONNIE: A friend.

MIKE: *(Gives her a hug.)* You've got one—always.

QUESTIONS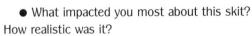

● What impacted you most about this skit? How realistic was it?

● Why do you think Kathy gave in and had sex with Scott? How might Scott and Kathy have avoided the trauma they experienced?

● What do you think Bonnie and Mike were talking about in this ending? What did Bonnie talk to her parents about? What does this story line illustrate about the value of friendship?

Read Genesis 2:24; Matthew 5:27-28; and 1 Corinthians 7:2-3.

● What do these passages suggest about the role of sex in relationships?

● Why do so many people today think that saving sex for marriage is such an archaic idea?

● Do you face pressure to have sex before marriage? If so, from whom? How can you deal with those pressures?

2. LET'S GET TOGETHER

(In this ending, all four teenagers are sitting together at a restaurant. To introduce the fact that kids are in a restaurant, you may want to have a Server walk out onstage, say, "I'll be right with you" to the actors, then deliver pizza to the audience members to enjoy during the skit.)

SCOTT:	*(To Kathy)* No way! Double pepperoni and extra cheese on a thick crust.
KATHY:	*(Teasing him)* You *are* a thick crust. Bonnie and I want a veggie pizza on a *thin* crust.
BONNIE:	But no olives.
KATHY:	Right, no olives.
SCOTT:	Pepperoni. Tell 'em Mike.
MIKE:	Pepperoni.
BONNIE:	Veggie.
KATHY:	Veggie.
MIKE:	OK, OK. We'll get one of each.

(Pause.)

SCOTT:	Hey, guys, can we talk about something serious for a moment?
BONNIE:	What? And spoil a perfectly good evening?
MIKE:	Go ahead. Spill your guts.
SCOTT:	I just wanted to thank you guys for being such good friends and helping me see what's really important.
KATHY:	I'll second that.
SCOTT:	I mean, if you weren't so willing to talk about such a sensitive topic, who knows where I'd be?
KATHY:	Certainly not with me.
MIKE:	Hey, it's no easy thing dealing with *(spelling the word quietly)* S-E-X in the nineties. I'm just glad we had a forum to talk about it in our youth group meeting.
BONNIE:	Even though it was the most excruciatingly embarrassing meeting we've ever had.
SCOTT:	But worth every blush.
MIKE:	Yeah. It's been a real kick to spend so much time with other people.

(Pause.)

KATHY: All right. Enough of the serious stuff. We still haven't chosen the soft drink du jour.

SCOTT: Mountain Dew.

BONNIE: No way—Diet Pepsi.

MIKE: *Diet?* I don't think so!

KATHY: Here we go again!

(All characters freeze in place.)

QUESTIONS ▼ ▼ ▼ ▼ ▼ ▼ ▼ ▼ ▼ ▼ ▼ ▼

● What do you think changed Scott and Bonnie's minds about playing around sexually? How can we as group members help each other make solid, Bible-based decisions about sexual behavior?

● Besides spending time with other people instead of time alone with a boyfriend or girlfriend, what are some other practical ways to avoid sexual pressures or temptations?

Read Genesis 2:24; Matthew 5:27-28; and 1 Corinthians 7:2-3.

● What do these passages suggest about the nature of sex?

● Why do you think the Bible says that sex is to be saved for the marriage relationship?

● How might your friends react if they heard that you chose to not play around sexually?

● Why do so many people think abstinence is such an old-fashioned idea?

● What do the four teenagers in this skit gain because they're saving sex for marriage?

▲ ▲ ▲ ▲ ▲ ▲ ▲ ▲ ▲ ▲ ▲ ▲ ▲ ▲ ▲

3. BACKWARD GLANCES

(Have the audience stand and spin clockwise in place while you call out years until you've gone about ten years into the future. For example, you might say, "1998, 1999, 2000 . . . " and so on through 2007. Then have audience members sit down to watch the skit ending. In this ending, Bonnie is talking on the phone with Kathy, and Scott is kneeling on the floor in prayer. Mike is nowhere to be seen. Scott remains frozen in place while we listen to Bonnie and Kathy's phone conversation.)

BONNIE: *(Upset)* Kathy, I had to talk with you. I don't know what to do.

KATHY: What's the matter?

BONNIE: It's Brian. He . . . he threatened to leave me.

KATHY: What? But when we went out the other night with you guys, everything seemed to be just fine.

BONNIE: It was. But last night we were talking, and it came out that I slept with Mike.

KATHY: That was years ago.

BONNIE: I know. But considering what happened to Mike, I had to say something. He was so angry and so hurt.

KATHY: So what are you going to do?

BONNIE: I don't know. All I feel like doing is crying.

KATHY: You know I'm here for you. Why don't you come by, and we can talk about it.

BONNIE: Maybe I will. Ashley is at preschool until three. I can be there in about twenty minutes.

KATHY: And meanwhile, I'll be praying for you guys.

BONNIE: *(Softly)* Thanks.

(Kathy and Bonnie freeze in position as Scott prays.)

SCOTT: Father, thank you so much for watching over me all these years. It's been a difficult road, and I never could have made it to this day safely without you. Thanks for giving me the strength to save sex for marriage.

You know how much I love Sheri, Lord. Thank you for sending her to me. As we head to the altar tonight, help us to focus on you and to truly believe the words we speak in our vows. And help us to live out those vows each day from now until the end of time.

Also, God, I ask that you be with Mike's family today. It's been a tough week for them. It's never easy to lose someone you love. Mike made plenty of mistakes in life, and I don't know if he knew you when he died, but I know you're a merciful God, and I ask that you comfort those he left behind.

Please help us to discover a cure for AIDS.

Amen.

QUESTIONS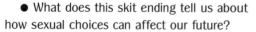

● What does this skit ending tell us about how sexual choices can affect our future?

● Which character would you rather be in this skit ending? Explain.

● What other things could have happened if the teenagers in this skit had all chosen to have sex before marriage? What things could have happened if they had all chosen to save sex for marriage?

● How would you feel if you were a member of Mike's family? How would you feel if you were Bonnie? her husband, Brian? What might you be thinking if you were Scott?

Read Genesis 2:24; Matthew 5:27-28; and 1 Corinthians 7:2-3.

● Why is marriage so special that the Bible tells us sex is only for marriage? What are some benefits of saving sex for marriage?

● How do most of your friends feel about the idea of abstinence? How would you respond to them if they said the idea was "stupid and old-fashioned?"

THEY'LL KNOW WE ARE CHRISTIANS

SCRIPTURE:

Matthew 11:11-19;
Matthew
28:16-20;
Romans 12:2; and
1 John 2:15

THEMES:

Drinking,
hypocrisy, parties,
sharing faith

THE SETTING:

A huge crowd of teenagers is partying at a local teen hangout. Many of the teenagers are drunk. Three Christian teenagers are talking to each other as they're walking to the party.

THE PROPS:

You'll need a large wall clock if you use ending options one or three. You'll need a sign that says, "One hour later, on the roof of the party house..." if you use ending option one. You'll need a sign that says, "One hour later, in a corner of the party house..." if you use ending option three.

THE CHARACTERS:

Sam, a teenage guy
Drew, a teenage guy
Jackie, a teenage girl
Tina, a non-Christian party-goer (if you use ending option one)
Crowd, a bunch of teenagers who are already at the party (if you use ending option two)
Jeff, a non-Christian party-goer (if you use ending option three)

THE SCRIPT:

(Sam, Drew, and Jackie are walking to a home where a rather wild party is in full swing. Have kids walk around the youth room to add to the illusion that they're walking to a party.)

SAM: I'm not so sure this is such a good idea.

DREW: So what's the big deal?

SAM: I just don't think we should be going to a party where there's beer... and who knows what else. Especially when we have to go to youth group later.

DREW: You don't have to drink any, and besides, lots of important kids are going to be there. If we don't make an appearance at this party, we'll never be invited to another.

SAM: I'm not sure I *want* to be invited to another party.

JACKIE: Don't you see, Sam? This is our big opportunity. This is our chance to make a difference—to set an example for other kids.

DREW: *(To Jackie)* You're not gonna turn into a Jesus freak and scare everybody away again, are you?

SAM: Scare everybody away?

DREW: *(To Sam)* Last time Jackie and I went to one of these parties, she started preaching to everybody about why they need Jesus and why drinking isn't the way to solve their problems.

JACKIE: They *do* need Jesus.

DREW: *I* know that. *(To Jackie)* But that doesn't mean you have to hit them over the head with it.

JACKIE: I was just doing my job as a Christian, unlike *some* people I know.

SAM: *(Stops walking.)* I think I'm going to turn around and head home. This doesn't sound like the kind of party I want to go to.

(Jackie and Drew turn and face Sam.)

JACKIE: But they *need* us.

DREW: And we need to be seen there. Look, Sam, it's just a bunch of kids talking, listening to music, dancing . . .

SAM: . . . and drinking.

DREW: Right. They're all misguided. But if we ever want to have a chance of reaching these kids, we need to reach them on *their* level.

(Sam, Drew, and Jackie start walking again.)

SAM: *(Sarcastically)* So we have to get drunk, swear, and put sex at the top of our list of goals for our final year of high school.

JACKIE: He doesn't mean that, Sam. *(To Drew)* Do you?

(Drew doesn't answer.)

JACKIE: Drew?

DREW: Well, I'm not sure there's anything wrong with drinking a little beer. My parents drink wine all the time. What's the difference? Besides, if I'm accepted by these kids, then maybe they'll hear me out about what I think is important.

JACKIE: What *is* important to you, Drew?

DREW:	You know, my faith . . . and all that stuff.
SAM:	All that stuff? *(Sarcastically)* You sound so convincing.
JACKIE:	Look, Sam. Drewski here may be a few light-years off in his methods, but his goals are good. We're called as Christians to reach out and share our faith with others. What better way than to meet them where they live and just tell them what we're all about?
SAM:	I'm not really into this evangelizing thing. I prefer a more subtle approach.
DREW:	You mean you'd rather hide in your room.
SAM:	I don't hide. I just don't do well in crowds.
JACKIE:	Well, you'd better learn to adjust pretty quickly. *(Points ahead as they walk toward the stage.)* Looks like quite a crowd today.

Freeze the skit. Then have participants or audience members choose from the following ending options to finish the skit. Choose additional actors if necessary.

1. On the House (new character: Tina, a non-Christian party-goer)

2. Revival Meetin' (new characters:
Crowd, a bunch of teenagers who are already at the party)

3. One for the Road (new character: Jeff, a non-Christian party-goer)

1. ON THE HOUSE

(Have a volunteer stand up onstage, hold up a clock, and move the hour hand forward one hour. Have another volunteer stand up on stage and hold up the sign that says, "One hour later, on the roof of the party house . . ." Sam, Drew, and Jackie, all drunk, are sitting side by side on the roof of the house.)

SAM:	*(With slurred speech, as if drunk)* This was some party. Don't you think, Jahgee?
JACKIE:	*(Dazed)* Huh?
DREW:	*(More sober than the others, but still drunk)* Didn't I tell you this would be a good idea?
JACKIE:	I don't feel so good.
DREW:	I think everybody really thought we were cool.

SAM:	Yeah, umspecially when Jahgee drank that beer upshide down.
JACKIE:	I really don't feel so good.

(Tina walks onstage, not drunk at all.)

TINA:	Excuse me.
SAM:	*(Looks at Tina.)* Oh, helooo there. Who are you?
TINA:	Tina.
DREW:	Wasn't that a great party, Tina?
JACKIE:	I mean it. I really don't feel well at all.
TINA:	It was OK.
SAM:	Hey, what are we doing up here on this roof?
JACKIE:	We're on a roof?
DREW:	Pretty cool, huh Sam?
JACKIE:	Now I'm really gonna be sick. *(Climbs on all fours away from the others and offstage.)*
TINA:	What's wrong with her?
DREW:	Can't hold her liquor, I guess.
SAM:	How did we get here?
DREW:	*(Ignores Sam and speaks to Tina.)* So what are you doing up here?
TINA:	I was hoping I could talk to you guys.
SAM:	To ush guysh?
DREW:	*(Burps)* What about?
TINA:	Well, you *are* the guys who go to church and stuff, aren't you?
SAM:	Only when we're not partying down! *(Does disco impersonation.)*
DREW:	Yeah, that's us.
TINA:	I thought you could help me, but now I'm not so sure.
DREW:	What seems to be the trouble?
TINA:	Well, I've been kinda down lately. Nothing seems to be going right. I just kinda feel empty.
SAM:	Then you need a freefill, a freefall—I mean a refill.
DREW:	Well, take it from me—Jesus is the answer.
TINA:	*(Stands up.)* Maybe this was a bad idea. *(Walks away sadly.)*

DREW:	Hey! Looks like we saved another one!
SAM:	*(Stands up and looks down.)* Wow! It's a long way down, isn't it?

QUESTIONS ▼ ▼ ▼ ▼ ▼ ▼ ▼ ▼ ▼ ▼ ▼ ▼

● What do you think happened to Drew, Jackie, and Sam in this skit? Why did they choose to give in and get drunk? What do you think Tina's perception of Christians is now?

● How might Drew, Jackie, and Sam have been able to help Tina if they hadn't been drunk?

Read Matthew 11:11-19.

● How might this passage be interpreted as support for the idea of drinking with non-Christians? What other ways can you interpret this passage? Can we assume that we have the same wisdom in our choices that Jesus did?

Why or why not?
Read 1 John 2:15.

● How does this verse relate to the skit topic? How can we interpret this verse for today? How might it apply to the methods we choose for sharing the Good News with others?

Read Matthew 28:16-20.

● How can you as individuals and as a group go out and teach others about Jesus? How can you avoid the mistakes that Drew, Jackie, and Sam made in this ending?

▲ ▲ ▲ ▲ ▲ ▲ ▲ ▲ ▲ ▲ ▲ ▲ ▲ ▲ ▲

2. REVIVAL MEETIN'

(The Crowd is standing in front of the audience, facing the stage. They're "whooping it up" until Jackie gets their attention.)

DREW:	*(Walking in the "door" to the party)* We're here! Now where's that keg?
SAM:	Drew!
DREW:	I just wanted to know where it was so I could steer clear.
JACKIE:	Well, here goes nothin'.
DREW:	*(Panicked)* Jackie, you're not going to . . .
JACKIE:	*(Interrupts in a loud voice.)* Excuse me, everyone. Excuse me. I have something to say.

(Sam looks on in awe while Drew slinks away and hides.)

JACKIE:	*(When everyone is quiet)* I know you're here to party and have a good time, but you're missing out on the greatest joy of all because you forgot to invite someone.
SAM:	*(To himself)* Who'd they forget to invite? Looks like the whole school's here.
JACKIE:	You forgot to invite Jesus!

(Crowd boos and hisses.)

DREW:	*(Groans.)* I'm ruined.
JACKIE:	No, wait. Hear me out. Why are you here? Because you like to feel good? Because you want to forget all your problems at home and at school? Well, if you think alcohol is going to make life better, you're wrong. But Jesus *can* make a difference. He can change your life from the inside out.

(Crowd murmurs but then quiets down to listen again.)

DREW:	*(To himself, in a surprised tone)* They're listening. They're actually listening!
JACKIE:	*(With passion)* Have you ever felt lost? Alone?
CROWD:	Yeah.
JACKIE:	*(With building intensity)* Have you ever felt hopeless? like nobody cared?
CROWD:	Yeah.
JACKIE:	*(Loudly and with excitement)* Have you ever wondered what's going to happen to you when this life is over?
CROWD:	Yes!
JACKIE:	*(Pleading)* Then give Jesus a chance. Just ask him into your heart. He'll always be there for you. Then you'll never be alone.
CROWD:	Amen!
JACKIE:	*(Even louder)* You'll be loved . . .
CROWD:	Yes!
JACKIE:	*(Yelling)* . . . and you'll have a home forever in heaven!

(Crowd claps and cheers.)

JACKIE:	Just come forward, and my friends and I will help you know how to ask Jesus into your heart.

(The whole Crowd walks forward, cheering.)

DREW:	*(To himself)* Jackie, someday you're gonna drive me to drink.

(Jackie is beaming as she listens to the crowd.)

SAM:	*(To Jackie)* I don't believe this. You actually did it.
JACKIE:	All it takes is a little faith.

QUESTIONS ▼ ▼ ▼ ▼ ▼ ▼ ▼ ▼ ▼ ▼ ▼ ▼

● How would you react if your "preaching" had an impact as big as Jackie's? What do you think would happen to Jackie and her friends if she tried this in real life? What role does risk-taking play in reaching others with God's love?

● What kind of impact can Christians have on people who disdain everything they believe in? What are some different ways Christians can reach out to others?

Read Romans 12:2.

● How does this verse relate to the skit topic? How can we interpret this verse for today? How might it apply to the methods we choose for sharing the good news with others?

▲ ▲ ▲ ▲ ▲ ▲ ▲ ▲ ▲ ▲ ▲ ▲ ▲ ▲

3. ONE FOR THE ROAD

(Have a volunteer stand up onstage, hold up a clock, and move the hour hand forward one hour. Have another volunteer stand up onstage and hold up the sign that says, "One hour later, in a corner of the party house . . . " Drew, Jackie, and Sam are standing in a corner, talking among themselves.)

DREW: Well, at least the pizza's good.

SAM: I really think it's about time for us to be going. Youth group starts in half an hour.

JACKIE: Yeah. No one seems to want to talk to me about Jesus anyway. They all just say, "Yeah, whatever" and walk away.

SAM: Well, maybe you've planted a seed or something.

DREW: I hope Sam's right. But we're just marking time here now. At least we showed up. Maybe some of these people will be more willing to talk to us another time.

JACKIE: I hope so.

(Jeff appears onstage and wanders over to where Drew, Sam, and Jackie are standing.)

SAM: How's it going, Jeff?

JEFF: Not too well, actually.

JACKIE: What's up?

JEFF: I'm just kinda getting sick of this party routine. All we ever do is drink until we're sick or someone calls the cops. Then we go home and lie to our parents, and we still have to get up the next day.

DREW: Doesn't sound like much fun to me.

SAM: So why do you keep coming?

JEFF: I don't know. Nothing else to do, I guess.

JACKIE:	Well, we usually go to youth group meetings on Saturdays. Maybe you'd like to come with us.
DREW:	There's no drinking, but we usually have lots of fun.
SAM:	Yeah, and our youth leader is great—he understands where we're coming from.
JEFF:	I don't know. Churchy stuff sounds awful boring to me.
JACKIE:	It's not bad. You just need an interpreter sometimes. That's what the youth leader is for.
SAM:	We're heading over to a meeting now. If we get there early, we can play a little basketball first.
JEFF:	I don't know.
DREW:	C'mon. You can call your folks from the church.
JEFF:	*(After a pause)* Oh, all right. Guess it can't be any worse than this dull routine.

(Drew, Jackie, Sam, and Jeff start walking away from the party.)

JACKIE:	I think I should warn you, Jeff. We talk about Jesus a lot at these meetings.
JEFF:	That's OK. My sister's always preaching to me at home. I'm used to it.
SAM:	Did you ever wonder if she was right?
JEFF:	Well, now that you mention it . . .

QUESTIONS ▼ ▼ ▼ ▼ ▼ ▼ ▼ ▼ ▼ ▼ ▼ ▼

● What kind of impact did these three teenagers have on the party-goers in this skit ending? How might their example have affected people like Jeff?

● Is it difficult for you to ask friends to your youth group meetings? If so, what makes it difficult? What can you do to help overcome those difficulties?

● What does this skit ending tell us about one way we can reach out to others? What are some other ways to spread the good news?

● What role does risk-taking play in reaching others with God's love?

Read Matthew 28:16-20.

● What does this passage say about the way Christians should relate to their non-Christian friends? Is the way Jackie, Drew, and Sam reached out to Jeff an example of following this passage?

▲ ▲ ▲ ▲ ▲ ▲ ▲ ▲ ▲ ▲ ▲ ▲ ▲ ▲

AT HOME WITH MISSIONS

SCRIPTURE:

Matthew 25:31-46

THEMES:

Hunger, missions, neighbors, serving others

THE SETTING:

Two teenagers are canvassing their neighborhood, collecting money and nonperishable food items to donate to a hunger-relief organization.

THE PROPS:

You'll need a few nonperishable food items (such as canned or boxed foods) for kids to collect during the skit. You'll also need an open box of doughnuts. You'll also need two boxes or bags.

THE CHARACTERS:

Pam, a teenage girl
David, a teenage guy
Neighbor 1, Neighbor 2, and Neighbor 3, three people who stand in three different places in the room and act as neighbors who donate items during the skit. Divide your nonperishable goods between Neighbor 1 and Neighbor 2. Give Neighbor 3 only the box of doughnuts.
Caseworker, a male or female social worker (if you use ending option two)

THE SCRIPT:

(Pam and David are holding bags or boxes, walking around the youth room as if wandering through a neighborhood.)

PAM:	*(Sarcastically)* So is this youth group event exceeding your wildest expectations, or what?
DAVID:	Hey, it's not so bad. At least we're helping out some people who really need it.
PAM:	I know, I know. I don't mean to be so negative. It's just not how I'd normally choose to spend two hours on a Saturday afternoon.
DAVID:	Well, at least we get to be outside.
PAM:	True.
DAVID:	*(Points to Neighbor 1.)* Let's try that house.
PAM:	OK.

(David and Pam walk over to where Neighbor 1 is and pretend to knock on the door.

Neighbor 1 answers the door.)

DAVID:	Hello. We're from First Christ Church over on East Street, and we're collecting food on behalf of the Emergency Assistance Team of Unselfish Philanthropists, or EAT-UP, to be given to people who have little or no food. Do you have any nonperishable food items you'd like to contribute?
NEIGHBOR 1:	Hang on a minute. *(Goes to collect the food, then returns and gives it to David and Pam.)*
PAM:	Thank you very much.

(Pam puts the food in her bag, and Pam and David begin walking again.)

DAVID:	That wasn't so bad. What did we get?
PAM:	*(Looking in the bag)* Beets, tomato sauce, a box of rice . . .
DAVID:	Like they don't have enough rice already.
PAM:	*(Still looking in the bag)* Oh, yes, and everybody's favorite—dark kidney beans in heavy syrup.
DAVID:	Yum.
PAM:	I don't get it. Why don't people ever give the good stuff—you know, pizza, chips, hot dogs . . .
DAVID:	Um . . . Pamela, my dear, those aren't nonperishable items.
PAM:	I don't know about you, but they never go bad around my house.
DAVID:	*(Points to Neighbor 2)* Let's try that one next. And it's your turn.

(David and Pam walk over to Neighbor 2 and pretend to knock on the door.)

NEIGHBOR 2:	*(Answers the door.)* Yes?
PAM:	We're wondering if you have any food.
NEIGHBOR 2:	What?
DAVID:	What she means is we're collecting food on behalf of the Emergency Assistance Team of Unselfish Philanthropists, or EAT-UP, to be given to people who have little or no food. Do you have any nonperishables you'd like to contribute?
PAM:	*(To David)* Thanks.
NEIGHBOR 2:	Yeah. I think we can help. Give me a minute to see what we have.

(Neighbor 2 retrieves the food items and gives them to David and Pam.)

NEIGHBOR 2:	I hope that helps.

DAVID: I'm sure it will. Thanks.

(David puts the food in his bag, and Pam and David start walking again.)

PAM: OK, what's the take this time?

DAVID: *(Looking in his bag)* Hey, this isn't too bad. Three cans of spaghetti rings (one with meatballs, two without), one can of tuna (packed in water), and a couple of cans of whole kernel corn.

PAM: Those people were sure generous.

DAVID: What do you think most people who get this stuff think about the people who donated it?

PAM: I don't know, but I'd be a little ticked off with most of the stuff we seem to get.

DAVID: *(Sadly)* Yeah, me too.

PAM: Well, we have time for a few more houses. How about that one? *(Points to Neighbor 3.)*

DAVID: OK. I guess that's as good as any.

(Pam and David walk up to Neighbor 3 and pretend to knock on the door.)

NEIGHBOR 3: *(Answering the door)* Yes?

PAM: Um . . . we're from the church down the road, and . . . we're collecting food—you know, for people in far away places that don't have any to eat? Do you want to donate anything?

NEIGHBOR 3: Well, let me see . . . hang on. I'll be right back. *(Neighbor 3 retrieves the box of doughnuts and returns after a moment or two. Neighbor 3 hands the open box of doughnuts to Pam and David, who look surprised.)*

Freeze the skit. Then have participants or audience members choose from the following ending options to finish the skit. Choose additional actors if necessary.

    1. Above and Beyond (no new characters)

    2. There's No Place Like Home (new character: Caseworker)

    3. Empty Boxes (no new characters)

1. ABOVE AND BEYOND

DAVID:	*(Takes the open box of doughnuts.)* Um . . . thanks.
NEIGHBOR 3:	Um . . . actually, those are for you guys. You looked kinda hungry.
PAM:	Oh . . . thanks. *(David and Pam start to walk away.)*
NEIGHBOR 3:	Hang on there, kids. I couldn't find any canned goods, so I thought I'd write you guys a check. You can take it to the agency you're working with.

(David and Pam turn around and walk back to Neighbor 3.)

DAVID:	Oh. That's great.
PAM:	Yeah, thanks. We forgot to say you could donate money.
NEIGHBOR 3:	Now what organization is this you're collecting for?
DAVID:	The Emergency Assistance Team of Unselfish Philanthropists, or . . .
NEIGHBOR 3:	*(Interrupting)* EAT-UP. Yeah, I know about them. *(Writes an imaginary check, tears it out, and gives it to Pam.)*
PAM:	*(Looking at check)* Um . . . I think you made a mistake here. It says five thousand dollars.
NEIGHBOR 3:	It's no mistake.
DAVID:	Wow! Um . . . are you sure you really want to do this?
NEIGHBOR 3:	Yes. Before I inherited all this money, I had to almost beg for food. And EAT-UP, in spite of its silly name, is a fine organization.
PAM:	Well, we don't know what to say.
NEIGHBOR 3:	Just say thanks.
DAVID:	Thanks.

(Pam and David leave and begin walking quickly back to the front of the room.)

PAM:	Can you believe that?
DAVID:	That's incredible.
PAM:	Just think how many people can be fed with that kind of money.
DAVID:	Now there's an unselfish person.
PAM:	This turned out to be a pretty good Saturday afternoon after all.

QUESTIONS ▼ ▼ ▼ ▼ ▼ ▼ ▼ ▼ ▼ ▼ ▼ ▼

● How would you have reacted if you had been Pam or David in this ending? What do you think was unrealistic about this ending?

● Pam seemed to be happy about the day's activities only after she got that big check. What does that say about her desire to help people?

● How is your desire to help people affected by the expected results? If you knew you'd spend three hours visiting door to door only to get three cans of food, would you choose to participate in the activity? Why or why not?

● In what little ways can you reach out to people in your community who need food or other assistance?

● How can we balance our efforts to help people locally and internationally?

Read Matthew 25:31-46.

● What do these verses tell us about our responsibility toward people who don't have much?

▲ ▲ ▲ ▲ ▲ ▲ ▲ ▲ ▲ ▲ ▲ ▲ ▲ ▲ ▲

2. THERE'S NO PLACE LIKE HOME

DAVID: Um . . . thanks.

(Neighbor 3 sits down or leaves. Pam and David walk away from Neighbor 3.)

PAM: That was kinda weird.

DAVID: It's the thought that counts.

PAM: Yeah, but a box of half-eaten doughnuts?

DAVID: Maybe that's all there was.

PAM: I doubt it. I think that was rather rude. I mean, who doesn't have at least one can of beans?

(David says nothing.)

PAM: *(Points to another "house.")* How about that one?

DAVID: *(Uncomfortable)* Um . . . I don't think so.

PAM: Oh, come on. So it's a little run-down. I'm sure the people there are nice.

DAVID: *(Stops walking while Pam continues.)* You go on. I'll wait here.

PAM: All right. You sit back and watch a master at work.

(Pam walks up to an imaginary door and is about to knock when the Caseworker steps out of the "house.")

CASEWORKER: *(Talking as if to someone inside the house, oblivious of Pam)* Once you get set up on that community food bank program, things will seem better. And don't be embarrassed. Sometimes you don't have a choice.

(The Caseworker turns, almost bumps into Pam, apologizes, then walks toward David. David tries to turn away so the Caseworker doesn't see him. Pam turns and watches the Caseworker walk up to David.)

CASEWORKER:	Is that you, David? How are you doing?
DAVID:	*(Quietly)* Um . . . fine.
CASEWORKER:	Don't worry too much. Things are going to get better soon.
DAVID:	I hope so.
CASEWORKER:	See you next week.
DAVID:	Bye.

(Caseworker leaves.)

PAM:	*(Surprised, walks toward David.)* Who was that?
DAVID:	A caseworker.
PAM:	A what?
DAVID:	You know, a person who helps needy families.
PAM:	*(After an awkward pause)* This is *your* house, isn't it?
DAVID:	*(Softly)* Yes.
PAM:	I'm sorry. I didn't know.
DAVID:	None of the youth group kids do. And I'd like to keep it that way.
PAM:	I won't say anything. But why didn't you tell *me?*
DAVID:	It's kind of embarrassing to admit you're on food stamps. It's nothing I'm proud of.
PAM:	But you seem so normal . . . *(stops herself)* . . . I'm sorry. That didn't come out right.
DAVID:	Don't worry about it. I know what you meant. We're not stupid because we're poor; we're just poor. Dad can't work since his accident, and Mom can only get part-time work, so we just don't have much money these days.
PAM:	And here we are, collecting donations to send overseas to people we don't even know. *(Pauses.)* I wasn't being very sensitive earlier. I'm sorry. I guess I never thought we had hunger problems right here in our own town.

QUESTIONS ▼ ▼ ▼ ▼ ▼ ▼ ▼ ▼ ▼ ▼ ▼ ▼

● What surprised you about this skit ending?

● What does this skit tell you about the varieties of needs in our world? How important is it to reach out to our own communities as well as to other countries?

● Why are people often embarrassed if they don't have much money or can't afford food?

● What are some hidden needs in your own youth group? in your church? How can you help people in your youth group and church with their needs?

● What are some ways we can help hungry people in our own community without depriving them of their dignity?

Read Matthew 25:31-46.

● What is a Christian's responsibility toward people who have little? What actions can we take to live out the message of these verses?

▲ ▲ ▲ ▲ ▲ ▲ ▲ ▲ ▲ ▲ ▲ ▲ ▲ ▲ ▲

3. EMPTY BOXES

DAVID: Um . . . thanks. *(Takes the box of doughnuts.)*

PAM: We're not supposed to take perishable foods. Don't you have any canned goods you could donate?

NEIGHBOR 3: I'm sorry. We really don't have much. I know the doughnuts really can't be used. But I wanted to give you the best thing we could. Maybe you can share them with people at your church.

PAM: We will. Thanks again.

(David and Pam start to walk away.)

DAVID: That's kinda sad.

PAM: Yeah. Can you imagine what it would be like to not even have enough food to donate one can?

DAVID: They said these doughnuts were the best things they had.

PAM: And they gave them to us.

DAVID: Who would've believed we'd have hungry people right here in our own backyard?

(Both stop and look at each other.)

PAM: Are you thinking what I'm thinking?

DAVID: I think so.

PAM: Do you think we should?

DAVID: *(Resolutely)* Yes. We should.

(Pam and David turn around and go back to Neighbor 3's house. They knock on the door.)

NEIGHBOR 3:	Yes?
DAVID:	We decided we didn't need the doughnuts. *(Hands them back.)*
NEIGHBOR 3:	But we really wanted to help.
PAM:	Tell you what. We'll take the doughnuts if you take this. *(Places the food they've already collected on the floor in front of Neighbor 3.)*
NEIGHBOR 3:	I . . . I don't know what to say.
DAVID:	Say "OK."
NEIGHBOR 3:	*(Handing back the doughnuts and picking up the canned goods)* But you were collecting these for someone else.
PAM:	No, I think we were collecting these for you.
NEIGHBOR 3:	Won't you get in trouble?
DAVID:	Hey, we were collecting food for people who needed it. You need it, so we're giving it to you. We're just doing what we set out to do.
NEIGHBOR 3:	Thank you so much. You don't know how much this means to us. God bless you.
DAVID:	He already has.

QUESTIONS ▼ ▼ ▼ ▼ ▼ ▼ ▼ ▼ ▼ ▼ ▼ ▼

● What do you think David meant when he said God had already blessed them? How does it feel to help people in need?

● How did the way Pam chose to trade the doughnuts for the food help preserve some of Neighbor 3's dignity in this skit ending? How important is it to respect people's dignity in circumstances such as these?

Read Matthew 25:31-46.

● How are Pam and David's actions an example of the message in these verses? How can we show responsibility for people who have unmet needs?

● Some people don't have food or money for legitimate reasons, while others may be trying to get "something for nothing." How can you distinguish between the two? Should we treat people who are just trying to get something for nothing differently than people who truly need and deserve help? Explain.

▲ ▲ ▲ ▲ ▲ ▲ ▲ ▲ ▲ ▲ ▲ ▲ ▲ ▲ ▲

THE TWO SHALL BECOME ONE

SCRIPTURE:
Malachi 2:14-16;
Mark 10:7-9; and
1 John 1:9

THEMES:
Divorce, friend-
ship, parents and
stepparents,
prayer, relation-
ships

THE SETTING:
Three teenage girls are talking in one girl's bedroom.

THE PROPS:
You'll need at least three throw pillows.

THE CHARACTERS:
Mary, a teenage girl
Laura, Mary's friend
Kerri, Mary's friend
Mr. Howard, Mary's dad
Mrs. Howard, Mary's mom

THE SCRIPT:

(Laura, Kerri, and Mary are sitting on the floor of Mary's room, talking. The throw pillows are scattered on the floor.)

KERRI: What about Jeremy?

MARY: No way. He's so conceited.

LAURA: Yeah, but that's because he *is* good looking.

KERRI: He's a Greek god.

MARY: Sorry, but I'd rather go out with Tom than that big-headed jerk.

LAURA: Tom Berg?

KERRI: *(Sarcastically)* Now there's a Greek god for you.

LAURA: More like a geek god.

MARY: So what if he's not the most handsome guy in school? He's really nice . . . and smart.

LAURA: That's a good point. I don't think I've ever heard a sentence longer than two words come out of Jeremy's perfect mouth.

KERRI: Yeah, but that doesn't matter if the sentence is "Kiss me."

(Mary and Laura throw pillows at Kerri.)

LAURA:	*(To Mary)* On a more serious note, what's up with your parents?
MARY:	*(Reluctantly)* Um . . . things aren't going so good.
KERRI:	I didn't know something was going on with your parents. They divorcing or something?
LAURA:	Miss Sensitivity speaks again.
KERRI:	Sorry.
MARY:	That's OK. You didn't know. Truth is, I'm not sure I really know either. They've been arguing so much lately, and I never used to see them argue. The word "divorce" hasn't come up, but if you ask me, I think they've already decided to call it quits. They're just letting us in on it slowly.
KERRI:	That's a bummer.
MARY:	I always thought they'd be together forever. You know, it was always other people's parents getting divorced. Mine were supposed to be immune, I guess.
LAURA:	Doesn't that go against what the Bible says? Divorce, I mean.
MARY:	Yeah. But lots of people believe that particular part of the Bible is outdated.
KERRI:	Well, there *are* lots of good reasons for divorce.
MARY:	Not in this case. I mean, I'd understand if Dad was beating up on Mom, or Mom was beating up on Dad . . .
KERRI:	*(Interrupting)* Now there's a funny picture: your petite mom pounding on that giant dad of yours . . .
LAURA:	*(Interrupting)* Kerri.
KERRI:	Sorry. Continue, Miss Howard.
MARY:	My parents are really good to each other. And *for* each other. At least they *were*. That's why I'm so confused. What changed?
KERRI:	People change.
LAURA:	I don't know what to say. My folks divorced so long ago that I really don't remember what it was like to have both of them together anyway.
KERRI:	Well, maybe it's not too late. Maybe they're just going through a difficult time.
MARY:	Maybe. I hope so. But I doubt it.

(Mr. Howard knocks on the bedroom door.)

MARY:	Who is it?
MR. HOWARD:	It's Dad. You got a minute?
MARY:	Kerri and Laura are here with me.
MR. HOWARD:	I can come back later.
MARY:	No, I'll be out in a sec.

Freeze the skit. Then have participants or audience members choose from the following ending options to finish the skit. Choose additional actors if necessary.

1. **Home Improvement** (new character: Mrs. Howard)

2. **Unhappily Ever After** (new character: Mrs. Howard)

3. **Step by Step** (new character: Mrs. Howard)

1. HOME IMPROVEMENT

LAURA:	We'll be praying for you . . .
KERRI:	Hang in there, Mary.

(Mary steps out of her room. Laura and Kerri pray silently until Mary returns.)

MR. HOWARD:	Mary, your mom and I want to talk with you about something very important.
MARY:	*(Nervously)* OK.
MR. HOWARD:	Let's go downstairs to talk.

(Mrs. Howard appears onstage and sits down in a different area of the stage. Mr. Howard and Mary walk to the part of the stage where Mrs. Howard is sitting. Mary and Mr. Howard sit down with Mrs. Howard.)

MRS. HOWARD:	Sorry to steal you away from your friends, Mary, but we thought we ought to talk to you as soon as possible.
MR. HOWARD:	This is pretty important.
MARY:	*(Starting to worry)* I don't know if I want to hear this. *(Stands up and starts to walk back to her room.)*
MRS. HOWARD:	Mary, wait. It's not bad news. Really, it isn't.
MARY:	You guys are getting a divorce, and that's not bad news?

(Mr. and Mrs. Howard look at each other, then back at Mary.)

MR. HOWARD:	Honey, we're not getting a divorce.
MRS. HOWARD:	No, we're in this marriage for the long haul.
MARY:	Then what is it? What's the big news?
MR. HOWARD:	I'm quitting my job and setting up my own business at home.
MARY:	You're what?
MRS. HOWARD:	Dad's been having to fight too many battles at work lately. Plus, there are a few questionable things going on. We've talked about this long and hard, even argued a bit *(smiles at Mr. Howard)*, but we both agree that it's best for the well-being of the family if he gets out of that situation as soon as possible.
MARY:	So why is this such a big deal for me?
MR. HOWARD:	Well, there's no guarantee that the business will succeed. We'll have to cut back quite a bit—at least at first.
MRS. HOWARD:	At worst, we may have to move into a smaller house. At best, things will stay the same as they are or even get better.
MARY:	*(Hugs her mom and dad.)* This is such great news! I'm happy for you, Dad. And don't worry. You'll do great.

(Mary races back to her bedroom.)

KERRI:	What was that all about?
LAURA:	Yeah, what's the big news?
MARY:	*(Smiling)* The big news? God answers prayer.

QUESTIONS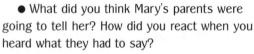

● What did you think Mary's parents were going to tell her? How did you react when you heard what they had to say?

● What does this ending say about marriage? about prayer? about jumping to conclusions? about communication with parents and stepparents?

● How would you react if you discovered one of your parents or stepparents was leaving his or her job? How would that feeling compare to the way you'd feel if you discovered your parents or stepparents were divorcing?

Read Malachi 2:14-16 and Mark 10:7-9.

● How valid are these verses for today? Why does God hate divorce? How does God feel about people who have been divorced?

Read 1 John 1:9.

● How might this verse apply to couples who divorce?

● What can we do to help friends whose parents are divorced or separated?

2. UNHAPPILY EVER AFTER

LAURA: We'll be thinking about you.

KERRI: Yeah. Hang in there.

(Mary walks out of her room to where her dad is standing.)

MR. HOWARD: Let's go downstairs to talk.

(Mr. Howard and Mary walk together to a different area of the stage and sit down together. Mrs. Howard enters and sits with them.)

MARY: *(After an awkward pause)* So what's this all about?

MR. HOWARD: Your mother has something to tell you.

MRS. HOWARD: *(Angrily, to Mr. Howard)* Why do I have to do all the hard things? You're supposed to be the leader of this household. You're supposed to take charge and be a man. But no. You defer all the tough jobs to me and take all the credit when something works out right.

MR. HOWARD: *(Upset)* Look, I work sixty hours a week to provide for this family. Maybe I need a break when I get home. Maybe I've had enough leading people and fixing problems at the end of the day.

MARY: *(Interrupting)* Stop it, you two! Stop arguing and get to the point. Are you divorcing or not?

(Mr. and Mrs. Howard look at Mary with surprised looks.)

MR. HOWARD: We are. How did you know?

MARY: It was pretty obvious with all the arguing going on.

MRS. HOWARD: We're sorry you had to see that.

MARY: So now what?

MRS. HOWARD: We signed the papers yesterday. Dad is moving out tonight. After that, I'm not sure.

MARY: *(Stands up while her mother is still talking.)* I can't stay. I've got friends up in my room. *(Runs quickly back to her room.)*

LAURA: *(When Mary has arrived back in the bedroom)* From the looks of your face, it's not good news.

MARY: *(About to cry)* No.

LAURA: Are they divorcing?

(Mary nods.)

KERRI: I'm sorry.

(Kerri and Laura hug Mary.)

KERRI: Is it OK if we pray for you?

MARY: I'm going to need all the help I can get.

KERRI: Dear God, comfort Mary right now . . .

QUESTIONS ▼ ▼ ▼ ▼ ▼ ▼ ▼ ▼ ▼ ▼ ▼ ▼

● What roles can friends take in helping someone through his or her parents' divorce?

● Why do you think there are so many divorces today, even in Christian homes? What can be done to reduce the divorce rate in this country?

● How might you feel (or did you feel) if your parents or stepparents were divorcing? What would you say to them? What would you want others to say to you?

Read Malachi 2:13-16 and Mark 10:7-9.

● Why do you think God gave these instructions about divorce? According to these verses, what does divorce do to people?

Read 1 John 1:9.

● Do you think this verse could help prevent divorce?

▲ ▲ ▲ ▲ ▲ ▲ ▲ ▲ ▲ ▲ ▲ ▲ ▲ ▲

3. STEP BY STEP

KERRI: We'll hang around until you're back.

LAURA: I hope it's not bad news.

(Mary steps outside of the bedroom to where her dad is standing.)

MARY: What's up, Dad?

MR. HOWARD: Well, you've probably noticed that your mom and I have been arguing a bit more than usual lately.

MARY: It's kinda hard to ignore.

MR. HOWARD: Well . . . *(he stops himself)* . . . Why don't we go downstairs and talk.

(Mr. Howard and Mary walk to a different area of the stage, where Mrs. Howard is sitting.)

MRS. HOWARD: Hi, honey. I forgot Kerri and Laura were here. If you'd rather, we can talk later, after they're gone.

MARY: No. They can wait.

MR. HOWARD: Well, as I was saying, your mom and I haven't been getting along well lately.

MRS. HOWARD: It has nothing to do with you, honey.

MARY: I know.

MR. HOWARD:	We've been having some financial difficulties.
MRS. HOWARD:	And we don't agree on how to deal with them.
MR. HOWARD:	Anyway, we just wanted to tell you that we're trying to work things out.
MRS. HOWARD:	We don't want you to worry too much about what's going to happen. Of course *we* don't know what's going to happen, but we're going to see a counselor next week.
MR. HOWARD:	I think she can help.
MRS. HOWARD:	I sure hope so.
MARY:	So this little discussion of ours . . . you just wanted to let me know you're working on things, right? You're not trying to hide something, are you?
MR. HOWARD:	No, we're not hiding anything.
MRS. HOWARD:	We didn't want you to worry needlessly.
MARY:	*(Hopeful)* I'm sure you guys can work things out. You always have before.
MR. HOWARD:	I hope you're right.
MRS. HOWARD:	We're just going to take things step by step.
MARY:	That's all I ever do.
MR. HOWARD:	We love you, Mary.
MRS. HOWARD:	We really do.

(Mary hugs each of her parents separately.)

MARY:	Well, I've got some friends upstairs.

(Mary walks back to her bedroom.)

KERRI:	So what's the scoop?
MARY:	Um . . . no scoop, really. They wanted to tell me not to worry about them—that they're trying to work out their differences.
LAURA:	And how does that make you feel?
MARY:	Like I still don't know what's going to happen. But at least they're trying.
KERRI:	I can't imagine having to work at a relationship.
LAURA:	That's because you've only dated one-dimensional people.
MARY:	Speaking of one-dimensional, weren't we talking about guys?

QUESTIONS ▼ ▼ ▼ ▼ ▼ ▼ ▼ ▼ ▼ ▼ ▼ ▼

● How realistic is this skit ending? What do you think will happen to Mary's parents?

● Why are financial issues so often at the core of marriage problems? How can couples who are planning to marry prepare for these kinds of difficulties?

● How do you think Mary feels, knowing that her parents are having troubles? knowing that they're working on their troubles?

Read Malachi 2:14-16 and Mark 10:7-9.

● Have you seen evidence that the things these verses say are true? If so, what? What do you think married couples can do to avoid divorce?

Read 1 John 1:9.

● How can this verse help people when their parents or stepparents divorce?

● How can we support group members whose parents or stepparents are divorced or going through difficult times?

▲ ▲ ▲ ▲ ▲ ▲ ▲ ▲ ▲ ▲ ▲ ▲ ▲ ▲ ▲

LOST IN CYBERSPACE

SCRIPTURE:

Matthew 26:31-56,
28:16-20; Mark
3:13-19, 6:7-13;
and Luke 5:1-11

THEMES:

Friendship, honesty, the Internet, relationships, technology

THE SETTING:

Two teenagers are sitting at their computers, communicating with each other online.

THE PROPS:

You'll need to set up two desk areas and place a computer (or a reasonable imitation) at each. Separate the two desk areas with a partition or another barrier. You'll need an alarm clock and a sign that says, "Room 222" if you use ending option one.

THE CHARACTERS:

Wolf324, the screen name for a teenage girl named Tony
Jettstar, the screen name for a teenage guy named Pat
Mrs. Noonan, Pat's mom (if you use ending option two)
Sarah, Tony's friend (if you use ending option three)
Jason, Pat's friend (if you use ending option three)

THE SCRIPT:

(Tell the audience that the two teenagers onstage are communicating via an online network. The audience will be listening to what the teenagers are actually typing. Tell the two actors to speak their lines slowly while they pretend to type on their computer keyboards—at sixty words per minute, of course.)

Wolf324:	Hello. I just noticed in your user profile that you're a Christian. Do you go online often?
Jettstar:	Hello. Yes, I do. I have been online all weekend.
Wolf324:	Me too! I'm surprised I haven't noticed you here before.
Jettstar:	I just joined this online network. I've been spreading my time between five or six other networks.
Wolf324:	Are you on Compuserve?
Jettstar:	Yes.
Wolf324:	AOL?
Jettstar:	Yep.

Wolf324:	Genie?
Jettstar:	Yep.
Wolf324:	Prodigy?
Jettstar:	Not any more.
Wolf324:	Me either. Your user profile sounds just like mine. Online all the time.
Jettstar:	So how's this network?
Wolf324:	This one is pretty cool. Have you checked out the download library yet?
Jettstar:	No, but I plan to. I really like to play computer games, so I'll probably try to see what I haven't already downloaded.
Wolf324:	Maybe I'll e-mail you some of my favorites from this system.
Jettstar:	Sounds great.
Wolf324:	So what does Jettstar mean?
Jettstar:	You mean my screen name? Nothing, really. I just like the way it looks. What about Wolf324?
Wolf324:	I really wanted just plain "wolf," but of course it was taken. So I added my birth date to make my name unique.
Jettstar:	You were born March twenty-fourth?
Wolf324:	Yes.
Jettstar:	My birthday is March twenty-fifth!
Wolf324:	What a coincidence.
Jettstar:	So how old are you?
Wolf324:	Sixteen.
Jettstar:	Is that your real age or just the one you tell everyone online?
Wolf324:	My real age. And you?
Jettstar:	Sometimes I pretend to be older, but I'm really sixteen.
Wolf324:	Wow! One day apart.
Jettstar:	Yeah, pretty creepy, huh?
Wolf324:	You don't find many Christian teenagers online.
Jettstar:	There are more than you think. They just don't always announce it.
Wolf324:	I wish they would. There's so much junk in cyberspace, it would help if a few more Christians got online to balance things out.

JETTSTAR:	I know what you mean. But the Christian adults I know don't seem to understand this online world.
WOLF324:	My mom certainly doesn't.
JETTSTAR:	Neither does mine.
WOLF324:	So what kinds of interests do you have?
JETTSTAR:	I'm into computers, computers, and computers.
WOLF324:	You must be my twin.
JETTSTAR:	Hang on a second. I need to check my account balance.
(Pause.)	
JETTSTAR:	I'm back. I just wanted to be sure I didn't exceed the credit limit my parents imposed.
WOLF324:	I assume you haven't.
JETTSTAR:	Nope. I've got at least three hours left this weekend.

● ● ● ●

Freeze the skit. Then have participants or audience members choose from the following ending options to finish the skit. Choose additional actors if necessary.

1. Don't I Know You? (no new characters)

2. Ghost in the Machine (new character: Mrs. Noonan, Pat's mom)

3. Unplugged (new characters: Sarah, Tony's friend; and Jason, Pat's friend)

● ● ● ●

1. DON'T I KNOW YOU?

(The skit continues as before, with Tony and Pat communicating online.)

WOLF324:	So where do you live?
JETTSTAR:	Lincoln, Nebraska.
WOLF324:	You're kidding, right?
JETTSTAR:	No.
WOLF324:	That's where I live.
JETTSTAR:	No way.
WOLF324:	Way.

JETTSTAR:	I suppose you go to West High?
WOLF324:	Yes, I do.
JETTSTAR:	This is incredible. We go to the same school!
WOLF324:	OK, here's the real test. Where is your locker?
JETTSTAR:	East wing, three places to the right of the men's room.
WOLF324:	Mine's in the west wing.
JETTSTAR:	Thus endeth the coincidence.
WOLF324:	Maybe not.
JETTSTAR:	What do you mean?
WOLF324:	What classes are you taking?
JETTSTAR:	Physics, advanced math, English lit., and a few others.
WOLF324:	OK, now we have something to go on. What hour do you have advanced math?
JETTSTAR:	Fourth, room 222.
WOLF324:	Aha. Me too. Who's your teacher?
JETTSTAR:	Danworthy.
WOLF324:	So we're in the same class!
JETTSTAR:	This is bizarre.
WOLF324:	Hang on. Looks like my time is about up. Maybe I'll see you in class tomorrow.
JETTSTAR:	I guess I've never noticed all the people in class before. What do you look like?
WOLF324:	Five-six, dark hair, and blue eyes. I usually wear jeans.
JETTSTAR:	I'm five-nine, and I have blond hair and blue eyes. I usually wear a plaid shirt.
WOLF324:	Oh—and what's your real name?
JETTSTAR:	Pat.
WOLF324:	OK, Pat. I'm Tony.
JETTSTAR:	Why don't we meet outside the classroom right after class?
WOLF324:	Sounds good. Bye.
JETTSTAR:	Bye.

(Clear the stage. Then have someone ring the clock's alarm to indicate the start of

classes. Have someone hang a sign on the stage that says, "Room 222." Pat enters the stage, looking around for someone. As he does this, Tony also appears onstage and looks around. Pat and Tony smile politely at each other but keep looking.)

PAT: Looking for someone?

TONY: Yeah. You too?

PAT: Yeah.

(Tony and Pat look around for a moment and then turn quickly to face each other again. They speak at the same time.)

PAT: You're Tony?

TONY: You're Pat?

(Tony and Pat speak at the same time.)

PAT: I thought you were a guy.

TONY: I thought you were a girl.

(Pat and Tony stare at each other for a second or two.)

PAT: *(Uncomfortable)* Um . . . well . . . I guess we'd better get to our next classes.

TONY: *(Embarrassed)* Yeah . . . see ya.

(Tony and Pat walk away in opposite directions.)

QUESTIONS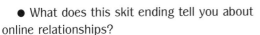

● What does this skit ending tell you about online relationships?

● What did you learn about Pat and Tony from their online communication? How well can you get to know someone online?

● Why didn't Pat and Tony notice each other at school?

● Why is it difficult for some people to initiate friendships? Why is the Internet an easy way for people to meet?

● What are the dangers of meeting someone online? the benefits? How can you be sure people online are telling you the truth?

● Do you think Pat and Tony will ever chat online again? Why or why not? How might you be a different person online compared to who you are in real life?

Read Mark 3:13-19, 6:7-13.

● What do these passages tell us about Jesus' relationship with his disciples?

● What roles do trust and honesty play in relationships? How are trust and honesty often applied in online relationships?

2. GHOST IN THE MACHINE

WOLF324: Well, I don't have much time left. Maybe we'll chat again soon.

JETTSTAR: That would be great. It's always nice to find someone with similar interests online.

WOLF324: Well, I've got to log off. I've got some friends coming over soon. We're going out for pizza.

JETTSTAR: OK, bye. Eat a slice for me. *(Talking to himself aloud while typing furiously)* Now, let's see. I still need to check out the software files and the news sections, and there are a few message boards I want to visit.

MRS. NOONAN: *(From offstage)* Pat, who are you talking to?

JETTSTAR: *(Ignoring her)* And I have to see what that section on nanotechnology is all about.

MRS. NOONAN: Pat? Are you in there? You've been on that computer all day long.

JETTSTAR: Maybe I ought to see what tomorrow's weather is going to be like.

MRS. NOONAN: *(Walks onto the stage and stands outside Pat's bedroom "door.")* Pat! Open your door this instant, or I'm going to pull the plug on that thing.

JETTSTAR: *(Still ignoring her)* What's this? I've got a message from the sysop. Let's see . . . it says, "Welcome to cyberspace. You've now exceeded your online limit by five seconds. Prepare to pay . . . What? I have almost three hours left.

MRS. NOONAN: Pat, I'm going to have to break down this door.

(Have the audience make a loud noise, simulating the sound of the door being broken, while looking away from the stage. While people are making this sound, have Pat slip offstage and have Mrs. Noonan "fall" into the room as if she's just broken down the door. Have the audience look back at the stage when Mrs. Noonan speaks again.)

MRS. NOONAN: *(Looking around the room)* Pat? Where did you go, Pat? *(Walks over to the computer.)* What does this say? *(Reading from the screen)* Help! I'm lost in cyberspace! *(Puzzled, stares at the screen for a moment.)* Hmm . . . I wonder what that means? Oh well. *(Looks around again.)* Pat? Where did you go? Pat? *(Exits the stage.)*

QUESTIONS ▼ ▼ ▼ ▼ ▼ ▼ ▼ ▼ ▼ ▼ ▼ ▼

● What does this skit ending say about the addiction of computers and, in particular, spending time online?

● Do you know anyone who spends more time with a computer than with other people? How does that person relate to other people?

● How is the way Wolf324 (Tony) seemed to be happy to log off to go eat pizza with friends an example of how to keep computer use in balance? How is the way Jettstar (Pat) ignored his mother an example of the dangers of spending too much time with a computer?

● Why is it important to balance solitary activities with activities enjoyed in the company of others? How can real relationships with people add to your life in ways that online relationships can't?

Read Matthew 26:31-56, 28:16-20. →

● What might life have been like for the disciples if they'd only communicated with Jesus via an online network? What can we learn from Jesus' relationships to help us relate to others better?

▲ ▲ ▲ ▲ ▲ ▲ ▲ ▲ ▲ ▲ ▲ ▲ ▲ ▲ ▲

3. UNPLUGGED

WOLF324: Well, I've got all night. I'm planning to stay up until I just can't type anymore.

JETTSTAR: Do you use a wrist-fatigue pad?

WOLF324: Yep.

JETTSTAR: How about wrist braces?

WOLF324: Sure do.

JETTSTAR: Then you're set for hours. I'm going to see if I can borrow time from tomorrow's allotment. Hang on a sec.

(At this time, Sarah walks into Tony's room and stands behind her. At the same time, Jason slips in behind Pat. Sarah and Jason speak their lines in unison.)

SARAH AND JASON: All right, you. It's time to get back to reality.

WOLF324 AND JETTSTAR: But I've still got online time left.

SARAH AND JASON: I'm sorry, but you need to spend a little time with your real friends.

WOLF324 AND JETTSTAR: No, wait. I just want to finish this conversation.

SARAH AND JASON: OK. *(Sarah and Jason lean over and type into the computers at the same time)* Goodbye. There. Now sign off.

WOLF324 AND JETTSTAR: But . . .

SARAH AND JASON: *(Firmly)* Sign off!

(Tony and Pat reluctantly type into their computers and then sit still in their chairs.)

SARAH AND JASON: OK, now let's go.

WOLF324 AND JETTSTAR: Go? Where?

SARAH AND JASON: We're going out for pizza with a few friends.

WOLF324 AND JASON: Pizza?

SARAH AND JASON: Yep. Food and real conversation.

WOLF324 AND JASON: But what will I say?

SARAH AND JASON: Just pretend you're typing on your computer. It'll come to you.

(Sarah leads Tony and Jason leads Pat offstage. Just before they exit, Sarah and Tony speak in unison again.)

SARAH AND JASON: Shield your eyes. It's bright in the real world.

QUESTIONS ▼ ▼ ▼ ▼ ▼ ▼ ▼ ▼ ▼ ▼ ▼ ▼

● How did Sarah and Jason's intervention help Tony and Pat? What might have happened to Tony's and Pat's real-life friendships if Sarah and Jason had not intervened?

● What are the risks of spending too much time online or in any other particular pursuit?

● Why do real relationships have to be nurtured? What happens if they're ignored?

● Who are you more like, Tony and Pat or Sarah and Jason? Explain. If you prefer to spend time alone, how can you expand your world to include relationships with other people? If you prefer to spend time with others, how do you balance that time with time alone?

Read Luke 5:1-11.

● What do you think gave Jesus and his disciples the kind of relationship they had? Should we be looking to these relationships as examples for our own?

● Do you think it's possible for us to apply what we learn to our own relationships? How?

● How can a relationship with Jesus help strengthen our relationships with others?

SERMON NOTES

SCRIPTURE:

1 Corinthians 12:12-31; Colossians 3:11-17; and Titus 2:1–3:8

THEMES:

The Church, helping others, relevance

THE SETTING:

Two teenagers are sitting in church, half-listening to the sermon and passing notes back and forth.

THE PROPS:

You'll need a sheet of paper, two pencils or pens, and some chairs set up in rows onstage, facing the audience.

THE CHARACTERS:

Robin, a teenage girl

Rachel, a teenage girl

Pastor Johnson, the church pastor, who is giving a sermon

Usher, someone to take the offering (if you use ending option one or two)

Diana, Robin and Rachel's friend (if you use ending option one)

Mrs. Johnson, the church pastor's wife (if you use ending option one)

THE SCRIPT:

(As the skit opens, Robin and Rachel are sitting in chairs onstage. They aren't directly next to each other, but they are within note-passing distance. Pastor Johnson stands behind the audience, facing the stage. Explain that the audience will be able to "listen in" on what Robin and Rachel are writing back and forth during the sermon, as well as hear portions of the sermon. You might want to include other people in this skit, to represent other congregation members. These people could sit in chairs around (and even between) Robin and Rachel.)

(Robin scribbles a note on a piece of paper.)

PASTOR JOHNSON: Let's take a look now at 1 Corinthians 13, verses 1 to 13. This is certainly a familiar passage for most of you. Let's start at the beginning, with verse 1. *(His voice trails off.)*

(Robin passes the note to Rachel.)

RACHEL: *(Reading Robin's note)* This sermon is waaaay boring. He's only on verse 1. That means 12 to go. Why does church have to be so boring?

(Rachel writes on the note.)

PASTOR JOHNSON: *(His voice fades back in.)* How many times have you just been a sounding gong or a crashing cymbal? I know I've been guilty of this many times. *(His voice fades out again.)*

(Rachel passes the note to Robin.)

ROBIN: *(Reading Rachel's note)* Talk about a crashing cymbal. Don't pastors live in the real world? The only places you'll ever hear about crashing cymbals are church or band practice.

(Robin writes on the note.)

PASTOR JOHNSON: *(His voice fades in.)* Let me put it another way. It doesn't matter how eloquent you are or what kind of command you have over language. You could have the oratorical skills of a Billy Graham, the elocution of James Earl Jones . . . *(His voice fades out.)*

(Robin passes the note to Rachel.)

RACHEL: *(Reading Robin's note)* Wasn't James Earl Jones the voice of Darth Vader? And what does electrocution have to do with anything? I sure wish I would've faked a temperature today.

(Rachel writes on the note.)

PASTOR JOHNSON: *(His voice fades back in.)* And let's look at verse 2. Look at what this says about love. How many of us have wished that we had the kind of faith that moved mountains? For that matter, how many of us have wished we had even a fraction of that kind of faith? But this passage isn't about faith. It's about love. *(His voice fades out.)*

(Rachel passes the note to Robin.)

ROBIN: *(Reading Rachel's note)* If I had faith that could move mountains, I might just move myself over to Diana Bergstrom's house. Did you hear her mother died? That is so sad. I wish I could help her.

(Robin begins writing on the note.)

PASTOR JOHNSON: *(His voice fades in.)* And in verse 3, the message is made even clearer. Imagine what people would think if you gave up everything you had—all your belongings: your new minivan, the house, down to the last piece of silverware. It would look pretty impressive to the neighbors, wouldn't it? But look at what it says next: It wouldn't mean a thing without love. *(His voice fades out.)*

(Robin passes the note to Rachel.)

RACHEL: *(Reading Robin's note)* I hadn't heard about Diana. She doesn't go to church, does she? I guess she probably could use a friend about now.

(Rachel begins writing on the note.)

PASTOR JOHNSON: *(His voice fades in.)* You've all read this next section, but I'd like to focus on just one of these sayings today. Love does not boast. What does that mean? *(His voice fades out.)*

(Rachel passes the note to Robin.)

ROBIN: *(Reading Rachel's note)* At least she doesn't have to sit through boring sermons. I wish I knew what we could do for her. Maybe I could send some flowers or something. What do you think?

(Robin begins writing on the note.)

PASTOR JOHNSON: *(His voice fades in.)* Love never fails. What a wonderful promise— and an incredible challenge. Love may never fail, but we often do. Our goal should not be to "be the most loving." No, that makes love a game, with God holding the score card. Our goal should be to let love rule our lives. *(His voice fades out.)*

(Robin passes the note to Rachel.)

RACHEL: *(Reading Robin's note)* Flowers would be good. They'll sure win us a few points with her. Maybe she'll let us in her little "clique" if we show her some kindness. I thought about inviting her to youth group tonight, but I'm glad I didn't.

(Rachel writes on the note.)

PASTOR JOHNSON: *(His voice fades in.)* And as we look at this final verse, pay close attention to the emphasis here. Faith and hope are not excluded from the formula, but love is given the highest esteem. *(His voice fades out.)*

(Rachel passes the note to Robin.)

ROBIN: *(Reading Rachel's note)* Yeah, the pastor's coming to talk about missions. Now that's *boring.* Maybe we should go visit her tomorrow after school.

PASTOR JOHNSON: *(His voice fades in.)* Amen. Now let us take a moment to give back to God a portion of what he has given us.

ROBIN: *(Whispering to Rachel)* Let's meet after church and make our plans.

(Rachel nods.)

● ● ● ●

Freeze the skit. Then have participants or audience members choose from the following ending options to finish the skit. Choose additional actors if necessary.

1. The Church Is Not a Building (new characters: Usher; Diana, Rachel and Robin's friend; and Mrs. Johnson, the church pastor's wife)

2. Collection Plate (new character: Usher)

3. Power Outage (no new characters)

● ● ● ●

1. THE CHURCH IS NOT A BUILDING

(The Usher walks among the congregation, pretending to collect an offering, then brings the offering to Pastor Johnson.)

PASTOR JOHNSON: Bless these gifts, Lord. Amen.

(Pastor Johnson walks "down the aisle" and past Rachel and Robin then off the stage. Rachel and Robin start to follow him offstage.)

RACHEL: He is so boring.

ROBIN: Yeah, I wish we had a more exciting pastor.

(Have the audience members make noises like cars starting and driving. Then have them "drive" as they turn around in place and face away from the stage. While they're facing away, have the actors clear the stage except for two chairs. The stage now represents Diana's house. Diana is sitting on a chair in the middle of the room. There is an empty chair next to her. When the stage is set, have the audience turn around and stop driving their "cars.")

ROBIN: *(Knocking on the door)* I hope she liked the flowers.

RACHEL: Do you think she got them yet?

(Diana stands up and answers the door.)

ROBIN: Hello, Diana. Rachel and I just thought we'd stop by and . . . you know . . .

RACHEL: Um, yeah, anything we can do?

DIANA: Thanks. I've already got some guests, but you're welcome to come in.

RACHEL: Oh, we don't mean to interrupt.

(Pastor Johnson and Mrs. Johnson enter from offstage and see Robin and Rachel. Pastor Johnson has the note from earlier in the skit in his pocket.)

MRS. JOHNSON: Hello, Robin, Rachel. Nice to see you here. *(Smiles.)*

PASTOR JOHNSON: It's good to see you, girls.

DIANA: I'll get some tea for everyone. *(Scurries offstage.)*

(Rachel and Robin look at Pastor and Mrs. Johnson with their mouths hanging open.)

ROBIN: *(To Pastor and Mrs. Johnson)* What are you doing here?

RACHEL: Yeah, we didn't know you knew Diana.

PASTOR JOHNSON: We're just getting acquainted. I heard that Diana's mother had died, so we thought we'd see what we could do for the family.

ROBIN: But how did you . . .

RACHEL: Where did you . . .

PASTOR JOHNSON: How did I find out about Diana's mom? Well, after church yesterday, I was helping clean up the sanctuary, and I found this. *(Pulls Rachel and Robin's note from his pocket.)*

(Robin and Rachel are completely embarrassed.)

ROBIN: We didn't mean . . .

RACHEL: What we wrote wasn't . . .

PASTOR JOHNSON: You don't need to explain. I was young once, too.

RACHEL: We're sorry.

ROBIN: Yeah. *(Pauses.)* So how did you have the guts to call up Diana and invite yourselves over?

MRS. JOHNSON: That's what the Church is all about, Robin: showing love to people, no matter what the cost.

PASTOR JOHNSON: Hmm . . . I think I did a sermon about that recently.

RACHEL: Oops.

ROBIN: I think we'll be listening a little more carefully next time.

(Diana returns to the room.)

DIANA: *(To Rachel and Robin)* Your pastor and his wife are so cool. I always thought church was such a waste of time, but with a pastor like this, I may have to change my mind. I'm so glad you told him about my mom.

(Rachel and Robin look at Pastor Johnson, who smiles at them.)

QUESTIONS ▼ ▼ ▼ ▼ ▼ ▼ ▼ ▼ ▼ ▼ ▼ ▼

● How many times have you felt the way Rachel and Robin felt about church in this skit? What makes church seem boring?

● What are some ways you can help make the church service more interesting? How can you contribute to the life of the Church to make it more meaningful to teenagers?

● What does this skit ending tell you about →

the real nature of church? Which is the better picture of church: the sermon time or the pastor and his wife's visit to Diana's house? Explain.

Read 1 Corinthians 12:12-31; and Titus 2:1-3:8.

● What do these passages tell you about the Church? Do you think the original Church cared much for what kind of building it met in?

2. COLLECTION PLATE

(The Usher walks among the congregation, "collects" the offering, then takes it to the pastor. Robin and Rachel are still in their seats as the pastor receives the tithes and offerings. The note is nowhere to be seen.)

PASTOR JOHNSON: As you know, we've moved our announcements to the end of the service to help you better remember what's coming up in the life of the church. So here we go. Tomorrow night there is a men's basketball game at St. Luke's . . .

ROBIN: *(Searches on the floor, then whispers to Rachel.)* Do you have the note?

RACHEL: *(Whispering)* You had it last.

PASTOR JOHNSON: And that's it for the announcements, except . . . wait, I think there's one here in the collection plate.

(Robin and Rachel suddenly look at the pastor, then at each other in horror.)

PASTOR JOHNSON: *(Reading from the note)* "This sermon is waaaay boring. He's only on verse 1. That means twelve to go. Why does church have to be so boring?" *(Clears his throat.)* Um . . . I guess that's not an announcement. *(Scans the room, then focuses on Rachel and Robin.)* Excuse me for a moment.

(Rachel and Robin squirm and try to hide as Pastor Johnson walks down the aisle and hands Rachel the note. He then returns to the pulpit. As the pastor returns to the pulpit, Robin and Rachel slide down in their chairs, trying not to be seen.)

PASTOR JOHNSON: I guess we do have one more announcement. I'll be available right after today's service to talk with the young people about how to make our service more interesting. Please plan on attending if you've ever wondered why church was so boring. I guess I've been out of touch lately, and I want to remedy that. *(Looks straight at Robin and Rachel.)* See you there?

(Rachel and Robin nod.)

PASTOR JOHNSON: Then let's close in prayer.

QUESTIONS ▼ ▼ ▼ ▼ ▼ ▼ ▼ ▼ ▼ ▼ ▼ ▼

● How would you have felt if you were Rachel or Robin? How would you have felt if you were the pastor?

● What do you think about the way the pastor handled the note? Would you have preferred that the pastor had ignored the note? Why or why not?

● Why does church often seem boring to teenagers? What aspects of church do you like the best?

● Who do you think is responsible to make church services more interesting? Do you think you share any responsibility to make it more meaningful to teenagers? Why or why not?

Read Colossians 3:11-17.

● What does this passage tell you about the Church? How does the church described in this passage compare to your church?

▲ ▲ ▲ ▲ ▲ ▲ ▲ ▲ ▲ ▲ ▲ ▲ ▲ ▲ ▲

3. POWER OUTAGE

PASTOR JOHNSON: Thank you, Lord, for giving us so much and for challenging us to love one another. As we go from here today... *(Begins to repeat himself as if he is a broken record.)* ... as we go from here today... as we go from here today...

(While Pastor Johnson continues to repeat himself, "stuck" on those words, Rachel and Robin look at each other, puzzled.)

RACHEL: Robin, what's going on?

ROBIN: You got me. *(Looks around.)* Look! No one else seems to notice anything wrong.

RACHEL: Go up there and tap him on the shoulder. Maybe he's forgotten where he was.

ROBIN: No, you go.

RACHEL: OK, we'll both go.

(Rachel and Robin sneak out of their chairs and walk up to where the pastor is still repeating "as we go from here today" and tap him on the shoulder. Nothing happens, so they tap him harder. This time, he says the phrase once more but his voice trails off as if his "power" has been turned off. Then he stands in the pulpit as if he is frozen.)

ROBIN: Um... Rachel... I don't think we're in Kansas anymore.

RACHEL: *(To the people—real or imaginary—in the sanctuary area onstage)* Um... hello? Does anyone else notice anything kinda weird going on here?

(Rachel gets no response.)

ROBIN: *(Walking over to an imaginary or real congregation member somewhere onstage)* Hey, Rachel, look at this.

(Rachel walks over to Robin.)

ROBIN: These people aren't even real. They're just big puppets. I'll bet the power went out.

RACHEL: You mean all these years we've been going to church, it's been nothing more than a big puppet show?

ROBIN: *(To the audience)* Kinda makes you think, doesn't it?

RACHEL: *(Starting to enjoy this)* Hey, here's something I've always wanted to do. *(Walks to the front of the church and stands next to the pulpit.)* Hello, people! *(Yelling)* Wake up and get real!

QUESTIONS ▼ ▼ ▼ ▼ ▼ ▼ ▼ ▼ ▼ ▼ ▼ ▼

● What did you think about this ending? Have you ever felt as if your church were nothing more than a show?

● What kinds of things make a church "real" and "awake"? How can you contribute to making the church feel alive?

● If you've ever felt that the Church didn't seem rooted in reality, what have you done to change that? How are the people of the Church the lifeblood of the Church?

Read Titus 2:1–3:8.

● What does this passage tell you about the Church? How true is the sentence "The church is not a building, but people" for the churches in your community? What can you do to make your church more like the Bible says the Church should be?

▲ ▲ ▲ ▲ ▲ ▲ ▲ ▲ ▲ ▲ ▲ ▲ ▲ ▲ ▲

I THINK I'LL GO EAT WORMS

SCRIPTURE:
Matthew 12:1-14;
20:17-28

THEMES:
Acceptance, friendship, loneliness, popularity

THE SETTING:
An unpopular teenager is sitting in the cafeteria at school, trying to make friends.

THE PROPS:
You'll need to set up at least two tables and some chairs to make the set look like a school cafeteria. Have food trays or sack lunches available so the actors can carry them onto the stage and eat or pretend to eat. You'll need a bell or an alarm clock if you use ending option three.

THE CHARACTERS:
Reggie, an unpopular teenage guy
Troy, a teenage guy
Randy, a teenage guy
CeCe, a teenage girl
Bonnie, a teenage girl
Jerry, a teenage guy
Bell Ringer, someone holding a bell or an alarm clock (if you use ending option three)

THE SCRIPT:

(Reggie is sitting at a table by himself in the cafeteria, picking at his food. Jerry is sitting quietly at another table, watching the conversations between Reggie and the other students. He doesn't speak until the script indicates that he should.)

REGGIE: I can't believe I have a table all to myself. What a great school this is. *(Looks offstage at Troy and Randy.)* Hey, those guys are in my English class. Maybe they'll sit at my table.

(Troy and Randy enter the cafeteria with their lunches. They look over at Reggie's table, then sit down at one of the other tables.)

TROY: *(To Randy)* Isn't that guy over there the one that went on and on in English about all that stuff nobody cared about?

RANDY: *(Looks at Reggie)* Sure is. I can't believe the teacher let him go on for so long.

TROY:	How could she stop him? He must be a real idiot.
REGGIE:	I wonder if they know I'm in their class. Maybe I'll say hi. *(Speaks in rapid-fire form to Troy and Randy.)* Hey, guys, what did you think of English class today? Kinda wild, huh? Can you believe what the teacher was trying to tell me about Shakespeare? As if I really didn't already know that. I mean, who doesn't? Only an idiot wouldn't know that about Shakespeare—don't you agree?
TROY:	*(Doesn't even look at Reggie.)* Yeah, whatever.
RANDY:	Look, we're busy here. Do you mind?
REGGIE:	*(Once again speaking uncontrollably)* Oh no, not at all. In fact I'm really quite used to keeping to myself. Usually that's because I'm so far beyond most people intellectually, you know. I'm sure they avoid me because they don't want to feel inferior. Who would? It's no fun to have a conversation with someone who's light-years ahead of you on the intelligence scale. Not that I wouldn't mind having someone stop for a chat once in a while, but . . .
RANDY:	*(Interrupting)* Excuse me, but I did say we were busy here.
REGGIE:	Oh, sorry. Enjoy your lunch!
TROY:	*(To Randy)* Can you believe that guy? If he would shut up for a few minutes, he might be tolerable. But the way he goes on and on about himself . . . I'll bet even his parents try to avoid him.
RANDY:	It's pathetic.
REGGIE:	*(To himself again)* Well, that was fun. They actually talked to me. Note for personal log: Cafeteria is a good place to make friends.

(CeCe and Bonnie enter the cafeteria, look over at Reggie's table, then sit at a different one.)

REGGIE:	*(Watching CeCe and Bonnie)* Well, look at that. Two of the most beautiful women I've ever seen. Methinks they're unprepared to handle my charming intellect. *(To CeCe and Bonnie)* Ladies . . .

(CeCe and Bonnie try to hide behind their lunches.)

REGGIE:	Ladies, did you know that the African canolaberry plant can reach heights of seventy-two feet? I know—hard to believe, isn't it? But it's true. Only one other plant not classified as a tree can grow higher, and that plant is the hukara plant, which is found only in the dense, humid South American jungles.
CECE:	Um . . . that's . . . really interesting.

BONNIE: (*Sarcastically*) You've really made my day.

REGGIE: Wow! Thanks, ladies! I know a lot about food, too. For example, the taco on today's menu: Did you know that federal beef regulations include allowance for up to 20 percent non-meat product in grade A beef? You know—bones, cartilage, hearts, et cetera. Not that the beef in that taco is likely to be grade A. In fact, it's probably grade B because B is cheaper. Now grade B can have up to . . .

(CeCe and Bonnie put down their food and make disgusted faces.)

RANDY: (*Interrupting Reggie*) Solomon! Give it a rest.

REGGIE: Oh. OK . . . *(looks at Randy and smiles)* . . . buddy.

RANDY: (*To Troy*) I can't believe that guy!

REGGIE: (*To himself*) Wow! Bonnie said I made her day. And CeCe talked to me, too. What a dilemma. They *both* like me. Note for personal log: Bonnie and CeCe both like me. Must make tough decision—which one will be my girlfriend.

(Jerry stands up to leave.)

REGGIE: (*Spies Jerry.*) Hey, Jerry! I didn't see you sitting over there. What did you think of my impromptu oral report on the life cycle of the moose this morning? I know most people say "mooses," but the proper plural usage is "moose." Isn't that unusual? The same word is both singular and plural . . .

JERRY: (*Interrupting*) Reggie, I think there's something I need to tell you.

Freeze the skit. Then have participants or audience members choose from the following ending options to finish the skit. Choose additional actors if necessary.

> **1. Doh!** (no new characters)
>
> **2. Duh** (no new characters)
>
> **3. Dude!** (new character: Bell Ringer)

1. DOH!

REGGIE: Sure, go right ahead. Did I misstate something in my report? Was the information incomplete? What did I forget?

JERRY:	It has nothing to do with your report.

(Jerry sits down at Reggie's table.)

JERRY:	Tell me . . . how has your lunch hour been so far?
REGGIE:	Great! I made two new friends, and I have a couple girls fighting over me. Then you came along. It really couldn't be much better.
JERRY:	*(Points to Randy and Troy.)* Are those your new friends?
REGGIE:	Yes.
JERRY:	I'm sorry to have to tell you this, but those guys aren't your friends. They don't even like you. In fact, they've been saying not-so-kind things about you all lunch hour.
REGGIE:	But they talked to me. They said hi to me.
JERRY:	They were being polite. Look, Reggie, you get on people's nerves. All your constant talking about subjects no one really cares about just makes people want to avoid you.
REGGIE:	So you didn't like my report on the life cycle of the moose?
JERRY:	Reggie, get back to reality. People don't like you because you're obnoxious. If you'd just relax a little, talk about one-tenth as much as you do now, and show some sincere interest in what others are saying, you just might have a chance of making a friend.
REGGIE:	But CeCe and Bonnie . . .
JERRY:	*(Completing his sentence)* . . . were being sarcastic. You didn't make Bonnie's day. In fact, you probably made her sick with all that talk about beef.
REGGIE:	*(In Homer Simpson style)* Doh! I've been such a dolt.
JERRY:	I won't argue with that.
REGGIE:	*(Sadly)* So Bonnie and CeCe *don't* like me.
JERRY:	If anything, they may feel sorry for you. But I can guarantee you won't be on the top of their list when it comes time to ask some-one to the Sadie Hawkins dance.

(Long pause.)

REGGIE:	So what can I do?
JERRY:	Slow down. Observe. Learn from others, and stop trying so hard. Useless trivia doesn't win friends; honesty and sincerity do.
REGGIE:	Will you teach me how to be more popular?

JERRY:	No. I'll teach you how to be real.
REGGIE:	I guess that will have to suffice.
JERRY:	Look, I gotta go. We'll talk some more another time.

(Jerry starts to leave.)

REGGIE:	Wait, Jerry. Why are you willing to do this—to help me, I mean?
JERRY:	That's what friends are for.

QUESTIONS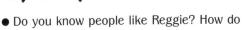

- Do you know people like Reggie? How do you relate to them?
- What does the last sentence imply about the nature of friendship? How do friends help each other succeed in life?
- What does it feel like to be unpopular? Have you felt this feeling? If so, when?
- How can you feel good about yourself when others ignore you or make fun of you?

Read Matthew 20:17-28.

- Why did these disciples want to have special places in heaven? How is that like the way people vie for "position" in school groups and cliques? What was Jesus' response to these requests?
- Do you think it's important to change in order to fit in our world today? Why or why not?
- What aspects of people's lives and personalities should they be willing to change to be more accepted? What aspects should they not be willing to change?

2. DUH

REGGIE:	Um . . . and that would be . . . ?
JERRY:	You're a real dweeb.
REGGIE:	Duh . . . I am? *(Smiling)* Well, thank you. I'm so glad you stopped by. Would you like to hear about my recent trip to the numismatics museum? It was quite fascinating in so many regards. Did you know that the most valuable penny is . . .
JERRY:	*(Interrupting)* I'm outta here.
REGGIE:	Bye! I'm glad we had this little chat. Maybe we can continue it after school. You know, I'm on the same bus as you, but you probably didn't know that since I sit up front near the bus driver. *(Jerry is long gone, but Reggie continues to talk.)* I've been a real bus driver's helper, if you will—reminding him when to initiate his directionals at precisely the right distance from an intersection, helping him to remember his route . . . those kinds of things. Well, 'bye.

(Randy and Troy stand up and start to walk out of the lunchroom.)

REGGIE:	Hey, guys, I really enjoyed our little time together today. Perhaps

we can get together over some java and discuss your free-thinking ideas about what the teacher ought to do with all those Shakespeare plays. While I personally don't agree with your rather concise assessment, I'm always up for a healthy debate. Disagreements can be so invigorating.

RANDY: *(To Troy)* What a jerk.

(Randy and Troy exit. CeCe and Bonnie stand up, look over at Reggie, then run out of the room as quickly as possible. Reggie talks to them even though they're gone in an instant.)

REGGIE: *(Standing and waving)* Hey, girls! Don't forget that next month is the Sadie Hawkins dance. It's first-come, first-served with me. I'll just need to know what color dress you're wearing so I can track down a complementary tux at Mr. Neat's.

(Reggie slowly sits down in his chair, still smiling.)

REGGIE: *(To himself)* What a truly spectacular day this has been. And there's so much more to look forward to. I can't wait to share this news with my parents. Note for personal log: First day of school is a resounding success. Made five new friends. This is going to be a great year.

QUESTIONS ▼ ▼ ▼ ▼ ▼ ▼ ▼ ▼ ▼ ▼ ▼ ▼

● What are your first thoughts about Reggie? What do you see in him that you've noticed in others in your school?

● How are you like Reggie? How are you different from him?

● Do you know any Reggies in your school? How do other people relate to them? How do you relate to them?

● Do you think Reggie has any clues about his unpopularity? Why or why not? If you were there to observe this little interaction in person, would you say anything to try to help Reggie? Why or why not?

● What things might Reggie need to change to find friends? What aspects of your personality are you willing to change to be more popular? What are you not willing to change?

● What's our role as Christians in relating to people like Reggie?

Read Matthew 12:1-14.

● How did Jesus react when the "big shots" of the time, the Pharisees, attacked him? What value did Jesus place on being in the "in" group? How can we learn from Jesus' example?

▲ ▲ ▲ ▲ ▲ ▲ ▲ ▲ ▲ ▲ ▲ ▲ ▲ ▲ ▲

3. DUDE!

REGGIE: What did you need to tell me?

JERRY: You are the coolest dude I've ever met.

(CeCe, Bonnie, Troy, and Randy all stop what they're doing and look over at Reggie and

Jerry. They pay close attention to every word Jerry says.)

JERRY:	You know so much about so many things . . . and the way you communicate with others—it's unreal.
REGGIE:	*(Taken aback)* Um . . . thanks. I think I'm speechless for the very first time. Well, that's not quite true. I think I was speechless once before. It was when my parents announced that I was going to have my own apartment at home. That was really so kind of them. I really didn't want to accept their gift, but they insisted that they wouldn't be worthy of sharing the same rooms with me. Of course I agree, but . . . *(stops)* . . . Why isn't anyone stopping me?
JERRY:	Stopping you? Why would we want to stop the coolest guy in school from telling another of his captivating tales of wonder?

(CeCe and Bonnie stand up and walk over to Reggie's table.)

CeCe:	You know, I think we misjudged you, Reggie. We really didn't notice how cool you were before.
BONNIE:	Yeah! Continue with your story. You were talking about your apartment.
REGGIE:	*(Soaking it all in)* Yeah, I was, wasn't I? Well, you see, it all started when I told my parents about how the ancient Babylonians used to send their teenage sons into battle . . .

(Bell Ringer enters and stands behind the actors.)

TROY:	*(Walking over to Reggie's table and interrupting)* Excuse me, but can we join you?
RANDY:	*(To Troy)* Don't interrupt him. It's just getting interesting.
TROY:	Sorry. Go on.
REGGIE:	Go ahead, guys. Sit down. I was just talking about the ancient Babylonians . . .

(Bell Ringer rings the bell, and all characters turn to look at him or her.)

JERRY:	Bummer. This was just getting good.
TROY:	Hey, Reggie, do you want to go play hoops or something after school?
RANDY:	Yeah, we'd like to hear the rest of the story.
REGGIE:	I don't fancy athletic activities much. I would enjoy a nice scoop or two of Mocha Delight ice cream and a stimulating conversation, however.

TROY:	Hey, that sounds much better than basketball. Count me in.
RANDY:	Me too.
JERRY:	I'll be there.

(Randy, Jerry, and Troy leave.)

CECE:	Say . . . Reggie, have you thought about the dance this Saturday? Um . . . I mean . . . have you asked anyone yet?
REGGIE:	Well, actually . . .
BONNIE:	*(Interrupting)* Don't you dare, CeCe. I saw him first. *(To Reggie)* Would you take me?
CECE:	No, take me.
REGGIE:	Ladies, ladies, I'd be glad to take you both.

(CeCe and Bonnie run up to Reggie and hug him, then leave, giggling with delight.)

REGGIE:	That was great.

(The audience closes its eyes for a moment while the actors re-enter the stage quietly and return to where they were at the midpoint of this skit. Reggie lays his head on the table as if he's sleeping. The audience opens its eyes.)

JERRY:	*(Standing in front of Reggie's table)* Hey, Dweeb, you're sleeping in your lunch.

(Bell Ringer enters, stands behind the actors, and rings the bell. All characters look up and leave the stage. Reggie looks around groggily.)

REGGIE:	Huh? Oh . . . thanks. *(Pauses.)* Even dweebs can dream.

QUESTIONS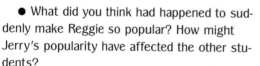

● What did you think had happened to suddenly make Reggie so popular? How might Jerry's popularity have affected the other students?

● Have you ever felt the way Reggie did? What was it like? Have you known people like Reggie? How have you related to them?

● What might Reggie need to do to be more likable?

● Is it easy for you to reach out to people who aren't popular or who are outcasts? Why or why not?

Read Matthew 12:1-14.

● Why didn't Jesus choose to appease the big shots of the time? What value did Jesus place on being in the "in" group? Where do you think Jesus got his sense of identity?

● If you could suddenly become popular at the snap of your fingers, would you do it? Why or why not? Why is popularity and having lots of friends so important to people?

JOIN THE TEAM

SCRIPTURE:
Matthew 28:16-20;
Mark 13:22-23;
John 14:6; and 1
Timothy 1:3-11;
4:1-16

THEMES:
Christian faith,
friendship, New
Age philosophies,
sharing faith

THE SETTING:
Two Christian teenagers are sitting on the bench at a softball game.

THE PROPS:
You'll need a long bench for kids to sit on and a variety of softball equipment (such as bats, gloves, and balls) to set around the stage.

THE CHARACTERS:
Dee, a teenage girl
Jacinda, a teenage girl
Melissa, a teenage girl

THE SCRIPT:

(Dee and Jacinda are sitting on a bench, looking out at the audience as if watching a softball game.)

DEE: *(Stands up and shouts while watching the game.)* Go, Donna . . . go . . . slide!

JACINDA: Yes! *(Shouting)* Way to run, Donna!

DEE: She's really good.

JACINDA: Yeah. I don't feel so bad sitting on the bench with people like Donna doing so well.

DEE: Did you hear her solo last Sunday?

JACINDA: Incredible, wasn't it?

DEE: I wouldn't be surprised if we see her face on a bunch of CDs someday.

JACINDA: Me either.

DEE: *(Straining to see someone in the other team's dugout)* Say . . . isn't that Melissa on the other team?

JACINDA: Yeah, I think so. Guess she's keeping the bench warm too.

DEE: You know I talked to her the other day, don't you?

JACINDA: Yeah. *(Shouting at the game)* She was safe! *(Talking to Dee)* How did that go?

DEE:	She seemed to be open to what I was saying, but you know how it is. You plant seeds, but you never know if they'll bloom.

(They both stand and shout at the game.)

DEE:	Go! Go! Hit the dirt!
JACINDA:	Way to go, Gina!

(Jacinda and Dee sit down.)

JACINDA:	So what kinds of things did you say?
DEE:	I just told her I was worried about her...about the choices she was making. I kinda probed to see what was driving her to act that way, you know. Then I told her about how Jesus has made my life so complete. I think she was most interested in the idea that God could give her peace. I guess she hasn't had much peace in her life lately.
JACINDA:	Hey—I think she's seen you. She's coming over.
MELISSA:	*(Walking over to Jacinda and Dee)* Hey, Dee, I've been thinking about what you said the other day. Got a minute?

Freeze the skit. Then have participants or audience members choose from the following ending options to finish the skit.

1. Mixed Vegetables (no new characters)

2. Peas (no new characters)

3. Beans (no new characters)

1. MIXED VEGETABLES

DEE:	Sure. I don't think I'm gonna get in the game for quite a while. What's up?
MELISSA:	I was thinking about what you said the other day, and I decided to do some of my own research. Anyway, you were right.
DEE:	I'm glad you...
MELISSA:	*(Interrupting)* Jesus is a really cool guy. I read some of his stuff in the Bible and thought it was so true.
JACINDA:	I'm really glad for you, Melissa.

DEE:	Me too. That is so great! Have you thought about my offer to take you to our church?
MELISSA:	I sure have, but I don't think your church is quite what I'm looking for.
DEE:	Well, there are lots to choose from in this town.
MELISSA:	True. But so many of them are so narrow.
JACINDA:	I . . . guess that's true.
MELISSA:	That's why I came over. I was wondering if you knew about a church that kinda covered all the spiritual bases, so to speak.
DEE:	*(Confused)* What do you mean?
MELISSA:	Well, you see, when I was studying about Jesus, I also found some books on Buddhism, Islam, and all kinds of other religions. You know, I wanted to check out the competition. But you know what I discovered? Those religions really have it right, too.
JACINDA:	But I thought you . . .
MELISSA:	And when I got to talking with my friend Maura, I learned all about this crystals and pyramids stuff—you know what I mean. Anyway, I really thought that stuff was so cool. I even found an old Ouija board we had when I was a kid. Did you know you could find out answers to just about any question from that silly little game?
DEE:	Well, actually, I . . .
MELISSA:	I feel like a new person, Dee. No more bad choices for me! With all this spiritual assistance, I'm on my way to nirvana . . . or enlightenment . . . or heaven . . . or reincarnation . . . or all of them!

(Jacinda looks at Dee.)

MELISSA:	And I owe it all to you! Thanks so much for opening my eyes.
DEE:	But I think you . . .
MELISSA:	*(Interrupting)* So do you know any churches like that?

QUESTIONS ▼ ▼ ▼ ▼ ▼ ▼ ▼ ▼ ▼ ▼ ▼ ▼

● Do you know anyone like Melissa? What went wrong with Dee's attempt to share Jesus with Melissa?

● Have you ever discovered that a friend was into New Age or other non-Christian kinds of spirituality? How did you feel?

● What are the most important aspects of faith in Christ that Christians must tell others about when sharing their faith?

Have kids form two groups, and assign each group one of these passages: Matthew 28:16-20 or Mark 13:22-23. Have groups read their passages and discuss the following questions before sharing insights with the whole group.→

● What do these passages tell us about the Christian faith and false doctrines? How easy is it to completely trust that these messages are true?

● Why do people (even some Christians) like to believe that all kinds of religions are viable options for today?

● How comfortable are you speaking about your faith with your friends? Which is easier: talking to someone who has no religious or spiritual beliefs, or talking to someone who has strong (but non-Christian) beliefs? Explain.

2. PEAS

DEE:	Sure, we can talk. What's up?
MELISSA:	Well, it's kinda weird, actually. I was sitting at dinner the other day, thinking about what you said. And . . . well . . . you're going to think this is pretty odd.
DEE:	Try me.
MELISSA:	OK. I started staring at the peas on my plate. I just stared at them, thinking about how tough life has been lately. Each one of those peas reminded me of one bad decision I've made. Am I making any sense?
JACINDA:	I think so.
DEE:	Yeah, you were thinking about all the bad stuff that's happened in your life.
MELISSA:	Yeah, and just like there were lots of peas on my plate, there's been a lot of junk in my life.
DEE:	We all make bad choices.
MELISSA:	Not as many as I have.
JACINDA:	But God can forgive them all.
MELISSA:	Hang on. You're getting ahead of me. So anyway, I was sitting there, staring at my peas, when suddenly I understood. What I needed was *peace*, not peas.

(Jacinda and Dee look at each other, puzzled.)

MELISSA:	I know. It's too weird, isn't it? But don't you get it? I was thinking about these peas—these problems I have—and then I realized I could have peace instead of peas—I mean, instead of these problems. It's what you said the other day, Dee. God can give you peace in the middle of storms.
DEE:	It's true.

MELISSA:	I know that now. Right there at the dinner table, I put down my fork and said a silent prayer, asking God to give me that kind of peace, you know.
JACINDA:	I'm so glad for you.
DEE:	That's great! I have been praying for you for so long, Melissa.
MELISSA:	I feel so much better now, but I know from what you said that things aren't going to be perfect just because I've asked Jesus into my life. So that's really why I'm here. I was wondering if you—and you too, Jacinda—could help me learn more about what it means to be a Christian.
DEE:	Sure, but we're no experts. We're learning all the time too.
JACINDA:	You should start coming to church with us—and to youth group. Hey, there's a youth group dinner tomorrow.
DEE:	Yeah, and it's going to be a lot of fun. It's a surprise meal. No one knows what we're having except the leader.
JACINDA:	And she promised it will be a meal we'll never forget.
MELISSA:	I'm so glad to have you guys as friends. The dinner sounds great! I'd love to come. *(Pauses.)* You don't think they'll serve peas, do you?

(Melissa, Jacinda, and Dee laugh.)

QUESTIONS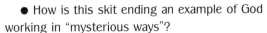

● How is this skit ending an example of God working in "mysterious ways"?

● Has someone you cared about ever come to the realization that he or she needs God? If so, how did you feel? What is the role of Christians in helping other people know Christ?

● Have you ever talked to your friends about a relationship with Christ? What did you say? Did you feel as if your words seemed to fall on deaf ears?

● What are the risks of sharing your faith with your friends? What are the rewards?

● How important is it for Christians to have relationships with other Christians? What are other ways people can grow in their faith?

Have kids form four groups, and have each group read one of the following passages: John 14:6 or 1 Timothy 1:3-11; 4:1-16. Then have kids form foursomes consisting of one person from each group to discuss the following questions:

● What do these passages tell us about avoiding false doctrines?

● What are Christians' responsibilities when it comes to false religions and doctrines?

● What makes Christianity incompatible with other religions?

3. BEANS

DEE:	Yeah, what's up? Did any of what I said make sense?
MELISSA:	I wasn't sure, but I wanted to find out.
JACINDA:	What did you do?
MELISSA:	Well, I was ready to try just about anything to stop all this pain, you know.
DEE:	Yes.
MELISSA:	So I talked to some other friends about what you said. *(Pauses.)*
DEE:	And . . . ?
MELISSA:	They laughed at me.
JACINDA:	Melissa, lots of people don't understand . . .
MELISSA:	*(Interrupting and starting to get upset)* You made me look like a fool, Dee. I poured out my heart to you, and you just gave me a bunch of religious baloney that only geeks and simps believe is true. That Jesus stuff doesn't amount to a hill of beans. It's all a big lie.
DEE:	But that's not true. Your other friends don't know . . .
MELISSA:	*(Interrupting)* They obviously know more than you do. *(Starts to leave.)* I'm sorry, Dee, but your pitiful attempt to turn me into a Jesus freak crossed the line. I can't consider you my friend anymore. Nobody who's anybody believes any of that Jesus stuff. *(Storms off.)*
(Pause.)	
JACINDA:	Wow. I bet that hurt. She seemed really upset.
DEE:	*(Looking down at the ground)* I'm sure it hurt Jesus a lot more than it hurt me.
(Pause.)	
JACINDA:	*(Looking at the game again)* So who do you think is winning?
DEE:	*(Looks at Jacinda.)* Well, this round may have gone to Satan, but the game's not over. *(Stands up and walks in the direction Melissa went.)* Melissa, hang on a second.

QUESTIONS ▼ ▼ ▼ ▼ ▼ ▼ ▼ ▼ ▼ ▼ ▼ ▼

● Have you ever told someone about your faith and been laughed at, ignored, or mocked? Why do some people think Christian faith is a sign of weakness?

● What role does persistence play in helping others know Christ? How might Dee have planted a seed in Melissa that may someday help her acknowledge Jesus as Lord?

● What is the most difficult aspect of sharing your faith with others? What are the biggest risks? the greatest rewards?

● How does the way we present the Gospel message factor into the way people react to that message? What are some different methods for sharing faith with others? Which have you tried? Are you better at some than at others? Explain.

● How do you think God feels when someone chooses to reject him?

Have kids form two groups, and assign each group one of these passages: John 14:6 or 1 Timothy 1:3-11; 4:1-16. Have groups read their passages and discuss the following questions before sharing insights with the whole group.

● According to these passages, what are some characteristics of many false doctrines and religions?

● What sets Christianity apart from other religions?

● What are some ways we can help keep other people from being deceived by false teachings?

CHRISTMAS PAGEANT

SCRIPTURE:

Psalm 31:24;
Psalm 37:7-8;
Proverbs 14:29-30;
Ecclesiastes 3:1-8;
Luke 2:11; and
John 19:17-30,
20:19-23

THEMES:

Christmas, failure,
miracles, planning,
responsibility,
stress

THE SETTING:

A group of teenagers prepares to direct the annual children's Christmas pageant.

THE PROPS:

You'll need a large plastic Santa Claus (or a cardboard facsimile), a flash-light, and cardboard crowns. You'll also need a tape recording of thunder-ous applause and a cassette player if you use ending option two. (You may be able to get this from your own church during a particularly good worship service.)

THE CHARACTERS:

Laura, a teenage girl
Carrie, a teenage girl
David, a teenage girl
Rob, a teenage guy
Steve, a teenage guy
Timmy, a child in the pageant (if you use ending option one)
Pastor Braun (if you use ending option two)

THE SCRIPT:

(During the first part of this skit, the audience will watch as five teenagers race on and off the stage while trying to coordinate the start of the children's Christmas pageant.)

(Laura races onstage, stops, and looks around.)

LAURA: Ben? Ben, where are you? Sheep are wonderful little animals. You don't have to cry about being a sheep. Ben... *(Runs offstage.)*

(Carrie and David race onto the stage from opposite sides, nearly knocking over each other.)

DAVID: Have you seen the wise men costumes?

CARRIE: No. I'm looking for the twinkling star. Didn't you put that away last rehearsal?

DAVID: Yeah, I left it right over... *(looks over on the floor and sees that the star isn't there)*... there. Somebody must have moved it. I'll check in the other room.

CARRIE: I'll go ask Steve about the costumes.

(They run offstage in opposite directions.)

LAURA: *(Walks onstage and looks around again.)* C'mon, Ben. Danny is going to be the shepherd this time. You can be a shepherd next year. Ben? Where did you go? *(Exits.)*

(Steve enters from one side of the stage while Rob races in behind him and almost runs into him because he's not watching where he's going.)

ROB: Oh, sorry, Steve. I was just trying to track down the Wilson twins. Have you seen them yet?

STEVE: No. I don't think they're here. Have you seen the Youngs or the Hammersmith boy?

ROB: Nope.

STEVE: What time do you have?

ROB: Five 'til nine.

STEVE: *(Suddenly frantic)* Five 'til nine? We have five minutes to get this show on the road! Quick—round everyone up and see who's missing. Let me know as soon as you find out.

ROB: Got it, chief!

(Rob races offstage. Carrie races back on.)

CARRIE: Steve, am I glad I found you. Where are the wise men costumes? I can't find them anywhere.

STEVE: David should know.

CARRIE: Already asked him. Hasn't seen 'em.

STEVE: OK. Did you check the men's restroom?

CARRIE: The men's restroom? Why would I check there?

STEVE: There's a storage closet there. The kids changed there yesterday. Maybe someone stuffed the costumes in the closet.

CARRIE: I'm not going in the men's room.

STEVE: Find Rob. Have him check.

(Carrie exits. Steve looks around the stage. David enters.)

DAVID: Have you seen the star?

STEVE: Practicing your lines for the play?

DAVID: They're not *my* lines unless that Hammersmith boy doesn't show up. No, I'm really looking for the star—the one we made out of Christmas lights, cardboard, tin foil, and duct tape.

STEVE: The star is missing too?

DAVID: I'll take it you haven't seen it either. (Checks his watch.) Yikes! Three minutes 'til the end of our theater careers!

(Steve and David run offstage. Rob and Laura run back on.)

ROB: Have you seen the Hammersmith boy? I think his name is Jake.

LAURA: Nope. One of the Wilsons just showed up, though.

ROB: Which one?

LAURA: The sheep.

ROB: What happened to the other one?

LAURA: Sick with the flu. Sorry.

ROB: Well, it looks like the Barber family isn't going to make it either. We're two wise men, one donkey, two angels, and one Joseph short with *(looks at watch)* two minutes 'til curtain!

LAURA: Add a sheep to that list unless I can find Ben. He's hiding because he doesn't want to be a sheep anymore. He wants to be a shepherd.

(Steve, David, and Carrie walk onstage. Carrie is carrying the plastic Santa, David is carrying a flashlight, and Steve is holding cardboard crowns.)

DAVID: The star is gone. We'll have to use a flashlight.

STEVE: And we couldn't find the wise men costumes, so we'll have to use these paper crowns.

LAURA: What's the plastic Santa for?

CARRIE: No one wants to be Joseph. We needed a stand-in.

(All characters look at their watches, at each other, then at the audience.)

EVERYONE: Oh no, it's show time!

(All characters race offstage.)

● ● ● ●

Freeze the skit. Then have participants or audience members choose from the following ending options to finish the skit. Choose additional actors if necessary.

1. Towering Inferno (new character: Timmy, a child in the pageant)

2. In the Nick of Time (new character: Pastor Braun)

3. Miracle on 34th Street (no new characters)

● ● ● ●

1. TOWERING INFERNO

(Have the audience members close their eyes and stand to give the "just finished" play a standing ovation. After the applause dies down, have the audience members sit down and open their eyes. When they open their eyes, Steve, Carrie, David, Rob, and Laura should be sitting on the floor of the stage, looking tired and depressed.)

STEVE:	That play is certain to go down as the worst production in church pageant history.
CARRIE:	People laughed when they were supposed to cry and cried when they were supposed to laugh.
DAVID:	Did you see how Tom Howland kept shining the flashlight out at the audience instead of on the manger?
CARRIE:	That was nothing. How about when Ben jumped out from behind the plastic Santa, shouting, "I'm a shepherd! I'm a shepherd!" right in the middle of the most important scene?
ROB:	You think that was bad? I had to go onstage to stop that fight between the two sheep.
LAURA:	At least they stayed in character, baaing and bleating as they fought.
STEVE:	So where did we go wrong?
ROB:	Poor planning.
DAVID:	The play was too difficult.
LAURA:	But we practiced the whole thing three times!
CARRIE:	David's right. Maybe we could've pulled it off, but these are little kids.
STEVE:	I don't think I want to help out with the pageants anymore.
DAVID:	Me neither.
LAURA:	Oh, come on. It wasn't so bad.
ROB:	It was. Just when I thought things couldn't get any worse, Mary wet her dress.

LAURA:	*(Disbelieving him)* No!
ROB:	It's true. Anyone sitting in the front row could see a small puddle growing just below Mary's feet.
STEVE:	Maybe there was no room in the inn's bathroom either.
CARRIE:	This isn't funny, Steve. We failed. And all the parents are going to hold us accountable for the embarrassment of their children.

(Laura, David, Rob, Steve, and Carrie sit, looking depressed and holding their heads in their hands.)

TIMMY:	*(Walks onstage and looks at the five teenagers.)* Excuse me.

(Laura, David, Rob, Steve, and Carrie look up at Timmy.)

DAVID:	Hello, Timmy.
TIMMY:	I just wanted to say . . . we had lots of fun doing this play. My mom said it was the best one yet. Do you think you might want to help us with next year's Easter pageant, too?

(Laura, David, Rob, Steve, and Carrie look at each other. Rob shakes his head no. The others glare at him, then he reluctantly nods.)

STEVE:	I think we might have one more play in us.
TIMMY:	Thanks. *(He leaves.)*
CARRIE:	Maybe it wasn't such a washout after all.
DAVID:	Maybe they couldn't see what was really going on, with Tom blinding them with the flashlight all the time.
LAURA:	See? I told you it wasn't so bad.

QUESTIONS ▼ ▼ ▼ ▼ ▼ ▼ ▼ ▼ ▼ ▼ ▼ ▼

● How do you feel when you fail at something? In what ways was this play a failure for these teenagers?

● What did Timmy say that helped the teenagers see their efforts in a different light? How can seeing situations from new perspectives turn failures into successes?

● What might the teenagers have done differently to better prepare for the pageant? What role does good planning play in being successful?

● What kind of stress did these teenagers face? How is that like the stresses you face?
Read Luke 2:11 and John 19:17-30, 20:19-23.

● How might people have viewed Jesus' life as a failure? Why do many people see his life as a success?
Read Psalm 31:24 and Psalm 37:7-8.

● What ideas do these passages give about dealing with stressful times? Why is it important to trust God when we're feeling stressed by our circumstances?

▲ ▲ ▲ ▲ ▲ ▲ ▲ ▲ ▲ ▲ ▲ ▲ ▲ ▲ ▲

2. IN THE NICK OF TIME

(Have someone play the tape of the thunderous applause offstage. After the applause dies down, Steve, Rob, Laura, David, and Carrie enter the stage and give each other hugs and high fives.)

STEVE:	That was the most incredible bit of work I've ever seen.
ROB:	Could you believe the Barber kids showed up with just seconds to spare?
LAURA:	Not only that, but they knew all their lines.
DAVID:	The star appeared at just the right time, too.
CARRIE:	Yeah! All we had to do was look up. I couldn't believe someone had already hung it from the ceiling. I'm just glad the wise men had their costumes with them when they showed up.
ROB:	And I'm glad we didn't have to use that Santa.
CARRIE:	You *did* make a handsome Joseph, Rob.
ROB:	Thank you.
LAURA:	You know, we were really stressed out just before the pageant. Maybe we should have been a little calmer.
DAVID:	Yeah, things did turn out just fine.
STEVE:	I don't know. I think stress kinda helps to keep us at our best.
CARRIE:	I could have done without it.
LAURA:	Me too.

(Pastor Braun enters.)

PASTOR BRAUN:	Hey, everyone. That was spectacular. Nice work.
STEVE:	Thanks.
PASTOR BRAUN:	So . . . ready for the second service?

(Steve, Rob, Laura, David, and Carrie look at each other in horror.)

STEVE, ROB, LAURA, DAVID, AND CARRIE:	*(Together)* The second service? Oh no!

(The characters speak the rest of their lines in rapid succession as they race around the stage.)

CARRIE:	I'll round up the kids. *(Runs offstage.)*
LAURA:	*(Stands up and starts looking around.)* Ben? Where did you go, Ben? *(Rushes offstage.)*

DAVID:	*(Frantic)* Somebody plug in the star! Somebody plug in the star! *(Runs offstage.)*
ROB:	Where's my Joseph costume? Who stole my Joseph costume? *(Hurries offstage.)*
STEVE:	Places, places everyone! *(Runs offstage after the others.)*

QUESTIONS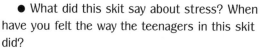

● What did this skit say about stress? When have you felt the way the teenagers in this skit did?

● How do you deal with stressful situations? What are some positive and negative ways to deal with stressful situations?

● What factors probably contributed to the success of this pageant? What role does planning play in successful ventures?

● How can stress help people do their best? How can it limit people's abilities?

● Describe one of your most stressful times. How did you survive the stress? How could others have helped you through the stress?

Read Proverbs 14:29-30 and Ecclesiastes 3:1-8.

● What do these passages say about dealing with stressful times? Do these verses encourage you? If so, how?

3. MIRACLE ON 34TH STREET

(The audience sings the last verse of "Silent Night" or any other Christmas song, then breaks out in applause. After the applause dies down, Laura and Steve walk in and sit down onstage. Carrie and David enter and sit down with them.)

DAVID:	That was pretty cool.
STEVE:	Yeah, the children did really well.
DAVID:	Oh, I don't mean the play. I mean Rob.
LAURA:	What about Rob?
CARRIE:	This little girl, Celia, came up to Rob right after the play, you know. And she asked him point-blank, "Do you love Jesus too?"
STEVE:	Oh, wow! What did he say?
LAURA:	I was worried about him helping out, I mean, since he isn't a Christian.
DAVID:	But that's the cool part. He smiled and said, "I don't know. Do you?"
CARRIE:	The little girl said yes and then, get this, started to tell him all about what it means to love God.
STEVE:	You're kidding.

CARRIE:	No. I was floored. This little girl knew just what to say.
LAURA:	Then what happened?
DAVID:	The little girl walked away, and Rob just sat there for a while.
CARRIE:	We were cleaning up, so we didn't see him leave. We thought he'd be with you guys.
STEVE:	No. Haven't seen him yet.

(Rob walks into the room.)

ROB:	Hey, guys, you got a minute?
STEVE:	Sure, sit down.
ROB:	I just spent the last ten minutes talking with your pastor. Guess what? I've asked Jesus into my life!
LAURA:	Wow!
CARRIE:	That's so cool.
STEVE:	Congratulations, Rob.
DAVID:	You made a great decision, Rob.
ROB:	Yeah. Now I understand what makes you guys tick.

(Long pause.)

DAVID:	Pretty good play, huh, Rob?
ROB:	The best.

QUESTIONS ▼ ▼ ▼ ▼ ▼ ▼ ▼ ▼ ▼ ▼ ▼ ▼

● What did you like about this ending? How does God sometimes use children to help people understand truth?

● What lessons have you learned from little children? Why do you think the Bible tells us to become as little children?

● In what ways was this pageant a success? How do you feel when you succeed at some important endeavor? How do you feel when you fail?

Read Luke 2:11 and John 19:17-30, 20:19-23.

● Do you think Jesus' life was a failure or a success? What standards do we use to define success?

● What are the benefits of inviting non-Christians to help with youth group activities? How can Christians help non-Christian friends learn about Christ in non-threatening ways?

▲ ▲ ▲ ▲ ▲ ▲ ▲ ▲ ▲ ▲ ▲ ▲ ▲ ▲ ▲

JAPANESE FOODS THAT HEAL

Using Traditional Japanese Ingredients to Promote Health,
Longevity and Well-Being

JOHN AND JAN BELLEME

TUTTLE PUBLISHING
Tokyo • Rutland, Vermont • Singapore

Published by Tuttle Publishing, an imprint of Periplus Editions (HK) Ltd., with editorial offices at 364 Innovation Drive, North Clarendon, Vermont 05759 U.S.A.

Library of Congress Control Number: 2006939305

ISBN-10: 0-8048-3594-2
ISBN-13: 978-0-8048-3594-7

Distributed by

North America, Latin America & Europe
Tuttle Publishing
364 Innovation Drive
North Clarendon, VT 05759-9436 U.S.A.
Tel: 1 (802) 773-8930
Fax: 1 (802) 773-6993
info@tuttlepublishing.com
www.tuttlepublishing.com

Japan
Tuttle Publishing
Yaekari Building, 3rd Floor
5-4-12 Osaki
Shinagawa-ku
Tokyo 141 0032
Tel: (81) 03 5437-0171
Fax: (81) 03 5437-0755
tuttle-sales@gol.com

Asia Pacific
Berkeley Books Pte. Ltd.
61 Tai Seng Avenue, #02-12
Singapore 534167
Tel: (65) 6280-1330
Fax: (65) 6280-6290
inquiries@periplus.com.sg
www.periplus.com

First edition
10 09 08   10 9 8 7 6 5 4 3 2

Line art illustrations by Masturah Jeffrey and Akiko Aoyagi

Illustration on page i: Harvesting at an organic tea plantation. Only the rarest and most expensive teas are still hand picked in Japan.

Printed in Singapore

TUTTLE PUBLISHING® is a registered trademark of Tuttle Publishing, a division of Periplus Editions (HK) Ltd.

For Takamichi Onozaki, whose open heart and gentle spirit made two foreigners feel at home. The experience of living with him and his family greatly deepened our understanding and appreciation of Japanese culture and foods. His wisdom, courage and confidence in us were our inspiration for making miso in the United States. We will be forever grateful.

やさしく広い心で二人の外国人を温かく迎えてくれた小野崎隆道さんに捧ぐ
小野崎さん一家と共に過ごした経験によって、私たちは日本の食文化に対する
理解と感謝の気持ちをさらに深めることが出来ました。
彼の知識と勇気、そして私たちへの信頼はアメリカで味噌をつくるきっかけと
なりました。

Japanese pronunciation is surprisingly easy. It isn't necessary to hear a word to know where to place the accent, since all syllables are given equal weight. Except for the letter e, which has two distinct sounds, the vowels have only one pronunciation, and none are silent. Although vowels can be either long or short, we will not go into that here. Our purpose is simply to help you feel comfortable in using the Japanese words, not in mastering the fine points of the language.

With only a few exceptions, the consonants are pronounced the same as in English. The only exception worth noting is the letter r. Whereas we retract our tongue to pronounce the letter r, the Japanese r is said with the tongue forward and touching the roof of the mouth, as it is when we pronounce the letter l. So, to pronounce the Japanese r, place your tongue as you would to make an l sound, then try to make an r sound. It should come out somewhere between the two, which is what you are looking for.

The vowel sounds are as follows:

a — like the "a" in father, though generally a little shorter. In the list below, it is written "a."

e — this can be either like the "e" in "send" or like the "e" in "obey." In the list below, the former is written "e," the latter "ay."

i — like the "i" in "machine," though usually shorter. Below it is written "ee."

o — like the "o" in "comb." Below it is written "o."

u — very similar to the double "o" sound as in "toot," but usually shorter. In the following list is it written "oo."

Amazake	a ma za kay	Kinpira	keen pee ra	Suribachi	soo ree ba chee
Arame	a ra may	Koji	ko jee	Surikoji	soo ree ko jee
Azuki	a zoo kee	Kombu	kom boo	Sushi	soo shee
Bancha	ban cha	Kukicha	koo kee cha	Takuan	ta koo an
Bonito	bo nee to	Kuzu	koo zoo	Tamari	ta ma ree
Daikon	da ee kon	Mirin	mee reen	Tempura	tem poo ra
Donabe	do na bay	Miso	mee so	Tofu	to foo
Fu	foo	Mochi	mo chee	Udon	oo don
Genmai cha	gen ma ee cha	Natto	nat to	Ume	oo may
Gobo	go bo	Nori	no ree	Umeboshi	oo may bo shee
Goma	go ma	Sake	sa kay	Ume su	oo may soo
Gomashio	go ma shee o	Seitan	say ee tan	Wakame	wa ka may
Hijiki	hee jee kee	Sencha	sen cha	Wasabi	wa sa bee
Hojicha	ho jee cha	Shiitake	shee ta kay	Yudofu	yoo do foo
Ita	ee ta	Shoyu	sho yoo		
Jinenjo	jee nen jo	Soba	so ba		
Kanten	kan ten	Somen	so men		

CONTENTS

FOREWORD

I have known John Belleme for twenty years and when I met him in 2004, I told him how much I loved our friendship. What? Let me clarify. I first "met" John in 1986 when a friend gave me Jan's and his cookbook, *Cooking with Japanese Foods*. Within a couple of weeks, I'd written an adoring fan letter thanking him for how much I had learned from that amazing book.

Macrobiotics was new to me back then. I was fresh off my recovery from my own struggle with cancer and I had an unquenchable thirst for more knowledge about this centuries-old way of life that had helped me save mine. I read everything I could get my hands on. Frankly, while many of the books were filled with valuable information, they were as dry as a rice cake, if you get my drift. Then John and Jan's book, with its warm style and easy recipes, made a whole world of exotic ingredients comfortably familiar.

Fast-forward sixteen years to my first Holistic Health Cruise and I finally met the man I had "known" and "loved" for all those years. John is as comfy as your favorite T-shirt, with intensely warm eyes and an easygoing style that belies his vast expertise.

It was another year before I met Jan, the yin to John's yang. Together they are balanced perfection and it shows in all they do. Jan's expertise is as deep as John's and she brings an elegance to the writing and recipes that only a woman like Jan could.

Now they honor me by asking that I write the foreword to their sophisticated, informative new book. By the table of contents alone, you will know that you are in for a treat. Not only are the recipes unique, distinctive and delicious (I am particularly fond of the Creamy Curried Carrot Soup and Udon and Mushrooms with Glazed Zucchini and Pineapple), the background information about the ingredients is written with a depth of understanding that only comes with time and experience. John and Jan have combined ancient wisdom with the latest nutrition research to create a comprehensive guide to the power of food in our lives.

I learned long ago that our health begins in the kitchen. I discovered that when I found my own health there. In that humble room, we create the life we live . . . and the quality of it. With this book to guide you, you can live a life of health, strength and vitality. You need look no further than your sauté pans.

CHRISTINA PIRELLO
Cookbook author, cooking instructor and Emmy Award–winning
host of the national public television series, *Christina Cooks*

The Onozaki household is in an old Japanese farming village in the mountains north of Tokyo. The family house, a three-hundred-year-old classic grass-roofed post-and-beam structure, is the center of village activities, a meeting place of predominately older, very traditional people. In the shade of towering cedar trees, in one corner of the family land, is a series of primitive tombstones and a small shrine commemorating the ancestors who have lived on this land for over five hundred years. Newcomers in the neighborhood are the families who have been here for less than two centuries. In the fall of 1979, the search for a place to study the traditional art of making miso led us to this peaceful corner of rural Japan, where no one spoke more than a few words of English.

With his wife, three daughters and mother looking on, Takamichi Onozaki, the fifty-year-old master of the house, asked us upon our arrival why we wanted to learn how to make miso. Struggling with dictionaries we tried to answer. As we talked about the virtues of learning the ancient art of making miso, Takamichi-san's eyes darted back and forth from us to his wife. We anxiously awaited Takamichi-san's verdict. If he refused to teach us traditional miso making, it was back to Tokyo and possibly the United States. Still not completely understanding our motives, almost on faith alone, he accepted us. "You are now a member of our family," he said, looking up and smiling confidently. The months that followed were a complete cultural immersion into traditional Japanese life and the labor-intensive art of making old style miso.

We worked hard alongside the Onozakis six and a half days a week for eight months. We lived in their beautiful old house with no heat, except that provided by a *kotatsu* (a small table with a heating unit underneath), and ate their traditional foods each day. The meals were usually very simple, but they were delicious and satisfying and were always made and presented with care. Some of the warmest memories we have of the Onozakis are connected to the simmering one-pot meals cooked right at the table on the coldest nights. Though the temperature inside the house was regularly below freezing on winter nights and early mornings, because of the appropriate selection of foods and cooking methods, we rarely felt uncomfortably cold.

There, in that small village, we saw and experienced the real value of the various aspects of traditional diet, lifestyle and health that we had been studying in the United States for several years in an abstract way. The strength, energy, good humor and stamina of the rural Japanese people clearly demonstrated to us the health-giving qualities of traditional diet and lifestyle. This book, born more than twenty-five years after that pivotal experience, draws on a lifetime of study, writing on and personal use of the healing Japanese foods.

Japanese Foods That Heal includes everything you will ever want to know about the healthy and delicious traditional foods of Japan—from nutritional and medical facts to recipes and tips for creating wholesome and flavorful meals. Our goals are to introduce traditional Japanese foods to you, provide the information necessary for you to determine the quality of the products or produce you purchase and offer recipes to guide you in their use.

Each chapter is divided into two sections—an introduction to the healing food, followed by easy-to-make recipes. Before diving into the recipes, please read the introductory sections. There you will find cultural and historical information; a discussion of the medicinal and nutritional qualities of each food, including up-to-date scientific information when available; an explanation of how the food is cultivated or produced, as well as an explanation of the difference between modern agricultural or production practices and those of natural or traditionally-made products; and a shopping guide, in which we give practical tips on how and where to shop for the highest quality foods.

Modern agricultural or food production processes often have a deleterious effect on a food's nutritional and healing properties, as well as its flavor. To steer clear of inferior foods, use this book as a shopping guide, ask questions at your local natural foods store, co-op or grocery store, and read labels carefully. Perhaps the most important question you can ask about what you eat is how it was made or grown—an important consideration for all conscientious cooks as well as natural foods manufacturers, wholesalers and retailers.

We are very fortunate that all of the traditional Japanese foods included in this book are now available in most natural foods stores and food co-ops, and, increasingly, in conventional grocery stores in the United States, Canada and Europe. In the United States, if your local natural foods store does not have some of these foods, ask them to order them for you from United Natural Foods Inc., the wholesale distributor that delivers to just about every natural foods store in the United States.

There are also several excellent mail order suppliers of these products, which are listed in the Shopping Resource at the back of this book. In some cases high quality Japanese foods can be found in Asian markets in the West, but again, read labels carefully.

The recipe section is a guide to using each food in a range of East and West cooking styles—from Thai Udon with Snow Peas to Vegan Lasagne and from Soba Salad with Spicy Peanut Sauce to Seitan Stroganoff with Tofu Sour Cream. Though many traditional Japanese foods may seem exotic to Westerners at first, they are easy to use. The simple recipes provided here should help you feel comfortable, and we hope they will soon serve as a springboard for your own creativity.

You will discover that Japanese foods are extremely versatile and can be incorporated into any style of cooking. For example, umeboshi (pickled Japanese plums) can be used instead of salt in many dishes and will add tangy flavor and unique health benefits to anything from o-kayu (rice porridge) to guacamole. Protein-rich seitan (seasoned wheat gluten) is equally at home in sukiyaki or pot pie.

We hope this book will encourage you to include these delicious and healthful foods in your everyday cooking. The quality of our food directly affects the quality of our lives. It is rewarding to prepare simple, wholesome meals and watch your family blossom and become healthier.

One last word of advice to help ensure success: Have fun! When you are giving your energy and creating with joy, positive energy flows through you and is received by all who eat your food.

John Belleme   Jan Belleme

Hippocrates, the father of modern medicine, knew well the role of food in maintaining health and preventing disease, proclaiming twenty-four centuries ago, "Let food be thy medicine." However, long before Hippocrates, Eastern traditional healers were prescribing foods as medicine. In fact, the ancient seal (above) is *Ishoku Dogen*, a profound Japanese saying that means "Food Is Medicine." It can also be translated as "Food is the key to health." Central to Asia's heritage of wisdom for thousands of years, this saying, even today, is the guiding principle of ancient healing systems such as Ayurvedic and Oriental medicine.

Today, modern science and medicine have begun to agree with this ancient wisdom. More and more, people are realizing that diet is directly connected to their health and well-being. There is a greater recognition of how the food we eat, what it is made of and how it is prepared affects us. This holistic point of view is a very important part of the traditional Japanese way of eating.

Japanese cuisine, though no longer untouched by industrialized food processing techniques, is still one of the healthiest in the world. By stocking up on the Japanese foods that heal, your kitchen pantry will literally become a medicine chest. Many of these foods, such as green tea, miso, shiitake, maitake and tofu, have been scientifically proven to cure and prevent degenerative disease, and to prevent premature aging. Vegetables from the sea are nature's mineral storehouse. Foods such as seitan and tofu are great substitutes for less healthy sources of protein, such as meat and dairy, and brown rice malt syrup and *amazake* are great substitutes for sugar, a sweetener utterly devoid of nutritional value. Adding these delicious and healthy foods to your everyday fare can create interest at mealtime while improving your health substantially.

The evolution in scientific information about diet and our health and well-being has produced a whole new field of study devoted to what are now called medicinal or "functional" foods—foods that have potential health benefits beyond their traditional nutritional value. These foods contain high concentrations of nutraceuticals or phytochemicals—natural plant substances that have been shown effective in the treatment and prevention of degenerative disease. Many of these phytochemicals are important to the plant's own survival. The powerful immune-boosting biochemicals found in shiitake and maitake mushrooms are nature's way of protecting these fungi from being destroyed by the natural defense mechanisms of their host. Ironically, as plants have evolved and adapted to survive and meet the challenges of their varied environments, nature has fortified them with powerful medicines that are very important to our own health and survival.

Ideally, the manufacturing and processing methods used to make the healing Japanese foods enhance their medicinal qualities. For example, the traditional fermentation process used to transform whole soybeans and grains into flavorful miso (soybean paste) helps destroy natural toxins found in grains and beans while increasing the concentration of cancer-fighting isoflavones and beneficial microorganisms. The slow natural aging process used by traditional miso makers digests miso's complex ingredients into less complex sugars, fats and amino acids, making them easy to assimilate.

Conventional agricultural practices and modern cost-saving manufacturing methods reduce or completely destroy the natural beneficial effects of medicinal foods. For example, many of the health promoting qualities of the soybean are lost when their oils are chemically extracted to produce the defatted soy meal used to make quick, modern soy sauce (shoyu and tamari). What's more, the rich and complex taste and aroma of long-aged, naturally brewed whole-bean soy sauce is lost.

Although today most Japanese foods are made using highly processed ingredients and time saving technologies or cultivated with toxic chemicals, there are still many traditional producers that have maintained high quality standards for centuries. These producers are committed to preserving the centuries-old traditions of their forefathers, and they carefully prepare or grow their products using time-honored methods and recipes. They use the finest ingredients, and many are the purest and most natural available. From invigorating, tangy organic green tea to hearty, robust Hatcho miso, these producers are dedicated to providing superior foods that promote and sustain health.

JAPANESE CIVILIZATION is ancient, yet the traditional diet has continued to survive to the present. Anyone interested in creating simple, nutritious, beautiful meals can benefit tremendously from learning its principles. The most basic principle—selecting and preparing food in harmony with the seasons and locale—is actually the foundation of all traditional diets and can be applied to any style of cooking.

The Japanese affinity with nature is reflected in the simplicity of the dishes and the balance within each meal. Only the freshest ingredients are selected in Japanese cuisine, and each is eaten in its own season. Like most age-old dietary principles, seasonal eating is simply common sense. We are attracted to lighter and cooler foods in summer. In winter hearty, warm dishes such as soups, baked beans, casseroles and stews with large chunks of root vegetables are appealing.

Japanese foods are simply prepared by methods that maintain and enhance their natural flavors, bright colors and nutritional value. Seasonings in dipping sauces and broths are generally light and subtle, allowing the essence of the principal foods to come through, but a meal will often include strong, stimulating flavors, too. The result is a meal that is deeply satisfying, natural, beautiful and delicious. When creating the recipes for this book, whether Japanese or Western ones, we consciously strove to follow this cooking philosophy.

Japanese Foods That Heal will show you how to incorporate the traditional foods of Japan into your daily diet. Learning to select and use high-quality, nutritious Japanese foods will enable you to create authentic Asian dishes as well as enhance the flavor and healthfulness of Western cooking. You will begin to feel a new vitality as the Japanese foods that heal begin to work their magic. As the months pass you to will come to learn, from personal experience, that the old Japanese saying, *Isoku Dogen* or "Food Is Medicine" is more than a proverb; it is the key to a healthier, more fulfilling life.

CHAPTER 1

MISO: A HEALTH SECRET TO SAVOR

Miso, a fermented soy product, is one of the world's most delicious and versatile medicinal foods. Having originated in China around 800 BCE miso was brought to the Japanese islands with Buddhism around 500 CE. Considered a "super food" by some ancient and contemporary healers, this ancient Far Eastern staple began appearing in alternative restaurants and food stores in the West in the 1970s, and today it is an essential ingredient in natural foods cuisine. Used to enhance every course, from appetizers to desserts, miso is found in basic natural foods dishes as well as fancy gourmet fare.

It is no wonder that miso has quickly become popular among health-conscious Americans. A good source of essential amino acids and some vitamins and minerals, miso is also low in calories and fat. Centuries of Japanese folklore and recent scientific studies indicate that the daily use of miso can reduce the risk of degenerative disease and contribute significantly to overall health.

It is not any one particular component of miso that makes it such an effective healing food, but rather a complex combination of ingredients and a unique double fermentation process that transforms soybeans and grains into a potent medicine. What's more, miso may be one of the most underrated foods in the natural foods pantry. After writing and researching more than one hundred twenty articles and four books about food, and having personally experienced the benefits of miso with our friends and family, we feel that using miso regularly is the best health insurance you can have.

Nutritional Benefits

Miso is a good source of iron, calcium, phosphorus, potassium, some B vitamins and protein. Because soybeans contain high amounts of protein, including all essential amino acids (the only such vegetable source), varieties of miso made with mostly soybeans, such as Hatcho and other soybean misos, can be considered an important source of complete protein for those eating a vegan diet. Miso also facilitates the body's absorption of calcium and magnesium.

Soybeans, which are about 20 percent oil, are an excellent source of high quality polyunsaturated fats such as essential fatty acids (EFAs), however, the majority of the soy oil sold in the United States is made by a process that destroys most of the delicate EFAs. The daily use of soybean miso, which is made with only soybean koji (cultured soybeans), salt and water, is a flavorful way to get EFAs. In fact, misos such as Hatcho are about 10 percent oil and more than 60 percent of this is linolenic (7.5 percent) and linoleic (55.9 percent) acid, two EFAs that are necessary for life but cannot be made by the body.

Miso as Medicine

Touted for centuries as a folk remedy for weak digestion, cancer, tobacco poisoning, acidic conditions, low libido and several types of intestinal infections, miso's reputation as one of nature's most healing foods is now being confirmed by modern medical science. These studies, many known mostly to scientists in the Far East, confirm what folk healers have known for centuries.

Atomic Radiation and Heavy Metal Poisoning. It may have been the fear of fallout from the impending nuclear holocaust or from nuclear power plant meltdowns that first attracted Westerners to miso. During the 1960s, students of macrobiotics and Zen began hearing about Shinichiro Akizuki, M.D., director of St. Francis Hospital in Nagasaki during World War II. Although Dr. Akizuki spent years treating atomic bomb victims just a few miles from ground zero, neither he nor his staff suffered from the usual effects of radiation. Akizuki hypothesized that he and his associates were protected from the deadly radiation because they drank miso soup every day.

Akizuki's theory was supported in 1989 by evidence demonstrating the protection miso offers to those exposed to radiation. Akihiro Ito, M.D., Ph.D. at Hiroshima University's Atomic Radioactivity Medical Laboratory read reports of European countries importing truckloads of miso from Japan after the accident at the Chernobyl nuclear power plant in the former Soviet Union. Ito reasoned that if people were protected from radiation by miso, then rats that were fed miso and radiated should develop less cancer than radiated rats that were not fed miso. Professor Ito was not surprised to find that the liver cancer rate for rats that were not fed miso was 100 to 200 percent higher than that of rats that were fed miso. Ito also reported that rats fed with miso had much less inflammation of the organs caused by radioactivity.

The Power of Numbers. Although Ito's radiation research is very impressive, it was wide-scale, long-term population studies conducted in Japan in the 1960s and '70s, and published in the '80s, that first alerted researchers to miso's potential as a powerful medicinal food. One study of more than 250,000 men and women showed that those who ate miso soup every day had fewer cases of certain types of cancer. The study also reported much lower incidents of coronary heart disease, liver cirrhosis, cerebrovascular disease and peptic ulcers.

Another more recent study involving more than 20,000 Japanese women (published in the June 2003 issue of *Journal of the National Cancer Institute*) showed that the breast cancer prevention effects of miso soup increase with daily consumption. With three bowls a day, the breast cancer rate was reduced by 40 percent!

Isoflavones: The Silver Bullet in Soyfoods

During the 1990s there was an explosion of exciting research pointing to the extraordinary health benefits of soy foods in general and miso in particular. Population studies in Japan, China and Singapore linked lower rates of several types of cancer, including kidney, uterine, breast, ovarian and prostate cancer with the consumption of traditional soy foods. This prompted scientists around the world to begin looking for a silver bullet in miso, tofu, soymilk, soy sauce, tempeh and even textured vegetable protein (TVP). What they found in the urine of people who ate these foods, and in the foods themselves, was a high concentration of a potent anticancer agent called genistein, a plant isoflavone.

Genistein's ability to destroy cancer cells has been demonstrated both in and out of the body in numerous studies. When added to tissue cultures of skin cancer cells, as reported in the *British Journal of Cancer*, genistein rapidly suppresses growth, and before long cancer cells look very different and begin to die. Genistein and miso have both been shown in laboratory experiments to have similar effects on animals with several types of cancer.

Genistein has been proven to be effective in both hormonal and non-hormonal types of cancer. Scientists believe that genistein, like several other plant compounds called phytoestrogens, may also have an influence on cancer via their estrogenlike action in the body.

The consumption of soy foods and isoflavones have been positively linked to improved mental function, protection against osteoarthritis, and stabilized blood sugar levels in diabetics. Scientists believe that these benefits may be related to the hormonal influence of isoflavones; these findings are inconclusive, however.

The Power of Fermentation

Studies have confirmed the fact that the fermentation of soybeans increases their concentration of isoflavones such as genistein and daidzein. Several years ago a group of scientists associated with the United States Department of Agriculture compared the isoflavone content of a wide variety of foods and plants, reporting in the *Journal of Alternative Complementary Medicine* that the isoflavone levels were relatively higher in fermented soy products such as soybean miso. When they compared the genistein and daidzein levels of unfermented soybeans with the same variety of fermented soybeans (soybean miso), the fermented soybeans had a thirty times higher concentration of these isoflavones. A research team at the National Cancer Center's Research Institute in Tokyo discovered that miso has about twenty times as much genistein as unfermented soy foods, such as soy milk and tofu. Researchers believe that during fermentation microbes cleave the bonds of genistein's precursor molecule genistin, converting it to the active anticancer substance.

Coronary Heart Disease

A body of more than fifty scientific studies has prompted the United States Food and Drug Administration (FDA) to endorse the heart benefits of soy foods. In 1999, the agency authorized manufacturers of foods that contain soy protein to state on the label that the food helps reduce the risk of coronary heart disease (CHD). The decision was based on a determination that soy protein lowers both total blood cholesterol and low-density lipoproteins (LDL), or "bad" cholesterol.

High total cholesterol and high LDL cholesterol levels are proven risk factors for CHD, the leading cause of death in the United States. Studies have shown that consuming 25 grams of soy protein per day lowers cholesterol levels. However, you would have to eat quite a lot of tofu, soymilk, or soy-based meat alternative foods to consume 25 grams of soy protein a day. Because miso has about twenty to thirty times as many isoflavones, it should only take about a gram of miso protein to have the same cholesterol lowering effect as at least four servings of other non-fermented soy foods. This is about one-and-a-half teaspoons of miso or the amount needed to make just one cup of miso soup. Besides lowering cholesterol, isoflavones may reduce blood clotting, which can reduce the risk of heart attacks and stroke. Finally, isoflavones may prevent the multiplication of cells that form artery plaque.

High Blood Pressure

Miso soup made with foods that are high in potassium, magnesium and calcium, such as wakame, fish stock (*bonito*), greens and carrots, has been found to lower blood pressure and to maintain healthy levels in people with normal pressure. A four-year study of elderly Japanese men and women with normal blood pressure, conducted by the School of Medicine, Showa University, Tokyo, revealed that two bowls of miso soup a day can prevent the development of high blood pressure. Another thirteen-year study of a large population of Japanese men and women showed that those who abstained from miso soup had a death rate from high blood pressure—related illnesses three and a half times higher than miso soup drinkers. Other studies have credited the daily use of miso with reduced risk of stroke, which is often associated with high blood pressure.

A Powerful Antioxidant

One of the biggest problems we face is that our bodies are having trouble producing enough antioxidants to neutralize all the damaging free radicals that our diet, environment and stressful lifestyles produce. Free radicals are highly unstable molecules that swim through our systems bumping into healthy cells and causing serious damage. They also steal electrons from healthy molecules, thus creating more free radicals in the body. The result is degenerative disease, bacterial and viral infections, and accelerated aging.

Researchers from Okayama University Medical School in Japan have now demonstrated that miso is a good source of antioxidants. In their experiments, miso was found to scavenge free radicals and inhibit lipid peroxidation, which can cause cell membrane damage. The scavenging ability of miso may be attributable to soybeans, its basic component, which contain known antioxidants including vitamin E, saponins (cholesterol-like plant compounds) and melanoidins, the dark pigments responsible for the color of long-aged miso. In a study at Japan Women's University in Tokyo, scientists attributed miso's antioxidative properties to miso's dark pigments. Furthermore, a study at the University of Shizuoka, in Shizuoka, Japan, identified daidzein, genistein and alpha-tocopherol as the active antioxidants in miso. Another study in Shenyang, China, at the Liaoning Institute of Basic Medicine, conducted by Chung Kuo Chung Yao Tsa Chih, concluded that miso protects cell membranes from aging and is, therefore, a "good natural agent for resisting aging."

Food Allergies

Allergists now know that it is the complex proteins in foods that cause the body's immune system to trigger an immune response. Miso is known to contain proteolytic enzymes that digest complex proteins, rendering them much less allergenic. As miso ferments, or ages, the enzymes supplied by the koji (grains or beans inculcated with *Aspergillus* culture) digest the proteins of the rice, barley or soybeans (depending on what type of miso is being made) into less complex amino acids. Not only are these amino acids much less allergenic, but they are also much easier to digest and assimilate.

The Miracle of Lactobacillus

Yet another key to miso's effectiveness as a medicine can be found in the unique lactobacillus fermentation process by which it is made. Not only does this process produce more isoflavones, numerous studies have confirmed that fermentation of food with lactobacilli increases the quantity, availability, digestibility and assimilability of nutrients while promoting a healthy pH in the digestive system. What's more, lactobacillus fermentation kills dangerous pathogens both in the foods before they are eaten and in the intestines.

Proponents of the macrobiotic diet have advocated the importance of the probiotic effects of beneficial microorganisms in unpasteurized miso for more than thirty years. George W. Yu, M.D., Clinical Professor of Urology at George Washington University Medical Center, has presented to the National Cancer Institute several case histories of terminal cancer patients who have failed to respond to conventional treatment, yet have successfully used a macrobiotic diet as their main source of treatment. Dr. Yu believes it may be the probiotic influence of the microorganisms in foods such as miso that is responsible for their anticancer effects. There is even research that shows that substances produced by lactic acid bacteria in miso prevent the growth of dangerous bacteria during and after fermentation. Research published in the *Journal of Applied Microbiology* showed that antibacterial substances produced by lactic acid bacteria inhibit the growth of undesirable bacteria in miso while not affecting the growth of beneficial bacteria.

Arginine

Misos made with a large proportion of soybeans and aged for one year or longer— long-aged misos such as Hatcho, barley, brown rice and soybean misos—are high in arginine, an important amino acid. Arginine is believed to retard the growth of tumors and cancer by enhancing immune function. Long-aged misos may benefit people suffering from AIDS and other diseases that suppress immune function. Arginine also stimulates the pancreas to release insulin, and has an important influence on liver function, fertility in men, weight loss and hormonal balance. Although there is no experimental evidence, the Japanese believe that miso soup's ability to almost instantly increase one's energy level is due to miso's rapid influence on the pancreas and its ability to rapidly adjust the body's blood sugar levels.

Osteoporosis

Some reports of osteoporosis in people who have a long history of eating a dairy-free natural foods diet have caused concern in the natural foods community. Although health statistics for people eating a mainly vegetable-based diet are good, cases of low bone density have been reported. Since most Americans get about 70 percent of their calcium requirements from dairy products, nutritionists assume that low bone density is caused by the absence of dairy products in vegan diets. However, according to a report published by the Japan Federation of Miso Manufacturers Cooperative, almost 90 percent of the calcium in the traditional Japanese diet comes from non-dairy sources, particularly miso soup. A bowl of miso soup with tofu, sea vegetables and a little fish contains about 233 milligrams of calcium. What's more, miso is known to facilitate the absorption of calcium and other minerals. Eating miso along with other high calcium foods can be an alternative to the use of dairy products or medications to increase bone density. In fact, daidzein, one of the isoflavones found in soybeans, is very similar to the drug Ipriflavone, which is used throughout Europe and Asia to treat osteoporosis.

Does Length of Aging Make a Difference?

Many but not all of miso's health-promoting and disease-fighting biochemicals, such as essential fatty acids, lecithin, saponins, isoflavones and melanoidins, come from its fermented soybean component. Since long-aged misos such as Hatcho, red (rice), barley and brown rice miso are made with more soybeans than misos that are aged for a lesser amount of time, such as mellow and sweet miso, long-aged miso should have the most medicinal properties of the two types. Four separate studies at Hiroshima University have actually confirmed this hypothesis. When longer- and shorter-aged misos were compared in animal dietary studies on radiation exposure and colon, lung and stomach cancers, long-aged misos were more effective in preventing the onset of these conditions. These results indicate that, at least for the prevention of some cancers and radiation sickness, long-aged misos, which are made with more soybeans, are a better choice. However, these studies also have found that sweeter, shorter-aged miso are effective, albeit less so. Also, shorter-aged misos may have benefits of their own not shared by long-aged misos. For example, shorter-aged misos, which have a higher grain component than long-aged misos, have been shown to contain a higher concentration of some vitamins, simple sugars and "friendly" lactobacillus bacteria.

Let Tradition Be Your Guide

It is wonderful when medical science confirms the medicinal properties of popular traditional foods, but researchers are not even close to understanding the importance of miso. Miso is a nourishing, high energy, whole food that helps maintain health and vitality. And because of the magic of lactic acid fermentation, miso is much more than the sum of its parts. During fermentation, the complex proteins, oils and carbohydrates of grains and soybeans are broken down into more readily digestible amino acids, fatty acids and simple sugars. This is why miso soup is considered an excellent food for people with weak digestion and is still used by Japanese women for weaning.

Even today, in some parts of China and Japan, drinking miso soup every day is associated with a long, healthy life. Starting the day with miso soup is said to alkalinize the body and help neutralize a buildup of acid caused by eating meat and sugar and drinking alcohol. Also, alkaline blood helps maintain health by making it easier for the immune system to fight off disease. For quick relief, miso is like a traditional Alka-Seltzer. Also, once established in the intestines, the acid-loving bacteria found in abundance in sweet, light, unpasteurized misos (those typically aged between two and eight weeks) promote health and stamina. For smokers, miso is thought to rapidly clear nicotine from the body, and miso broth is still used in the Japanese countryside to clean tar from smoker's pipes. Research aside, let long tradition be your guide. Miso is the world's most effective medicinal everyday food, and it tastes good, too!

For centuries Japanese craftsmen have used natural fermentation to transform soybeans and grains into many types of miso—a thick, savory paste used for flavoring a wide variety of dishes. Throughout Japan each region has developed its own particular type of miso; like fine wines, each has its own distinct flavor, color and aroma. And though many Japanese today include Western cuisine in their diet, most still start their day with a steaming bowl of miso soup.

During our apprenticeship in 1979 with miso master Takimichi Onozaki, in Yaita, a small city in Tochigi Prefecture, we learned the age-old methods for making traditionally crafted miso. Although methods used for making miso differ depending on the type of miso being made and the level of technology employed, the basic process used in the Onozaki shop dates back to pre-industrial Japan. Cooked soybeans are mixed with koji (grains or beans inoculated with *Aspergillus* culture), salt, and water. This mixture is placed in old cedar casks to naturally ferment at

At the Onozaki shop in Yaita, Japan, rice koji is placed in wooden boxes, which are stacked around the koji room. By the next morning the koji is mature and ready to be mixed with soybeans to make miso.

room temperature for up to two years, depending on the type of miso. Gradually, enzymes supplied by the koji, along with microorganisms from the environment, break down the complex structure of beans and grains into readily digestible amino acids, fatty acids and simple sugars. By varying the type of koji used (usually rice, barley or soybean) and the proportions of ingredients in the recipe, traditional makers like Onozaki are able to create a wide range of misos, from light and sweet to dark and robust.

Although there are a few exceptions, misos can be divided into two types based on color and taste. Sweet, or short-term, miso is usually light in color (beige or yellow) and high in carbohydrates. It is marketed as "mellow miso," "sweet miso" or "sweet white miso." Being high in koji and low in soybeans and salt, sweet miso ferments in just two to eight weeks, depending on the exact recipe and temperature of aging. These misos developed and became popular around Kyoto, Japan's southern regions and later Hawaii. The sweet, light misos, or blends of light and dark misos, are perfect in summer soups, dips, spreads, sauces and salad dressings.

Long-term miso, with its higher salt content, lower koji content and proportionately more soybeans, is darker in color and saltier in taste than sweet miso. It must be fermented longer, usually at least one summer, but as long as two to three years in very cold climates. This type of miso is marketed as "red miso," "brown rice miso" or "barley miso." Soybean misos, such as *mame* and Hatcho, are also dark and savory. Salty, long-aged misos are more popular in Japan's central and northern regions. In the West we find their earthy tones and hearty flavor excellent for winter soups, stews and sauces.

In Japan the names used to describe miso are usually clear and indicate not only what type of miso it is, but often what part of the country it is from. In the West, such names as "mellow red" or "mellow barley" can be confusing, because the word mellow indicates a sweet or light miso, and words such as "red" and "barley" usually indicate a darker, saltier, long-aged miso. To avoid confusion, just check the sequence of the ingredients on the package. In the United States, FDA regulations require that a product's ingredients must be listed on the package in descending order by weight. For true sweet or mellow misos, the first ingredient will be the koji, usually listed as cultured rice or barley. In saltier, long-aged misos, the first ingredient is soybeans. The difference between these types of miso can be very important when it comes to following specific recipes.

Distinguishing Quality Miso

Miso is such a unique and vital food that it is important to understand what factors influence its taste, medicinal qualities and nutritional value. The two most important influences on all three of these qualities are manufacturing methods and the quality of ingredients used.

Basically, there are two methods for making miso—modern and traditional. The modern process employs accelerated temperature-controlled fermentation in plastic or stainless steel holding tanks. The rice and salt used in the commercial method are often processed and have less nutritional value.

The slower, traditional method employed by Onozaki, and the few other remaining traditional miso makers, uses handmade koji and natural aging in large, wooden fermentation casks at the temperature of the environment. Also, traditional manufacturers use whole ingredients and natural sea salt.

When shopping for miso, look for the words *traditionally made* or *naturally aged* on the package. The finest quality misos are also made from 100 percent organic ingredients and sun-dried sea salt. Look for the word *organic* on the front of the package and check the ingredient list for sea salt. Unpasteurized miso, which is usually stocked in the refrigerator, is generally preferred to pasteurized miso, which is sold in unrefrigerated sealed plastic bags. However, there are several excellent Japanese-made, pasteurized misos that are sold in natural foods stores. Keep in mind that most of the health-promoting qualities of miso are not reduced by the low temperature of pasteurization.

Miso should be firm, not wet or runny. Refrigerated miso should not have a strong alcohol smell—this usually indicates that it was not manufactured or shipped properly. Sweet and mellow miso should be light yellow or beige in color rather than orange. With the exception of 100 percent soybean misos, such as Hatcho or mame miso, which are usually a dark chocolate color, typical long-aged rice and barley misos should not be dark brown, but rather russet, light brown, or have shades of red. The dark color of many unpasteurized misos sold in American natural foods stores indicates that they have been fermented too long, resulting in an inferior taste and aroma. Long-aged misos should look and smell appetizing.

COOKING WITH MISO

 The key to fine miso cooking is not to overpower dishes with a strong miso taste. The more subtle aspects of miso's color and flavor should be integrated to create a gentle balance with other ingredients. The light color, sweet taste and creamy texture of mellow white or sweet white miso is suggestive of its application in American-style cooking: it is an excellent dairy substitute. For example, try a little white miso instead of milk in mashed potatoes or creamed soups.

Experiment with tofu, mellow miso and lemon or rice vinegar to make creamy dips and spreads. To realize the full potential of sweet or mellow miso, explore its uses in salad dressings and sauces. Sweet or mellow miso and good-quality rice vinegar create a delicate tartness that is both refreshing and cooling. Sweet or mellow miso combined with sake or mirin makes excellent sauces for baked, broiled or stir-fried fish or vegetables. Think of sweet miso for festive occasions and light summer cooking. In southern climates, mellow or sweet miso is excellent for year-round cooking. Note: Though sweet and mellow white miso are similar, they are not exactly the same, so in some recipes sweet white miso is specified first because it would be the first choice in that application.

The readily digestible amino acids, fatty acids and simple sugars, and the relatively low salt content of sweet miso make it ideal for the delicate constitutions of babies and young children. A very dilute sweet miso broth is readily accepted by most children starting at age twelve months.

In contrast, Hatcho miso and the saltier varieties of dark miso are excellent for basic winter cooking in cold climates. Its hearty quality combines nicely with beans, gravies, baked casseroles and vegetable stews and soups. Try dark miso in thick soups with root vegetables such as burdock, carrots and daikon. A lentil loaf made with red miso warms the body and supplies a large quantity of high-quality protein. Remember that dark miso is stronger in taste than sweet miso, so use it sparingly.

Any discussion of miso is incomplete without considering its use in miso soup. Miso soup and rice, accompanied by a side dish of pickles and a cup of tea, constitute a meal by Japanese standards. In Japan, the dynamic flow of ingredients, texture and colors of miso soup reflects seasonal changes and geographic location. In the south, sweet barley miso, which gives miso soup a beautiful yellow to beige color, is preferred. In the north, hearty red miso is the popular choice. Often combined with carrots, burdock and wakame, red miso produces soup with a very earthy color and flavor. Don't be afraid to experiment with the many possibilities of miso soup. However, since miso is the dominant taste here, unpasteurized miso is preferred. Miso should be added to soup near the end of the cooking time. Miso (in miso soup) may be briefly simmered, but not boiled. Boiling alters the fresh miso flavor and destroys beneficial enzymes and microorganisms. The miso should be dissolved in some of the soup stock before being added to the soup.

According to ancient Japanese mythology, miso was a gift from the gods. An integral part of a traditional Japanese diet, miso has evolved with other foods in that diet. Not only is miso closely associated with the Zen Buddhist grain-centered vegetarian diet, it is also linked with such foods as rice vinegar, sake and mirin, which were often used with miso for the purpose of balance.

Samurai Miso Soup

Tokugawa, the most famous Samurai, was said to have favored Hatcho miso, which is highest in soy isoflavones. Miso soup is often used to help restore health or prevent disease. When making miso soup for medicinal purposes, we add vegetables and other foods that have well documented healing properties. Although Hatcho miso is recommended, you can substitute any dark miso that lists soybeans as the first ingredient.

> 6 cups (1.5 liters) Kombu-Shiitake Stock (see page 176)
> $^{1}/_{2}$ onion, thinly sliced into half moons
> 4 fresh or reconstituted dried shiitake mushroom caps, thinly sliced
> 2 carrots, thinly sliced on the diagonal
> $1^{1}/_{2}$ cups (125 g) chopped kale
> 4 tablespoons Hatcho miso or another dark miso

1. Combine the stock, onion and shiitake in a saucepan and bring to a boil. Lower the heat and simmer for 5 minutes.

2. Add the carrots and kale and simmer for 10 minutes more, or until the kale is tender.

3. Dissolve the miso in some of the broth and add it to the soup. Remove from the heat and allow to steep for a minute before serving.

SERVES 4 TO 5

Preparation time: 10 minutes
Cooking time: 20 minutes

Creamy Curried Carrot Soup

There is a fairy tale about a king who wanted warm ice cream. I do not remember how the king eventually got his wish, but the idea of something cool and warm is how I would describe this soup. The heat of the curry is contrasted with the cooling, creamy and refreshing qualities of coconut milk to create an experience that our minds cannot quite find a reference for.

This recipe calls for Madras curry, which is a specific, hot blend from the Madras region of India. McCormick carries this blend in their "Gourmet Collection." Other companies also offer this particular blend of curry. If you use a more generic blend, you may have to adjust the amount you add in order to get the heat and flavor you want.

1 tablespoon extra virgin olive oil
$1^1/_2$ onions, diced
3 cloves garlic, minced
4 large carrots, sliced
$^1/_4$ teaspoon sea salt
$2^1/_2$ cups (625 ml) water
One 14-oz (420-ml) can coconut milk
2 teaspoons Madras curry powder, or to taste
$^1/_8$ teaspoon freshly ground black pepper, or to taste
2 tablespoons sweet or mellow miso (any variety)
2 tablespoons grated carrot

1. Heat the oil in a large saucepan over medium heat. Cook the onion and garlic, stirring frequently, for 2 to 3 minutes, or until the onion is translucent.

2. Add the carrots and salt and cook 2 minutes more, stirring frequently.

3. Pour in the water and coconut milk, bring to a boil, then reduce the heat and simmer, covered, for 20 minutes or until vegetables are tender.

4. Stir in the curry powder and black pepper and simmer for 2 minutes more.

5. If you have an immersion blender, add the miso to the soup, insert the blender wand into the soup pot and blend until smooth. Be sure that the blender is fully immersed in the liquid before blending. If using a regular blender, half fill it with some of the soup, add the miso and blend well. (Caution! Blending hot soup can be dangerous. Do not fill the blender more than half full.) Pour the pureed soup into a large bowl and continue blending portions until all of it has been pureed.

6. Return the soup to the pot, stir in the grated carrots and bring just to a simmer. Remove from the heat and serve hot.

SERVES 4

Preparation time: 15 minutes
Cooking time: 30 to 35 minutes

Szechuan Shrimp

This is a delicious choice for those who like it hot. It is especially good served with or over white rice.

$^1/_2$ cup (50 g) thinly sliced yellow or green bell pepper

1 small, dried Japanese chile, seeded and minced, or $^1/_4$ teaspoon dried red
  pepper flakes

$1^1/_2$ tablespoons chopped fresh parsley

2 teaspoons minced garlic

1 teaspoon peeled and minced fresh ginger

1 generous tablespoon spaghetti sauce

1 teaspoon red, brown rice or barley miso thinned with 1 teaspoon water

1 teaspoon brown rice vinegar

1 teaspoon mirin

Scant $^1/_4$ teaspoon chili-flavored sesame oil

Pinch of sea salt

2 tablespoons sesame oil (untoasted)

10 oz (300 g) fresh shrimp, deveined

1. In a small bowl, combine the bell pepper, chile, parsley, garlic and ginger.

2. In a separate bowl combine the spaghetti sauce, thinned miso mixture, rice vinegar, mirin, chili-flavored sesame oil and salt.

3. Heat 1 tablespoon of the sesame oil in a skillet over medium-high heat. Add the shrimp and stir-fry for 1 minute. Transfer shrimp with a slotted spoon to a bowl.

4. Add the remaining 1 tablespoon of oil to the pan along with the bell pepper mixture. Stir-fry 1 minute.

5. Return the shrimp to the pan and add the spaghetti sauce mixture. Sauté 1 minute more, or until the shrimp is heated through and well coated with the sauce.

6. Transfer shrimp to a serving dish and serve immediately.

SERVES 2

Preparation time: 20 minutes
Cooking time: 5 minutes

Red Lentil Pâté

This simple pâté makes a tasty and nutritious spread for crackers and bread, or a filling for small tarts, quartered bell peppers or celery boats. Spread on a slice of bread and top with slivered red onion, lettuce and sprouts for a satisfying sandwich. Red lentils impart a golden color that is much more tempting than the same dish made with green lentils.

1 cup (175 g) dried red lentils
3 cups (725 ml) water
$1/2$ teaspoon sea salt
2 tablespoons extra virgin olive oil
$1/2$ cup (50 g) minced onion or sliced green onion (scallion)
2 to 3 cloves garlic, minced
$1/2$ teaspoon dried marjoram
Dash of freshly ground white or black pepper
1 tablespoon fresh lemon juice
3 tablespoons chopped fresh parsley
1 tablespoon chopped fresh basil
2 teaspoons red, brown rice or barley miso thinned in 2 teaspoons water

1. Wash and drain the lentils.

2. In a saucepan, bring the lentils and water to a boil. Reduce the heat to a simmer and cook, covered, for 20 to 25 minutes, or until tender.

3. Stir in the salt and simmer, uncovered, for 10 minutes more, or until nearly all the liquid has been absorbed.

4. Remove from the heat and let cool briefly. Mash the lentils with a potato masher and set aside.

5. Meanwhile, heat 1 tablespoon of the oil in a small skillet over medium heat. Sauté the onion and garlic for 2 to 3 minutes, or until the onion is translucent.

6. Stir in the marjoram and ground pepper and sauté 1 minute more.

7. Combine the onion mixture with the lentils. Add the lemon juice, parsley, basil, thinned miso and the remaining 1 tablespoon of olive oil; mix well.

8. Let the pâté cool to room temperature before serving. It will thicken as it cools. The pâté will keep for about 6 days if stored in the refrigerator in a covered container.

MAKES 2$1/2$ CUPS (550 G)

Preparation time: 15 minutes
Cooking time: 45 minutes

Kyoto-Style Miso Soup

Although one mellow miso may generally be substituted for another, this is the exception to the rule. The beautiful color of this savory soup can only be achieved by using fresh mellow white miso. Other vegetables may be added or substituted, but simplicity and a flavorful stock are the keys to this authentic miso soup.

> 4 cups (1 liter) Kombu-Bonito Stock (see page 176)
> 4 oz (125 g) tofu, cut into $^{1}/_{2}$-in (1-cm) cubes
> 1 or 2 green onions (scallions), thinly sliced
> $^{1}/_{2}$ cup (25 g) baby spinach leaves
> 4 tablespoons mellow white miso

1. Bring the stock to a simmer in a saucepan. Add the tofu and green onion, and simmer for 2 minutes.

2. Stir in the spinach and simmer 30 seconds more, then remove the pan from the heat.

3. In a small bowl, combine a ladleful of the hot stock and the miso. Mix thoroughly and add back to the pan. Let the soup rest briefly before serving.

SERVES 4

Preparation time: 5 minutes
Cooking time: 6 to 8 minutes

Comfort Gravy

This hearty gravy does as much for mashed potatoes as Grandmother's does, and is also delicious over grains, especially bulghur and millet. The nutritional yeast adds a concentrated source of B vitamins to soothe your body and soul. Nutritional yeast is grown on mineral enriched molasses. Once mature, the culture is pasteurized to kill the yeast. A terrific food supplement, it is a complete protein and is rich in a variety of minerals and vitamins. Being rich in the B-complex vitamins, it is particularly good for stress reduction. Nutritional yeast is especially valuable to the vegetarian, as it is one of the rare vegetarian sources of B-12.

> $1^{1}/_{2}$ tablespoons extra virgin olive oil
> 1 small onion, diced
> 1 to 2 cloves garlic, minced
> 4 small fresh shiitake or cremini mushrooms, stemmed and sliced
> 3 tablespoons unbleached white flour
> 3 tablespoons nutritional yeast
> $1^{2}/_{3}$ cups (400 ml) Shiitake Stock (see page 92) or water
> 3 tablespoons sweet or mellow miso thinned with 3 tablespoons water
> 1 tablespoon mirin or white wine
> 2 tablespoons chopped fresh parsley
> 2 teaspoons minced fresh basil or $^{1}/_{4}$ teaspoon dried

1. In a medium skillet, heat the oil over medium heat. Add the onion and garlic, and sauté for 1 minute, then add the mushrooms and sauté 2 to 3 minutes more, or until the onion is soft and translucent.

2. Reduce the heat to low. Add the flour and nutritional yeast, stirring constantly for 1 to 2 minutes.

3. Slowly add $1^1/_2$ cups (375 ml) of the stock while stirring briskly. Increase the heat to medium, and continue to stir frequently for about 10 minutes, or until the gravy begins to simmer and thicken.

4. Reduce the heat to medium-low and add the miso, mirin or white wine, parsley and basil. Stirring occasionally, simmer gently, uncovered, for 15 minutes, or until the gravy is thick and smooth. Use immediately.

MAKES ABOUT 2 CUPS (475 ML)

Preparation time: 10 minutes
Cooking time: 35 minutes

Coconut-Lime Salad Dressing

Creamy coconut milk and tangy lime juice give this unique dressing a Caribbean flavor that can turn a summer salad into an exotic experience. You can substitute other sweeteners such as honey, if you like.

4 tablespoons fresh lime juice
4 tablespoons thick coconut milk
2 tablespoons sweet or mellow miso (any variety)
1 tablespoon plus 1 teaspoon pure maple syrup
2 tablespoons water
$^1/_2$ cup (125 ml) canola or grapeseed oil
$^1/_3$ cup (30 g) shredded unsweetened coconut

1. In a blender or food processor blend all ingredients well except the oil and coconut. Slowly drip the oil into the food processor or blender while it is running for better emulsification. Add the shredded coconut and pulse briefly to mix.

2. Pour the dressing into a jar, and if time permits, chill before serving. Shake well before using.

3. Refrigerated, this dressing will keep for about one week.

Note to Cook
If you prefer to use thin or light coconut milk, increase the amount of coconut milk to $^1/_3$ *cup (75 ml). Do not add the 2 tablespoons of water.*

MAKES ABOUT $1^1/_2$ CUPS (375 ML)

Preparation time: 5 to 10 minutes

胡
麻
油

TOASTED SESAME OIL: THE COOKING OIL SUPREME

The dark, aromatic toasted sesame oil of Japan, Korea and China is one of the most intriguing flavors of Asia. Like coffee beans, when sesame seeds are toasted, biochemical changes take place that radically alter their taste and aroma. This fragrant, delicious and nutritious oil complements any grain, pasta or vegetable, and will add pleasing character to your sauces and dressings.

Sesame seeds are among the most important oil seeds of mankind. In fact, sesame may be the oldest cultivated seed known to man, dating back five to seven thousand years to equatorial Africa. Food historians believe that the golden oil pressed from sesame seeds was first used as a fuel and lubricant before its fine cooking qualities were discovered. By the sixth century BCE, affluent Persians were using sesame oil in cooking, and as an ointment and medicine. For centuries, sesame oil has been immensely popular in India, where it is used for therapeutic massage as part of the ancient medical system known as Ayurveda. Although almost all toasted sesame oil is now made in large factories using modern equipment, there are a few shops in Japan that still use methods dating back to the 1800s.

Sesame oil is rich in vitamins A, B and E, as well as the minerals iron, calcium, magnesium, copper, phosphorus and the important nutrient silicic acid. What's more, research has shown that sesame oil facilitates the absorption and digestion of some vitamins.

Sesame oil is very high in linoleic acid, one of the two essential fatty acids (EFAs) our bodies cannot produce. EFAs are necessary for normal growth and for healthy blood, arteries and nerves. They keep the skin and other tissues youthful and healthy by preventing dryness and scaliness. Recent scientific research has shown that EFAs also play an important role in regulating blood pressure, cholesterol metabolism and the flow of biochemicals across cell membranes. Overall, EFAs are involved with producing life energy in our body from food substances, and moving that energy through our system. Since the advent of food processing, particularly oil and grain refinement, EFA deficiencies and imbalances have begun to show up in some people. Linoleic acid deficiencies include hair loss, skin eruptions, mood swings, arthritis-like conditions, susceptibility to infections, poor wound healing and, in extreme cases, heart, liver and kidney disease.

Sesame oil is also rich in oleic acid, the major constituent of olive oil. Unrefined oils that are high in oleic acid are thought to benefit cardiovascular health.

Modern medical research has shown that the consumption of sesame oil lowers cholesterol and is beneficial for the heart and kidneys. In laboratory experiments, researchers at the United States Food and Drug Administration (FDA) reported that a diet high in sesame oil significantly lowered cholesterol levels in animals.

Research in Japan has shown that a diet rich in sesamin, a natural phytoestrogen found in sesame oil, reduces the risk of renal hypertension and cardiac disease. In India, research showed that sesame oil used with medication significantly lowered blood pressure.

Unrefined sesame oil contains an antioxidant called sesamol, which protects it from becoming rancid. Antioxidants are also scavengers of free radicals, which are known to cause degenerative disease. One study performed at the University of Pharmacy and Life Sciences in Tokyo actually demonstrated that sesamol inhibits the damage caused by free radicals on DNA. Sesamol has been used by the meat industry to help preserve the color and flavor of refrigerated meats. A Harvard Medical School study showed that mice with damaged intestines recovered much faster on a diet rich in sesame oil. Moreover, blood levels of interleukin, an important disease fighting blood component, were markedly higher on the sesame oil diet.

The effectiveness of sesame oil and sesamol as preventive agents with regard to cancer may go beyond their function as antioxidants. Researchers at Howard University's School of Pharmacy explained that the "potent" beneficial effect that these substances have on skin cancer in mice cannot be solely explained by the effect of free radical absorption, and they recommended further research.

When applied to the skin, sesame oil has amazing properties. Those who use it daily have found that they have fewer bacterial infections and less joint pain. Also sesame oil restores moisture to the skin, keeping it soft, supple and young looking. Its chemical structure gives it the unique ability to penetrate the skin, making it a popular massage oil in many cultures.

More than 99 percent of the world's toasted sesame oil is made in large manufacturing facilities. Many of these companies make excellent oil using large-scale production methods. However, *Tama shibori*, or simple pressing, is the traditional process that was used at the turn of the century, and is still used in a few small Japanese family shops in present-day Japan. Without high temperatures or modern powerful equipment, this centuries-old method produces sesame oil with a fresh, nutty taste and aroma, while retaining most of the oil's original healthful qualities.

The traditional Tama shibori process begins with the selection of golden sesame seeds, the very best available. The seeds are slowly toasted in a unique, wood-fired toasting machine. According to Kichisaburo Hiraide, the fifth generation head of a traditional toasted sesame oil shop in Aizu Wakamatsu, Japan, "Wood toasting heats the seeds from the inside out." In contrast, says Hiraide, "Electric toasting, used in large modern factories, heats from the outside in, which gives typical toasted sesame oil a subtle harshness not found in wood-fired oils."

Next, the toasted seeds are crushed by rollers and lightly steamed for a few minutes. Steaming heats and moistens the seeds, which allows the oil to flow more freely.

The steamed sesame meal is then placed in a wooden pressing tub that is lined with two types of filters—one made of

Japan's purest and most delicious toasted sesame oil is made in small quantities using simple filters and presses. Here steamed sesame seeds are gently pressed to extract their golden oil.

paper and the other made of human hair. (The few remaining Japanese oil makers who still use filters made from human hair claim it gives their oil its characteristic "soft texture.") The tub of warm sesame meal is then pressed.

With gentle pressure, the crushed sesame seeds easily release their rich, golden oil, which passes through the filter and drips from the bottom of the tub. This first pressing is called *ichiban shibori*; its warm, nutty aroma fills the old workshop. Filtered once more, this time through handmade Japanese paper, the oil is bottled immediately without the use of preservatives.

When stored at room temperature and exposed to air and light, most natural vegetable oils gradually turn rancid. Fortunately, a minute amount of sesamol, a natural component of sesame seeds, protects sesame oil from oxidation. This is why sesame oil, of all the edible oils, is the least subject to rancidity and loss of flavor over time.

The simple, but labor-intense methods used by the Hiraide family and other traditional producers may seem impractical by modern manufacturing standards. These small shops produce a modest thirty quarts (30 liters) of oil for a full day's work. In contrast, large oil companies produce thousands of gallons (1 gallon = 3.8 liters) a day with little effort. However, the traditional Tama shibori process produces a silky-smooth, aromatic and delicious oil that cannot be duplicated by modern technology.

Making Good Quality Oil in a Large Factory

Most natural-food quality toasted sesame oils are made by first roasting sesame seeds at about 400°F (200°C) and then pressing out the oil using a mechanical press. The degree of toasting determines the color and taste of the oil. Toasting the seeds for a shorter time makes lighter oils. Many types of toasters are used. The heat source can be electric, steam or gas, and the seeds are usually moved through the toaster on a conveyor belt. Once the sesame seeds are toasted, they are placed in an expeller press where the oil is forced out of the seeds by the turning of a screw. Using a slow screw process keeps the temperature low, which protects delicate vitamins and essential fatty acids from oxidation. Although some heat is generated in the process due to friction, no heat is added as in the high temperature extraction process used to make low quality sesame oils. Some manufacturers blend toasted and untoasted sesame oil to produce various colors and milder flavors. Marketing names often associated with the simple mechanical process described above are "cold pressed" or "unrefined."

SHOPPING FOR TOASTED SESAME OIL

Today, there are many excellent toasted sesame oils available in natural foods stores, ranging from light-colored, mild-tasting brands to more intensely flavored, dark varieties. When searching for a natural-food quality toasted sesame oil, make certain that, at the very least, the oil isn't refined. Unrefined toasted sesame oil is made by simply toasting sesame seeds, mechanically pressing out the oil, then filtering and bottling it. Except for mildly toasting the seeds, no heat or chemicals are added. This product may be labeled "unrefined." Refined toasted sesame oil is also mechanically pressed, but undergoes a non-chemical process to deodorize and remove some free fatty acids. Refined oils can be used at higher temperatures without burning or smoking, but they lack the rich flavor and natural fatty acid spectrum of the unrefined oil.

The lowest quality toasted sesame oils are made by a harsh chemical process that includes bleaching, deodorizing and high temperature chemical extraction of oil. The industrial oil extraction process increases the amount of oil extracted but strips the oil of its flavor, aroma, natural color and nutritional value, and can leave behind toxic residues. This type of toasted sesame oil is sold in grocery stores and Asian food markets, but usually not in natural foods stores.

There are many fine quality toasted sesame oils in natural foods stores and shops specializing in authentic ethnic foods. A few products are even made with organic sesame seeds. Some of these oils are quite dark in color and have an intense taste. Others are lighter and milder in flavor. The labor-intensive traditional process described above makes the most delicious and nutritious toasted sesame oils. These have the taste of freshly toasted sesame seeds and a distinctively soft and silky texture. However, there are other good toasted sesame oils made in larger factories. Most natural foods brands describe the process on the label. They may or may not use the term *unrefined*. The ingredient list should read "sesame oil" only.

COOKING WITH TOASTED SESAME OIL

 The delightfully nutty flavor and aroma of good quality toasted sesame oil is a distinctive characteristic of Asian cooking. Like other oils, toasted sesame oil seals in water-soluble nutrients and aids in the assimilation of fat-soluble ones and prevents burning when sautéing and pan-frying, but its tempting fragrance and full-bodied flavor make this oil most highly prized as a seasoning.

Use a small amount of toasted sesame oil in marinades, vinaigrettes, sauces and dressings. Toasted sesame oil is often added after cooking to enhance the flavor of fried noodles and sautéed or stir-fried dishes. When used in this way, it is especially important that the oil is a mild tasting, traditionally made product so it does not overpower the flavor of other ingredients. Add about 10 percent toasted sesame oil to the oil used for tempura or deep-frying. This will give the cooking oil a rich background flavor. In sautéeing, toasted sesame oil may overpower some mild-flavored vegetables if used alone, but it is delicious when used in combination with another vegetable oil, such as light, untoasted sesame, grapeseed, canola or safflower.

The easiest way to take advantage of toasted sesame oil's rich flavor is in braised vegetable dishes. Simply sauté a few thin slices of ginger in two or three teaspoons of toasted sesame oil. Add sturdy vegetables such as broccoli, kale or cabbage and a pinch of salt. Sauté briefly, then add a little water. Cover and simmer until the vegetables are tender.

Wok-Flashed Udon, Tofu and Vegetable Medley

Here's a delicious and satisfying complete meal that is quick and simple to prepare. Ponzu sauce, a distinctive Japanese dipping sauce, is available bottled, and can be found at Asian markets and natural foods stores. Not all sauces, however, use organic ingredients. I use Mitoku brand ponzu sauce, a high-quality product available from the Natural Import Company.

8 oz (250 g) dried udon noodles
3 cups (175 g) broccoli florets
1 carrot, cut into thin matchsticks
$1^1/_2$ tablespoons toasted sesame oil
$1^1/_2$ teaspoons minced garlic
$1^1/_2$ teaspoons peeled and minced fresh ginger
Pinch of ground red pepper (cayenne) (optional)
$^1/_2$ block (about 200 g) firm or extra-firm tofu, cubed
2 tablespoons ponzu sauce (Japanese dipping sauce)
Pinch of sea salt
Pinch of freshly ground black pepper
1 tablespoon shoyu (Japanese soy sauce)
2 teaspoons mirin
Toasted sesame seeds, for garnish

1. In a large saucepan, bring 8 cups (2 liters) water to a rolling boil and add the noodles. To prevent them from sticking together, stir until the water returns to a boil. Cook until tender but still firm. Immediately drain noodles and rinse them briefly under cold running water or in a cold-water bath. Drain and set aside.

2. Bring 4 cups (1 liter) water to a boil in a saucepan and boil the broccoli and carrots for 2 to 3 minutes, or until tender-crisp. Drain immediately, drop vegetables into a cold water bath, then drain and set aside.

3. Heat the oil in a wok or large skillet over medium heat and sauté the garlic, ginger and ground red pepper, if using, for 1 to 2 minutes.

4. Add the tofu and half of the ponzu sauce, and sauté over medium-high heat for 3 minutes. Add the vegetables, sprinkle with salt and black pepper and the remaining ponzu sauce, and sauté 2 minutes more.

5. Add the noodles, shoyu and mirin and toss for 1 to 2 minutes, or until the noodles are heated through.

6. Garnish with toasted sesame seeds and serve immediately.

SERVES 2 TO 3

Preparation time: 10 minutes
Cooking time: 15 minutes

Kinpira

This adaptation of a traditional Japanese recipe is our family's favorite way to enjoy the long, slender root vegetable known as burdock, especially during the late fall and winter months. *Kinpira* refers to a cooking style that Westerners know as braising, which is a technique of sautéing and then simmering in a small amount of liquid. In Japan, it is commonly used to cook root vegetables such as carrots, burdock and lotus root.

Burdock root has long been prized in Asia for its pleasant, crunchy texture and earthy flavor, as well as for its medicinal qualities. It is highly regarded in Asian medicine as a blood purifier. Cultivated burdock roots are available in better supermarkets and natural foods stores.

3 burdock roots (each approximately 12 in/30 cm long)
2 to 3 teaspoons toasted sesame oil
1 small, dried Japanese chile, seeded and minced, or $^1/_8$ to $^1/_4$ teaspoon dried red pepper flakes
2 large carrots, cut into thin matchsticks
$^1/_4$ teaspoon sea salt
2 tablespoons mirin
1 tablespoon tamari

1. Scrub the burdock well and cut into very thin, 2-inch (5-cm)-long matchsticks. Immediately submerge strips in cold water to prevent discoloring.

2. Heat the oil in a frying pan or heavy saucepan over medium heat. Add the chile and sauté it for 15 seconds, then add drained burdock and sauté for 3 minutes. Add 1 to 2 tablespoons water, if necessary, to prevent scorching. Cover and cook over medium-low heat for 10 to 15 minutes, or until burdock is nearly tender.

3. Add the carrots, salt and 1 tablespoon of the mirin. Sauté briefly. Cover and let cook for about 10 minutes. Check often to be sure vegetables are not sticking to the bottom of the pan.

4. When the liquid in the skillet has been absorbed and the carrots are nearly tender, add the remaining 1 tablespoon of mirin and the tamari. Toss, cover and cook briefly until tender, adding 2 tablespoons water if necessary. Transfer to a bowl and serve hot.

SERVES 4

Preparation time: 15 minutes
Cooking time: about 30 minutes

Vegetable Soba Salad

Vary the vegetables according to availability. Fresh peas, red and green bell pepper, and radishes are good, colorful options. A touch of chili-flavored sesame oil in the dressing gives the salad a mildly spicy quality. Chili-flavored sesame oil is available in most well stocked natural foods stores, Asian food stores and some specialty shops and supermarkets.

8 oz (250 g) dried soba (buckwheat) noodles
1 carrot, cut into $1^1/_2$-in (4-cm) long matchsticks
$1^1/_2$ cups (100 g) broccoli florets
1 cup (125 g) frozen corn kernels
2 green onions (scallions), very thinly sliced on the diagonal
3 tablespoons minced fresh parsley or coriander (cilantro)

Sesame Oil Dressing
3 tablespoons brown rice vinegar
2 tablespoons shoyu (Japanese soy sauce) or tamari
2 tablespoons toasted sesame oil
$1/_4$ teaspoon chili-flavored sesame oil or a pinch of dried red pepper flakes
$1/_4$ teaspoon sea salt
1 clove garlic, finely minced

1. Break the noodles into 3 or 4 even lengths and cook according to the directions on the package. When just tender, rinse noodles under cold running water, drain and set aside.

2. Cook the carrots, broccoli and corn in boiling water for 2 minutes only. Rinse under cold running water and drain well.

3. Combine all the vegetables with cooked noodles in a serving bowl.

4. Whisk the sesame oil dressing ingredients together in a small bowl and pour over the noodle mixture. Toss gently and serve.

SERVES 3 TO 4

Preparation time: 10 minutes
Cooking time: about 12 minutes

Rice Salad with Sesame-Orange Dressing

This colorful salad has an interesting blend of tastes and textures. Unlike most salads, it keeps well in the refrigerator for a couple of days, so we like to keep some on hand for a quick lunch on busy days.

$1^1/_3$ cups (250 g) white basmati rice
4 tablespoons diced dried mango or papaya
$^1/_3$ cup (50 g) tamari-roasted almonds, coarsely chopped
4 tablespoons raisins
3 green onions (scallions), thinly sliced
$^1/_2$ green bell pepper, deseeded and diced
1 tablespoon minced fresh coriander (cilantro)

Sesame-Orange Dressing
$^1/_2$ cup (125 ml) orange juice
2 tablespoons tahini (ground sesame seed paste)
$1^1/_2$ tablespoons fresh lemon juice
1 tablespoon fresh ginger juice (finely grate fresh ginger and squeeze to extract juice)
1 tablespoon brown rice malt syrup
1 tablespoon toasted sesame oil
1 tablespoon shoyu (Japanese soy sauce)
1 tablespoon minced fresh coriander (cilantro)
1 teaspoon Dijon mustard
$^1/_8$ teaspoon freshly ground black or red pepper

1. Wash and drain the rice several times until rinse water is nearly clear. Combine with 2 cups (475 ml) water in a small saucepan, bring to a boil, reduce the heat to a simmer and cook, covered, for 30 minutes.

2. Toss the dried fruit with rice as soon as rice is done cooking. Cover and let sit 10 minutes, then transfer to a bowl and let cool to room temperature.

3. Add the almonds, raisins, green onion, bell pepper and coriander to the bowl and mix well.

4. Combine the dressing ingredients in a blender and blend until smooth.

5. Toss $^1/_3$ to $^1/_2$ cup (75 to 125 ml) of the dressing with the salad and serve. Store the remaining dressing in the refrigerator for another use.

SERVES 4

Preparation time: 15 to 20 minutes
Cooking time: 35 minutes plus time for rice to cool

Sesame-Crusted Sea Bass

The flavor and aroma of fresh ground sesame seeds and toasted sesame oil combines perfectly with this delectable and succulent fish. Try serving it with a hearty grain, such as wild rice, and Glazed Acorn Squash (page 194). Grouper filets can be used instead of sea bass, if desired.

Shoyu Marinade
2 tablespoons shoyu (Japanese soy sauce)
1 tablespoon fresh lemon juice
2 teaspoons mirin, sake or white wine
1 teaspoon fresh ginger juice (finely grate fresh ginger and squeeze to extract juice)

....

$1^1/_3$ lb (600 g) sea bass, cut into 4 fillets
4 tablespoons sesame seeds
2 tablespoons unbleached white flour
$^1/_4$ teaspoon sea salt
Pinch of freshly ground black or white pepper
$1^1/_2$ to 2 tablespoons toasted sesame oil

1. Combine the marinade ingredients and pour 2 tablespoons of the mixture into a baking dish or pie plate. Reserve the rest for basting fish.

2. Roll the fish fillets in the marinade to coat all surfaces and let the fish marinate for up to 20 minutes while you prepare the sesame coating.

3. In an unoiled skillet over medium heat toast the sesame seeds for 1 to 2 minutes, or until they are fragrant or begin to pop. Do not overtoast or they will become bitter.

4. In a *suribachi* (Japanese grinding bowl) or mortar, grind the seeds until about 40 to 50 percent are crushed. Add the flour, salt and pepper, and mix well.

5. Preheat the oven to 400°F (200°C).

6. Spread the toasted, ground sesame seeds in a platter and roll the skinless surfaces (top and sides) of the fish in the mixture to coat evenly. Place the fish in a lightly oiled baking dish, skin side down.

7. Using a pastry brush, gently dab all of the sesame-coated surfaces of the fish with the toasted sesame oil.

8. Bake for 15 minutes, then baste the fish with the remaining marinade. Continue baking for 10 minutes, or until just tender, flaky and opaque throughout. The baking time will vary depending on the thickness of the fish.

SERVES 4

Preparation time: 15 to 20 minutes
Cooking time: 25 to 30 minutes

醤
油

SHOYU: KING OF CONDIMENTS

Few foods have so profoundly influenced the Japanese diet and culture as the
dark, rich soy sauce known as *shoyu*. Typical dishes such as sushi, sashimi, tempura
and sukiyaki could not be eaten without it, and in Japan it is even used to
enhance the flavor of Western-style cooking. Moreover, shoyu is one of the
ingredients of dashi (page 176), the basic stock used to make typical noodle
broths, soups and dips. In fact, shoyu is so omnipresent in Japanese cooking that
it is often called "the flavor of Japan."

The complex savory flavor of naturally brewed shoyu cannot be described
by the four basic tastes: sweet, salty, sour or bitter. The intricate flavor created by
the fermentation of equal proportions of soybeans and roasted wheat produces
a unique blend of flavorful amino acids that is difficult for Westerners to
describe. The Japanese consider this flavor to be a fifth taste, which they call
umami, their word for flavor. According to author and shoyu historian Norio
Tanaka, the umami flavor, which is also present to a lesser degree in other
Japanese foods, stimulates the appetite for large amounts of rice. This makes
shoyu the perfect condiment for the Japanese rice-based diet. Since rice is the
main source of nourishment and calories in the Japanese diet, shoyu has indirectly
played a central role in the history of this island nation.

A TASTE FOR SHOYU

Like miso and tamari, shoyu's lineage can be traced back to ancient China where the dark liquid extracted from a mixture of fermented grains, beans and fish was used as a seasoning. This early condiment, however, was very different from today's shoyu, which is made by a complex process that came of age during Japan's "cultural flowering" in the seventeenth, eighteenth and early nineteenth centuries—an era that also saw the development of the tea ceremony, flower arranging, poetry and Zen Buddhism. However, since the seventeenth century, the production of shoyu was dominated by a few large manufacturers around the capital of Tokyo. Although it was difficult for small, family-run businesses to compete with the large cartels, a few managed to survive.

The West's love affair with Japanese soy sauce may have begun with Dutch traders who were stationed in Nagasaki in the 1600s. Those early middlemen sent barrels of this liquid treasure back to Europe, some of which ended up in the French royal kitchens of Louis XIV. It was rumored around the court that the king's secret ingredient came from the other side of the globe, where it had been fermented for almost two years in tall wooden casks. Since that time, Japanese soy sauce, with its rich, fermented fragrance and salty, slightly sweet flavor, has secured an international reputation as a versatile and delicious seasoning.

HEALTH AND WELL-BEING

Because shoyu is a fermented soy food, like miso, it shares many of miso's medicinal and nutritional properties while avoiding the problems associated with unfermented soy foods. It is said to aid in the digestion of grains and vegetables while being rich in several minerals.

Scientists have given particular attention to the high concentration of brown pigment in shoyu, because of its strong antioxidant and anticancer properties. In fact, a recent study by the National University of Singapore reports that dark soy sauce has antioxidant properties that are ten times more potent than the antioxidants in red wine and 150 times more effective than vitamin C. Though research leader Barry Halliwell, Ph.D. guards against consuming too much soy sauce, as the high level of sodium could lead to high blood pressure, he also states that "it may potentially slow down the rate of cardiovascular and neurodegenerative diseases." Antioxidants combat the effects of free radicals, which attack human cells and tissues, and are linked to aging as well as a number of diseases including heart disease, Parkinson's disease and cancer.

Making high quality traditional shoyu in the few remaining small, family-run shops in Japan is both an intuitive craft and a demanding skill. Uncompromising when it comes to quality, small-scale shoyu makers carefully perform each step of the traditional process handed down through generations of family artisans. The result is a delicious, savory seasoning with an irresistible aroma and a complex, full-bodied flavor.

The traditional process of making shoyu begins with the roasting and cracking of whole, organic winter wheat and the steaming of whole, large, high-protein soybeans. These ingredients are then mixed together in approximately equal parts and inoculated with the spores of *Aspergillus*, a natural microorganism. After a three-day incubation period in a warm, humid room, the wheat and soybeans are covered with a fragrant, fluffy mycelium that is high in natural enzymes. Now called *koji*, the mixture is added to a solution of water and sea salt. In temperate climates, the thick mixture of koji and brine, called *moromi*, is placed in seasoned cedar casks to ferment for about eighteen months (or at least two full summers).

During the long aging process, enzymes from the koji and the naturally occurring yeasts and bacteria slowly break down the complex carbohydrates, proteins and oils of the wheat and soybeans into sweet sugars, aromatic alcohol and flavorful amino and fatty acids. The mature fermented moromi is then placed in cotton sacks and pressed under great force to extract its dark liquid, a mixture of shoyu and crude soy oil. The oil, which rises to the surface, is removed. Now, the shoyu is ready for settling, low-temperature pasteurization and bottling. The entire process takes about twenty-four months.

Naturally brewed shoyu is gently stirred occasionally to assist the fermentation process. Only a very small amount of Japan's shoyu is made by the traditional process.

According to traditional shoyu makers, the most important point in making high quality shoyu is aging it for six to eight seasons in old wooden casks. Each of the four seasons, with their different temperatures and humidity, influence the fermentation process in a way that cannot be simulated by artificially adjusting the temperature. Like other natural processes, traditional shoyu fermentation depends on a delicate balance of activity and rest. The speedy pace of microbial activity in the warmer months is balanced by the gradual slowing down of activity during the cooler months. Only by this gentle, natural process can the complex proteins, fats and carbohydrates of soybeans and wheat be transformed into the simple amino acids, sugars, fatty acids and aromatic alcohols of rich and fragrant natural shoyu.

SHOPPING FOR SHOYU

 Although Westerners now indiscriminately sprinkle soy sauce on everything from beef to popcorn, experienced cooks use it with discretion to enhance the subtle, natural flavors of foods. But beware: the dark, thick seasoning enjoyed by yesterday's European aristocrats is very different from most of the soy sauce sold in supermarkets today. Almost half of the eighty million dollars Americans spend annually on soy sauce is for a product containing soy extract, ethyl alcohol, sugar, salt, food coloring and preservatives. Not fermented, this product is the result of a one-day chemical process. Nearly all of the remaining soy sauce sold in the West is made using hexane-defatted soybean meal and contains sodium benzoate as a preservative. High-tech, accelerated methods and temperature-controlled fermentation are used in the manufacturing of this product, which can be made in as little as three to six months in stainless steel or fiber glass tanks.

The strongest objection to high-tech soy sauce is the substitution of hexane-defatted soy meal for whole soybeans. Hexane is a highly toxic organic solvent used in the chemical industry to dissolve fats and oils. One major concern is the possibility of hexane getting into finished soy sauce. Some critics are just as concerned about the fact that the manufacture of defatted soy meal is an environmental and occupational hazard.

According to Tokuji Watanabe, co-author of *Nature's Miracle Protein: The Book of Soybeans* (Japan Publications, 1984), the fat extraction process begins when whole soybeans are heated, cracked, hulled and rolled into flakes. The flakes are mixed with hexane and agitated to facilitate the oil extracting process. The soy oil is processed further and sold as cooking oil, while the soy meal is washed with hot water and steam to remove hexane, then sold to food processors.

Testing for hexane is not part of the soy sauce industry's daily quality control program. The FDA and solvent extraction industry have set acceptable limits for hexane in soy meal at 25 parts per million. However, advocates of higher standards of food quality are concerned about the cumulative effect of toxins in the diet.

High quality, whole-bean shoyu made by the traditional process accounts for less than one percent of Japan's production. If you want to experience the true flavor of traditional Japanese shoyu, read labels carefully. Traditional shoyu is made with water, cultured whole soybeans, whole wheat and sea salt, and is unhurriedly aged in wooden casks at natural temperatures for eighteen months to two years. (Tamari is another type of traditional soy sauce related to shoyu, but it is wheat-free and has slightly different cooking qualities than shoyu.) Shoyu contains no artificial preservatives; traditional producers rely on naturally occurring alcohol from wheat fermentation, which acts as a preservative. A few traditional shoyu producers add high quality mirin (sweet rice wine) as a natural preservative.

The issue of genetically modified organisms (GMOs) in food is a health and political concern in many countries. Most of the soybeans used to make Japanese soy foods such as tamari, miso, natto, shoyu and tofu come from the United States, China and Canada. A large proportion of the soybeans exported by the United States have been genetically modified to simplify certain standard agricultural practices. Due to complex biochemical changes that take place during the fermentation process, it is difficult to determine if a soy food, such as shoyu, has been made from genetically modified ingredients after it has been fermented. Since there are no federal laws regulating the use or labeling of foods containing genetically modified organisms, the only way to ensure that the shoyu you purchase has not been made with genetically modified soybeans is to use shoyu made with organic ingredients. The guidelines for organic standards prohibit the use of GMOs. Therefore, when shopping for shoyu, check the ingredient list to see if it has been made with organic soybeans.

COOKING WITH SHOYU

 It's no wonder that shoyu has gained worldwide recognition as an outstanding and versatile seasoning. A few drops of this rich, dark fermented liquid bring out the natural sweetness and subtle hidden flavors in almost all foods, including fish, grains, vegetables, soups, sauces and salads.

A complex chemical makeup gives traditional shoyu its extraordinary full flavor and irresistible aroma. Amino and fatty acids, released by the fermentation of whole soybeans, stimulate the taste buds and add a heartiness to meatless meals. Glutamic acid, a natural form of monosodium glutamate, makes traditional shoyu an excellent flavor-enhancer and tenderizer, perfect for marinating, pickling and sautéing. The fermentation of roasted cracked wheat yields natural sugars and alcohol, which impart a rich, savory aroma and subtle sweetness not found in tamari (pages 47–54), shoyu's wheat-free cousin. With at least twenty identified flavor components, traditional shoyu can best be described by the term deep-flavored.

In general, when using shoyu as a seasoning, it should be added during the last few minutes of cooking. Brief cooking enables it to harmonize with and heighten other flavors in the dish. In longer cooking, shoyu's slightly alcoholic qualities and delicate flavor are diminished. Tamari is generally preferred when longer cooking is needed. Shoyu is an excellent substitute for salt in a wide variety of recipes.

When using shoyu to season soups, sauces or sautés, a little sea salt can be added in the early stages of cooking to deepen the flavor of the ingredients. Add the shoyu shortly before serving. A spray bottle is ideal for applying a light, even mist of shoyu to dishes such as sautés, fried rice or noodles, and steamed vegetables.

If you want to take full advantage of shoyu's rich bouquet and complement of flavors, there are several ways to use it uncooked. Combined with a little stock, mirin and grated daikon or ginger, shoyu makes a delicious dip for tempura and other deep-fried foods, as well as for fish, pan-fried or baked mochi, and sushi. For a simple and tasty cold weather pickle, cover thinly sliced rutabaga or carrots with a mixture of half shoyu and half water for two to four days. When the vegetables are pickled enough to have lost their raw taste, they should be refrigerated. Of course, shoyu can also be used as a table condiment.

To preserve the fine qualities of traditionally-made shoyu, tightly close the cap after each use and, if you do not expect to use the bottle within a month or two, store it in the refrigerator. Prolonged exposure to heat and air can adversely affect shoyu's flavor and aroma.

You will find many recipes using shoyu throughout this book. Here are a variety of simple recipes that are enhanced by the addition of this uniquely delicious seasoning.

Festive Tofu Soup

Garnished with "flowering carrots," this elegant, light soup is the perfect beginning to a large, festive meal. You will need a garnish cutter to create the flowers that make this soup so charmng. Garnish cutters come in various shapes and can be used to cut slices of sturdy vegetables, such as carrots, to add interest to simple soups and dishes.

Broth
6 cups (1.5 liters) Kombu-Bonito Stock (see page 176) or Kombu-Shiitake Stock (see page 176)
2 tablespoons shoyu (Japanese soy sauce)
1 1/2 tablespoons mirin
1 teaspoon sea salt
. . . .
1 large carrot, cut into 24 "flowers"
8 oz (225 g) fresh tofu, cubed
1 bunch watercress, cut into 2-in (5-cm) pieces
1 teaspoon finely grated peeled, fresh ginger

1. Combine the stock, shoyu, mirin and salt in a saucepan and bring just to a simmer. If not using immediately, remove from the heat and reheat just before serving.

2. Slice the carrot into thin rounds and punch out the shapes with a flower cutter.

3. Steam or boil carrot flowers for 4 to 5 minutes, or until just tender. Drain and set aside.

4. Steam or parboil tofu for 1 to 2 minutes. Drain and set aside.

5. Evenly distribute the carrot flowers, tofu and watercress in six small soup bowls. Add a pinch of the ginger to each bowl and cover with piping hot broth. Serve immediately.

SERVES 6

Preparation time: 10 minutes
Cooking time: 10 minutes

Udon and Mushrooms with Glazed Zucchini and Pineapple

A harmonious blend of all five essential tastes makes this simple dish delicious and satisfying. A little broiled pineapple adds a touch of sweetness. I use canned pineapple chunks in their own unsweetened juice, which I use to enhance the flavor of the vinaigrette.

Pineapple Juice Vinaigrette
3 tablespoons brown rice vinegar
3 tablespoons shoyu (Japanese soy sauce)
3 tablespoons unsweetened pineapple juice
1 tablespoon mirin
1 tablespoon water
2 tablespoons chopped fresh parsley

. . . .

1 tablespoon plus 1 teaspoon toasted sesame oil
1 tablespoon minced fresh ginger
1 tablespoon plus 1 teaspoon peeled and minced garlic
Pinch of ground red pepper (cayenne)
2 cups (125 g) sliced fresh baby portobello mushroom caps
Pinch of sea salt
2 small zucchini (about 5 in/13 cm long)
$^{2}/_{3}$ cup (125 g) canned pineapple chunks (reserve juice for the vinaigrette)
8 oz (250 g) dried udon noodles

1. In a large pot bring 2 quarts (2 liters) of water to a boil.

2. Meanwhile, combine the vinaigrette ingredients in a small bowl and set aside.

3. Heat the oil in a large skillet over medium heat. Add the ginger, garlic and ground red pepper and sauté for 1 minute. Add the mushrooms, sprinkle with salt, and sauté 3 to 4 minutes more, or until they become tender.

4. Add the vinaigrette to the mushrooms and toss well to coat. Remove the skillet from the heat.

5. Turn on the broiler. Cut the stems off the zucchini and cut them lengthwise into thirds. Stack the 3 slices and cut lengthwise into thirds again, to make 9 spears from each zucchini. Place the zucchini and pineapple chunks in a single layer on a baking sheet. Dip a brush into the vinaigrette and mushroom mixture that you've set aside, and liberally coat the vegetables. Broil for 3 to 4 minutes or until lightly browned. Brush with the vinaigrette again, and broil 1 to 2 minutes more. Set aside.

6. When the water comes to a rolling boil, add the udon, stir to prevent noodles from sticking together, and cook until tender but still firm. Drain and immediately toss with the mushrooms and vinaigrette. Divide onto dinner plates or pasta bowls. Arrange the zucchini and pineapple on top of the pasta. Serve immediately.

SERVES 2 TO 3

Cooking time: 20 minutes
Preparation time: 15 minutes

Asian-Style Fish Soup

This delicious and nutritious soup takes only 25 minutes from start to table. Japanese seven-spice, or *shichimi togarashi*, a mixture dominated by crushed red pepper, is a zesty addition. It is available in Asian grocery stores. If using it for the first time, add just a little at a time until you reach the level of spicy heat that you prefer.

> 6 cups (1.5 liters) Kombu-Shiitake (see page 176) or Shiitake Stock
>   (see page 176)
> $1/2$ teaspoon sea salt
> 2 carrots, thinly sliced on the diagonal
> 10 to 12 oz (300 to 350 g) fresh white fish fillet
> 2 cups (150 g) sliced Chinese (napa) cabbage, with the leaves and stalks separated
> 2 cups (100 g) baby spinach leaves, washed and drained
> 8 oz (250 g) fresh tofu, cut into $1/2$-in (12-mm) cubes (optional)
> 2 tablespoons shoyu (Japanese soy sauce)
> 1 teaspoon fresh ginger juice, or to taste (finely grate fresh ginger and
>   squeeze to extract juice)
> 1 green onion (scallion), thinly sliced on the diagonal, for garnish
> Japanese seven-spice (shichimi togarashi) (optional)

1. In a soup pot bring the stock to a simmer. Add the salt and carrots and simmer for 5 minutes.

2. Cut the fish into bite-size cubes and add to the soup along with the sliced Chinese cabbage stalks. Simmer for 2 minutes.

3. Stir in the sliced cabbage leaves and simmer for 3 minutes.

4. Add the spinach, tofu, if using, and shoyu. Simmer for 1 minute more.

5. Remove from the heat and add the ginger juice.

6. Serve hot, topped with a pinch of the slivered green onion. Set out the Japanese seven-spice on the table so people can sprinkle it on their soup if they like a little more pepper and heat.

SERVES 4

Preparation time: 15 minutes
Cooking time: 20 minutes

Scallops in Red Velvet Sauce

This tasty and attractive dish goes well with rice and steamed greens.

> Red Velvet Sauce
> 1 cup (235 ml) Shiitake Stock (see page 92) or Vegetable Stock (see page 183)
>   or water
> 3 tablespoons natural ketchup
> 1 tablespoon mirin
> 2 teaspoons shoyu (Japanese soy sauce)
> 1 teaspoon brown rice vinegar
> $1/4$ teaspoon sea salt
> Pinch of freshly ground black pepper
> $1^1/2$ tablespoons crushed kuzu starch
>
> . . . .
>
> 2 tablespoons peanut or sesame oil (untoasted)
> 1 tablespoon minced garlic
> 2 teaspoons peeled and minced fresh ginger
> 1 green bell pepper, deseeded and diced
> 6 fresh shiitake mushrooms (optional)
> 1 lb (450 g) sea scallops
> Pinch of sea salt and freshly ground pepper
> 4 green onions (scallions), sliced into $1/4$-in (6-mm) pieces
> 1 tablespoon sake or white wine

1. Thoroughly combine the sauce ingredients in a small bowl.

2. Heat the oil in a wok or large skillet over medium heat. Sauté the garlic and ginger for about 15 seconds. Add the green pepper and, if using, the shiitake mushrooms and sauté for 2 to 3 minutes.

3. Increase the heat slightly and add the scallops and a pinch of salt and pepper. Sauté for 3 to 4 minutes, or until scallops turn opaque.

4. Stir in the green onions and sake.

5. Make a well in the center of the scallop mixture, stir the red velvet sauce and pour it into the well. Stir constantly until sauce thickens. Simmer gently for 1 to 2 minutes.

6. Remove from the heat and serve immediately.

> SERVES 3
>
> *Preparation time:* 15 minutes
> *Cooking time:* 10 minutes

Leafy Greens with Japanese Dressing

Lightly cooked greens add vibrant color and concentrated nutrition to any meal. The simple dressing in this recipe complements the slightly bitter flavor of the greens. Carrots and sesame seeds provide an interesting contrast of color and texture.

> 1 bunch leafy greens such as mustard, collards or kale, washed and stemmed
> Pinch of sea salt
> 1 carrot, sliced into thin matchsticks
>
> Dressing
> 2 teaspoons toasted sesame oil
> 1 tablespoon brown rice vinegar
> 1 tablespoon plus 1 teaspoon shoyu (Japanese soy sauce)
> . . . .
> 1 tablespoon toasted sesame seeds, for garnish

1. Fill a large pot halfway with water and bring to a boil. Add the salt and as many whole leaves as will comfortably fit. Boil the greens until just tender (about 7 minutes for collards and kale, a little less for other greens).

2. When the greens are tender, immediately remove them from the pot and plunge them into a bowl of cold water to stop the cooking and hold their color. Drain, gently squeeze out excess water and thinly slice. (If the leaves are very large, cut in half lengthwise first.)

3. Cook, cool and slice the remaining leaves.

5. Boil the carrots for 2 to 3 minutes, remove and cool under cold running water. Drain and set aside.

6. In a small bowl, whisk together the sesame oil, vinegar and shoyu.

7. In a mixing bowl, toss the greens and carrots with the dressing. Place the mixture in a serving bowl, garnish with the toasted sesame seeds and serve.

SERVES 4

Preparation time: 5 minutes
Cooking time: about 20 minutes

CHAPTER 4

溜

TAMARI: THE WHEAT-FREE SOY SAUCE

Little known outside of its home in central Japan, traditional wheat-free tamari is a rich, dark soy sauce made by naturally aging soybeans in brine for eighteen months. Tamari is particularly favored among people who have allergies to wheat. And around the world it is appreciated by a growing number of cooks—both those interested in natural foods and those who specialize in Asian cuisine—for its seasoning and cooking qualities. For simmered dishes, in particular, tamari is the seasoning of choice. Even today, however, hundreds of years after its invention, very few people understand tamari's importance and uniqueness as a flavoring agent. Indeed, tamari may be one of Japan's best-kept secrets, and one of its fading arts.

The few remaining authentic tamari shops in Japan are small family businesses located in Aichi prefecture on the Chita peninsula in central Japan, where soybeans were traditionally grown. These shops are virtual tamari museums. Inside their old wooden storehouses, rows of towering hundred-year-old wooden casks, held together with huge hoops of braided bamboo, are filled to capacity with fifteen tons of thick, rich tamari. The air is filled with the heady aroma of fermenting soy sauce, and, if you listen carefully, you can hear the sound of bubbling brew, particularly on hot summer nights.

Unlike shoyu, tamari does not contain wheat and is an excellent seasoning for those on a wheat-free diet. Like shoyu and miso, tamari is a fermented soy food, and it shares many of miso's medicinal and nutritional properties (pages 12–17) while avoiding the problems associated with unfermented soy foods. Scientists have given particular attention to the high concentration of "brown pigment" in tamari because of its strong antioxidant and anticancer properties. Tamari is said to aid in the digestion of grains and vegetables while being rich in several minerals. Since many of the health-promoting qualities of fermented soy foods are due to the soybean content, tamari, with its high soybean content, is often considered the most health-promoting variety of soy sauce.

HOW TRADITIONAL TAMARI IS MADE

In ancient times, tamari was simply the dark liquid that pooled on the surface of fermenting miso. Tamari has been collected from miso since eighth-century Japan and may have originated in China more than two thousand years ago. By 1290, the first commercial Japanese tamari shop was established. Gradually, central Japan, because of its ideal climate, choice soybeans and high quality water, became a tamari center. Around the fourteenth century, an intentionally wetter soy miso was prepared; after fermentation, its flavorful liquid was pressed out, filtered and bottled. This was the beginning of Japan's small tamari soy sauce industry, which survives today in Aichi, Mie and Gifu prefectures. Another factor contributing to tamari's growing popularity in central Japan during the 1600s was the patronage of Japan's most famous warlord, shogun Tokugawa Ieyasu, who loved its flavor and gave it to his workers and samurai.

The original thick, concentrated tamari that is closely associated with soybean miso contained no wheat and had a ratio of two parts soybeans to one part water. This so-called go-bu tamari is expensive, time consuming to make, and requires skills that can only be learned over generations and must be passed from one touji, or brewmaster, to another. In present day Japan, go-bu tamari is a dying tradition and only a few dedicated producers have survived.

Although some of these small tamari shops have bought some new equipment for washing, cooking and mixing, they still use the traditional recipes and techniques of their forefathers. Whole natural ingredients, handmade soybean koji (cultured soybeans), a high ratio of soybeans to water and long, natural aging in wood are the hallmarks of making traditional tamari.

In the fall, when natural conditions are ideal for making koji, tamari shops begin the day by soaking large, high-protein soybeans in well water. The next morning, the swollen beans are placed in a large capacity steamer. After cooking, the soft beans are crushed into small balls the size of marbles called miso dama. These balls are dusted with a mixture of Aspergillus spores and roasted barley flour and then placed in a special room to incubate for about three days. During this time, the tamari maker carefully controls the temperature and humidity. (According to historical records, before the advent of laboratory methods to isolate *Aspergillus*, balls of cooked soybeans were hung outside to be naturally inoculated by wind-blown *Aspergillus* spores.)

The sweet smelling, fluffy, pale yellow balls, now called koji, are removed from the incubator and placed on bamboo mats to dry for two weeks. This unique drying process is said to give go-bu tamari its extra thick, rich quality and concentrated flavor.

The dried koji is mixed with a brine solution (sea salt and water) and placed in 10-foot (3-m)-tall cedar vats to ferment. This fermenting mash, called *moromi*, is actually a thick paste that is pressed with 1,000 pounds (450 kilograms) of river stones. The weight of the stones on the moromi creates the ideal oxygen and humidity requirements for fermentation.

During the long aging process, enzymes from the *Aspergillus* culture and naturally occurring yeasts and bacteria slowly break down the moromi. The complex carbohydrates, proteins and oils of the soybeans are transformed into simple sugars, aromatic alcohols and dark, flavorful amino and fatty acids. The mature fermented moromi is then placed in cotton sacks and pressed under great force to extract its dark liquid, a mixture of tamari and crude soy oil. The oil, which rises to the surface, is removed. The tamari is finally ready for settling and bottling. The entire process takes about eighteen months.

SHOPPING FOR TAMARI

 Traditionally made tamari—which is long-aged in wooden vats, contains no wheat and is made with only whole soybeans—accounts for a very small part of the world's tamari production. According to Japanese Agriculture Standards (JAS), even a product made with 20 percent wheat can be called tamari. Besides adding wheat, modern tamari manufacturers make a much more diluted product than that made by small, traditional producers. Authentic tamari is made from two parts whole soybeans and one part water. Therefore, authentic tamari moromi is very thick, making it difficult to press and extract the rich, concentrated tamari.

To save time and money, modern tamari makers use a ratio of ten parts soybeans to ten parts water, resulting in a thinner, less flavorful product. What's more, most tamari is made by a rapid commercial process using soybeans defatted with the industrial solvent hexane. This type of tamari is fermented at high temperatures for three to six months and often bottled with additives. Manufacturers of temperature-controlled, defatted tamari claim that their closed, heated system is more efficient and produces a comparable or superior tasting product. Advocates of the traditional brewing process counter that the vigorous fermentation of summer and subtle activity of winter each influence the developing tamari, slowly transforming and mellowing the mixture in a way that cannot be duplicated by artificial temperature controls. Christopher Dawson, CEO of Clearspring, Europe's largest importer of traditional Japanese foods, compares brewing to raising children. "If you leave children inside year round, with air-conditioning and artificial heat, they will not develop the resistance, strength, health and character of children that play outside in the extremes of winter and summer." Likewise, he explains, "temperature-controlled tamari lacks vitality, character and complexity."

When shopping for authentic tamari, the first thing to look for is the country of origin. As of the writing of this book, the only whole soybean tamari, naturally aged in wooden vessels, is made in Japan. The labels on these traditional products usually proudly mention the authentic process described above. The only ingredients on the labels of traditional tamari are cultured soybeans, water, sea salt and a trace of barley flour. The finest tamari is preserved with about 2 percent sweet rice wine, or mirin. Other manufacturers use a little ethanol as a preservative.

The issue of genetically modified organisms (GMOs) in our food is a growing health concern. The only way to ensure that the tamari you purchase has not been made with genetically modified soybeans is to buy tamari made with organic ingredients. The guidelines for organic standards prohibit the use of GMOs. Therefore, when shopping for tamari, check the ingredient list to see if it has been made with organic soybeans.

COOKING WITH TAMARI

Tamari is a uniquely delicious, versatile seasoning that adds immeasurably to the flavor of soups, sauces, vegetables and main dishes. It is a flavorful substitute for salt in a wide variety of savory preparations.

Unlike shoyu, which derives much of its flavor from the natural alcohol produced by wheat fermentation, tamari's rich flavor comes from an abundance of amino acids, which are derived from soy protein. Because amino acids are not volatile, they don't evaporate the way alcohol does. This makes tamari the better soy sauce to choose when lengthy cooking is required. Tamari also contains more flavor-intensifying glutamic acid than shoyu. Bland foods like tofu and tempeh are enhanced when simmered in a seasoned liquid. For dishes that require this long simmering process, tamari is the preferred seasoning. Its slightly thicker consistency and deeper taste also make it good for dipping sauces and pickling.

Hawaiian-Style Teriyaki Tofu

This flavorful dish is a great way to introduce someone to tofu. Serve it with brown rice and steamed vegetables for a quick and simple, nutritious meal.

1 large block (about 1 lb/450 g) firm or extra-firm tofu
2 tablespoons unsweetened pineapple juice
2 tablespoons tamari
1 tablespoon mirin or sweet white wine, such as Reisling
1 teaspoon fresh lime or lemon juice
1 teaspoon fresh ginger juice (finely grate fresh ginger and squeeze to extract juice)
1 clove garlic, crushed
2 teaspoons toasted sesame oil
2 tablespoons minced green onion (scallion), for garnish

1. Cut tofu crosswise into six or eight equal slices. Arrange the slices in a single layer on one end of a clean, dry kitchen towel. Cover the tofu slices with the other half of the towel and gently press to remove excess moisture.

2. Lay the slices flat on a platter or baking dish. Combine the pineapple juice, tamari, mirin or sweet white wine, citrus and ginger juices, and garlic, and pour the mixture over the tofu slices. Coat tofu on all sides and let marinate for 20 minutes. Turn the slices once or twice while marinating.

3. Heat the oil in a large cast-iron or other heavy-bottomed skillet over medium-low heat. Remove the tofu from the marinade and set the marinade aside. Drain excess liquid from tofu and fry on one side until lightly browned. (Browning will enhance tofu's flavor and appearance, but be careful not to burn.)

4. Carefully turn the slices and cook 2 to 3 minutes more.

5. Add the marinade and cook another 30 to 60 seconds.

6. Place the tofu slices on serving dishes. Garnish with the green onion and serve hot.

SERVES 3 OR 4

Preparation time: 10 minutes plus 20 minutes for marinating
Cooking time: 10 minutes

Caribbean Black Bean Soup

Black bean soup is a thick, substantial Caribbean favorite that, traditionally, is spicy-hot. This version is quite mild; if you prefer to turn up the heat, simply add fresh or dried hot pepper to taste, along with the other vegetables and spices.

2 cups (375 g) dried black "turtle" beans
8 cups (2 liters) water
1 tablespoon extra virgin olive oil or sesame oil (untoasted)
2 cloves garlic, minced
1 onion, diced
2 carrots, diced
1 rib celery, sliced
1 bay leaf
$1^1/_2$ teaspoons ground cumin
2 teaspoons sea salt
$1/_4$ teaspoon freshly ground black pepper
$1^1/_2$ tablespoons tamari
3 to 4 tablespoons minced fresh parsley
2 tablespoons fresh lemon juice (optional)
6 sprigs fresh parsley or coriander (cilantro), for garnish

1. Pick over and rinse the beans. Soak the beans for 8 hours in water, covered, or boil them for 2 minutes, remove from the heat, and soak, covered, 1 to 2 hours.

2. Drain the beans, combine with 8 cups (2 liters) of fresh water in a large pot, and bring to a simmer over medium heat. Reduce the heat to medium-low and simmer until tender about $1^1/_2$ to 2 hours. If you're in a hurry, pressure cook the beans in 6 cups (1.5 liters) water for 45 to 50 minutes.

3. While the beans are cooking, heat the oil in a skillet over medium heat. Sauté the garlic and onion until the onion is translucent.

4. Add the carrots, celery and a pinch of salt and sauté for 2 to 3 minutes. Add 2 cups (475 ml) of water, simmer for 10 minutes, then remove from the heat.

5. When the beans are tender, add the vegetables, bay leaf, cumin, salt and pepper, and simmer for 10 minutes. Stir in the tamari and simmer for 10 minutes more, or until the vegetables are tender.

6. Add the minced parsley during the last minute or two of cooking.

7. Remove the soup from the heat and stir in the lemon juice, if desired. Remove and discard the bay leaf. Ladle into bowls and garnish each with a sprig of parsley.

SERVES 6

Preparation time: 20 minutes plus soaking time for beans
Cooking time: about $2^1/_2$ hours

Fall Harvest Soup with Curried Cornmeal Dumplings

Here's a special treat that features autumn's colorful harvest.

    1 tablespoon extra virgin olive oil
    3 thin slices fresh ginger
    1 onion, thinly sliced into half moons
    8 button or other small mushrooms, stemmed, caps cut into quarters
    2 leeks, white part only, slit lengthwise to center, rinsed well and thinly sliced
        on the diagonal
    $^1/_2$ rutabaga, diced
    2 carrots, cut into bite-size chunks
    1 red potato, diced
    1 rib celery, sliced
    5 cups (1.25 liters) Kombu Stock (see page 176) or water
    $^1/_2$ bay leaf
    $^1/_2$ teaspoon sea salt
    $^1/_2$ teaspoon dried marjoram
    12 green beans, cut into 1-in (2.5-cm) lengths
    $1^1/_2$ to 2 tablespoons tamari (to taste)
    3 tablespoons crushed kuzu starch

Curried Cornmeal Dumplings

$1/3$ cup (45 g) whole-wheat pastry flour

$1/3$ cup (50 g) cornmeal, preferably stoneground

1 teaspoon arrowroot

1 teaspoon baking powder

$3/4$ teaspoon curry powder

$1/4$ teaspoon sea salt

$1/3$ cup (75 ml) plain rice milk or soymilk

$1^1/2$ tablespoons vegetable oil, such as canola or safflower

1. Heat the oil in a large soup pot over medium heat. Add the ginger and sauté briefly, then add the onion and sauté for 3 to 5 minutes, or until it is translucent.

2. Add the mushrooms, leeks, rutabaga, carrots, potato, celery and a pinch of salt. Cook briefly while stirring frequently, adding a little water if needed to prevent scorching.

3. Add the stock or water, bay leaf, salt and marjoram and simmer for 25 minutes, or until the rutabaga is nearly tender.

4. Remove the ginger slices.

5. To prepare dumpling batter, combine the flour, cornmeal, arrowroot, baking powder, curry powder and salt in a small bowl. In a separate bowl combine the rice milk and oil and add it to the dry mixture, stirring with a fork until just combined.

6. Add the green beans and tamari to the soup. Thoroughly dissolve the kuzu in 3 tablespoons cold water and add it to the soup while stirring. Continue stirring until the soup returns to a simmer and thickens. Remove the bay leaf and discard.

7. Drop the dumpling mixture from a large spoon to make 4 large mounds on top of the simmering stew. Tightly cover and gently simmer for 12 minutes. (Do not uncover before at least 10 minutes are up.)

8. To test for doneness, insert a toothpick into one of the dumplings. If it comes out clean, the dumplings are done.

9. Carefully ladle the stew and dumplings into bowls. (For the nicest appearance, gently lift one dumpling out with a spatula and set it aside. Fill one bowl with stew and top it with a second dumpling from the pot. Continue in this way, topping the last bowl with the dumpling you set aside.)

SERVES 4

Preparation time: 25 to 30 minutes

Cooking time: 50 minutes

Hot and Spicy Chinese Noodle Soup

This soup and its cousin, Szechuan Soup (page 203), are two favorites in our household. Ginger and chili-seasoned sesame oil give this one an authentic Asian flavor. The oil is available in well-stocked natural foods stores, Asian foods stores, specialty shops and many supermarkets. It is very hot, so use it sparingly. Bifun noodles are delicate, transparent Chinese noodles made from rice starch, sometimes called "cellophane noodles." They are also sold at natural foods and Asian foods stores.

$^1/_2$ package (about $2^1/_2$ oz/70 g) bifun noodles
6 cups (1.5 liters) Shiitake Stock (see page 92) or Kombu-Bonito Stock (see page 176) or Vegetable Stock (see page 183)
2 thin slices peeled fresh ginger
1 teaspoon sea salt
2 teaspoons tamari
$^1/_2$ cup (30 g) sliced mushrooms of your choice
$^1/_2$ cup (60 g) thinly sliced carrots
$^1/_2$ cup (40 g) diced red bell pepper or thinly sliced celery
12 snow peas, trimmed and sliced on the diagonal in half or thirds
$^1/_2$ teaspoon chili-flavored sesame oil

1. In a saucepan, bring 6 cups (1.5 liters) water to a boil, add the bifun and cook for 5 minutes.

2. Drain noodles and rinse under cold running water, drain well and chop into 2-inch (5-cm) lengths. Divide the noodles among six individual serving bowls.

3. In a soup pot, combine the stock, ginger, salt, tamari, mushrooms, carrots, and red pepper or celery. Bring to a boil and gently simmer for 10 minutes. Remove and discard the ginger.

4. Add the snow peas and simmer 1 to 2 minutes more. Add the chili-flavored sesame oil and remove from the heat.

5. Ladle the hot soup over the noodles and serve.

Note to Cook
Somen noodles, a delicate Japanese noodle, could be substituted for bifun noodles, though the soup would no longer be authentically Chinese.

SERVES 6

Preparation time: 10 minutes
Cooking time: 30 minutes

甘
酒

AMAZAKE: SWEET AMBROSIA

The first time you taste *amazake,* you will not believe that the sweet, ambrosial flavor of this puddinglike substance comes entirely from grain. Amazake, literally "sweet sake," is a nonalcoholic fermented food made by incubating a mixture of cooked rice and *koji,* rice cultured with an *Aspergillus* mold, for several hours. The surprisingly concentrated sweetness develops as the abundant digestive enzymes in koji break down the complex starches in rice into easily digestible, natural sugars. This naturally sweet rice preparation has been used in Japan for centuries as the base of a delicious, warming drink. In the past, it was sold by street vendors wherever people gathered, and it is still popular at inns and teahouses. Japanese prepare the drink by combining equal parts of amazake and water then heating it just to a simmer. They always serve it hot, often topping it with a pinch of finely grated ginger.

Throughout its long history as an important, enjoyable part of traditional Japanese cuisine, amazake has been prepared and served almost exclusively in this simple way. Amazake's brief history in the West is quite a different story. Westerners quickly discovered many ways to use this sweet, creamy food: as a dairy substitute; for puddings, frozen pops and "ice cream"; in breads, cakes, and cookies; and as the basis of delicious salad dressings and quick pickles.

Brown rice amazake is high in fiber and complex carbohydrates, as well as the B vitamins niacin and thiamin, and is low in fat. Since brown rice amazake is made with whole brown rice and brown rice koji, it contains all the beneficial nutrition of brown rice. Whole brown rice contains a generous supply of B vitamins, plus calcium, phosphorus and iron. Also, because the natural process leaves the rice germ intact, traditional amazake contains important fatty acids not found in highly processed, commercial amazake made with white rice.

Unlike other intensely sweet foods, which are usually made up of mostly simple sugars, amazake provides a slow but prolonged source of energy that is calming and soothing. The carbohydrates in whole grain amazake consist of about 50 percent simple sugars, primarily maltose, and 50 percent complex carbohydrates. Maltose, being a disaccharide, takes up to one-and-a-half hours to be assimilated, and complex carbohydrates require up to three hours to digest. Thus, this composition supplies the body with fuel over an extended period of time, rather than a large dose all at once, which makes it an excellent food for athletes and other active people.

Amazake is the perfect food for people suffering from poor digestion, since its ingredients are predigested into simple nutrients by the traditional fermentation process. For this reason, it is also considered an excellent food for young children. Like miso, amazake has an abundance of active enzymes that help your body break down proteins, fats and complex carbohydrates into simple amino acids, fatty acids and simple sweet sugars. In fact, the strong enzymatic action of amazake is used in making several traditional Japanese pickles.

HOW AMAZAKE IS MADE

Amazake's natural sweetness develops as the abundant digestive enzymes in the koji break down the complex starches in the rice into easily digestible, natural sugars. When making amazake, you can help determine how sweet it will be by the amount of koji you use—the more koji, the sweeter your amazake.

The basic recipe calls for two parts water, one part sweet brown rice and one-half to one part koji, depending on the sweetness desired. After the rice is pressure cooked with the water, it is cooled until it is moderately hot to the touch. While the rice is still warm, the koji is added and the mixture is placed in a warm place to ferment for approximately eight hours. During this time, it is stirred once ever hour or so. A pinch of salt is added after the first stirring to help develop the sweetness. When finished, the amazake has a sweet aroma and taste. The finished product is sold refrigerated or made shelf stable by high temperature sterilization.

Although the Japanese traditionally used milled white rice to make amazake, natural home-style amazake is made from brown rice or sweet brown rice and rice koji using the same traditional fermentation methods that were used in the Japanese countryside before the industrial revolution. Natural amazake is dairy-free, wheat-free and contains no added sugar or processed ingredients.

SHOPPING FOR AMAZAKE

 Typical amazake found in Asian food stores is made with white rice and white rice koji. In some cases, white sugar is added to enhance sweetness. This style of amazake is more of a confection than a natural treat. Besides being almost completely devoid of nutrition, sugar-laced white rice amazake lacks the natural balance of the traditionally made, whole-grain product.

Among natural foods brands, the most significant difference between brands made using the traditional, small scale approach and that of mass-market producers is that large manufacturers substitute one or more laboratory-produced enzymes, such as alpha-amylase, beta-amylase and glucosidase, for some or all of the koji. The enzymes may or may not be listed as ingredients on the label.

Traditional makers contend that there is a distinct qualitative difference between amazake made with koji and that made with enzymes. Whereas the enzymes in koji are part of a living cell, in the laboratory they are isolated from the rest of the cell and are, therefore, no longer part of a living system. While using isolated enzymes offer producers more control over their finished product, the use of koji is the natural way to ferment rice to make amazake and other traditional fermented foods. With koji, many enzymes are at work holistically digesting proteins and fats as well as carbohydrates. According to traditional makers, this results in a more complex flavor and provides other subtle but important benefits, but they admit that this is difficult to prove in the laboratory.

Producers who use enzymes can control the percentages of maltose (a disaccharide) and glucose (a monosaccharide) in the final product. That is, when isolated enzymes are used to make amazake, producers can tailor their choice of enzymes to achieve a specific result. For example, since glucose tastes twice as sweet as maltose, if a sweeter flavor is desired, more of the enzyme that produces glucose is added. Another incentive for using enzymes is that they help ensure product consistency, which is critical to large manufacturers. When koji is used, the flavor and degree of sweetness varies somewhat with each batch.

Although we enjoy several of the mass-produced, natural food–quality amazake products on the market, for the best flavor and health benefits, we prefer to purchase traditionally made amazake or amazake products or to make our own at home.

The ingredient list on traditionally made amazake packages should say water, rice, koji and, sometimes, sea salt. Most natural products are made with organic sweet rice, although some high quality amazake is made with conventional brown rice.

COOKING WITH AMAZAKE

 Brown rice amazake drinks and other foods made with amazake are a favorite with children and adults alike. For a hardy winter breakfast, just heat the amazake gently and serve with a hint of ginger or dilute with water and serve hot for a wholesome, warming drink. As a sweetener, amazake is a natural in puddings, pie fillings and custards. It adds a rich, moist quality to breads, scones, pancakes, waffles, cakes and cookies. Use amazake for delicious quick pickles, to add body and mild sweetness to salad dressings, and to make scrumptious, dairy-free "milk shakes." The recipes that follow offer a variety of ways to enjoy this wholesome comfort food.

Homemade Amazake

Many people make amazake with regular brown rice or white rice. I prefer to use sweet brown rice. Rice koji is available at well-stocked natural foods stores. If your local shop does not carry it, ask the manager to order some for you. I prefer using a pressure cooker because it makes the rice softer and easier for the koji to penetrate and break down. However, if you don't own a pressure cooker, using a pot will also work. Start making amazake early in the day, because it needs to incubate for 6 to 10 hours.

> 2 cups (400 g) sweet brown rice
> 4 cups (1 liter) water
> 1 cup (150 g) rice koji
> Pinch of sea salt

1. Rinse the sweet brown rice under cold running water. Combine it with the 4 cups (1 liter) water in a pressure cooker. (If cooking rice in a saucepan, add 5 cups/1.25 liters of water.) Bring the rice up to pressure and cook for 40 minutes. (Or simmer for 1 hour in the saucepan, tightly covered.)

2. Allow the pressure to come down, then transfer the rice to a large ceramic or glass bowl and beat vigorously with a rice paddle or large wooden spoon for 5 to 10 minutes. Beating helps to cool the cooked grain quickly, and, if you crush some of the grains against the side of the bowl as you go, the koji will be able to penetrate and do its work faster. After beating, you should be able to plunge your finger into the rice and hold it there without burning, although it will still be quite hot.

3. Add the koji and mix well. Cover the bowl and place it in a warm but not hot oven: the temperature should not be higher than 140°F (60°C). If this is not possible, place the bowl on a radiator, hot water heater or another warm spot.

4. Let the mixture incubate for 6 to 10 hours, stirring once every hour or so and adding a small pinch of salt during the first or second stirring. Incubation helps facilitate fermentation. When finished, the amazake will have a rich, sweet aroma and taste. You will soon learn how much or how little fermentation you like.

5. If you prefer a smooth consistency, put the amazake through a food mill or place it in blender and puree. Keep it refrigerated in a covered container. Enjoy as is, or use it in any of the following recipes.

Note to Cook

Occasionally amazake gets "stuck"—that is, the fermentation stops for no apparent reason. A small amount of calcium is needed for complete fermentation. Hard water usually contains enough calcium to make good amazake, but if you are using purified or distilled water, you may need extra calcium. Simply crush one-fourth of a natural calcium supplement tablet and add it to the cooked rice along with the koji.

MAKES 5 CUPS (1.25 LITERS)

Preparation time: about 20 minutes

Cooking time: about 1 hour plus 6 to 10 hours fermentation time

Strawberry Shake

Colorful and full of fresh, fruity flavor, shakes or smoothies are a hit with all ages. Strawberry is a favorite, but experiment by adding or substituting other fruits. For example, try it with raspberries, or reduce the amount of strawberries to one cup and add one small banana.

    1 cup (235 ml) amazake (homemade, see opposite, or an undiluted
      commercial brand)
    1 to 1 1/2 cups (250 to 375 ml) almond milk
    2 cups (250 g) fresh or frozen strawberries
    1/4 teaspoon pure vanilla extract
    2 tablespoons rice syrup, or to taste (optional)

1. Puree all ingredients thoroughly in a blender. For a smooth texture, pour through a fine-mesh strainer to remove rice hulls. (Press solids dry, and save them in a container in the refrigerator for making cookies, quick breads and pastries.)

2. Serve well chilled.

   MAKES 2 CUPS (475 ML)

   Preparation time: 5 minutes plus chilling time

Amazake Custard

Enjoy this simple dessert as is, use it as a filling for cream pies and tarts, or layer it with fresh fruit or fruit sauce for delicious parfaits.

    2 cups (475 ml) Almond Shake (see page 61) or Strawberry Shake (see above)
    2 to 3 tablespoons brown rice malt syrup (to taste)
    1 1/2 tablespoons kanten flakes
    1 1/2 tablespoons crushed kuzu starch
    1/2 teaspoon pure vanilla extract

1. In a saucepan combine the amazake and rice syrup. Sprinkle the kanten flakes on the surface, heat to a simmer over medium heat without stirring, then simmer for 2 minutes more, stirring gently until kanten is dissolved.

2. Thoroughly dissolve the kuzu in 2 tablespoons cold water and add it to the pan while stirring briskly. Gently simmer 2 minutes more, stirring frequently until the mixture thickens.

3. Remove from the heat and stir in the vanilla. Pour into custard cups or small bowls and chill until firm, about 2 hours.

4. If desired, garnish with fresh berries, toasted coconut flakes or toasted slivered almonds before serving.

   SERVES 4

   Preparation time: 5 minutes plus 2 hours to cool and set
   Cooking time: 5 minutes

Amazake Tea Scones

The Scots invented scones to eat with their afternoon tea. They have always known that for best results the dough should be worked as little as possible, then popped in the oven quickly once the leavening agent and the liquid have been combined. Scones are best eaten the day they are made, still warm and with butter and jam.

$^1/_2$ cup (125 ml) amazake (homemade, see page 58, or an undiluted commercial brand)

4 tablespoons soymilk or almond milk

$^1/_3$ cup (50 g) currants or chopped raisins

2 teaspoons finely grated lemon zest

$1^1/_2$ cups (175 g) whole-wheat pastry flour

$^1/_2$ cup (65 g) unbleached white flour

2 teaspoons baking powder

$^1/_2$ teaspoon baking soda

$^1/_2$ teaspoon sea salt

$1^1/_2$ teaspoons ground cinnamon

3 tablespoons vegetable oil, such as canola or safflower, or 4 tablespoons unsalted butter, melted

1. Preheat the oven to 400°F (200°C) and oil or butter two baking sheets.

2. Combine the amazake and soymilk in a blender and process until fairly smooth.

3. Pour the mixture into a small bowl. Stir in the currants and lemon zest.

4. Sift together the dry ingredients into a mixing bowl. With a fork, stir in the vegetable oil or butter, then rub the mixture between your hands until it resembles coarse sand.

5. Make a well in the center of the flour mixture. Add amazake-soymilk mixture, and mix lightly with a fork until the flour is evenly moist. Knead the dough gently a couple of times and form a ball. The dough should be soft and slightly sticky. If it is too sticky, mix in a little more flour; if it is too dry, add a bit more liquid.

6. On a floured board, quickly press or roll the dough out to an even $^1/_2$-inch (1.25-cm) thickness, first sprinkling a little flour on the surface of the dough and on the rolling pin to prevent sticking.

7. Cut out rounds with a biscuit cutter or glass and place them on the baking sheets. Roll out the scraps and cut them into biscuits as well.

8. Bake for 10 to 15 minutes. Scones should be golden, but still soft, not crisp.

MAKES ABOUT EIGHTEEN 3-INCH (8-CM) SCONES

Preparation time: 15 minutes

Cooking time: 10 to15 minutes

Original Amazake Drink

Served hot, this is a creamy cup of comfort. Cooled to room temperature or slightly chilled, it makes a delicious summer drink.

$3/4$ cup (175 ml) amazake (homemade, see page 58, or an undiluted commercial brand)
$3/4$ cup (175 ml) water
Pinch of peeled and finely grated fresh ginger or a pinch of grated nutmeg and a few drops of pure vanilla extract

1. If you prefer a smooth consistency, puree the amazake and water in a blender. Transfer the puree to a saucepan and bring just to a simmer over medium-low heat, stirring occasionally.

2. Remove from the heat and add the ginger or nutmeg and vanilla. Serve immediately or let cool if making a chilled drink.

MAKES 1^1/$_2$ CUPS (350 ML)

Preparation time: 2 minutes
Cooking time: 2 minutes

Almond Shake

Roasted almond butter is the key to the richness of this popular drink. Ground toasted almonds just don't do the trick. Almond butter is a delicious nut butter made from roasted almonds. Almond butter and almond milk are both available in most natural foods stores. If you cannot find almond milk, prepare fresh almond milk by following the recipe on page 102.

1 cup (235 ml) amazake (homemade, see page 58, or an undiluted commercial brand)
1 to 1^1/$_2$ cups (250 to 375 ml) almond milk
3 tablespoons roasted almond butter
Scant pinch of sea salt
$1/2$ teaspoon pure vanilla extract
$1/8$ teaspoon pure almond extract

1. Puree all the ingredients thoroughly in a blender. For a smooth texture, pour through a fine-mesh strainer to remove rice hulls. (Press solids dry, and save them in a container in the refrigerator for making cookies, quick breads and pastries.)

2. Serve well chilled.

MAKES 2 CUPS (475 ML)

Preparation time: 5 minutes plus chilling time

Amazake Salad Dressing

This slightly sweet yet tart dressing makes a tossed salad sing. Similar to a creamy Italian, it was inspired by salad dressing recipes from Grainaissance, a California-based mochi and amazake producer.

> $^1/_2$ cup (125 ml) amazake (homemade, see page 58, or an undiluted commercial brand)
> 2 tablespoons sesame oil (untoasted)
> 2 tablespoons extra virgin olive oil
> 4 tablespoons brown rice vinegar
> 1 tablespoon red (rice) miso
> 1 clove garlic, sliced

Combine all the ingredients in a blender and process until smooth. Serve with mixed greens or pasta salads. It will keep in the refrigerator for about 2 weeks.

MAKES ABOUT 1 CUP (235 ML)

Preparation time: 3 to 5 minutes

Amazake Summer Pickles

Pickles aid digestion and provide important nutrients. This refreshing, quick pickle is perfect with summer meals. Use vegetables with a variety of colors for an especially appealing side dish. Our favorites are carrots, cucumbers, daikon, red radishes and turnips. Thick-skinned vegetables, such as daikon and turnips, should be peeled. Thin-skinned vegetables do not have to be peeled, unless they are not organic or have been waxed.

> 2 cups (475 ml) amazake (homemade, see page 58, or an undiluted commercial brand)
> 2 tablespoons sea salt
> 1 cup (about 75 g) peeled, if necessary, and thinly sliced vegetable(s) of your choice

1. In a small saucepan, bring the amazake slowly to a simmer while stirring frequently to prevent scorching. Remove from the heat and let cool to room temperature.

2. Mix in the salt and store in a jar in the refrigerator until ready to use.

3. The day before, or at least 2 to 3 hours before serving, toss the vegetables with enough of the pickle mix to coat each slice. (Return the remaining pickle mix to the refrigerator for later use. It will keep for about 1 month in the refrigerator.) Set aside at room temperature until mealtime.

4. To serve, shake off excess pickle mix and arrange the pickles attractively in a pickle dish or small serving plate.

MAKES 1 CUP

Preparation time: 10 minutes plus 2 to 3 hours for pickling
Cooking time: 3 to 5 minutes

甘
酒

KUZU: THE WONDER ROOT

Roots are the reservoir of a plant's energy. This is why roots have always occu-
pied a special place in man's diet, as well as in his medicine chest. Popular roots
such as ginseng, burdock, radishes, beets and carrots are prized for their concentrated food value and healing power. No wonder kuzu (*Pueraria lobata*) root
one of the world's largest vegetable roots, is considered big medicine in Japan
and China. Averaging 200 pounds (90 kg), the kuzu root is an Asian giant.

In its native land, kuzu has always enjoyed an excellent reputation. Asians
seem to have no problem using kuzu as fast as it grows. Since ancient times, the
leaves and roots have been used for food. The strong fibrous stems have been
used as thread to weave fabrics and baskets. But it is kuzu cuisine that has become
a fine art in Japan. The purest white kuzu root powder is sought out by high-
quality confection manufacturers and chefs of fine restaurants.

Kuzu, better known as kudzu in America, also has a dark side. A sea of green kuzu tendrils and leaves blankets seven million acres of the southeastern United States from May to October, smothering utility poles, trees and barns. This prolific vine causes hundreds of millions of dollars in damage each year. It's no wonder that kuzu has been jokingly referred to as a vegetable form of cancer and the weed that ate Dixie.

Ironically, while irate farmers and utility companies have been killing kuzu by spraying and burning the plants, for years Asian people in the United States have been importing kuzu roots and root powder for medicinal and culinary use.

Kuzu's schizophrenic existence in America began around 1900, shortly after it was introduced from Japan. With purple wisteria-like flowers perfuming the summer air and cattle grazing on its large, high-protein leaves, kuzu seemed like a perfect plant for southern farmers. Moreover, kuzu's large, penetrating root system and nitrogen-fixing capability made it ideal for building soil and preventing soil erosion.

By the 1950s, however, many of kuzu's advocates had become disillusioned. Indeed, it was kuzu's incredible vitality that was causing the problem. Unchecked by its natural Asiatic enemies, kuzu enjoyed perfect growing conditions in the South and began to grow out of control. Under these conditions, according to Japanese foods scholar and author William Shurtleff, co-author of *The Book of Kudzu: A Culinary and Healing Guide* (Avery, 1985), kuzu can grow one foot (30 cm) a day. One acre of neglected vines will cover 13,000 acres (5,260 hectares) in one hundred years!

In the 1960s, kuzu was partially redeemed because of America's growing interest in all things Japanese. Students of macrobiotics, Zen and Oriental medicine began learning about kuzu's nutritional and medicinal value. Among them, it was even rumored that kuzu was the main food of the mysterious *sennin*, Japanese mountain hermits who attained immortality by living a life of simple austerity and self-purification.

Kuzu soon became a respected food and medicine among macrobiotic and health-conscious consumers. Basic kuzu cream with *umeboshi* (Japanese pickled plum) has been found to be a very effective remedy for an acid stomach and for intestinal inflammation. Kuzu's mild taste, translucent sheen and good jelling ability have made it popular in puddings, sauces, stews and glazes.

In the East, kuzu, a member of the legume family, has enjoyed an excellent reputation and has been part of the cuisine and pharmacopoeia of China and Japan for more than two thousand years. The starch that makes kuzu an outstanding jelling and thickening agent in cooking is partly responsible for its medicinal action. Some of kuzu's complex starch molecules enter the intestines and relieve the discomfort caused by overacidity, bacterial infection, and—in the case of diarrhea—excess water. In many cases of abdominal aching and intestinal irritation, a cup of Kuzu Cream (page 69) brings quick relief, particularly for children who often do not like the taste of over-the-counter stomach medications.

According to Subhuti Dharmananda, Ph.D., director of the Institute for Traditional Medicine and Preventive Health Care in Portland, Oregon, kuzu also contains a very high concentration of flavonoids, the likely source of the plant's strong medicinal effect on the digestive and circulatory systems. Flavonoids, which occur naturally in kuzu and other plants, are fairly well known as antioxidants. However, they also have the ability to inhibit the contraction of smooth muscle tissue, thereby increasing blood flow and relieving cramping in the intestines.

Compelling Research

The medicinal effects of kuzu's flavonoids were proven during numerous clinical studies in China in the 1970s. The results, published in several important Chinese medical journals, showed that crude kuzu root preparations or its extracted flavonoids, given as injections or taken orally, reduce high blood pressure, regulate blood sugar, relieve chronic migraine headaches and ease aches in the shoulders and neck. In China, kuzu flavonoids have successfully treated sudden deafness, which can be caused by restricted circulation. Researchers report that flavonoids also lower cholesterol levels, reduce the risk of the formulation of blood clots, protect the heart against cardiovascular disease and protect the brain by dilating cerebral microvessels to increase the blood flow.

Like some soy foods, kuzu root contains high concentrations of phytoestrogens, a group of plant biochemicals that can have a substantial influence on the human hormonal system. In fact, kuzu's ability to regulate estrogen levels in mammals was demonstrated at the National Institute of Health and Nutrition in Tokyo, Japan, where it was shown to prevent the bone loss induced by estrogen deficiency. Scientists stated, "Kuzu root may represent a potential alternative medicine for hormone replacement therapy in the prevention of osteoporosis in postmenopausal women."

Recently, research on kuzu has focused on its use as a treatment for an entirely different type of problem: alcohol abuse. Fascinated by reports of Chinese physicians using kuzu to treat chronic alcoholism, Harvard medical researcher Wing-Ming Keung, Ph.D., traveled to China to collect clinical information. During his visit, Keung interviewed thirteen traditional and modern physicians and compiled three hundred case histories. "In all cases," said Keung, "the medication (a tea made from kuzu root and other herbs) was considered effective in both controlling and suppressing appetite for alcohol and improving the function of alcohol-affected vital organs. No toxic side effects were reported by the Chinese physicians."

When Keung returned to Harvard, he conducted his own research, which confirmed what he had learned in China: kuzu, for reasons still not understood, can curb the desire for alcohol as well as its ravages on the body.

Obviously, research on the medicinal value of kuzu will continue, both in the United States and in Asia, although kuzu's capabilities are far more extensively studied and documented in the East than they are in America. For example, key Chinese medical texts describe the properties and uses of tablets made from kuzu root extract for a wide range of both minor and serious illnesses.

Although kuzu may not be well known to Western herbalists, it is commonly prescribed by American acupuncturists trained in Oriental herbology, to be used in conjunction with acupuncture treatments. Acupuncturist Mary Cissy Majebe, O.M.D., director of the Chinese Acupuncture and Herbology Clinic in Asheville, North Carolina, uses teas made from kuzu root and complementary herbs for specific conditions requiring the elimination of accumulated heat (as with head colds, influenza and muscle stiffness) with "excellent results." However, she stresses that similar symptoms do not always indicate the same underlying cause of illness. If you have a condition that you think would benefit from kuzu or another herbal remedy, talk with a trained healthcare professional.

Kuzu Remedies

As a remedy, kuzu root is used in two ways: as powdered starch and as whole dried root. Kuzu starch remedies can be used to treat minor indigestion; some experts use it to treat colds and minor aches and pains as well. Eating lots of foods made with kuzu starch can have the same effects and is considered good preventive medicine. Teas can be used when a different type of medicine is needed: for chronic headaches, stiff shoulders, colitis, sinus troubles, tonsillitis, respiratory ailments, hangovers, allergies (especially hay fever), bronchial asthma and skin rashes.

In his book *Healing Ourselves* (Avon Books, 1973), holistic health practitioner Naboru Muramoto recommends a drink called Kuzu Cream (page 69) for colds, general body pains, stomach cramps and diarrhea. Kuzu Cream is also recommended for neutralizing stomach acidity and for relaxing tight muscles. When made with the addition of ginger juice and minced umeboshi, the drink is especially potent. The ginger aids digestion and circulation, while the salt plum neutralizes lactic acid and eliminates it from the body.

Kuzu Cream and other remedies are made using kuzu root starch while medicinal kuzu teas are usually made using pieces of the whole kuzu root, which contains more water-soluble medicinal flavonoids, some of which are lost during starch production. Kuzu root tea (*kakkon*) is found in herbal shops and some natural foods stores; it frequently contains several other herbs with medicinal properties, including ginger, licorice and cinnamon.

The techniques for processing kuzu root powder were probably brought to Japan from China. By the twelfth century, farmers around the city of Kyoto had discovered how to process kuzu root in such a way that the starch was separated from its tough inedible fibers. About that time, kuzu root powder began to be used in food preparation around the cities of Kyoto and Nara.

The first facility in Japan to produce kuzu starch for commercial purposes was established in the Yamato province in the early 1600s, at the foot of Mount Yoshino. However, as civilization gradually pushed out into the mountainside, land became too valuable to grow wild kuzu and kuzu root powder manufacturers were forced to move to Japan's more remote southern island of Kyushu. Today, almost all the kuzu root powder used in Japan comes from a few large producers in Kyushu.

Japan's largest kuzu root starch producer is the Hirohachido Company, located at the edge of Kagoshima Bay, in southern Kyushu. Hirohachido makes 300 tons of kuzu root powder annually. This represents about two-thirds of Japan's total production. Fifth-generation president Kazuhiro Taguchi is head of the family-run business, which was founded in 1875. The original shop was in Akizuki, a small town in northern Kyushu. In 1953, the march of civilization pushed the Taguchi family farther south to their present location.

Averaging 200 pounds, the kuzu root is one of the largest roots in the world. The starch extracted from the kuzu root is the world's finest culinary thickening agent.

Akizuki's climate and water are ideal for processing kuzu root powder. The 120-day-long traditional process of making kuzu begins in December, when the kuzu plant has focused its energy back underground and its roots are swollen with starch. The backbreaking work of hand digging roots in the mountains and backpacking them to the nearest road continues until the roots begin sending out their first shoots in the spring. In a good year, the roots will have about 13 percent extractable starch. If, however, there has been too much rain, too little sun, or if the previous autumn's typhoon has damaged the plant's leaves, the roots will produce less starch. When the starch level falls below 10 percent, it is not profitable for the Taguchis to process the roots.

The method of separating the starch from the fibrous kuzu root requires that the root be cleaned, cut and mashed into a gray paste. The crude paste is washed and filtered through silk screens many times to remove plant fibers and bitter tannins. After settling, the kuzu paste is again dissolved in cold water and filtered. The washing, filtering and settling process continues until a pure white, claylike starch is formed.

The starch is cut into 6-inch (15-cm)-thick blocks and placed in paper-lined boxes to dry for about sixty days. The drying process is critical. Kuzu cannot be dried in direct sunshine or heated ovens, as this will affect the purity of its color and impair its jelling qualities. Oven drying makes the kuzu too brittle and hard to dissolve in water. Proper drying takes place in a long wooden shed with large windows that are opened to circulate the air. Every few days, the boxes of kuzu are moved around to make sure each block dries evenly.

If the water used during the filtering process is not cold and pure, the kuzu will begin to ferment during drying. Too much humidity will cause bacterial fermentation and totally destroy the drying kuzu. When properly dried, each block of kuzu should contain about 16 percent moisture. Once dried, the kuzu is carefully dusted with a brush, crumbled and packaged.

SHOPPING FOR KUZU

 Making kuzu even in an automated factory is still a three-month-long, expensive process. The roots must still be dug by hand and then washed, filtered and dried to extract the starch. In comparison, starch from sweet potatoes can be extracted in just three or four days with twice the yield as kuzu.

Because of kuzu's high price, many cooks use potato starch or arrowroot powder instead of kuzu in Asian recipes. To reduce cost, some kuzu manufacturers mix potato starch with the kuzu powder. Neither potato starch nor arrowroot has the medicinal or culinary properties of authentic kuzu powder. Properly made, high quality kuzu dissolves quickly, has superior jelling ability and gives foods a beautiful satin sheen.

Shoppers must read labels carefully to be sure they are buying 100 percent kuzu powder. Kuzu sold in American Asian food markets is sometimes an inferior mix of potato and kuzu starch. It is best to buy kuzu at a natural foods store.

In addition to drinking the rejuvenating tonics Kuzu Cream (below) or Apple Kuzu Drink (page 70) when we are not feeling well, we can enjoy the preventive benefits of kuzu and its culinary assets in a wide range of dishes from soups to desserts. Kuzu is unsurpassed as a thickening agent. It produces sparkling, translucent sauces, adds a shiny gloss to soups, and provides a smooth texture with no starchy or interfering taste. Vegetables and fish that have been dusted with kuzu powder and then deep-fried have a light, crisp coating. Since kuzu helps balance the acidity of sweets, it is ideal in desserts such as kantens and puddings, and it is the perfect ingredient in icings, shortcake toppings and pie fillings.

Store kuzu in a sealed jar. When you buy kuzu, the powder will be in small chunks. Crush the chunks with the back of a spoon before measuring. Use approximately 1 tablespoon crushed kuzu per 1 cup (235 ml) liquid for sauces and gravies, and 2 tablespoons per 1 cup (235 ml) for jelling liquids. For most preparations, completely dissolve the measured amount of kuzu in a little cold water, then add it to the other ingredients near the end of cooking time. Gently bring the mixture to a simmer, stirring constantly while the kuzu thickens and becomes translucent.

Kuzu should not be confused with cornstarch, arrowroot or potato starch. Cornstarch, in particular, is not recommended because it is highly processed and treated with chemical bleaches and toxic extracting agents. Potato starch is also mass-produced and chemicals are used to accelerate the extraction process. While arrowroot is made by a simple, natural process, kuzu is far superior in jelling strength, taste, texture and healing qualities.

Kuzu Cream

This restorative tonic is most effective when taken about 1 hour before meals (preferably in the morning when the stomach is empty). This recipe makes a thick, puddinglike cream. If you'd prefer to make a thinner drink, reduce the amount of kuzu to 1 rounded teaspoon.

> $1^1/_2$ tablespoons crushed kuzu starch
> 1 umeboshi plum, pitted and minced, or 1 teaspoon umeboshi paste
> $^1/_4$ to $^1/_2$ teaspoon fresh ginger juice (finely grate fresh ginger and squeeze to extract juice)
> $^1/_2$ to 1 teaspoon shoyu (Japanese soy sauce) (optional)

1. In a small enamel or nonmetallic saucepan, thoroughly dissolve the kuzu in 1 cup (235 ml) cold water. Add the umeboshi and bring to a simmer over medium heat, stirring frequently. As soon as the mixture begins to bubble around the edges, stir constantly until kuzu thickens and becomes translucent.

2. Gently simmer for 1 to 2 minutes, then remove from the heat. Add the ginger juice and, if desired, shoyu to taste.

MAKES 1 CUP (235 ML)

Preparation time: 5 minutes
Cooking time: 3 to 5 minutes

Apple Kuzu Drink

For a quick pick-me-up or for small children, good tasting kuzu beverages are ideal. In his book *Macrobiotic Home Remedies* (Square One Publishers, 2007), macrobiotic teacher Michio Kushi recommends Apple Kuzu Drink for constipation and fevers and to stimulate the appetite. Apple Kuzu Drink has a soothing effect that is useful for calming hyperactive children. When making this tonic for young children, replace $^1/_2$ cup (125 ml) of the apple juice with water.

> 1 cup (235 ml) apple juice
> Scant pinch of sea salt (optional)
> 1 rounded teaspoon crushed kuzu starch
> 1 to 2 tablespoons water for dissolving kuzu

1. Heat the apple juice and salt in a small saucepan over medium heat just until bubbles begin to appear around the edges. Remove from the heat.

2. Thoroughly dissolve the kuzu in water, add it to the juice while stirring, then return the saucepan to the burner. Stir constantly until kuzu thickens and becomes translucent. Simmer 1 minute more, then remove from the heat.

3. Let the drink cool for a few minutes before serving.

> MAKES 1 CUP (235 ML)
>
> *Preparation time:* 1 minute
> *Cooking time:* 5 minutes

Vanilla Pudding

Vanilla pudding and the flavor variations suggested below are delicious when eaten plain or when topped with fresh fruit or Fruit Sauce (page 73). These puddings also make great fillings for pies, parfaits, trifles, cream puffs, and shortcakes. For an especially rich and creamy result, use Homemade Almond Milk (page 102).

> 2 cups (475 ml) unflavored almond milk
> $^1/_2$ cup (125 ml) brown rice malt syrup or 4 tablespoons pure maple syrup
> $^1/_8$ teaspoon sea salt
> 2 level tablespoons kanten flakes
> $1^1/_2$ tablespoons crushed kuzu starch
> 1 teaspoon pure vanilla extract
> 1 tablespoon unsalted butter (optional)

1. Combine $1^3/_4$ cups (425 ml) almond milk, rice syrup, and salt in a small saucepan. Sprinkle kanten flakes over the top. Bring to a simmer over medium heat without stirring. Gently simmer for 2 to 3 minutes, stirring until kanten is dissolved.

2. Thoroughly dissolve kuzu in the remaining 4 tablespoons almond milk and add to saucepan while stirring briskly. Return to a simmer and cook 1 to 2 minutes. Remove from the heat.

3. Mix in vanilla and butter and divide among four small dessert cups. Chill, uncovered, for about 2 hours, or until firm.

Variations

Lemon Pudding. Add $1^1/2$ tablespoons fresh lemon juice and $1^1/2$ teaspoons grated lemon zest along with the vanilla. (Lemon zest is the bright yellow outer peel of the lemon. Avoid the deeper white layers as they are bitter.)

Berry Pudding. Follow directions for Vanilla Pudding except blend $1^1/2$ cups (200 g) fresh raspberries or strawberries with the almond milk before heating, and reduce the vanilla to $^1/2$ teaspoon.

SERVES 4

Preparation time: 5 minutes
Cooking time: 8 minutes plus 2 hours to cool and set

Clear Sauce

Unlike most sauces or gravies, this simple recipe contains no oil or flour, yet it has a full, delicate flavor and pleasing texture. Serve it over grains, vegetables or noodles.

2 cups (475 ml) Kombu-Shiitake Stock (see page 176)
$^1/4$ teaspoon sea salt
$^1/2$ bay leaf
1 to 2 green onions (scallions), thinly sliced, or 1 to 2 shallots, minced
1 tablespoon shoyu (Japanese soy sauce)
$^1/2$ tablespoon mirin or sake
$2^1/2$ tablespoons crushed kuzu starch

1. Combine the stock and salt in a small saucepan and bring to a simmer. Add the bay leaf and green onions or shallots, and simmer for 5 minutes.

2. Add the shoyu and mirin or sake and remove from the heat.

3. Dissolve the kuzu in 3 tablespoons water and slowly add to sauce while stirring briskly. Return pan to the heat and bring to a simmer, stirring constantly. Simmer for 1 to 2 minutes. If too thin, add a small amount of kuzu, dissolved in water; if too thick, add a little water or stock.

Variation

The addition of mushrooms and onion sautéed in a little sesame oil adds rich flavor to this basic sauce. Substitute $^1/4$ medium onion, minced, for the green onions. To prepare, heat two teaspoons of toasted or untoasted sesame oil in a small saucepan and sauté the onion and 4 sliced button mushrooms over medium-high heat until fairly tender. Add the stock, salt and bay leaf, and simmer for 10 minutes, then continue with Steps 2 and 3.

MAKES $1^2/3$ CUPS (400 ML)

Preparation time: 5 minutes
Cooking time: 10 minutes

Tempeh Bourguignon

Unusually rich in flavor, this delicious and nutritious main course is especially appealing served over egg noodles, but any light, flat noodle is a good option.

8 oz (250 g) tempeh
2 tablespoons extra virgin olive oil
1 1/2 cups (375 ml) dry red wine
1 cup (235 ml) water or Vegetable Stock (see page 183)
2 tablespoons shoyu (Japanese soy sauce) or tamari
2 teaspoons fresh thyme or 1/2 teaspoon dried thyme
1/4 teaspoon freshly ground black or white pepper
About 30 pearl onions (do not peel)
10 white button mushrooms, cut into pie-shaped wedges
2 cloves garlic, minced
Pinch of sea salt
1 bay leaf, broken in half
2 tablespoons crushed kuzu starch
4 tablespoons chopped fresh parsley

1. Cut the tempeh into quarters, cut each quarter in half by thickness, then dice each section into bite-size squares.

2. Heat 1 1/2 tablespoons of the oil in a large skillet over medium-high heat. Add the tempeh and brown on both sides, about 2 to 3 minutes on each side.

3. In a bowl, combine the wine with the water or stock, shoyu, half of the thyme and the pepper. Add the browned tempeh and set aside to marinate while completing Steps 4 through 6. Place a small plate on the tempeh to keep it submerged.

4. In a small saucepan, bring 3 cups (700 ml) water to a boil, add the pearl onions and simmer for 5 minutes.

5. Drain the onions, then cover with cold water until cool enough to handle. Slice the tip off the root end and pinch to squeeze out the onion. Set aside.

6. Heat the remaining 1/2 tablespoon of oil in the skillet and sauté the mushrooms and garlic with a pinch of salt for 3 to 5 minutes, or until the mushrooms begin to give off some liquid.

7. Add the tempeh and marinade to the mushrooms and bring to a simmer. Add the bay leaf and peeled onions, cover and gently simmer for 30 minutes.

8. Thoroughly dissolve the kuzu in 2 tablespoons cold water and add it to the tempeh mixture while stirring. Simmer for 3 to 5 minutes.

9. Spoon the hot stew into bowls as is or over a bed of noodles or rice. Garnish with the remaining parsley and serve.

SERVES 3

Preparation time: 20 minutes
Cooking time: 1 hour

Fruit Sauce

This light fruit dessert is delicious when eaten as is. It can also be used to dress up other simple desserts. It makes a great topping for Vanilla or Lemon Pudding, pies or tarts with a vanilla-pudding base, and shortcake, vanilla cake, pancakes or waffles. This fruit sauce is a scrumptious filling for crepes. Refrigerated in a covered container, it will keep for several days.

> $2^1/_2$ cups (325 g) sliced or whole fresh fruit (strawberries, blueberries, raspberries, nectarines, peaches, pitted cherries, etc.)
> 1 cup (235 ml) apple juice
> $^1/_3$ to $^1/_2$ cup (75 to 125 ml) brown rice malt syrup (use smaller amount with sweet fruits, larger amount with tart ones)
> Pinch of sea salt
> 2 tablespoons crushed kuzu starch

1. Cut larger fruits into bite-size pieces. Small berries can be left whole.

2. Combine the juice, rice syrup and salt in a saucepan. If cooking the fruit is recommend (see note below), add it to the saucepan and bring to a simmer, uncovered, over medium heat. Remove from the heat.

3. Thoroughly dissolve the kuzu in 2 tablespoons cool water and add to fruit mixture while stirring briskly. Place over medium-low heat and stir constantly until mixture returns to a simmer and thickens.

4. If using fruit that does not require cooking, place fruit in a ceramic or glass bowl and pour the hot liquid over it. Mix gently and cool in the refrigerator. If fruit is already mixed in, transfer contents of the pot to a bowl and cool. The sauce will thicken as it cools.

Note to Cook

Delicate, tender fruits such as strawberries and raspberries should not be cooked. Ripe nectarines do not need cooking, but firmer fruits such as blueberries, cherries and apples should be simmered with the juice.

MAKES ABOUT 3 CUPS (700 ML)

Preparation time: 5 minutes
Cooking time: 5 minutes plus about 1 hour to cool and thicken

Lemon Meringue Pie

This beautiful and delicious version of a classic pie is easy to make and substitutes healthful ingredients for the cornstarch and sugar.

$1^3/_4$ cups (700 ml) water
$^1/_2$ cup (125 ml) pure maple syrup
$^1/_8$ teaspoon sea salt
2 tablespoons kanten flakes
2 tablespoons crushed kuzu starch
2 large eggs at room temperature
1 tablespoon plus 1 teaspoon freshly grated lemon zest
$^1/_3$ cup (75 ml) fresh lemon juice (about 2 lemons)
Whole Wheat Pie Crust, halve recipe for single shell, prebaked (see page 106)
2 tablespoons pure maple syrup

1. Combine the water, maple syrup and salt in a saucepan. Sprinkle the kanten flakes over the top. Bring to a simmer over medium heat without stirring. Gently simmer for 2 to 3 minutes, stirring until kanten is dissolved.

2. Thoroughly dissolve the kuzu in 2 tablespoons cold water and add it to the saucepan while stirring briskly. Continue stir ring until mixture thickens; then gently simmer over low heat for 3 to 5 minutes.

3. Separate the eggs. Set the whites aside and beat the yolks with 1 teaspoon water.

4. Remove the saucepan from the heat and slowly drizzle in the beaten egg yolks while stirring. Return to the stovetop and gently simmer for 2 to 3 minutes while stirring. Remove from the heat.

5. Add the lemon zest and lemon juice, pour mixture into a glass or ceramic bowl and let cool for at least 30 minutes.

6. Preheat the oven to 325°F (160°C).

7. With an electric mixer, beat egg whites until they are stiff but not dry, then drizzle in the 2 tablespoons maple syrup while beating constantly until whites are firm enough to hold a peak.

8. Pour the lemon filling into the prebaked pie shell (see page 106 for instructions on how to prebake a pie shell). Cover filling with the beaten egg whites, spreading them to the edges. With a butter knife, swirl the meringue to form soft peaks.

9. Bake for 10 minutes, or until peaks are browned. Remove and let cool for 2 to 3 hours, or until firm.

MAKES ONE 8-INCH (20-CM) PIE, TO SERVE 8
Preparation time: 25 minutes
Cooking time: 40 minutes plus 2 to 3 hours to cool and set

玄
米
酢

BROWN RICE VINEGAR: A TRADITIONAL TONIC

Vinegar may be humankind's oldest seasoning. Since ancient times, people from all over the world have let wild acetic-acid bacteria turn their alcoholic beverages to vinegar. Each with its distinctive flavor, aroma and color, naturally brewed vinegars are derived from sugar cane, molasses, fruit or grain. Vinegars are vital as food preservatives, and they play important roles in products such as health and beauty aids, antiseptics, cleaning solutions and medicines. All vinegars share a mouth-puckering acidity that refreshes tired taste buds and stimulates the appetite.

Rice is the main source of carbohydrates for a large part of the world's population, and vinegar made from rice is a delicious and refreshing condiment used daily by billions of Asians. Japanese food historians believe that the traditional method of making rice vinegar was brought from China to southern Osaka, in central Japan, during the era of the Emperor Ojin, who flourished in the early fifth century CE. Although sake, or rice wine, can naturally turn to vinegar, the complex, controlled process of adding a specific amount of cooked rice and cultured rice (koji) to water and letting the mixture ferment for a specific time and at a specific temperature is the basic method used for centuries by Japanese housewives and commercial vinegar makers alike.

In his best-selling book *Folk Medicine* (Fawcett, 1995), Dr. D. C. Jarvis, an authority on old Vermont folk remedies, described an extraordinary experiment. He asked twenty-four people to keep a daily record of the food they ate for two years. They were to check the acid-alkaline reaction of their urine each day using a simple litmus-paper test. Comparing his patients' medical records with their urine tests, Jarvis saw a clear pattern. A few days before the onset of an illness, a patient's urine shifted from acid to alkaline. The alkaline reaction usually corresponded with eating specific foods. Jarvis was surprised to learn that one of Vermont's oldest and most popular tonic drinks, two teaspoons of apple cider vinegar and a teaspoon of honey in a cup of water, shifted the urine reaction back to a healthy acidic condition. Old-timers, as Jarvis discovered, used vinegar for fatigue, headache, high blood pressure, dizziness, sore throat, obesity and a host of other ailments that afflicted both humans and farm animals.

Medical researchers now believe it is the amino acids present in vinegar that are partly responsible for its medicinal effects. In particular, these amino acids help counter the effects of lactic-acid buildup in the blood, which can cause fatigue, irritability, stiff and sore muscles, and can contribute to disease.

In Japan, scientific interest in authentic vinegar's health benefits is revitalizing the small Kyushu brown rice vinegar industry. Yoshio Takino, M.D. of Shizuoka University has confirmed the importance of vinegar's amino acids. According to Takino, the twenty amino acids and sixteen organic acids found in authentic rice vinegar help prevent the formation of toxic fat peroxides. He explains that when unsaturated fatty acids from vegetable oils and other foods are heated and exposed to light in cooking or oxidized during metabolism, fat peroxides can form, which contribute to aging and to cholesterol formation on blood vessel walls.

Paul Pitchford, author of *Healing with Whole Foods* (North Atlantic Books, 2002), is a leading U.S. authority on the synthesis of Asian traditions and modern nutrition. In his book he lists many medicinal effects of vinegar, such as its ability to help circulate energy in the body, remove stagnant blood, elevate mood and neutralize poisons in the body. Vinegar relieves what Chinese medicine calls "damp" conditions such as edema, overweight and excess mucus. One of vinegar's best applications, according to Pitchford, is in cases of nausea from eating old foods, overly fermented foods or poor food combinations.

When applied directly to the skin, vinegar has long been a folk remedy for everything from bleeding to bug bites. Even in modern times, a solution of vinegar and water has been used to fight common athlete's foot.

Vinegar's extreme acidity and sour taste is a double-edged sword. The ancient Chinese believed the sour taste reduced accumulations in the liver and abdomen. Ayurvedic medicine, the traditional medical lore of India, claims that sour foods such as vinegar spark digestion and add savor to foods. However, both traditions, as well as the folklore of several other cultures, warn against the overuse of this powerful food because, under certain conditions, it can create imbalance in the body.

One of the world's most nutritious and delicious vinegars is still made in Japan from 100 percent brown rice wine (sake) that is fermented in earthenware crocks that are buried in the ground. This unique thousand-year-old method survives only on Japan's southern island of Kyushu. Because it is made from brown rice, with its bran and germ intact, kuro-su (black vinegar) has a high concentration of essential amino acids. It is recognized not only for its mellow taste but also for its medicinal quality. The finest Kyushu brown rice vinegar in the world is made in a remote area of Kyushu, away from industrial pollution. Due to the growing interest in natural Japanese foods, this fine product is available in most natural foods stores.

Kyushu brown rice vinegar making begins at sake shops where a thick, primitive-type sake is made from only two ingredients: brown rice and spring water. The sake maker steams brown rice, sprinkles it with spores from an *Aspergillus* culture, and sets it to incubate in a warm, humid room. The spores germinate and the culture begins to produce digestive enzymes using the brown rice as a nutrient source. After two days, the fermented rice and *Aspergillus* become koji (the ubiquitous starter used in most Japanese fermented foods). The sake maker next com-

On Japan's southern island of Kyushu brown rice vinegar is made in old earthenware crocks partly buried in the ground. This unique thousand-year-old process keeps the temperature of the fermenting brown rice vinegar stable year round.

bines the koji with water and cooked brown rice, then pours the mixture into 100-gallon (378-liter) wooden casks.

Gradually, the enzymes in the koji convert the proteins, carbohydrates and fats of the brown rice into amino acids, simple sugars and fatty acids. Next, naturally occurring yeast converts the sugars to alcohol.

After about eight weeks, when its alcohol content reaches about 20 percent, the thick, heady brown rice sake automatically stops fermenting, which inhibits yeast growth. It is then delivered to the vinegar shop, where it is mixed with spring water and seed vinegar (good vinegar from a previous batch). Finally, the liquid is poured into partially buried crocks that are sealed with thick, natural-fiber paper and wooden or ceramic lids.

The crocks, many more than a hundred years old, are aligned in rows running north to south so each crock can receive maximum warmth as the sun travels from east to west. In the summer, when warm temperatures could cause the vinegar to overheat, the grass is left to grow tall around the crocks to provide cooling shade. In winter, the grass is cut short to expose the upper third of the crocks to the warming sun.

Within two to four months, depending on the season, the acetic-acid bacteria transform the alcohol of the brown rice sake into golden rice vinegar. The vinegar-maker pumps the vinegar from the crocks, dilutes it with water to reduce its acidity, and puts it in large tanks where it is left to age and mellow for about ten months. Once aged, the vinegar is filtered through cotton, flash-pasteurized and bottled. The Kyushu vinegar process takes over a year to complete.

Kyushu brown rice vinegar is unique among natural rice vinegars because it is fermented outdoors. For centuries, Kyushu vinegar makers have buried their brown, twenty-five gallon, glazed crocks about two-thirds in the ground. According to master brewer Tetsunori Ezaki, "This technique keeps the vinegar temperature constant over a narrow range. Daily and seasonal temperature fluctuations are very important, because they give the vinegar deep character and richness." Yet, Ezaki warns, "temperature extremes can destroy the vinegar completely."

SHOPPING FOR BROWN RICE VINEGAR

 Authentic Kyushu brown rice vinegar accounts for less than 1 percent of Japan's annual 100-million-gallon (378-million-liter) vinegar production. During the Second World War, a shortage of rice encouraged the development of a much cheaper, quicker process. According to Togo Kuroiwa, author of *Rice Vinegar* (Kenko Igakusha, 1977), who spent most of his life trying to reestablish authentic rice-vinegar production in Japan, industrial rice-wine vinegar (sake cake vinegar) dates back to the early nineteenth century but became popular when the Japanese government rationed rice in 1942.

The quicker, industrial process for making rice vinegar does not use rice koji. Instead, sake lees, the dregs left from sake manufacturing, are mixed with distilled grain alcohol. This mixture is fermented under controlled temperatures, and, in less than a month, bacteria will convert the alcohol to acetic acid (distilled vinegar). Much more than flavor is lost in this short-cut process. Because the alcohol is distilled by boiling, most of the amino acids are left behind in the process. According to the Japan Food Research Laboratories, authentic rice vinegar has five times the amount of amino acids—the component most responsible for its medicinal powers—as sake-lees vinegar.

When shopping for rice vinegar, read labels carefully. The highest-quality products are made from either brown rice or sweet brown rice and water. Although many vinegars sold in Asian food stores are half the price of natural foods brands, keep in mind that these lower-priced products are invariably made from distilled alcohol and sake lees. Some brands include wheat, rice, corn, sake lees and alcohol in their ingredient lists, while other brands list no ingredients at all. We recently found an inexpensive so-called natural rice vinegar in our local natural foods store that listed "rice vinegar and water" as the ingredients. Of course, rice vinegar is an end product, not an ingredient, and there was nothing on the label to indicate how it was made. The labels of authentic, traditionally made vinegars will proudly provide information about how the product is made. Although brown rice vinegar is darker than other rice vinegars, it is impossible to judge the quality of rice vinegar by its color since some Asian food brands have added coloring agents.

COOKING WITH BROWN RICE VINEGAR

 Refreshing and delicious, naturally brewed rice vinegar is a wonderfully versatile seasoning. Characterized by a light sweetness, it is full-bodied yet mild, without the sharpness often associated with industrial vinegars. You can enjoy brown rice vinegar in all the ways you enjoy other natural vinegars. A stimulating contrast of flavors, brown rice vinegar brings almost any food to life.

Besides being a mainstay in salad dressings, pickling mixtures and marinades, rice vinegar also perks up sauces, dips, spreads and main dishes. Japanese housewives add a little rice vinegar to cooked summer rice to prevent it from spoiling. To make beans more digestible, add a little vinegar to the cooking liquid once the beans are tender. Brown rice vinegar also enhances the flavor of grain, vegetable and fish dishes. It can help balance salt and fats, and reduce cravings for strong sweets.

Following are some of our favorite ways to enjoy the benefits of brown rice vinegar. You will find many more recipes calling for this delicious and healthful vinegar in other chapters of this book.

Broiled Tofu with Miso Marinade

A natural with tofu, miso marinade is also great for flavoring fish, poultry, tempeh and vegetables before grilling, broiling or roasting.

Miso Marinade
2 tablespoons red, barley or brown rice miso
3 tablespoons mirin
3 tablespoons dry red wine
1 tablespoon brown rice vinegar
1 teaspoon toasted sesame oil
1 clove garlic, minced
1 teaspoon fresh ginger juice (finely grate fresh ginger and squeeze to extract juice)

. . . .

1 lb (450 g) firm tofu
2 tablespoons snipped fresh chives

1. Combine all of the miso marinade ingredients in a bowl and mix well.

2. Cut the block of tofu crosswise into 6 equal slices. Place the slices on one half of a clean kitchen towel, fold the other half over the top of the tofu and press gently to remove excess water.

3. Pour the marinade into a pie plate or baking pan. Dip all surfaces of the tofu into the mixture and marinate for 1 hour, turning the tofu slices 2 or 3 times.

4. Preheat the broiler. Place the tofu slices on a lightly oiled baking sheet, reserving the marinade. Broil for 5 minutes or until the tofu begins to brown. Baste with the reserved marinade, turn the tofu, baste the other side, and broil 5 minutes more. Remove tofu from the oven and baste it again.

5. Pour the remaining marinade into a small saucepan, bring it to a boil over medium-high heat, and cook, uncovered, for 3 minutes, or until the volume is reduced to about half and the marinade has a sauce consistency.

6. Spoon 1 to 2 teaspoons of the sauce over each piece of tofu, sprinkle with chives and serve.

SERVES 3

Cooking time: 15 minutes
Preparation time: 10 minutes plus 1 hour to marinate tofu

Dilled Potato Salad

Potato salad is a sentimental favorite, and this version is terrific. Strangely enough, we got the idea for it from a friend in rural Japan. We've brought it to several potluck dinners and everyone seems to agree that this is yet another example of the Japanese talent for imitating something foreign and improving on the original.

3 teaspoons sea salt, or to taste
8 large potatoes, peeled and cut into $^1/_2$-in (1-cm) cubes (about 10 cups)
2 carrots, cut in half lengthwise and thinly sliced into half moons
$^1/_2$ red onion, minced
3 radishes, cut in half lengthwise and thinly sliced
4 to 5 romaine lettuce leaves, halved lengthwise and thinly sliced
3 tablespoons chopped fresh parsley
4 tablespoons snipped fresh dill
1 cup (225 g) mayonnaise
2 tablespoons brown rice vinegar
2 to 3 teaspoons umeboshi vinegar (ume su)
$^1/_2$ teaspoon freshly ground black pepper

1. Half-fill a large soup pot with water and bring to a boil.

2. Add 2 teaspoons of the sea salt and the cubed potatoes and simmer until the potatoes are nearly tender, but still underdone.

3. Add the carrots and simmer for 3 minutes more. The potatoes should be just tender and the carrots tender-crisp.

4. Place the potatoes and carrots into a large colander, run cold water over them to prevent them from cooking more and drain well.

5. Sprinkle the remaining 1 teaspoon of salt over the cooked vegetables and toss to mix evenly. Let cool to room temperature.

6. While the vegetables are cooling, in a large bowl combine the onion, radishes, lettuce, parsley and dill.

7. In a small bowl combine the mayonnaise, vinegar, umeboshi vinegar and pepper.

8. Toss the cooked vegetables with the raw vegetables. Add the dressing and toss well to coat. Chill slightly before serving.

SERVES 8 TO 10

Cooking time: 30 minutes
Preparation time: 25 minutes

Chickpea Salad

Chickpea Salad, though light enough for the warmest spring and summer days, is no nutritional lightweight. The combination of chickpeas and broccoli makes this an especially nutritious dish that is rich in protein, calcium and iron.

1^1/$_2$ cups (100 g) broccoli florets
2 tablespoons extra virgin olive oil
2 tablespoons brown rice vinegar
1 tablespoon fresh lemon juice
1 clove garlic, finely minced or pressed
Sea salt, to taste
Freshly ground black pepper, to taste
2 cups (400 g) cooked chickpeas (garbanzos)
^{1}/$_2$ small red or white onion, diced
3 tablespoons minced fresh parsley, plus extra for garnish
1 tablespoon minced fresh basil, mint or dill (optional)
12 to 15 tender lettuce leaves (to line salad bowls)

1. Steam or boil the broccoli for 3 minutes, or until bright green and just tender-crisp. Immediately remove from the heat, drain and let cool.

2. In a small bowl combine the oil, vinegar, lemon, garlic, salt and pepper. Mix well.

3. In another bowl combine the chickpeas, broccoli, onion, parsley, and optional herbs.

4. Pour the dressing over the bean mixture and toss. Let the salad sit for at least 30 minutes before serving. Stir occasionally to marinate evenly. Store in a covered jar or bowl in the refrigerator. This salad is at its best a day or two after it is made.

5. To serve, line small bowls with the lettuce leaves, fill with the bean salad and garnish with parsley.

SERVES 4 TO 5

Preparation time: 10 minutes plus at least 30 minutes to marinate
Cooking time: 5 minutes

Creamy Miso Salad Dressing

Light, sweet misos make wonderful creamy salad dressings. We consider this our "house dressing." Always popular with guests, it's the one we keep coming back to.

^{1}/$_3$ cup (75 ml) safflower oil
4 tablespoons water
3 tablespoons sweet or mellow white miso
1^1/$_2$ tablespoons brown rice vinegar
2 teaspoons rice syrup or 1 tablespoon mirin
1 rounded tablespoon chopped onion
^{1}/$_4$ to ^{1}/$_2$ teaspoon dried mustard powder or 2 tablespoons snipped fresh dill

1. Place all of the ingredients in a blender and blend until smooth. Transfer to a jar with a lid.

2. Use immediately or chill until ready to serve. Shake well before using. The dressing will keep for 2 weeks in the refrigerator.

MAKES ABOUT 1 CUP (235 ML)

Preparation time: 5 minutes

Marinated Mushrooms

This light, piquant appetizer requires only 10 minutes preparation time. It must be made at least 12 hours before serving and can be made up to 3 days ahead.

3 to 4 cups (about 1 lb/450 g) fresh button mushrooms, preferably small
1 cup (235 ml) water
1 slightly rounded teaspoon sea salt
1 teaspoon shoyu (Japanese soy sauce)
$^1/_2$ cup (125 ml) brown rice vinegar
1 bay leaf, broken in half
1 to 2 cloves garlic, sliced or quartered
2 tablespoons snipped chives
2 to 3 sprigs fresh basil
2 to 3 sprigs fresh thyme, or $^1/_2$ teaspoon dried
2 tablespoons extra virgin olive oil
2 green onions (scallions), very thinly sliced on the diagonal
2 tablespoons minced fresh parsley

1. Wash the mushrooms, remove and discard the stems, and place the caps in a heat-proof bowl.

2. Combine the remaining ingredients except the green onions and parsley in a small saucepan, bring to a boil, simmer no more than one minute, then pour over the mushrooms. Let cool, then cover the bowl and refrigerate for at least 12 hours before serving. Toss occasionally to ensure that the mushrooms marinate evenly.

3. To serve, drain mushrooms and remove bay leaf, garlic and fresh herbs. Toss the mushrooms with the green onion and parsley, and place in a serving bowl.

MAKES 3 TO 4 CUPS (700 ML TO 1 LITER)

Cooking time: 3 minutes
Preparation time: 10 minutes plus 12 hours for marinating

Sunomono

Sunomono means "things of vinegar" in Japanese. A popular and refreshing side dish, it is most commonly made with cucumbers, but whatever vegetables are used, it is dressed with sweetened rice vinegar. In this version, rice syrup replaces cane sugar.

> One 4-in (10-cm) section of a small (1-in/2.5-cm diameter) daikon, peeled
> and cut into very thin slices
> 2 pickling (Kirby) cucumbers, peeled, if waxed, and thinly sliced
> 1 teaspoon sea salt
> 4 tablespoons brown rice vinegar
> 2 tablespoons brown rice malt syrup
> 2 teaspoons shoyu (Japanese soy sauce)
> 2 teaspoons mirin

1. In a small bowl, toss together the vegetables and salt, mixing well, and let stand for 15 minutes. Rinse with water to remove excess salt and drain well.

2. In a small saucepan, combine the vinegar, rice syrup, shoyu and mirin and warm it over low heat just until the syrup thins enough to mix easily with the liquids.

3. Combine the vinegar mixture and vegetables in a small bowl, toss well and let stand for at least 30 minutes, mixing occasionally to allow the vegetables to marinate evenly.

4. Serve in small individual bowls.

SERVES 4

Preparation time: 10 minutes plus 45 minutes for marinating

Creamy Dill Dip

High in protein and low in calories, this versatile dip combines the health benefits of tofu, miso and rice vinegar. It is great with chips or vegetables, as well as in a variety of appetizers such as canapés or as a spread for crackers or rice cakes.

> 8 oz (250 g) fresh tofu
> 3 tablespoons white miso
> 2 tablespoons sesame oil (untoasted)
> 2 tablespoons brown rice vinegar
> 1 tablespoon brown rice malt syrup
> 1 to 2 cloves garlic, sliced
> 4 tablespoons snipped fresh dill

1. Crumble the tofu into a blender along with all remaining ingredients and blend until smooth. If the mixture is too thick, add a little water or plain soymilk.

2. Refrigerate the dip for 2 hours to allow flavors to heighten.

MAKES 1¹/₂ CUPS (375 G)

Preparation time: 10 minutes plus 2 hours to chill and allow flavors to blend

椎
茸

SHIITAKE: MIRACLE MUSHROOM

One of Asia's most exotic and delicious foods, shiitake's delicate yet woodsy taste adds gourmet flair to almost any dish. Shiitake (*Lentinus edodes*) can easily be incorporated into Western style fare, so it is a great introduction to the healthy foods of Japan. Moreover, this mushroom is packed with health-promoting and medicinal qualities. Because of its appealing flavor and rich nutritional makeup, vegetarians sometimes use shiitake as a substitute for animal protein.

Shiitake is native to the Far East. Its primitive beginnings date back to the Cretaceous period, more than one hundred million years ago, and scientists believe this mushroom spread throughout China, Japan, Korea, Taiwan and Indonesia by windblown spores. The Chinese were the first to cultivate shiitake more than six hundred years ago. Today, shiitake is the second most widely cultivated mushroom in the world.

Since ancient times shiitake has been highly valued as both food and medicine. Wu Ri, a famous physician from the Chinese Ming Dynasty (1368–1644 CE), wrote extensively about this mushroom, noting its ability to increase energy, cure colds and eliminate worms. Indeed, traditional Chinese physicians knew the power of this dark, meaty, capped, forest mushroom to activate the qi or "life force" and promote longevity.

Dried shiitake contains up to 25 percent protein; all eight essential amino acids are present in a ratio similar to the "ideal" protein for human nutrition. Shiitake is rich in the amino acids leucine and lysine, which are deficient in many grains. It has high levels of the nonessential amino acid glutamic acid, which is considered to be "brain food" due to its ability to stimulate neurotransmitter activity as well as its ability to transport potassium to the brain.

Shiitake is also a good source of vitamins and minerals, including the elusive B-12 (Vitamin B-12 is synthesized solely by bacteria and fungi, and is not available from vegetables). Other nutrients include thiamin, riboflavin, niacin, copper, potassium, selenium, zinc, dietary fiber and enzymes. Shiitake also contains ergosterol, which can be converted by sunlight into vitamin D.

It is, however, shiitake's medicinal possibilities that are getting worldwide attention. In the last three decades, scientists have isolated substances from shiitake that may play a role in the cure and prevention of modern civilization's dreaded illnesses: heart disease, cancer and AIDS.

The person most responsible for stimulating the current medicinal interest in shiitake is Japan's Kisaku Mori, Ph.D. In 1936, Dr. Mori established the Institute of Mushroom Research in Tokyo. Until his death in 1977, Dr. Mori worked with scientists from around the world to document the medicinal effects of shiitake. Using analytical techniques, Mori found shiitake high in many enzymes and vitamins that are not usually found in plants. His findings, published in the book *Mushrooms as Health Foods* (Japan Publications, 1974), were impressive. Working for years with human subjects, he discovered that shiitake is effective in treating a long list of ailments including high cholesterol, gallstones, hyperacidity, stomach ulcers, diabetes, vitamin deficiency, anemia and even the common cold.

Mori's work gained notoriety, particularly in Japanese medicinal circles, and, beginning in the 1960s, scientists launched an extensive search to uncover the secret of shiitake's legendary healing powers. Their studies—several hundred in all—have focused on shiitake's ability to rapidly lower serum cholesterol, as well as this mushroom's potent antitumor, antiviral and antibiotic properties.

Cardiovascular Disease

High levels of blood cholesterol have been linked to serious diseases such as arteriosclerosis and stroke, so investigators were excited when, in 1966, they isolated a substance from shiitake that dramatically lowered blood cholesterol. This substance, now called eritadenine, was given to rats on a high-cholesterol diet. In just a few days, as reported in *The Journal of Nutrition*, the blood cholesterol level of the rats dropped 25 to 45 percent. Eritadenine has been associated with the water-soluble fiber of shiitake, but its action is even stronger when the whole mushroom is consumed. Studies with humans have shown that consuming only three ounces (85 g) of shiitake (five to six mushrooms) a day for one week can lower cholesterol by 12 percent.

The Immune System

"Many of the human diseases currently increasing throughout the world have no specific cures," notes mycologist John Donoghue, co-author of *Shiitake Growers Handbook* (Kendal Hunt, 1990). "Immune system failure or dysfunction is a common element in cancer, viruses and immune-deficiency diseases," writes Donoghue. He and other scientists around the world contend that there is increasing evidence that the health-promoting compounds found in medicinal and edible fungi, including shiitake, stimulate the immune system.

Scientists now believe that a polysaccharide called lentinan and viruslike particles found in shiitake trigger the increased production of various serum factors associated with immunity and inflammation. These so-called lymphokines, such as interferon and interleukin, stimulate the defense system, spurring the proliferation of killer cells called phagocytes, including macrophages and other immune fighters that attack cancer cells, bacteria and viruses. This so-called cell-mediated immune response is the body's natural defense against disease.

Cancer

The most dramatic experiment demonstrating shiitake's antitumor effect was performed on animals. At the National Cancer Research Center in Tokyo, mice suffering from sarcoma, a type of virally-induced cancer, were treated with small doses of shiitake extract over short periods of time. In 1970, the results, published in the journal *Cancer Research*, showed that six out of ten mice had complete tumor regression. At slightly higher concentrations, shiitake was 100 percent effective—all mice showed tumor regression.

In a 1996 study at Drew University, a protein-bound polysaccharide extracted from shiitake was found to have strong antitumor properties. In the study, ten cancer patients were treated with the compound and all showed significant improvement.

Similar studies have shown that shiitake extract helps prevent transplanted tumors from taking hold, and "excellent results" were obtained by Japanese scientists in a four-year follow-up study of patients with advanced and recurrent stomach and colon cancer. Shiitake extract is even being tested for use with modern chemotherapy drugs to lessen their toxic effects on healthy tissue and the immune system.

HIV/AIDS

The most recent development in shiitake medical research involves the use of shiitake extract to inhibit the reproduction of human immunodeficiency virus (HIV) in tissue culture. Researchers working at Yamaguchi University School of Medicine in Ube, Japan have reported that shiitake extract has a "protective effect" that inhibits the usual cell-destroying effects of the HIV virus. Researchers have noted that substances such as shiitake, which both enhance the immune response and have antiviral effects, should be further evaluated for the treatment of HIV/AIDS.

Potent Antibiotic

In addition to fighting cancer, inhibiting the growth of viruses and lowering cholesterol, shiitake has potent antibiotic effects against other organisms. A substance called cortinelin, a broad-spectrum antibacterial agent that has been isolated from shiitake, kills a wide range of pathogenic bacteria. A sulfide compound extracted from shiitake has been found to have an effect against the fungus that causes ringworm and other skin diseases. One preliminary trial suggested that shiitake might be useful for people with hepatitis B. Supplementation of lentinan from shiitake has been shown to significantly reduce the recurrence rate of genital warts (*Condyloma acuminata*) and reduce blood clots. Shiitake are also known to reduce hypertension.

HOW SHIITAKE ARE CULTIVATED

 Biologists consider shiitake and other mushrooms to be fungi, a group of primitive plants. Since they have no green pigments (chlorophyll), they cannot make food from sunlight as other plants, but must live by eating plants or animals. Shiitake's favorite food is dead hardwood trees. The word *shii* is derived from the shii tree (*Quercus cuspidatea*), an oak of central and southern Japan upon which shiitake most often grow; *take* means "mushroom" in Japanese.

The part of shiitake that we eat, the fleshy cap, is actually a primitive reproductive structure. You may have noticed a gray or beige powder on the undersurface of opened mushrooms. These are billions of microscopic spores. Like sperm and eggs (ova) of animals, the spores are sex cells. Each spore carries half of the genetic information of the parent mushroom. Mushroom spores move about the forest with the help of wind and rain. When two compatible spores get together, they fuse their cytoplasm and genetic material and, if food is available, grow into a new mushroom. This new plant is a white filimentous subterranean growth called a mycelium. In the case of shiitake, mycelium grows inside the log, using its powerful enzymes to change wood into food. After a period of time, environmental stresses such as food depletion or temperature and humidity changes cause the mycelium to form a reproductive structure—the mushroom—and the cycle is complete.

Left to its own devices, shiitake would probably rather reproduce by the sexual cycle outlined above. However, to ensure crop quality and consistency, shiitake growers inoculate their logs with the mushroom mycelium rather than spores. The so-called vegetative (asexual) method begins by growing shiitake mycelium on wood chips, paper disks or "enriched" sawdust. Shiitake cultivators then insert these "spawn" into holes or cuts made in hardwood logs.

In early fall, as trees shed their leaves in preparation for a dormant winter, the carbohydrate level in the tree trunk rises, making an ideal food for shiitake growth. When about 10 percent of the leaves have fallen, shiitake growers fell trees and cut them into 3-foot (1-m) lengths. Next, about twenty to twenty-five evenly spaced holes are drilled into each log. Then wood chips (plug spawn) are hammered into the holes. When sawdust spawn are used, they are placed in holes using a special transfer tool. In both cases, the holes are sealed with hot wax.

After the logs are inoculated, they are carried into a pine forest and placed in a spot where there is an ideal balance of sunlight and shade. Usually, by the following fall, the shiitake mycelium has completely penetrated the logs, and, with seasonal temperature changes, mushrooms begin to push through the bark.

From just one inoculation, logs can be expected to produce crops of shiitake every fall and spring for five to seven years, until the logs are completely decayed. The variety of shiitake called *donko* is superior in both flavor and medicinal qualities to the *koshin* variety. In its natural effort at self-preservation, donko shiitake produces a thick cap with strong viable spores to protect against harsh environmental conditions.

The timing of the shiitake harvest is critical. If the mushroom is left on the log too long, it will completely open and shed

The finest shitake are grown outdoors on hardwood logs under the shade of evergreens and harvested several times a year.

its spores, producing a mushroom that is thin, flat, dark and lacking in vitality. Premium donko shiitake (picked at the right time) should not be more than 70 percent open and should have thick, fleshy, slightly rounded caps. These cost more but are prized for their excellent flavor and healthfulness.

A Growing Controversy

The "natural log" method of growing shiitake is still practiced by most of the Japan's shiitake farmers. However, in the West, where shiitake farming is relatively new, and more recently in China, Korea and Taiwan, the high-tech method of growing shiitake indoors under controlled temperature and humidity on "synthetic sawdust logs" (actually sawdust blocks) is used by approximately 80 percent of the large commercial growers. A much smaller number of growers use natural logs under controlled conditions.

The method of growing shiitake on sawdust logs is a direct outcome of the biotechnical revolution that has taken place since World War II. Drawing on the latest technology, exotic mushroom cultivators mix various nutrients into sawdust, which is then formed into a block, sterilized and inoculated with shiitake mycelium. The blocks are then placed in semi-sterile growing rooms under ideal conditions to maximize mushroom growth. Ideal growing conditions usually create an opportunity for other fungi to grow and compete with the shiitake on the synthetic logs. As a result, most high-tech cultivators are forced to spray their growing rooms with pesticides and fungicides. However, there are exceptions. A few companies in the United States and Asia grow shiitake indoors without the use of toxic chemicals. These are usually certified organic.

The controversy over which method of cultivation produces the most delicious and nutritious mushrooms is a heated debate in the exclusive world of exotic mushrooms. Fusataro Taniguchi and other traditional shiitake growers feel that shiitake grown on synthetic sawdust logs look and taste inferior to their natural log-grown mushrooms. In addition, they believe that the fungicides used to control pests in the semi-sterile growing rooms pose a health threat to consumers and workers.

By looking at the life cycle of shiitake, it is possible to understand which set of growing conditions will enhance its medicinal properties. Mushrooms sit close to the lowest rung in the ecosystem, thriving on decaying materials in a very hostile environment. During the growing stage shiitake sends out thin hairs called mycelia that secrete powerful enzymes to digest food outside the cell. Since the mushroom needs to absorb the digested food, it must first deactivate any natural pathogens by utilizing its unique polysaccharide peptide properties. Mushrooms are also very proficient at expelling undesirable chemicals and contaminants that are absorbed during ingestion. In order for shiitake and other mushrooms to compete and thrive, their very existence depends on their biologically unique, aggressive and adaptive immune system. Therefore, shiitake grown outdoors, subject to the rigors of the natural wild environment, should have more concentrated medicinal properties than shiitake that are protected and pampered in growing rooms.

SHOPPING FOR SHIITAKE

Shiitake's culinary and health-promoting qualities are concentrated greatly during the drying process. When it comes to flavor, nutrition and medicinal potency, chefs, healers and growers all agree that dried shiitake are superior to fresh. The highest quality dried shiitake will not be fully open and will have thick, fleshy, slightly rounded caps. The world's finest dried shiitake is called Sun-Dried Donko. These delicious, thick, fleshy mushrooms are said to have 20 percent more vitamin D than typical oven dried varieties.

When shopping for dried shiitake look for an indication on the label that the mushrooms have been grown on logs outdoors. A few companies offer Certified Organic shiitake and carry the certifying agency's seal. Shiitake grown on sawdust are usually cultivated in greenhouses under very controlled temperature and humidity, so they tend to be uniform in size and shape. Shiitake logs are usually placed outside where there is a lot of environmental variation, so these mushrooms also have a lot of variation. This is very apparent in a bag of dried shiitake.

Fresh shiitake are much more delicate in flavor and texture than dried varieties. At their peak they are firm and the caps are not completely open. Choose smaller firm mushrooms that have thick fresh-looking caps. Avoid caps that appear wilted or dry. The underside should be light, not mottled or spotty in color. Because fresh shiitake are usually not sold in packages it is difficult to know if they have been grown on logs. However, many natural foods stores sell organically grown fresh shiitake.

COOKING WITH SHIITAKE

 Shiitake is a tasty and healthful addition to our daily diet. The famed Dr. Mori recommended four shiitake a day for the maintenance of health. However, when using shiitake as part of a therapeutic regimen, larger amounts are usually recommended.

The temperatures of cooking do not seem to destroy shiitake's healing qualities and cooking greatly enhances the mushroom's flavor. You can cook fresh shiitake in all the ways you are used to enjoying other mushrooms—in soups, stews, sauces and gravies. The mushrooms are a flavorful addition to stir-fries, fried rice and noodle dishes. They are particularly delicious in tempura or when baked with a seasoning of shoyu, mirin and fresh ginger. For a special treat, brush shiitake caps with olive oil and grill for 3 to 5 minutes.

To clean fresh shiitake, simply wipe them with a damp cloth or soft brush. Fresh shiitake can also be rinsed under cold water and patted dry, but be careful not to soak them or they will become soggy.

Dried shiitake are readily available in Asian markets and natural foods stores and are becoming more popular in supermarkets. Though the texture of reconstituted dried shiitake is not as tender as that of the fresh mushrooms, shiitake's exquisite flavor is even more concentrated with drying. To reconstitute, submerge dried shiitake in water for at least an hour or two and preferably overnight. After soaking, cut off and discard the tough stems and slice the caps. The soaking water makes a rich stock for soups, stews, sauces and gravies. Used with their soaking water and other ingredients, such as carrots and greens, shiitake are a superb addition to miso soup.

Regardless of the type of food you enjoy, shiitake will add depth of flavor and vitality to your diet. Following are two recipes using dried shiitake, including a medicinal preparation, and several of our favorite fresh shiitake recipes.

| Shiitake Stock |

This simple and versatile stock works well as the basis of almost any type of soup, stew or sauce.

> 4 to 5 dried shiitake mushrooms
> 6 cups (1.5 liters) water

1. Place the shiitake in the water and let them soak for at least 2 to 3 hours. A small plate or saucer inverted and placed on top of the shiitake will keep them submerged.

2. Pour the soaking water into a saucepan. Remove and discard the stems from the reconstituted shiitake, then thinly slice the caps and return to the water. Bring to a boil, lower the heat, and gently simmer, covered, for about 15 minutes. For a clear stock, remove the shiitake caps.

3. Use right away or refrigerate in a covered container for up to 5 days.

Note to Cook

If you want your soups, stews or sauces to have the flavor and health benefits of shiitake, but don't have time to soak shiitake for 2 to 3 hours, try the following two shortcuts.

- *Soak the shiitake for 20 minutes before bringing to a boil. Reduce the heat and gently simmer for 15 minutes. If time allows, let the shiitake steep in the liquid for 30 minutes.*

- *When you're extremely pressed for time, simply add the dried shiitake to the water when making soup. When the soup is done, remove the shiitake and reserve for another use.*

MAKES ABOUT 4 CUPS (1 LITER)

Preparation time: 1 minute
Cooking time: 20 minutes plus 2 to 3 hours soaking time

| Shiitake Tea |

This is a traditional folk remedy to relax and soothe. Considered a medicinal tonic, shiitake tea should be drunk in $^1/_2$ cup (125 ml) portions at a time.

> 1 dried shiitake mushroom
> 2 cups (475 ml) water
> Pinch of sea salt

1. Soak the dried shiitake in the water for 1 hour. Use a saucer to keep the shiitake submerged.

2. Remove and discard the stem, cut the mushroom cap into quarters. Pour the soaking water into a small saucepan. Add the quartered shiitake and the salt. Simmer for 10 to 20 minutes over medium heat, or until the liquid is reduced by half. Shiitake tea keeps for up to 2 weeks in the refrigerator.

SERVES 2

Preparation time: 5 minutes
Cooking time: 10 to 20 minutes plus 1 hour soaking time

Mushroom Gravy

This full-flavored gravy goes especially well with millet or mashed potatoes.

$1^1/2$ tablespoons extra virgin olive oil

1 small onion, diced

1 to 2 cloves garlic, minced

6 fresh shiitake mushroom caps, sliced

Pinch each of sea salt and freshly ground black pepper

3 tablespoons unbleached white or whole-wheat pastry flour

$1^2/3$ cups (400 ml) Shiitake Stock (see opposite) or Vegetable Stock (see page 183)

$1/4$ teaspoon sea salt

2 teaspoons barley, brown rice or red miso mixed with 2 teaspoons water

2 teaspoons fresh thyme or $1/2$ teaspoon dried

1 tablespoon mirin or sweet white wine, such as Reisling

1 tablespoon chopped fresh parsley

1. In a skillet, heat the oil over medium heat. Add the onion and garlic, and sauté for 2 to 3 minutes, or until the onion is soft and translucent.

2. Add the shiitake and a pinch of salt and pepper, and continue to sauté for 2 to 3 minutes or until the mushrooms are soft.

3. Reduce the heat to low. Sprinkle the flour over the vegetables and cook, stirring constantly, for 2 to 3 minutes.

4. Slowly add the stock while stirring briskly. Increase the heat to medium and continue to stir frequently for about 10 minutes, or until the gravy begins to simmer and thicken. Add the rest of the salt, miso, thyme and mirin or wine.

5. Stirring occasionally, gently simmer over medium-low heat, uncovered, for 15 minutes or until the gravy is thick and smooth. Add the parsley during the last minute of cooking. Use immediately.

MAKES ABOUT $1^1/2$ CUPS (350 ML)

Preparation time: 10 minutes

Cooking time: 35 minutes

Shiitake and Veggie Kabobs

Simple, appealing and delicious, these kabobs, flavored with an Italian medley of herbs, can be grilled or broiled. Substitute other tender vegetables or firm tofu, if desired, but use a colorful combination of ingredients for an attractive presentation. Vary the marinade herbs according to your preference or what you have on hand.

24 red or white pearl onions (do not peel)
24 fresh small shiitake mushroom caps, left whole, or 6 large shiitake mushroom caps, quartered
2 small (5 to 6-in/12 to 15-cm) zucchini, cut into twelve $3/4$-in (2-cm)-thick rounds
2 small yellow squash, cut into twelve $3/4$-in (2-cm)-thick rounds
1 red or orange bell pepper, deseeded and diced into twelve 1-in (2.5-cm) squares

Italian Marinade
$2/3$ cup (175 ml) extra virgin olive oil
3 tablespoons balsamic vinegar
1 small clove garlic, sliced
$1/2$ teaspoon sea salt
$1/8$ teaspoon freshly ground black pepper
2 tablespoons thinly sliced fresh basil leaves or $1 1/2$ teaspoons dried basil
1 teaspoon chopped fresh oregano or marjoram or $1/4$ teaspoon dried oregano or marjoram
$1/2$ teaspoon chopped fresh thyme or $1/8$ teaspoon dried thyme
1 teaspoon shoyu (Japanese soy sauce)

1. In a saucepan, bring 3 cups (700 ml) of water to a boil, add the pearl onions and simmer for 5 minutes.

2. Drain the onions, then cover with cold water until cool enough to handle. Slice the tip off the root end and pinch to squeeze out the onion. Set aside.

3. If you're using bamboo skewers, presoak 12 of them in water.

4. Blend the marinade ingredients together in a large bowl. Add all of the vegetables and stir to coat evenly. Marinate for at least an hour, stirring occasionally.

5. Preheat the broiler or prepare an outdoor grill.

6. Thread the mushrooms onto the skewers alternating with the onions, pepper and squash pieces. Reserve the marinade for basting and place the skewers on a rack over an outdoor grill or in a broiler pan, 3 inches from the heat source.

7. Cook, turning skewers occasionally and brushing with marinade as needed, for 10 minutes, or until the vegetables are tender. Serve immediately.

MAKES 12 KABOBS TO SERVE 4 AS A MAIN COURSE

Preparation time: 20 minutes plus at least 1 hour for marinating
Cooking time: 15 minutes

Udon with Shiitake

Based on a classic Italian pasta dish, this version starts with the traditional *aglio e olio* (garlic and oil), but incorporates the healthful qualities of shiitake and Japanese udon, which is more tender and easier to digest than Italian pasta. This is a simple dish, but careful timing is crucial to achieving the best results. Therefore, prepare all the vegetables and toast the almonds before you begin cooking the noodles or vegetables.

> 2 tablespoons extra virgin olive oil
> Salt and freshly ground black pepper, to taste
> 8 oz (250 g) dried udon noodles
> 2 cups (about 4 oz/125 g) fresh shiitake mushroom caps, sliced
> 1 tablespoon minced garlic
> 4 tablespoons finely chopped fresh parsley
> $1/3$ cup (25 g) very thinly sliced fresh basil leaves
> 1 teaspoon balsamic vinegar
> 2 green onions (scallions), thinly sliced
> $1/3$ cup (40 g) slivered almonds or pine nuts, lightly toasted

1. In a large bowl, combine 1 tablespoon of the olive oil and a pinch of salt and pepper and set aside.

2. In preparation for cooking the udon, add 8 to 10 cups (2 to 2.5 liters) of water to a large pot and bring to a full rolling boil. Add the udon to the rapidly boiling water and stir to prevent the noodles from sticking together.

3. Immediately heat the remaining tablespoon of oil in a large skillet and toss in the shiitake and garlic and a pinch each of salt and pepper. Sauté over medium heat for 2 to 3 minutes.

4. Stir in the parsley and basil and cook for 1 to 2 minutes more.

5. Add the balsamic vinegar and toss, then remove from the heat.

6. When the udon is tender but still firm, after about 7 to 9 minutes, drain, rinse briefly and toss with the olive oil, salt and pepper in the large bowl.

7. Immediately add the udon to the shiitake mixture, toss well and transfer the noodles and vegetables to a serving bowl. Garnish with some of the green onions and nuts and serve immediately. Set out the remaining nuts and onions, so they can be added to individual servings.

SERVES 2 TO 3

Preparation time: 10 minutes
Cooking time: 15 minutes

Flounder in a Blanket

Baking fish in a parchment paper or aluminum foil packet is a great way to keep all the natural juices in, resulting in a succulent, melt-in-your-mouth texture. Other mild white fish, such as scrod, haddock, pollock or sea bass can be substituted for the flounder, but of course, thicker cuts of fish require longer cooking. Sole or orange roughy fillets can be substituted for the flounder, if desired.

> 1 tablespoon extra virgin olive oil
> 1 clove garlic, minced
> 2 shallots, minced
> 5 oz (150 g) fresh shiitake mushrooms, stems removed and caps sliced
> Pinch each of sea salt and freshly ground black pepper
> Four 4-oz (120-g) flounder fillets
> Pinch of dried red pepper flakes
> $1/2$ lemon, quartered
> Spray of extra virgin olive oil
> 1 small zucchini, sliced into thin matchsticks
> 1 carrot, sliced into thin matchsticks

1. Preheat the oven to 425°F (220°C).

2. In a skillet, heat the olive oil over medium heat and sauté the garlic and shallots for 1 minute. Add the sliced shiitake, salt and pepper, and sauté for 3 minutes. Set aside.

3. Place each piece of fish on a piece of lightly oiled parchment paper or aluminum foil and sprinkle with salt and red pepper flakes. Squeeze the lemon juice over each fillet and spray lightly with olive oil.

4. Top the fish with the shiitake mixture, spreading it evenly over the surface of the fillets. Add the zucchini and carrot. Lightly sprinkle with salt and pepper and spray with olive oil.

5. To be sure the juices are kept in, wrap the fish by bringing the two ends of the parchment paper or foil together over the fish and crimp the edges twice with $1/2$-inch (1.25-cm) folds. (It helps to brush the edges of the paper with water.) Next fold each side in toward the center at least twice.

6. Place the fish packages on a baking sheet and bake for 25 minutes. If using a parchment packet, it should be puffed and golden brown.

7. If using aluminum foil, carefully unwrap the packet, transfer the fish to individual plates and serve immediately. Foods cooked in parchment are generally served in the paper. When guests slit the paper open with their knives, a puff of steam will carry up the appetizing bouquet. Have everyone carefully lift the fish out of the paper onto their plate. Discard the paper.

SERVES 4

Preparation time: 20 minutes
Cooking time: 30 minutes

玄
米
水
飴

BROWN RICE MALT SYRUP: HEAVENLY SWEET WATER

Rice malt syrup is among the oldest and most versatile of sweeteners. In ancient times, rice malt syrup was believed to be of divine origin. As if by some heavenly plan, the addition of a few sprouts of barley to rice resulted in golden sweet liquid. Rice was considered a gift of the gods, and its transformation into ambrosial syrup was only allowed to take place in shrines and sacred places.

In modern Japan, traditional rice malt syrup, called *mizu ame* (sweet water), is hard to find. In fact, you may be more likely to find authentic rice malt syrup in an American or European natural foods store than in a modern Japanese supermarket. This reflects the trend in Japan is away from traditional foods and toward Western-style foods, and the fact that the few producers of this type of rice malt syrup have focused more on the natural foods export markets.

Sugars are the fuel of life, and sweeteners are something everyone instinctively desires. How we satisfy this craving for sweets can have a significant effect on our health and happiness. The quick energy lift from refined white sugar, brown sugar, fructose, honey and maple syrup can cause rapid mood shifts on a daily basis. Over long periods of time, this can result in mental illness, hypoglycemia, diabetes and other hormonal and degenerative diseases.

When choosing sweeteners, it is important to consider their quality and the amount you use. There is, of course, a world of difference between using lots of white sugar, which has no nutritional value, and using a moderate amount of honey or maple syrup, which has some nutritional value. However, even regular consumption of these higher quality sweeteners can cause rapid upsurges in blood sugar levels, followed soon after by dramatic plummets. This cycle, often referred to as the "sugar blues," is due to a high concentration of simple sugars. The next time you start the day with pancakes drenched in maple syrup, pay particular attention to your emotions over the next few hours. The first sign of the sugar blues is usually anxiety or irritability, typically followed by low energy or depression.

If you are eating a healing diet, or if you simply want to enjoy the highest quality sweeteners available, choose naturally malted whole-grain sweeteners such as rice malt syrup. Like many of the traditional foods discussed in this book, rice malt syrup is made by a slow, natural enzymatic process as the whole grains are partially broken down to yield a thick, rich, sweet liquid.

Rice malt syrup contains about 30 percent soluble complex carbohydrates, 45 percent maltose (grain malt sugar), 3 to 4 percent glucose, and 20 percent water. The glucose is absorbed into the blood almost immediately. The maltose takes up to one-and-a-half hours to digest, and the complex carbohydrates are gradually digested and released for up to four hours. Unlike most other concentrated sweeteners, which are almost entirely simple sugars, rice malt syrup provides a slow but prolonged source of energy that is calming and soothing.

Another advantage of rice or brown rice malt syrup is that it has many of the B vitamins and minerals that are found in rice and sprouted barley. Characteristically rich but mild flavored, rice malt syrup complements simple foods, whereas honey, maple syrup and molasses have stronger, often overpowering tastes.

Before Commodore Perry's ships forced open Japan's ports to American trade more than 150 years ago, the Japanese sweet tooth was usually satisfied with the subtle sweetness of amazake (fermented sweet rice pudding), mirin (sweet rice wine) or rice malt syrup. Today, after more than a century of experimenting with white sugar, and especially so after WWII, the Japanese are also singing the "sugar blues." But scattered throughout Japan are a few small traditional shops that still make rice and brown rice malt syrup exactly the way it was made before the introduction of white sugar.

One of the world's few remaining authentic brown rice malt syrup shops is the Uchida Toka Company in Fukuyama, a small city on Japan's Inland Sea. As with other traditional Japanese foods, making brown rice malt syrup is a complex craft requiring a great deal of labor, knowledge and fine-tuned intuition.

Gunichi Uchida, head of this family-run business, begins the process of making his irresistibly sweet-yet-subtle, thick syrup with crushed and dried organic sprouted barley. The barley is traditionally grown and processed in the mountains around Japan's former capital of Kyoto. Organic barley grains are simply soaked in water until they sprout. They are then dried and crushed, which preserves the delicate enzymes that seeds naturally produce in order to convert their starch into usable sugars for sprouting. Uchida is particularly interested in the enzymes that change the starch into maltose, a disaccharide sugar used by seeds for sprouting.

To begin, Uchida flakes brown rice. This is the process of passing grain between two rubber rollers to press it into a flake. Flaking increases the surface area and breaks down the bran so it will cook faster and be more ready digested by enzymes. The flakes are then soaked overnight. The following morning he steams the flakes for one hour, adding a little water to form a thick porridge called kayu. Then, as the porridge is gently stirred, sprouted barley is added.

Thick, sweet amber rice malt syrup is made by flaking and steaming rice and then adding water to make porridge. Sprouted barley is added to start the malting process.

The delicate enzymes in the sprouted barley are easily destroyed by heat, so Uchida does not let the temperature of his rice porridge go above 158°F (70°C). After adding the sprouted barley, Uchida transfers the mixture to a vat, and keeps it at a temperature between 140–158°F (60–70°C) for several hours. During this short time, the carbohydrates, proteins and fats of the brown rice are broken down into less complex sugars, amino acids and fatty acids. The longer it is kept, the darker and sweeter the porridge becomes. However, if left for too long, the mixture begins to develop an alcoholic smell and taste. In fact, making rice porridge is one of the steps in the traditional process of making rice wine.

Long before any alcohol develops, Uchida's years of experience tell him it is time to stop the fermentation process by heating the mixture above 158° F (70° C.). The pasteurized porridge is then transferred to cotton sacks and pressed. As the thick amber liquid drips from the press, it is collected and filtered through cotton cloth.

Finally, the clear-filtered brown rice malt syrup is cooked down for several hours, first by direct cooking and then by steaming. When Uchida feels the malt has reached the perfect thickness, it is filtered one final time and then bottled.

SHOPPING FOR BROWN RICE MALT SYRUP

 There are several types of rice syrup available in natural foods stores, Asian grocery stores and even large supermarkets around the world. Syrup quality varies from Uchida-style brown rice malt syrup to white rice syrup that is made with enzymes and added sugar. The most common variation on the traditional method is to substitute laboratory-produced enzymes for the sprouted barley.

Naturally occurring digestive enzymes, such as those in sprouted barley or *koji*, are part of a living cell. In the laboratory, enzymes are isolated from the rest of the cell and are, therefore, no longer attached to a living system. Producers who use enzymes can control the percentage of maltose and glucose in the final product, and the process is much quicker and more economical.

However, traditional makers of rice malt syrup contend that there is a distinct qualitative difference between their product and enzyme-converted rice syrup. "In nature, a cell wouldn't let you use just one or two enzymes," explains food chemist and rice syrup authority Jim Allen. "With sprouted barley many enzymes are at work holistically digesting proteins and fats as well as carbohydrates." Gunichi Uchida claims there is a difference in the taste. He feels that with laboratory-produced enzymes you simply cannot get the full range of tastes that you get with sprouted barley.

If you are confused about which rice syrup to buy, simply read the label. Look for sprouted barley in the ingredients list. Authentic brown rice malt syrup, such as the Uchida product, contains whole grain rice, sprouted barley and water. Enzyme-converted rice syrup usually lists rice and water as the only ingredients. Another grain can be substituted for the rice. For example, the Uchida Toka Company makes the ultimate sweetener (especially for a healing diet) by substituting *hato mugi* (Job's tears) for brown rice in the malt recipe.

Rice malt syrup is a natural food in every sense of the word. The process begins with whole grains and simply lets nature take its course. With gentle warming and occasional stirring, rice malt syrup actually makes itself. No wonder the ancient Japanese considered rice malt syrup to be a gift from the gods. It is!

Brown rice malt syrup has a full, slightly nutty flavor with a hint of butterscotch. Its gentle, balanced sweetness provides the perfect alternative to refined sugar in many snacks and desserts. Brown rice malt syrup is excellent in salad dressings and dips, as well as in vegetable dishes such as candied yams and pickles.

Rice syrup is considerably less sweet than cane sugar, honey or maple syrup. To achieve an equivalent sweetness, substitute one and a half parts of rice syrup to one part white sugar and two parts rice syrup to one part maple syrup or honey. When substituting liquid sweeteners for sugar, it is necessary to reduce the total amount of liquid that is called for in the recipe.

If a sweeter taste is desired in the following recipes, or when substituting brown rice malt syrup for more concentrated sweeteners in other recipes, use a combination of rice syrup with honey or maple syrup. If you're new to the flavor of rice syrup, a good rule is to initially substitute rice syrup for one-half of the maple syrup or honey that is called for in a recipe. Gradually increase the proportion of rice syrup until your taste buds are satisfied by desserts that are sweetened with rice malt syrup only.

The texture or thickness of rice malt syrup varies according to the brand and to the temperature at which it is stored. If the syrup is too stiff to pour, place the uncovered jar in a saucepan with 2 inches (5 cm) of water and let it simmer for a minute or two. When the syrup warms up, it will pour easily.

Peach Melba

For a perfect ending to a summer meal, make this simple and pretty dessert. Sliced fresh strawberries can be substituted for the raspberries. If you have a taste for summer in the dead of winter, frozen organic raspberries and canned organic peaches can be substituted.

> 4 ripe peaches (substitute canned peaches off-season)
> 2 cups (250 g) fresh raspberries or strawberries (substitute frozen berries off-season)
> 4 tablespoons brown rice malt syrup, warmed
> $1/2$ teaspoon pure vanilla extract
> 1 pint (425 g) vanilla or raspberry non-dairy frozen dessert

1. Drop the peaches in boiling water for 1 minute. Remove with a slotted spoon. When cool enough to handle, slip off the skins. Cut the peaches in half and remove their pits.

2. Place two halves, cut side up, in each of four serving bowls.

3. In a bowl, mash the raspberries. Mix in the rice syrup and vanilla.

4. To serve, top the peaches with a scoop of frozen dessert and some raspberry sauce.

SERVES 4

Preparation time: 10 minutes

| Blueberry Pie |

Nothing satisfies like a homemade fruit pie. This one is extra quick and easy to prepare. For an extra special treat, try it warm from the oven with a scoop of non-dairy frozen dessert.

2 pints (500 g) blueberries, washed and stemmed
$^1/_2$ cup (125 ml) brown rice malt syrup
4 tablespoons pure maple syrup or honey
4 tablespoons (50 g) granulated tapioca
1 recipe Whole-Wheat Pie Crust (see page 106)

1. Preheat the oven to 375°F (190°C).

2. In a mixing bowl, gently but thoroughly combine the blueberries, sweeteners and tapioca. Set aside.

3. Line the bottom of a 9-inch (23-cm) pie plate with a layer of the pie dough.

4. Pour the fruit mixture into the pie shell.

5. Cover with top crust and trim, leaving about $^1/_2$ inch (1 cm) dough overhanging the rim of the pie plate. Fold top crust under bottom crust and flute the edges to seal.

6. With a butter knife or paring knife, make several slits in the top crust to allow steam to escape.

7. Bake for 50 to 60 minutes.

8. Cool thoroughly on a wire rack before slicing and serving.

MAKES ONE 9-INCH (23-CM) PIE

Cooking time: 50 to 60 minutes
Preparation time: 20 minutes

| Homemade Almond Milk |

Use almond milk as a substitute for dairy milk or soymilk in any dessert recipe. Puddings and pie fillings are particularly tasty when almond milk is used.

$^1/_2$ cup (65 g) shelled almonds
1 tablespoon brown rice malt syrup
$^1/_2$ tablespoon vegetable oil, such as canola or safflower oil
Pinch of sea salt
2 cups (475 ml) cold water

1. Bring a small saucepan of water to a boil. Drop in the almonds, boil for 10 seconds, turn off the heat and let sit for 2 to 3 minutes. Drain and rinse almonds under cold running water. When cool enough to handle, remove and discard almond skins.

2. In a blender, combine the peeled almonds, rice syrup, oil, salt and cold water. Blend for 1 to 2 minutes.

3. Strain the mixture through cheesecloth, squeezing out all the liquid into a container.

4. Reserve almond meal in a covered container in the refrigerator. Use meal within 5 to 6 days in cookies or other pastries.

5. If not using immediately, store almond milk in a covered container in the refrigerator, where it will keep for about 6 days.

Note to Cook

Almond meal can be used in a variety of cookie or muffin recipes. Simply combine up to $^1/2$ cup (100 g) of meal with the liquid ingredients before mixing the liquid and dry ingredients together.

MAKES ABOUT 2 CUPS (475 ML)

Preparation time: 10 minutes
Cooking time: 2 minutes

| Raspberry Sherbet |

Light and creamy, with a fresh raspberry flavor, this is sure to be a crowd-pleaser.

12 oz (375 g) fresh or frozen unsweetened red raspberries
1 cup (235 ml) plain almond milk, rice milk or soymilk
2 teaspoons kanten flakes
$^1/3$ cup (75 ml) water
1 to $1^1/4$ cups (250 to 300 ml) brown rice malt syrup, to taste
2 teaspoons fresh lemon juice

1. Thaw the berries, if frozen, and pick over fresh berries to remove any debris. Puree berries and almond milk in a blender and strain to remove seeds.

2. Sprinkle the kanten flakes over the water in a small saucepan (do not stir in), and slowly bring to a simmer over low heat. Simmer gently for 2 to 3 minutes, stirring occasionally. Remove from the heat.

3. Stir in the rice syrup and lemon juice, then mix in raspberry puree.

4. Pour the mixture into a baking pan, casserole dish or undivided ice trays, cover with foil or plastic wrap, and freeze until solid, at least 6 hours.

5. Up to a day before serving, scrape the frozen mixture with a fork until it resembles finely crushed ice.

6. Spoon half the mixture into a chilled food processor bowl or a blender and process quickly until it is light and smooth but not thawed. This amount will make about 1 pint, or enough to serve 4. If you're serving the entire amount, process the other half or save for another time.

7. If you like sherbet soft, serve it immediately. For a firmer texture, place the sherbet in a container, cover and freeze for 1 to 3 hours, or up to 24 hours. If stored longer, it becomes less creamy and more icy.

MAKES ABOUT 1 QUART (1 LITER)

Cooking time: 5 minutes
Preparation time: 10 to 15 minutes

Banana Crème Pie

With a pudding filling and a flaky crust, this sensuously cool and creamy, wonderfully rich and delicious, pie is sure to be a hit for kids and grown-ups alike.

2 cups (475 ml) Homemade Almond Milk (see page 102)
$^1/_2$ cup (125 ml) brown rice malt syrup
Pinch of sea salt
2 tablespoons kanten flakes
$1^1/_2$ tablespoons crushed kuzu starch or 2 tablespoons arrowroot
1 teaspoon pure vanilla extract
1 tablespoon unsalted butter or non-hydrogenated margarine
3 ripe bananas
Whole-Wheat Pie Crust, halve recipe for single shell, prebaked (see page 106)
3 tablespoons unsweetened coconut flakes, for garnish

1. Combine $1^3/_4$ cups (400 ml) of the almond milk with the rice syrup and salt in a small saucepan. Sprinkle the kanten flakes over the top. Bring to a simmer over medium heat without stirring. Gently simmer for 1 to 2 minutes, stirring until the kanten is dissolved.

2. Thoroughly dissolve the kuzu in the remaining 4 tablespoons almond milk and add to saucepan while stirring briskly. Return to a simmer and cook for 1 to 2 minutes. Remove from the heat.

3. Mix in the vanilla and butter. Slice one of the bananas and fold into the pudding.

4. Slice the remaining 2 bananas and arrange them in the prebaked pie shell (see page 106 for instructions on how to prebake a pie shell).

5. In a dry skillet over medium heat, toast the coconut flakes, stirring constantly for about 2 minutes, or until golden. Remove from the heat.

6. Pour the pudding into the pie shell, garnish with toasted coconut, and chill for 1 to 2 hours, or until firm, before serving.

SERVES 8

Preparation time: 10 minutes plus 1 to 2 hours to chill and set
Cooking time: 10 minutes

Jam-Filled Cookies

Quick and easy to make, these cookies are certain crowd pleasers.

$^1/_3$ cup (75 ml) vegetable oil, such as canola or safflower
$^2/_3$ cup (150 ml) brown rice malt syrup
1 teaspoon pure vanilla extract
$^1/_8$ teaspoon pure orange extract
$1^1/_2$ cups (200 g) whole-wheat pastry flour
$^1/_2$ cup (50 g) rolled oats
4 tablespoons shredded coconut
1 tablespoon arrowroot
$^1/_8$ teaspoon sea salt
$^1/_4$ teaspoon baking soda
1 tablespoon grated lemon zest
Natural fruit-sweetened strawberry, apricot or blueberry preserves

1. Preheat the oven to 375°F (190°C). Oil two baking sheets.

2. In a mixing bowl, combine the oil, sweetener, vanilla and orange extract and beat well.

3. In a separate bowl, combine the flour, rolled oats, coconut, arrowroot, salt, baking soda and lemon zest.

4. Gradually add the dry ingredients to the liquids, mixing well. The dough should be very stiff. If necessary, add a little more flour.

5. Drop dough by rounded teaspoons onto the prepared baking sheets. Leave at least 1 inch (2.5 cm) between the cookies, as they will spread while baking. Press cookies with a fork to about $^3/_8$-inch (8-mm) thickness. Dip a teaspoon in a cup of water, shake off any excess water and use the back of the spoon to make a shallow well in the center of each cookie.

6. Add about 1 teaspoon of jam to fill the "wells" in the cookies.

7. Bake for 12 to 15 minutes or until bottoms and edges are golden.

MAKES 25 TO 30 COOKIES

Preparation time: 20 minutes
Cooking time: 12 to 15 minutes

Whole-Wheat Pie Crust

This recipe can be a little tricky until you get some experience with it. It's important to measure your ingredients as accurately as possible. Even so, the amount of liquid needed may vary slightly, since different flours absorb more or less liquid. For a single-crust pie, simply halve the recipe.

> 2 cups (275 g) whole-wheat pastry flour
> 1 cup (135 g) unbleached white flour
> $^1/_2$ teaspoon sea salt
> $^1/_2$ cup (125 ml) safflower oil
> $^1/_2$ cup (125 ml) ice-cold water

1. Thoroughly combine the flours and salt.

2. Add the oil all at once, and quickly and lightly work it into the flour with a fork until the mixture resembles small pebbles. (Do not use your hands to mix pie dough or the crust will be less flaky.)

3. Add all the water and, with the fork, quickly mix the dough until it forms a ball in the center of the bowl. Knead lightly a few times if necessary to form the ball. The dough should just come together to form a ball, with no dry unmixed portions. If too dry, add a little more water to prevent the dough from cracking while rolling it out. If too sticky, stir in a bit more flour with a fork. If not using immediately, wrap dough in waxed paper and refrigerate.

4. Roll out half of the dough on an unfloured work surface, between sheets of waxed paper if you prefer. Start by rolling out from the center in all directions using light, short strokes. As the dough becomes thinner use longer strokes and more pressure.

5. When the dough is the desired size, gently loosen it from the board with a narrow spatula. Fold in half, carefully lift onto the pie plate and unfold. If using waxed paper, peel off the top layer of paper, invert dough over pie plate and peel off remaining layer. Trim the edges.

6. Roll out the top crust. After filling the pie, lay the top crust over it and trim so about $^1/_2$ inch (1.25 cm) hangs over the edge of the plate. Fold the excess under the bottom crust and seal by pressing with tines of a fork all the way around the edge of the crust. Slit top crust in several places to allow steam to escape.

7. If prebaking a pie shell, prick the sides and bottom of the crust several times with a fork to prevent it from bubbling. Prebake shell for 15 to 20 minutes at 375°F (190°C). When the crust is golden, remove from the oven.

MAKES TWO 9-INCH (23-CM) SINGLE CRUSTS OR ONE DOUBLE CRUST

Preparation time: 15 minutes
Cooking time: 15 to 20 minutes for prebaked crusts

梅
干
し

UMEBOSHI: VENERABLE PICKLED PLUMS

In some Japanese cities it is not unusual to see a small, seventeenth-century, tile-roofed Buddhist temple nestled between gleaming glass office towers. Even in the more traditional countryside, the contrast between old and new can be stark. While one family sits at a contemporary Western-style dinner table eating juicy steak, their more typical neighbors are seated on the floor eating rice and miso soup with chopsticks. However, when it comes to Japanese pickled plums, or *umeboshi* (dried plum), everyone seems to agree that there is no modern substitute for its zesty palate-cleansing flavor and fast-acting medicinal effects. Even today, some traditional Japanese people begin the day with one or two pickled plums and a cup of tea. British author and Japanese food authority Robbie Swinnerton compares umeboshi's taste to the culinary equivalent of a cold shower. Swinnerton writes, "The abrupt, searingly tart, tangy, salty taste jolts the eyes open, shakes the stomach awake, sandpapers off any staleness from the taste buds, and gets the day off to an unforgettable start."

Besides their dramatic flavor, Japanese pickled plums have remarkable medicinal qualities. Their powerful acidity has a paradoxical alkalinizing effect on the body, neutralizing fatigue, stimulating digestion and promoting the elimination of toxins and the absorption of calcium. In addition, umeboshi is said to help the liver process excess alcohol, restore the skin, help regulate sugar metabolism, prevent or cure anemia and relieve acute stomach and intestinal pain due to gas. In addition umeboshi is thought to be an antidote to food poisoning as well as a natural tranquilizer.

Umeboshi is the Far Eastern equivalent to both two aspirins and a daily apple. Not only is it a potent hangover remedy for mornings after; more than that, an umeboshi a day is regarded as one of the best preventive medicines available.

Although umeboshi can be a strong medicine, there are never any side effects. Its main function is to cure by gently helping the body function smoothly rather than being used as a special medicine for a particular ailment. Because of this, it can cure opposite conditions for which you would normally have to take two very different remedies. For example, plum extract (see below) can cure both diarrhea and constipation.

Like many of Japan's ancient medicinal foods, the origin of the pickled plum is obscure. One theory traces it to China, where a dried smoked plum, or *ubai*, was discovered in a tomb built over two thousand years ago. The ubai is one of China's oldest medicines and is still used for a variety of medicinal purposes such as counteracting nausea, reducing fevers and controlling coughs.

The oldest Japanese record of pickled plums being used as a medicine is in a medical text written about one thousand years ago. Umeboshi was used to prevent fatigue, purify water, rid the body of toxins and cure specific diseases such as dysentery, typhoid and food poisoning. Slowly, extensive folklore developed about umeboshi's ability to prevent and cure certain diseases.

During Japan's furious samurai period, which lasted through most of the Middle Ages, the pickled plum was the soldier's most important field ration. It was used to flavor foods such as rice and vegetables, and its high acidity made it an excellent water and food purifier, as well as an effective antidote for battle fatigue.

Almost two hundred years ago, the Japanese began experimenting with ways to concentrate the healing powers of umeboshi. Finally, a dark liquid called *bainiku ekisu* (plum extract) was developed. To make the extract, sour green ume plums are slowly cooked down to obtain their most active ingredients in a highly concentrated form. The resulting dark, sticky, thick liquid is usually mixed with hot water and honey and is drunk as a tonic. Dried plum extract is also formed into pills, called *meitan*. In both plum extract and meitan, the plums' citric acid content is concentrated tenfold, which is equivalent to about twenty-five times that of lemon juice. Also, neither of these products contains salt, which makes them more effective than umeboshi for the treatment of high blood pressure and other conditions that are not helped by high sodium levels.

Many natural healers feel that these concentrated forms of Japanese plums are among the world's most effective natural medicines. Ume extract, when applied to the skin, has been found to cure conditions such as ringworm and athlete's foot.

The center of Japan's pickled plum industry is in Wakayama Prefecture, on the main island of Honshu. Even before the first orchards were planted, wild plum (ume) trees covered Wakayama hillsides. The area's mild temperatures, year-round plentiful rain and sheltered geographic situation serve to bring forth the finest and most plentiful fruit in the country.

In the heart of Japan's pickled-plum region is Ryujin village, home of some of Japan's oldest and most traditional pickled plum producers. Using their own variation on the traditional methods used in Japan for centuries, Ryujin producers make a mellow, tasty pickled plum that is not as salty as typical Japanese pickled plums. The process used by all pickled plum producers is technically known as "lactic-acid fermentation," one of the oldest and safest ways of preserving food. The secret to making good pickled plums is getting lactic-acid-forming bacteria (the desirable type) to grow before other competing bacteria have a chance to multiply. While lactic-acid bacteria are salt-tolerant, many undesirable species are not. To help establish beneficial bacteria, traditional makers use the proper amount of salt and store the fermenting plums in a cool, dark place. Lactic-acid bacteria multiply rapidly under these conditions. Once flourishing, they produce enough lactic acid and carbon dioxide to create an acidic environment that further inhibits the growth of undesirable microorganisms and enzymes. The carbon dioxide also contributes to a favorable anaerobic (low oxygen) condition and further stimulates the growth of lactic-acid bacteria.

Plums are picked green and placed in a brine solution. Over several months, lactic-acid fermentation slowly transforms them into tart umeboshi.

At Ryujin, plums are picked around the end of June, when they are still green and their juice is at its peak of acidity. This guarantees that the umeboshi will have as tart a taste as possible. If picked too early, the plums are too hard and their color never changes from green, but if left too long on the branch, the resulting pickles will be soft, mushy and tasteless.

By the last week in June, the activity at Japanese pickled plum shops is intense and nonstop from dawn to dusk. All the plums reach their full size at the same time and must be picked within a week or two. Any delay means the plums begin to ripen, reducing their acidity, flavor and medicinal qualities.

Next, the harvested plums are washed and then soaked overnight in water to remove any bitterness. The following day, the soaked plums are placed in large vats. A layer of jade green plums is topped with glistening white sea salt, followed by another layer, then another, until each vat is filled with about 5,000 pounds (2,270 kg) of plums and 600 pounds (270 kg) of salt. This brings the salt content to about 12 percent. (In earlier times, before the link between strokes and salt consumption was clear, the salt content of pickled plums was over 25 percent!)

The salt immediately begins to draw out the juice from the plums. A flat pressing lid topped with a heavy weight is placed on the plums to keep them submerged in the liquid. As the salt penetrates the flesh of the fruit, the pickling process begins; the plums are left to ferment until the end of July, which is also the end of the rainy season. The pickled plums are removed from the vats, placed on wooden racks and left outside to dry for anywhere from four to seven days, depending on the weather.

Although the pickling process is now complete, the wrinkled and shriveled plums do not have the dramatic red color and aromatic flavor of prized Ryujin organic pickled plums. To make these finest umeboshi, producers must soak the plums in plum vinegar along with leaves of the beautiful, scented red shiso (perilla) plant.

An herb that is related to mint, shiso has a slight lemony taste yet a unique flavor of its own. Its red, heart-shaped leaves are reminiscent of red meat, hence comes one of its English names, "beefsteak plant." Besides adding color and flavor to umeboshi, shiso has strong preservative and antibacterial qualities both in the pickling process and for the person who eats them. It is the latter quality that makes shiso such a perfect garnish in the sushi shop, where raw fish is consumed.

To add the essence of shiso leaves to their pickled plums, Ryujin producers mix the leaves with the liquid (brine) that is left from the pickling process. The shiso leaves turn the liquid a brilliant red, and the umeboshi are left to steep in this liquid for five days. When the plums are removed from the plum vinegar, they are placed in vats and left to age for up to one year. The remaining red liquid is bottled and sold as umeboshi vinegar, one of Japan's most unique and delicious condiments.

SHOPPING FOR UMEBOSHI

 Although there are several natural producers of pickled plums in Japan, few use the year-long traditional process described above. Fewer still use organically grown plums and high-quality sea salt. In fact, the umeboshi found in many Asian food stores are made in just a few weeks using red dye, organic acids and commercial salt. Some of these are made in Japan but most are processed in Korea and China. To be sure that you are buying the finest-quality pickled plums, check the ingredients on the label. The finest pickled plums are made with organic plums, organic shiso leaves and sea salt.

Umeboshi and umeboshi paste are lively, versatile seasonings that add a pleasing tartness to salad dressings, cooked vegetables and sauces. Umeboshi is also commonly served in Japan as a condiment with rice or tucked inside a nori-wrapped rice ball. In the summer, thick cucumber rounds spread thinly with umeboshi paste are a cooling treat. Sparingly dabbed on cooked corn-on-the-cob, it is a delicious, healthful alternative to butter and salt. Umeboshi also goes especially well with members of the cabbage family, including broccoli, kale and cauliflower.

When using whole pickled plums, it is usually necessary to remove the pit and mince the flesh before adding it to recipes. Ready-to-use umeboshi paste (pitted, pureed umeboshi plums) can be substituted for whole umeboshi in virtually any recipe.

The shiso leaves that are often packaged with umeboshi are also delicious when chopped and used as a seasoning inside nori rolls or when tossed in with steamed or sautéed vegetables.

Umeboshi vinegar, also known as plum vinegar or *ume-su*, contains many of the healing qualities and nutrients associated with pickled plums, and it is easy and convenient to use. Pleasingly tart and salty, umeboshi vinegar is a versatile seasoning that is especially refreshing on hot afternoons. Use umeboshi vinegar to liven up salad dressings, pickles and tofu spreads. It adds a pleasantly pungent flavor to cooked cabbage and other leafy greens, cauliflower, broccoli and green beans. Steam, boil or sauté vegetables until tender but still colorful. Drain, if necessary, place in a serving bowl and toss with umeboshi vinegar to taste. When substituting umeboshi vinegar for other types of vinegar, substantially reduce the amount used, or eliminate the salt in the recipe. The following recipes will familiarize you with umeboshi and umeboshi vinegar and will soon have you discovering new ways to use these delicious and healthful seasonings.

East Meets West Guacamole

Our nontraditional guacamole is delicious as a dip or as a spread for toast, rice crackers and flatbread. Be creative and use it as a stuffing for celery or cucumber "boats." In order to avoid discoloration, prepare shortly before serving. Use mature avocadoes. When ripe, an avocado will give slightly to gentle thumb pressure.

  1 large or 2 small ripe avocadoes, peeled and pitted
  1 tablespoon grated onion
  1 tablespoon umeboshi vinegar
  2 teaspoons fresh lemon juice

1. Mash the avocado in a bowl with a fork. Add the onion, vinegar and lemon juice and mix well.

2. Transfer to a small bowl and serve.

   MAKES ABOUT 1³/₄ CUPS (350 G)

   Preparation time: 5 minutes

Sautéed Cabbage with Umeboshi

Umeboshi and cabbage are a match made in heaven.

> $^1/_2$ head cabbage
> 2 teaspoons sesame oil (toasted or untoasted)
> 1 tablespoon plus 1 teaspoon umeboshi paste or minced umeboshi

1. Cut the cabbage in half lengthwise, and then cut the 2 sections in half again to form 4 quarters. Remove and thinly slice the core. Cut the cabbage quarters crosswise into $^1/_4$-inch (6-mm) slices.

2. Heat the oil in a large skillet, add the umeboshi, and sauté for 10 to 15 seconds. Add the cabbage, including the sliced core, and toss with the umeboshi. (At first, the umeboshi will not disperse evenly, but as you continue tossing and sautéeing, it will evenly coat the cabbage.) Sauté until the cabbage and umeboshi are well mixed.

3. If the cabbage hasn't released any juice, add 1 to 2 tablespoons of water, cover and simmer over low heat for 15 to 20 minutes, or until tender. Serve hot.

> SERVES 3 TO 4
>
> *Preparation time:* 5 minutes
> *Cooking time:* about 20 minutes

Sesame-Ume Salad Dressing

This versatile dressing is delicious on pasta salads or grain salads, and it is also a perfect seasoning for steamed or blanched broccoli, cabbage, cauliflower or green beans.

> 2 tablespoons tahini (ground sesame seed paste)
> 1 tablespoon umeboshi paste or minced umeboshi
> 1 teaspoon toasted sesame or extra virgin olive oil
> 1 tablespoon plus 1 teaspoon fresh lemon juice
> 3 tablespoons chopped fresh parsley, preferably flat-leaf
> 2 tablespoons thinly sliced green onion (scallion) or 1 tablespoon snipped chives
> 4 tablespoons water or fresh-squeezed orange juice
> 1 small clove garlic, minced (optional)

Add all the ingredients to a blender and blend until smooth, adding more water if needed. The dressing should have body, but it should be thin enough to pour easily.

> MAKES ABOUT $^3/_4$ CUP (175 ML)
>
> *Preparation time:* about 7 minutes

Asian Slaw

Toasted sunflower seeds add concentrated nutrition and extra flavor to this more healthful version of an American favorite.

$^1/_2$ head cabbage
$^1/_2$ teaspoon sea salt
1 large carrot, peeled if not organic, and finely grated
$^1/_3$ cup (75 ml) vegan or natural mayonnaise
2 teaspoons umeboshi vinegar
$1^1/_2$ teaspoons brown rice vinegar or fresh lemon juice
1 teaspoon brown rice malt syrup
4 tablespoons sunflower seeds, for garnish

1. Cut the cabbage half in half again lengthwise. Remove the tough core. Slice the cabbage crosswise, as thinly as possible.

2. Rinse cabbage and drain well (shake to remove excess water or use a salad spinner), then place in a large bowl. Add salt, toss well and knead (squeeze by handfuls to help soften the fibers). Set aside for at least 20 minutes, then squeeze out excess water.

3. Add the carrot to the cabbage and toss until evenly mixed.

4. Make the dressing by combining the mayonnaise, umeboshi vinegar, brown rice vinegar or lemon juice, and rice syrup. Add the dressing to vegetables and toss well.

5. Toast the sunflower seeds in a dry skillet over medium heat, stirring constantly for about 5 minutes, or until golden and fragrant. Transfer to a small bowl.

6. If time permits, chill the salad slightly in the refrigerator.

7. To serve, top with a sprinkling of the toasted seeds. Serve remaining seeds on the side to be added to individual servings, as desired.

SERVES 4

Preparation time: 15 minutes plus at least 20 minutes to allow salt to draw liquid from the cabbage

Cooking time: 5 minutes

Scallops in Japanese Plum Sauce

This tangy and succulent dish is based on one of Lisa Turner's recipes in *Mostly Macro* (Healing Arts Press, 1995). It is easy to prepare and can be enjoyed as is, or try serving it over ribbon pasta, such as parsley garlic ribbons.

2 tablespoons umeboshi paste
2 teaspoons brown rice malt syrup or agave syrup
2 tablespoons fresh lemon juice
1 tablespoon tahini
2 teaspoons crushed kuzu starch, dissolved in 2 tablespoons cool water
1 tablespoon toasted sesame oil
1 tablespoon minced garlic
$1^1/_2$ tablespoons minced fresh ginger
$1^1/_4$ lbs (600 g) sea scallops, rinsed and drained
Pinch of freshly ground black pepper
$^1/_2$ cup (125 ml) dry white wine
2 tablespoons snipped chives
4 tablespoons chopped fresh parsley, preferably flat-leaf

1. In a small bowl combine the umeboshi paste, syrup, lemon juice, tahini and kuzu and set aside.

2. In a medium sauté pan heat the oil over medium heat, add the garlic and ginger and sauté for 15 seconds.

3. Add the scallops and a pinch of pepper and toss to coat the scallops with the oil and herb mixture. Add the wine, bring to a simmer, lower the heat, cover and gently simmer for 2 minutes.

4. Add the chives and parsley, then add the umeboshi mixture and stir it into the wine. Continue stirring until the liquid returns to a simmer and the sauce begins to thicken.

5. Cover and gently simmer for 5 minutes, or until the scallops are just cooked through. Do not overcook or they will become tough. Serve immediately.

SERVES 4

Preparation time: 10 to 12 minutes
Cooking time: about 10 minutes

餅

MOCHI: SWEET RICE CAKES

Mochi, a delicious whole-grain food, is made from a glutinous, high-protein variety of rice called sweet rice. The rice is soaked, steamed and pounded; then it is allowed to dry until it is firm enough to slice.

Late in December, traditional Japanese villages resound with the rhythmic pounding of sweet rice as families prepare mochi for the festive New Year's meal. A large, smooth bowl made from a hollowed-out log (carved generations before) and a heavy wooden mallet are set in place as the annual mochi-pounding custom begins. It is usually the grandmother who begins the ritual by placing steamed rice into the hollowed log. After each resonant stroke of the grandfather's mallet, the grandmother turns the rice. The elders work together quickly and rhythmically. Grandmother bobs in, turns the mound, then leans aside each time the mallet crashes down, releasing billows of steam from the hot rice.

After being pounded into a homogenous mass, the mochi is formed into small, flat cakes or balls known as *o-hagi*. Coated with sesame seeds, azuki bean paste or peanuts, o-hagi is a children's favorite. The remaining mochi is allowed to dry, then it is stored in a cold place or refrigerated for later use.

Although some rural families in Japan still pound mochi by hand, most homemade mochi is prepared using small electric machines that do the pounding. Several small mochi shops make a delicious shelf-stable mochi for the natural foods market. Some of these are even made with organic brown rice. In one family shop in Nagoya, the seven-day process begins by steaming 1,200 pounds (545 kg) of sweet brown rice, which yields about 1,600 pounds (725 kg) of mochi. The steamed rice is passed through a grinder that is similar to, but much larger than, the hand grinder used to chop meat. Grinding changes the whole grains of sweet brown rice into a sticky dough.

Next, the sweet rice dough is pounded about sixty times by a uniquely designed automatic pounding machine. During the pounding stage, individual grains of rice are further broken down until they form a smooth, sticky mass. Mochi makers feel this hard pounding is what gives mochi its concentrated energy.

On the days leading up to the New Year the sound of steamed sweet rice being pounded into mochi can be heard in the Japanese countryside.

After pounding, while the mochi is still warm and soft, it is placed in molding boxes to set. The boxes are then placed in a refrigerator for three days.

The chilled mochi is cut easily into small blocks about the size of dominos.

To prevent spoilage, mochi is quickly vacuum-packed and sterilized using steam heat, which gives mochi a one-year shelf life and enables it to be shipped around the world.

In Japan, as well as in natural foods stores in the United States, the most popular mochi is made with 100 percent sweet brown rice. However, adding millet, mugwort or black sesame seeds to the sweet brown rice makes other types of different colored mochi with various flavors.

Because brown rice mochi is made with whole sweet brown rice, it contains all the beneficial nutrition of brown rice. Whole brown rice contains a generous supply of B vitamins, plus calcium, phosphorus and iron. Also, because the natural process leaves the rice germ intact, whole grain mochi contains important fatty acids not found in highly processed commercial white rice mochi.

Japanese folklore and traditional medicine attest to mochi's ability to warm the body and increase energy. According to traditional Eastern medicine, mochi's sweet taste nourishes the pancreas, spleen and stomach.

Physically strengthening and easy to digest, mochi is an excellent food for people who are in a weakened condition. Japanese farmers and laborers favor mochi during colder months because of its reputation for increasing one's stamina.

Mochi is recommended for such health problems as anemia, blood sugar imbalances and weak intestines. Pregnant or new mothers benefit, because it strengthens both mother and child, and encourages a plentiful supply of milk in nursing women. Mochi made with the herb mugwort, which grows wild throughout Japan, is particularly high in calcium and iron and is traditionally given to women after childbirth. Mugwort mochi is also good for people who are anemic and those who want to gain weight.

Some words of caution: It is possible to eat too much mochi. It has a way of growing in your stomach. Oddly, in Japan the antidote for eating too much mochi is more rice! *Nanakusa* (seven herbs of spring) is a simple rice gruel cooked with seven herbs that is often served around the holidays to relieve a bloated stomach. However, we have discovered that the best way to survive a mochi feast is to take a long walk.

SHOPPING FOR MOCHI

Although mochi is still hand-pounded for the holidays, most of the pure white mochi found in Japanese supermarkets and Asian food stores in the United States is made from 100 percent white sweet rice squeezed through a modern grinder/extruder. Pounding mochi is backbreaking work, but mochi produced this way tastes better than the extruded product. What's more, some traditionalists feel extruded mochi lacks the healing qualities of the traditional pounded variety. Also, some modern mochi makers actually cook their products while sterilizing it in the package rather than cooking the rice before packaging and then sterilizing. According to traditionalists, this makes a difference in taste and digestibility of mochi.

Mochi is now available in many natural foods stores. It can usually be found in the refrigerator or freezer, packaged in rectangular blocks weighing about 1 pound (450 g). One Japanese-made product, which is sold in vacuum packages containing nine small cakes, appears on the dry foods shelf. Many Asian markets carry mochi made from white sweet rice. Often four or more small flat cakes of white mochi are packaged together on a foam tray and wrapped in plastic. This type is likely to contain additives, preservatives or sugar, so be sure to check the label before purchasing.

Mochi is versatile and easy to cook. Fresh, homemade mochi can be used immediately to make a variety of tasty o-hagi, a traditional Japanese treat (opposite). Store-bought mochi or homemade mochi that has been shaped and dried can be baked, broiled, grilled, pan-fried or deep-fried. When prepared using any of these methods, mochi puffs up to nearly double its size, developing a crisp exterior and a soft, melting interior. If cooked too long, the surface will crack and the soft inside will ooze out. So watch mochi carefully while it cooks.

Baked, broiled or grilled mochi is often eaten with a sweet miso topping. Baked mochi can also be diced and added to soups during the last minute of cooking. Pan- or deep-fried mochi needs nothing more than a light seasoning of soy sauce or a soy-ginger dip. Mochi can also be rolled in rice malt syrup, then coated with walnut meal and eaten as dessert or served as a healthy snack. Melt a couple pieces of mochi in a waffle iron, then top the delicious whole-grain waffle with warmed rice malt syrup and chopped, toasted pecans or walnuts.

Occasionally mochi becomes dry and begins to crack. Soaking very dry mochi for several hours in cold water will cause it to soften. It can then be prepared in any way.

The recipes in this chapter will show you how to make your own mochi at home as well as providing a variety of ways to prepare this delicious and popular whole-grain treat.

Homemade Mochi

Mochi is fun to make at home, and it enables you to enjoy o-hagi (opposite), which cannot be made with store-bought mochi. In Japan, many people make mochi at home with a specially-designed mochi machine. We find that a standard food grinder—either hand-powered or electric—will make mochi almost effortlessly. Whatever brand of food grinder or chopper you use, it is important to use the fine grinding plate so the grains of cooked rice cannot pass through it intact. A plate with $^1/_8$-inch (3-mm) holes works perfectly, whereas $^3/_{16}$-inch (4-mm) holes are slightly too large. We use a pressure cooker to cook the sweet rice, because it makes the grains softer, but pot-boiling is fine if you do not have a pressure cooker. Although we usually make larger batches of mochi and keep some on hand, the following is a good amount to start with.

    2 cups (400 g) sweet brown rice
    2 cups (475 ml) water
    2 pinches of sea salt

1. Wash the rice, drain well and combine it with the water and salt in a pressure cooker. Cover and bring to pressure over high heat, then reduce to low and cook for 40 minutes. (If boiling, use $1^1/_2$ cups [375 ml] water per 1 cup [200 g] sweet rice, bring to a full boil, then lower the heat and simmer, covered, for 1 hour.)

2. Remove pressure cooker from the heat and allow pressure to return to normal. Open cooker and fluff rice with a fork, then let it rest for a few minutes.

3. Set up the food grinder and place a bowl under the mouth of the grinder to catch the ground rice as it comes out.

4. Fill the hopper and press the rice down with a wooden stamper (never use your fingers!) while grinding. Continue until all the rice has been ground.

5. To make cleanup easy, immediately disassemble the grinder, place the parts in the empty rice pot, fill it with hot water and let them soak.

6. At this point the mochi is sticky and moist. It can be used immediately to make o-hagi (opposite) or allowed to become firm and reserved for later use. If you wish to store some or all of the batch, dust a baking sheet with arrowroot and place the mochi in the center. Sprinkle arrowroot over the surface and roll or pat the fresh mochi into a $1/2$-inch (1-cm)-thick rectangle.

7. Allow the mochi to dry in a cool place for 1 to 2 days before slicing. In warm weather the mochi should be left out for no more than 24 hours, then covered loosely and refrigerated.

8. When it is firm enough to slice and hold its shape, it can be cooked in any of the recipes that follow.

> **Note to Cook**
> During very warm (above 75°F/24°C) or humid weather we recommend storing mochi in Ziploc® sandwich bags. Fill the bags with mochi as it comes out of the grinder. Flatten to an even thickness, seal and refrigerate. After 2 to 3 days these handy, convenient packs will be quite firm and ready to be sliced and cooked. If you want to freeze some, wait until the mochi becomes firm. Otherwise, it will be too sticky and moist when thawed.

MAKES ABOUT 4 CUPS (900 G)
Preparation time: 15 to 30 minutes plus 2 days to dry if not using as fresh mochi
Cooking time: about 1 hour

O-hagi (Mochi Balls)

O-hagi are balls of freshly made mochi that are rolled in any of a number of coatings. Slightly salty coatings best complement the sweet taste of the mochi. For example, gomashio (toasted sesame seeds ground with sea salt) is preferable to unsalted ground sesame seeds.

> 3 cups (675 g) fresh Homemade Mochi (see opposite)
> 1 cup (150 g) Gomashio or Toasted Walnut Meal (see page 120)

1. Moisten the palms of both hands and roll pieces of mochi, about the size of golf balls, between cupped palms until smooth.

2. Roll the balls in Gomashio or Toasted Walnut Meal and arrange on serving platters.

MAKES ABOUT 15 MOCHI BALLS
Preparation time: 15 minutes

Gomashio (Sesame Salt)

In addition to its use in making o-hagi, gomashio is often sprinkled on rice or other grains, noodles or vegetables for added flavor and concentrated nutrition. The essential amino acids in sesame seeds perfectly complement those in brown rice, so these two foods eaten together provide high quality complete protein.

1 cup (150 g) brown sesame seeds
1 teaspoon sea salt

1. Place the sesame seeds in a dry skillet over medium heat and stir constantly for 1 to 2 minutes, or until they are fragrant and begin to pop. Test by squeezing a seed between your thumb and fourth finger. If it crushes easily, the seeds are toasted.

2. As soon as they are done, transfer the seeds from the skillet to a suribachi (Japanese grinding bowl) or mortar to prevent overcooking, which results in a bitter taste. Add the salt.

3. Grind the seeds with the surikoji, or pestle, using a steady, gentle pressure and a circular motion until the mixture is fragrant and about 80 percent of the seeds are crushed. Some oil will be released, giving a moist yet flaky texture.

Note to Cook

If you do not have a suribachi and surikoji or a mortar and pestle, place the seeds between two pieces of wax paper and crush them with a rolling pin.

MAKES 1 CUP (150 G)

Preparation time: 5 minutes
Cooking time: about 2 to 3 minutes

Toasted Walnut Meal

Besides its use in making o-hagi, Toasted Walnut Meal is a delicious condiment on vegetables, grains and salads. When summer squash is in season, we love to briefly steam slices of it, toss the slices in olive oil and minced fresh basil, and generously sprinkle walnut meal over each slice. Pecans can be substituted for the walnuts.

1 cup (125 g) walnuts
1/4 teaspoon sea salt or a dash of shoyu (Japanese soy sauce) or tamari

1. Toast the walnuts in a dry skillet over medium heat, stirring constantly for 3 to 5 minutes, or until crisp and fragrant.

2. Grind the nuts into a fairly fine meal in a blender, suribachi (Japanese grinding bowl) or mortar. If using a blender, transfer the ground walnuts to a shallow bowl.

3. Mix in the sea salt or a little shoyu, to taste.

MAKES 1 CUP (125 G)

Preparation time: 5 minutes
Cooking time: 5 minutes

Mochi Waffles

Here's a quick, whole-grain waffle that's sure to keep you satisfied through the morning hours.

> $^1/_3$ cup (50 g) chopped pecans or walnuts
> 8 pieces mochi, approximately 2 x $2^1/_2$ x $^1/_2$ inches (5 x 6.5 x 1 cm)
> Approximately 4 tablespoons warmed brown rice malt syrup

1. In a dry skillet, toast the nuts over medium heat, stirring constantly, for 3 to 5 minutes, or until lightly browned, crisp and fragrant. Set aside.

2. Heat and oil a waffle iron. Cook 2 pieces of mochi at a time—the iron's lid will press down on the mochi and begin to melt it so it will spread and form a waffle. Check occasionally and remove when the surface is crisp. Re-oil the waffle iron between each batch of mochi.

3. Serve hot, with a drizzle of warmed rice syrup and a sprinkling of toasted nuts.

> SERVES 4
>
> Preparation time: 5 minutes
>
> Cooking time: 20 minutes

Sweet Pecan Mochi

Sweet Pecan Mochi is a delicious and satisfying dessert, snack or special breakfast treat.

> 1 cup (125 g) pecan halves
> $^1/_8$ teaspoon sea salt
> 8 pieces mochi (approximately 2 x $2^1/_2$ in/5 x 6.5 cm)
> $^1/_3$ cup (75 ml) brown rice malt syrup, warmed

1. In a dry skillet over medium heat, toast the pecans, stirring constantly for 3 to 5 minutes, or until crisp and fragrant.

2. Transfer pecans to a *suribachi* (Japanese grinding bowl) or mortar, and grind into a coarse meal. Add salt, toss well and taste. Add more salt, if desired. Set aside.

3. Pan-fry the mochi (see Pan-Fried Mochi with Shoyu-Ginger Dipping Sauce, page 123).

4. When tender, dip each piece in rice syrup to coat. Shake off excess syrup, then roll pieces in a generous amount of toasted pecan meal. Enjoy!

> SERVES 4
>
> *Preparation time: 10 minutes*
>
> *Cooking time: 15 minutes*

| O-zoni (New Year's Mochi Soup) |

Symbolizing longevity and wealth in Japan, mochi is traditionally included in the first meal of the New Year, usually in soup or stew.

1 burdock root (*gobo*)
1 large carrot
8 cups (2 liters) Shiitake Stock (see page 92) or Kombu Stock (see page 176)
$^1/_2$ teaspoon sea salt
8 fresh shiitake or button mushrooms, sliced
6 pieces mochi (approximately 2 x $2^1/_2$ in/5 x 6.5 cm)
4 Chinese (napa) cabbage leaves (or other tender greens), chopped
3 green onions (scallions), trimmed and cut into 1-in (2.5-cm) lengths
1 tablespoon mirin
$^1/_4$ to $^1/_3$ cup (50 to 75 g) mellow white miso, or to taste, or 2 tablespoons shoyu (Japanese soy sauce)

1. Scrub the burdock. Cut it into 2-inch (5-cm)-long, thin matchstick strips. Immediately place in cold water to prevent discoloration.

2. Cut the carrot into slightly thicker matchsticks.

3. Drain the burdock and combine with the stock and salt in a saucepan. Simmer for 10 to 15 minutes, or until the burdock is nearly tender.

4. Add the mushrooms and carrots and simmer for 10 minutes.

5. While the soup is cooking, preheat the oven to 350°F (175°C). Cut the mochi squares into bite-size pieces and place on a lightly oiled baking sheet. Bake until slightly brown and puffy. (The time will vary significantly depending on the mochi's firmness. Check frequently to avoid overcooking.) Remove and set aside.

6. Add the cabbage, green onions and mirin to the soup, and cook 5 minutes more.

7. When the cabbage is just tender, add mochi and miso or shoyu. (If using miso, dissolve it in a little of the broth before adding it to the soup.) Gently simmer 1 minute only. The mochi will dissolve if overcooked. Serve immediately.

SERVES 5 TO 6

Preparation time: 20 minutes
Cooking time: about 30 minutes

Pan-Fried Mochi with Shoyu-Ginger Dipping Sauce

Cooked mochi is often served with a shoyu-and-ginger dipping sauce, as in this recipe. If you are missing ingredients for the dip, the cooked pieces can be rolled in a mixture of equal parts shoyu and water, then wrapped in 1-inch (2.5-cm)-wide strips of toasted nori. Either way, it is a quick, wholesome and delicious treat.

Shoyu-Ginger Dipping Sauce
$^2/_3$ cup (175 ml) Kombu Stock (see page 176) or Kombu-Shiitake Stock (see page 176)
1 tablespoon shoyu (Japanese soy sauce)
2 teaspoons mirin
1 teaspoon finely grated fresh ginger
3 tablespoons peeled and finely grated daikon (optional)
. . . .
2 teaspoons toasted sesame oil
6 pieces mochi (approximately 2 x $2^1/_2$ in/5 x 6.5 cm)

1. To prepare the dipping sauce, combine the stock, shoyu and mirin in a small saucepan and bring to a simmer for 1 minute. Remove from the heat.

2. Add the ginger and, if desired, daikon. Serve in small individual bowls.

3. To cook the mochi, heat the oil in a large frying pan. Add the mochi and cook, covered, over low heat for 5 minutes, or until the mochi bottoms are slightly browned.

4. Flip mochi pieces. If you are using very firm mochi, add 1 to 2 teaspoons water to create some steam to soften the mochi, cover again and cook a few minutes more. To prevent the mochi pieces from melting, remove them from the heat as soon as they are cooked.

SERVES 3

Preparation time: 5 minutes
Cooking time: 10 minutes

Fried Mochi in Broth

Deep-fried mochi is delicious when served with a dip or wrapped in toasted nori strips, but we like it best when it is served in broth.

2 cups (475 ml) Shiitake Stock (see page 92) or Kombu Stock (see page 176)
$2^1/_2$ to 3 tablespoons shoyu (Japanese soy sauce)
2 tablespoons mirin
Vegetable oil, such as canola or safflower, for deep-frying
9 pieces mochi (approximately 2 x $2^1/_2$ in/5 x 6.5 cm)
$^1/_3$ cup (60 g) peeled and finely grated daikon
2 green onions (scallions), minced

1. In a small saucepan, combine the stock, shoyu and mirin. Simmer briefly and keep hot but not boiling.

2. In a pot, heat 2 inches (5 cm) of oil to 325°F/160°C (until a drop of flour-water batter sinks to the bottom of the pot and immediately rises to the surface). With a slotted spoon, gently place mochi, 2 to 3 pieces at a time, into the oil and fry, turning occasionally until the outside is crisp and golden. Drain on paper towels. Continue until all the mochi has been fried.

3 In individual serving bowls, place 2 pieces of mochi on the bottom and 1 piece on top to form a pyramid. Pour about $^1/_2$ cup (125 ml) hot broth over each bowl of mochi. Top with the grated daikon and a sprinkle of green onion.

SERVES 3

Preparation time: 10 minutes
Cooking time: 10 to 15 minutes

麺

NOODLES: TRADITIONAL JAPANESE PASTA

The Japanese are experts when it comes to making and cooking noodles. It is believed that noodles originated in China and were passed to Japan, where they have been a favorite food for centuries. More noodles are probably eaten in Japan today than any other food except rice—the numerous, crowded noodle bars that abound in Japanese cities attest their popularity. The Japanese feel that their traditional fast food must be eaten immediately, before the piping hot broth has made the noodles limp. This means you must take in a cooling breath with each bite. The resultant slurping sounds can be strange to Western ears, but it is a sign of enjoyment and good etiquette in Japan. In fact, eating noodles slowly and quietly is offensive to the cook.

Although Italian-style pastas are still better known in the West, Asian noodles are becoming very popular in the United States, Canada and Europe. Light and easy to digest, delicious and satisfying, Japanese egg-free noodles are a versatile food. They make a filling lunch, convenient snack or, when served with one or two side dishes, a complete dinner. Quick to prepare, they provide the perfect solution when you have unexpected guests or find yourself at mealtime with "nothing in the works."

Japanese noodles have unique characteristics and health-promoting properties that are not found in traditional Western-style pasta. Generally speaking, Japanese noodles have less gluten than typical durum wheat pasta and so they are considered more digestible and may cause much less of an allergic reaction in wheat-sensitive people. The small quantity of salt, usually found in Japanese noodles, also helps to aid digestion.

Soba

The main ingredient of soba is buckwheat—a primitive grain that is rarely eaten in the United States. However, buckwheat is the best and, in some cases, the only source of some bio-compounds that are vital to the healthy functioning of cells and enzymes. This is why adding soba, particularly 100 percent buckwheat soba, to your diet can have a positive effect on your health.

Buckwheat is unusually rich in protein (12 to 15 percent) and the essential amino acid lysine (5 to 7 percent), which is lacking in most cereal grains. Buckwheat is also abundant in lipids, minerals (iron, phosphorus and copper), and vitamins B1 and B2.

This wonder grain is very high in rutin (4 to 6 percent), an essential nutrient that is not found in other grains, such as rice and wheat, or beans. Rutin is important, because it strengthens capillaries and thus helps people suffering from arteriosclerosis and high blood pressure. Rutin belongs to a group of plant compounds called bioflavonoids that also include the important catechins of green tea and polyphenols of red wine. Recent studies have shown that bioflavonoids are powerful antioxidants that fight free radicals. Free radicals are said to be responsible for as much as 90 percent of diseases, such as cancer, arteriosclerosis, strokes and age-related senility. Research in Japan has shown that 30 milligrams of rutin per day meets the body's needs. Because one serving of high protein soba contains about 100 milligrams of rutin, one serving of soba a day is more than enough.

Vitamin P is similar to rutin in that it increases capillary strength, but it also has an important synergistic effect on vitamin C absorption. Although vitamin P is found in trace amounts in some vegetables, buckwheat is the only significant source.

Choline, another important micronutrient found in buckwheat, plays an important role in metabolism, particularly regulating blood pressure and liver function. As a neutralizing agent, choline can support the liver when it is overburdened by alcoholic beverages. It makes sense that soba noodles and broth are often served in Japan after big parties.

After centuries of eating soba noodles, the Japanese have come to respect the healing power of soba, which has been confirmed by medical researchers. The high dietary fiber in 100 percent buckwheat soba helps the body eliminate cholesterol. Further, the regular consumption of protein-rich soba has also been associated with reduction in body fat.

Although eating soba noodles that are made with 80 to 100 percent buckwheat is the best way to get the nutritional benefits of buckwheat, there are several varieties of soba, such as cha soba, mugwort soba and jinenjo soba, that add the powder of important medicinal plants to a basic soba recipe. Cha (tea) soba, made by adding green tea powder—one of nature's most medicinal foods—to soba, is both colorful and healing.

Mugwort soba is made with the addition of wild mugwort (*yomogi*) powder, which gives this noodle a striking green color. Mugwort is high in several minerals and is often recommended for anemic conditions. Jinenjo (mountain yam) soba is a very popular noodle in Japan. A strengthening food rich in digestive enzymes, jinenjo helps bind the buckwheat flour, resulting in smooth, silky noodles that are easy to digest. Not surprisingly, jinenjo is considered an important Japanese folk remedy for people with weak digestion. Some of these varieties are available in the West at natural foods stores or via mail order sites (see the Shopping Resource, page 221).

Udon and Somen

Japanese wheat noodles, such as udon and somen, are low in fat and high in complex carbohydrates for sustained energy. Although udon and somen do not have the high protein and mineral content of some soba noodles, they are an excellent source of high quality protein, and brown rice udon contains some complementary amino acids of rice and wheat.

Udon is legendary in Japan for its digestibility. Laboratory experiments in Japan using digestive enzymes and controlled temperatures have shown that udon is digested much faster than other noodles and three times faster than beef. Japanese scientists believe that the kneading of flour during the manufacturing process enhances the digestibility of udon. Kneading develops and concentrates the wheat protein, which then mixes with the starch molecules and makes them more available to digestive enzymes in the body. Udon digests so quickly that large amounts of blood are not rushed to the stomach, so the body retains heat in the extremities. What's more, experiments have shown that udon creates body heat that lasts much longer than heat produced by ramen, soba or Western-style durum wheat pastas. This is why udon and dashi broth is a popular winter food for traditional Japanese who do not heat their homes, even in the northern regions. It is also a favorite food for people with the flu, because it quickly provides sustained energy and warmth that promotes healing.

HOW AUTHENTIC JAPANESE NOODLES ARE MADE

 Although you simply cannot beat the fresh taste and texture of professionally made *te-uchi* (handmade) noodles at a noodle bar, there are a few small shops in Japan that still manufacture soba and udon with the highest quality ingredients in a simple, uncomplicated way that duplicates the handmade process.

The traditional process begins by adding sea salt brine to freshly stone-ground organic flour. The correct salt content is critical for developing the right amount of gluten in the dough and for insurance against rancidity. The dough is thoroughly mixed and kneaded, then allowed to rest to develop the gluten.

After several hours, the dough is checked for the correct level of stickiness. It is then passed through a series of rollers to form thin, long, continuous sheets. The last roller has a cutter attached, which can be changed to cut the dough into either thin *ito* (thread) soba and somen or thick, traditional udon or soba noodles. Whether thick or thin, the long strands emerging from the cutter are chopped into six-foot sections and carried to a special drying room.

Not willing to compromise quality, traditional producers, like generations before them, still hang their noodles over bamboo rods to dry at natural temperatures. Fans are employed in the drying rooms to keep the air circulating. Artificial heat, common in modern processing to speed up the drying process, is not used because it adversely affects quality. From start to finish, the methods used to make traditional Japanese noodles are based on the way noodles are made at home.

Traditional Japanese pasta is slowly air-dried and then cut and packaged.

After drying for at least thirty hours, the noodles are cut into shorter lengths for packaging. The whole process takes about four times as long as the modern process, which can be completed in an eight-hour day.

SHOPPING FOR JAPANESE NOODLES

Only noodles made by the slow, time-honored methods outlined above have the mouth-feel, flavor and healing energy of traditional Japanese noodles. The drying process is very important, and quick, commercial drying with hot air can destroy some of the noodle's healing qualities and flavor. In fact, research in Italy has shown that drying pasta too quickly can cause wheat protein to break up into toxic substances. On the other hand, careless, prolonged drying can cause mold and bacteria to grow on noodles. Only careful, natural drying, such as in a traditional noodle shop, will produce a high quality product with all the flavor and health benefits of traditional noodles.

Japanese noodles made with preservatives and bleached white flour are very common in Asian supermarkets. Commercial salt that has been bleached and stripped of all its micronutrients is added to most noodles that are not made for the natural foods market. When shopping for Japanese noodles, check the ingredients on the package carefully. Look for noodles made with organic flour and sea salt. When buying ramen, be sure that it does not contain oil or preservatives.

During the heat of summer, Japanese noodles are wonderfully refreshing when served floating in a bowl of ice water and accompanied by a chilled dipping sauce. In winter, noodles are commonly served in hot, shoyu-seasoned broth. Whether in soups or salads, sautéed with vegetables, baked or topped with sauce, noodles are always delicious.

In addition to the recipes in this chapter, which present a wide range of cooking styles and tastes, you will find a number of recipes calling for Japanese noodles in other sections of this book, including the most popular and traditional Japanese dish, Noodles in Broth (page 193). With the interesting variety of Japanese noodles available and the many ways to prepare them throughout the year, we never tire of this traditional Japanese "fast food." Quick to prepare, noodles provide the perfect solution when you have unexpected guests. In the time it takes for the water to boil and the noodles to cook, you can prepare a broth or sauce and a vegetable dish and voilà! You have created a nutritious and satisfying meal.

Choosing the Right Noodle

Although there are many varieties within each type, there are two main categories of Japanese noodles: those made from buckwheat (soba) and those made from wheat (udon and somen). Because buckwheat requires cooler, drier growing conditions, the thin brownish-gray soba noodle is most popular in northern Japan. Natural foods stores and Asian markets offer a wide variety of soba noodles. One hundred percent buckwheat soba is a hearty, delicious, wheat-free noodle that comes in salt-free and salted varieties. Most soba noodles are made from 40 to 80 percent buckwheat flour, with the remainder being unbleached white flour. Ito soba, which contains 40 percent buckwheat flour, is a thin, delicate noodle that cooks quickly and easily absorbs the flavor of broths, sauces or seasonings.

Udon is a thick, chewy, beige wheat noodle that resembles linguine and is favored in Kyoto and southern Japan. The varieties sold in natural foods stores are made from 100 percent whole-wheat flour, or a combination of whole wheat and unbleached white flour. One hundred percent whole-wheat udon is a sturdy noodle with a robust whole-wheat flavor and textured appearance. For a noodle that will readily absorb the flavors of broths, sauces and seasonings, use lighter, smoother udons—typically those made with some unbleached white flour. Brown rice udon (*genmai udon*), a combination of brown rice flour and wheat flour, is not a traditional Japanese food, but rather was developed especially for the natural foods market.

Though Japanese noodles are well suited to a variety of cooking styles and preparations, it is important to choose the right noodle for the dish you want to prepare. For example, while typical soba and udon are excellent choices for stir-fried noodles, thin, delicate varieties of soba, such as ito and cha soba, are not recommended for frying, and 100 percent soba is also a poor choice. Somen, a thin wheat noodle, is too delicate for frying. The following guidelines will help you choose the variety of Japanese noodle that will give the best results in different types of dishes.

Noodles in Broth. In Japan most noodles are enjoyed in a shoyu-seasoned dipping broth. Any Japanese noodle can be used in this way. When using soba, the broth is usually a little more intensely flavored. That is, more shoyu and mirin are added than when serving udon or somen. Also, whereas broth for soba is traditionally seasoned with wasabi, Japanese seven-spice is more commonly used with udon.

Fried Noodles. Stir-fried Japanese noodles with vegetables and tofu or tempeh is a tasty, complete meal that can be prepared in short order. Udon or typical soba and jinenjo soba (containing 40 to 60 percent buckwheat) are the best choices when making stir-fried noodle recipes. Cook the noodles until they are nearly but not completely tender, rinse and drain well, then add them with your vegetables or other ingredients to your stir-fry for the last minute or two of cooking.

Noodles with Sauces. Although any type of Japanese noodle can be matched with a sauce, udon is more versatile than soba, because it has a less assertive flavor.

Noodle Salads. Soba is surprisingly well suited to noodle salads, especially when a spicy or Asian-style dressing is used. Two examples are Vegetable Soba Salad (page 34) and Soba Salad with Spicy Peanut Sauce (page 136). Somen is the noodle of choice for light salads and those with fruity dressings such as Sesame-Orange Dressing (page 35).

Noodles for Dipping. Delicate cha soba and ito soba are perfect for dipping in chilled broth. Somen noodles are also ideally suited for this popular summer staple.

Noodle Rolls. The same light, delicate noodles recommended for dipping are called for when preparing nori-wrapped Noodle Rolls (page 182).

NOODLE COOKING BASICS

In addition to choosing the right noodle, it is important to cook them properly. There are some significant differences in the way Italian and Japanese noodles are cooked, so if you are not already an expert, be sure to read these two basic cooking methods and tips. Experiment with both methods to decide which you prefer. The "shock" method, which some cooks swear by, is the more traditional way to cook Japanese noodles. I find that both methods work, and when harried I prefer the ease of the first method. Note that because most Japanese noodles are made with salt, it is not necessary or advisable to add salt to the cooking water. Regardless of which method you use, be sure to add plenty of water— using too little water will result in sticky, unevenly cooked noodles.

> 8 oz (225 g) dried noodles (serves 2 to 3 people)
> About 8 cups (2 liters) unsalted water

Method One

1. In a large pot, bring the water to a full rolling boil. Add only about 3 to 4 ounces (90 to 125 g) of the noodles at a time so as not to completely stop the boiling. If too many noodles are added at once, the water will not quickly

return to a boil and the noodles will be overcooked on the outside and undercooked on the inside. Stir gently until the water is boiling rapidly again to prevent the noodles from sticking to the bottom of the pan.

2. Cook the noodles over medium-high heat to maintain a continuous boil. (Go to Step 2 in Method Two.)

Method Two (known as the "shock" method)

1. Follow Step 1 in Method One. Once all the noodles have been added to the pot and the water returns to a rolling boil, add 1 cup (235 ml) of cold water to "shock" the noodles. When the water returns to a boil again, another cup of cold water is added. This is repeated three or four times until the noodles are cooked.

2. Test the noodles often to avoid overcooking. The noodles should be cooked until they are tender yet still firm, the equivalent of the Italian "*al dente.*" A properly cooked noodle should be slightly chewy. When broken in half, the noodle should be the same color throughout.

3. Once cooked, immediately drain and briefly rinse the noodles in a cold-water bath or under cold running water to prevent further cooking and to keep the noodles from sticking together. When they have cooled enough to handle, drain and set aside until ready to assemble your dish.

Serving Tips. If cooked Japanese noodles have been drained and sitting too long, they may become a little dry. When using them in a salad or other recipe that is not served hot, simply rinse them under cold water and drain again before serving. If reheating is necessary, undercook the noodles slightly. Then, just before serving, briefly dip them into boiling water or broth, one serving at a time. until just heated through. Drain well and serve.

Udon, Spinach and Shiitake with Pecan Topping

This East-West dish starts off with the classical Mediterranean duo of olive oil and garlic, then veers East with the addition of shiitake, udon and shoyu. Toasted, ground pecans add flavor and protein.

Pecan Topping
$^2/_3$ cup (100 g) pecans
$^1/_4$ teaspoon sea salt
. . . .
8 oz (250 g) dried udon noodles
1 tablespoon plus 1 teaspoon extra virgin olive oil
3 cloves (about 2 teaspoons) minced garlic
3 cups (250 g) fresh shiitake mushroom caps, thinly sliced
2 pinches of sea salt
2 pinches of freshly ground black pepper
4 teaspoons shoyu (Japanese soy sauce)
6 oz (175 g) spinach (about 6 cups)

1. To prepare the topping, toast the pecans in a skillet over medium-high heat for about 5 minutes, or until they begin to brown and become fragrant. Transfer the pecans to a *suribachi* (Japanese grinding bowl) or mortar, add the salt and pound the nuts to a coarse meal.

2. In a large saucepan, bring 8 cups (2 liters) of water to a rolling boil and add the noodles. To prevent them from sticking together, stir until the water returns to a boil. Cook until tender but still firm. Immediately drain the noodles and rinse them briefly under cold running water or in a cold-water bath. Drain and set aside.

3. In a large skillet, heat the oil over medium heat, add the garlic and sauté for 15 seconds. Add the shiitake and 1 pinch each of salt and pepper and sauté for 2 to 3 minutes. Add 1 teaspoon of the shoyu and stir.

4. Add the spinach and an additional pinch of salt and pepper. Cook for 1 to 2 minutes. Sprinkle with an additional teaspoon of the shoyu.

5. Add the cooked udon and the remaining 2 teaspoons of shoyu. Toss well. Add a little more shoyu, if desired. Continue cooking for 1 to 2 minutes, then serve immediately. Place the pecan topping on the table so it can be added to individual servings.

SERVES 2

Preparation time: 10 to 15 minutes
Cooking time: 30 minutes

Thai Udon with Snow Peas

This quick and easy noodle dish is deeply satisfying and full of flavor. It's one of our family favorites.

$2^1/2$ cups (about 6 oz/175 g) snow peas, tips and strings removed
$1/2$ red bell pepper, deseeded and cut into thin strips
12 oz (350 g) dried udon noodles
1 tablespoon toasted sesame oil
4 green onions (scallions), sliced
1 tablespoon peeled and minced fresh ginger
1 tablespoon minced garlic
$3/4$ cup (175 ml) light coconut milk
$1/2$ cup (125 ml) water
$1/3$ cup (75 ml) tomato paste
2 teaspoons curry powder
$1/2$ teaspoon sea salt
Dash of ground red pepper (cayenne)
3 tablespoons minced fresh coriander (cilantro), $1/2$ set aside for garnish

1. In medium saucepan, bring 4 cups (1 liter) of water to a boil for the vegetables, and in a large pot, bring 10 cups (2.5 liters) of water to a rolling boil for the noodles.

2. Add the peas and bell pepper to the saucepan, simmer for 2 to 3 minutes, then drain well and set aside.

3. Add the noodles to the pot of boiling water. To prevent them from sticking together, stir until the water returns to a boil. Cook until tender but still firm. Immediately drain the noodles and rinse them briefly under cold running water or in a cold-water bath. Drain and set aside.

4. While the noodles are cooking, heat the oil in a medium skillet, add the green onions, ginger and garlic, and sauté over medium-high heat for 1 to 2 minutes.

5. Stir in the coconut milk, water, tomato paste, curry powder, salt and ground red pepper, and bring to a boil. Reduce the heat and simmer for 5 minutes, stirring frequently. Add $1^1/_2$ tablespoons of the fresh coriander during the last minute of cooking.

6. In a large bowl, combine the noodles, vegetables and coconut milk mixture, tossing well. Sprinkle with the remaining fresh coriander and serve.

SERVES 3 TO 4

Preparation time: 15 minutes
Cooking time: 20 minutes

| Udon with Miso-Tahini Sauce |

The recipe below is simply garnished with green onion. For a heartier version, top the noodles and sauce with a colorful assortment of steamed vegetables.

8 oz (250 g) dried udon noodles
4 tablespoons sweet white miso
3 to 4 tablespoons tahini (ground sesame seed paste)
$^1/_3$ cup (75 ml) water
2 tablespoons brown rice vinegar
1 tablespoon mirin
2 teaspoons fresh ginger juice (finely grate fresh ginger and squeeze to extract juice)
Pinch of dried basil or thyme (optional)
Minced green onion (scallion), for garnish

1. In a large saucepan, bring 8 cups (2 liters) water to a rolling boil and add the noodles. To prevent them from sticking together, stir until the water returns to a boil. Cook until tender but still firm. Immediately drain noodles and rinse them briefly under cold running water or in a cold-water bath. Drain and set aside.

2. Combine the miso and tahini in a saucepan. Add the water, a little at a time, and mix well to form a smooth sauce. Add remaining ingredients and bring just to a simmer. If too thick, add a little more water; if too thin, simmer briefly to thicken.

3. To serve, place the noodles in individual serving bowls, spoon the sauce over the top and garnish with the green onion.

SERVES 2 TO 3

Preparation time: 5 minutes
Cooking time: about 20 minutes

Summer Soba

Cooling and refreshing when little else appeals, this traditional noodle dish is a favorite Japanese lunch on hot summer days. Light, delicate varieties such as ito soba and cha soba are ideal noodle choices.

Dipping Broth

3 cups (700 ml) Kombu-Bonito stock (see page 176) or Kombu-Shiitake Stock (see page 176)

$1/4$ teaspoon sea salt

3 tablespoons shoyu (Japanese soy sauce)

2 tablespoons mirin

8 oz (250 g) dried soba (buckwheat) noodles

Condiments

1 teaspoon wasabi powder plus $1/2$ teaspoon water

1 teaspoon finely grated fresh ginger

$1/4$ sheet nori, toasted and sliced into very thin ribbons

1 green onion (scallion) very thinly sliced on the diagonal

1. Combine the stock, salt, shoyu and mirin in a small saucepan, bring to a boil, and simmer for 1 to 2 minutes. Pour the broth into a bowl and refrigerate until chilled.

2. In a large saucepan, bring 8 cups (2 liters) of water to a rolling boil and add the noodles. To prevent them from sticking together, stir until the water returns to a boil. Cook until tender but still firm. Immediately drain the noodles and rinse them briefly under cold running water or in a cold-water bath. Drain and set aside.

3. To make wasabi paste, add the $1/2$ teaspoon of water to the powder and mix to form a thick paste. Prepare the other condiments.

4. To serve, divide cooked noodles and put them into small noodle baskets, plates or soup bowls. (If noodles are beginning to stick together, rinse under cold water and drain thoroughly before serving.) Pour chilled dipping broth into separate small individual bowls. Set out prepared wasabi, ginger, nori and green onion on the table so everyone can add them to the broth to suit their own taste.

5. Dip each bite of noodles in the broth. If the dipping sauce becomes diluted and bland, replace it with fresh broth.

Note to Cook

If you're unsure about what ratio of dipping sauce to condiments will be tasty, we recommend starting with about 2 teaspoons of green onion and $1/8$ teaspoon wasabi paste or ginger to $1/2$ to $2/3$ cup (125 to 150 ml) of broth.

SERVES 2

Preparation time: 10 minutes

Cooking time: 20 minutes

Stir-Fried Soba and Vegetables

Medium-thick soba noodles with a 40 to 60 percent buckwheat content, such as Jinenjo and mugwort, are delicious briefly stir-fried with vegetables and seasoned with shoyu and mirin. Thin, delicate sobas and hearty 100 percent buckwheat soba are not good choices for frying. Udon noodles can be substituted for the soba in this recipe.

8 oz (250 g) dried soba (buckwheat) noodles

$1^1/_2$ tablespoons toasted sesame oil

1 dried Japanese chile, seeded and minced, or $^1/_4$ teaspoon dried red pepper flakes (optional)

2 to 3 shallots, minced

1 carrot, sliced into thin matchsticks

3 cups (225 g) thinly sliced Chinese (napa) cabbage

1 handful snow peas, or other edible pod peas, tips and strings removed and cut into 2 or 3 pieces

4 to 5 green onions (scallions), thinly sliced on the diagonal

1 tablespoon minced fresh ginger

Pinch of sea salt

2 to $2^1/_2$ tablespoons shoyu (Japanese soy sauce) or tamari

2 tablespoons mirin

1. In large saucepan, bring 8 cups (2 liters) of water to a rolling boil and add the noodles. To prevent them from sticking together, stir until the water returns to a boil. Cook until tender but still firm. Immediately drain the noodles and rinse them briefly under cold running water or in a cold-water bath. Drain and set aside.

2. Heat the oil in a large skillet over medium heat and sauté the chile and shallots briefly. Increase the heat to medium-high, add the carrot and sauté for 1 to 2 minutes, then add the Chinese cabbage and continuing sautéing for another 2 minutes. Add the peas, green onions, ginger and a pinch of salt and sauté 1 to 2 minutes more. The vegetables should still be crunchy, but not raw tasting.

3. Add the cooked noodles, shoyu and mirin and toss until the noodles are heated through and evenly mixed with vegetables and seasonings. Serve immediately.

SERVES 2 TO 3

Preparation time: 15 to 20 minutes

Cooking time: 30 minutes

Soba Salad with Spicy Peanut Sauce

Vary the vegetables according to what is available. Fresh peas, corn, red or green bell peppers and red radishes are tasty, colorful options. The spicy peanut sauce is also delicious served with baked or broiled tofu.

12 oz (375 g) dried soba (buckwheat) noodles
4 cups (250 g) small broccoli florets
2 cups (150 g) thinly sliced Chinese (napa) cabbage
1 large carrot, cut into thin matchsticks
3 green onions (scallions), thinly sliced
1 pickling (Kirby) cucumber, quartered lengthwise, peeled (if waxed) and
   sliced (optional)

Spicy Peanut Sauce
$^1/_2$ cup (125 g) smooth all-natural peanut butter
$^1/_2$ cup (125 ml) warm water
2 tablespoons peanut oil
1 teaspoon minced garlic
1 tablespoon minced fresh ginger
3 tablespoons shoyu (Japanese soy sauce)
1 tablespoon plus 1 teaspoon rice vinegar
1 tablespoon plus 1 teaspoon fresh lime juice
1 tablespoon mirin
$^1/_2$ teaspoon dried red pepper flakes

1. In a large pot, bring 10 cups (2.5 liters) of water to a rolling boil, break the noodles in half and add them to the pot. To prevent noodles from sticking together, stir until the water returns to a boil. Cook until tender but still firm. Immediately drain the noodles and rinse them briefly under cold running water or in a cold-water bath. Drain and set aside in a large serving bowl.

2. Drop the broccoli florets into 4 cups (1 liter) of boiling water in a medium saucepan. Boil for 2 to 3 minutes or until bright green and tender-crisp. Remove the cooked broccoli with a slotted spoon: do not discard the cooking water. Immediately rinse the broccoli under cold water, drain well, and add it to the bowl with the soba.

3. Bring the broccoli cooking water to a boil again, add the Chinese cabbage and carrot and boil for 1 minute. Place the vegetables in a colander, rinse under cold water and drain well. Add the cabbage and carrot to the noodles and broccoli, along with the green onion and cucumber, if using.

4. To prepare the peanut sauce, combine all ingredients in a blender and puree until smooth. Add to noodle mixture, toss gently and serve.

SERVES 4

Preparation time: 15 minutes
Cooking time: 20 minutes

CHAPTER 13

豆
腐

TOFU: THE SQUARE EGG

Tofu's popularity in the West has prompted one American food writer to say, "Tofu is an essential ingredient for modern living." A bold statement, perhaps, but as more people become concerned about their health and the poor quality of animal protein, tofu is becoming a mainstay in the Western diet. Although it is best known in the West by its Japanese name, tofu actually originated in China over two thousand years ago, where legend has it that a cook over-seasoned a soymilk-based soup with too much sea salt. The salt caused the soymilk to coagulate, and the rest is history.

Like many other Chinese foods, tofu's introduction to Japan in the eighth century is closely associated with the spread of Chinese Buddhism. At first tofu was the fare of the more affluent Japanese, but by the sixteenth century, the general population had adopted tofu into their diet and small family shops were preparing several varieties.

Tofu's spread to North America has taken a two-fold path. By 1900 several small tofu shops were supplying tofu to Asians living in large U.S. and Canadian cities. However, tofu's introduction to non-Asians began in the 1960s, and was influenced by the spread of Zen Buddhism and macrobiotics, a philosophy of life that relates eating with health and happiness. Students of Zen and macrobiotics began making tofu and preparing simple recipes just as tofu started to gain popularity in hippie and vegetarian communities. By the 1980s, everything Japanese was becoming the rage and tofu began appearing as little white cubes in the miso soup served in the thousands of sushi bars that had cropped up in Western cities. However, it took American entrepreneurship to push tofu over the top and into supermarkets everywhere. First, cooks and chefs noticed that blended tofu has the mouth-feel and much of the nutrition of dairy foods, so they transformed tofu into a plethora of spreads, dips, shakes and desserts that would have shocked traditional Japanese tofu makers. Next, ambitious natural foods manufacturers began making meat analog products such as tofu burgers and tofu hot dogs. Meanwhile, behind the scenes, soy foods manufacturers were prompting the United States Food and Drug Administration (FDA) to allow health claims on soy foods packaging that touted its ability to reduce the risk of cardiovascular disease. In 1999, when the FDA allowed the health claim, tofu sales and interest in tofu started skyrocketing. In just thirty years, tofu has gone from an esoteric ethnic food to a healthy all-American staple.

In addition to being enjoyed fresh, tofu can be freeze-dried into one of the world's most concentrated forms of complete protein. Invented nearly eight centuries ago by a Buddhist priest, freeze-dried tofu may be the original convenience food. The 2 x 2 $^1/_2$-inch (5 x 6 $^1/_2$-cm) pieces are reconstituted when briefly soaked in plain water. Like a sponge, this food is ready to pick up the flavor of seasonings, sauces and marinades. It cooks in minutes and is delicious when simmered, stir-fried or deep-fried. Freeze-dried tofu adds interest, flavor and nutrition to any style of cooking.

In addition to its ease of use and versatility in the kitchen, tofu is one of the healthiest foods on the planet. It is low in calories and packed with nutrition. In fact, some vegan writers have dubbed tofu the "square egg."

More than most soy foods, tofu is a concentrated source of easy-to-digest complete soy protein. One 4-ounce (115-g) serving of firm tofu contains about 12 grams or 20 percent of the daily requirement of protein. This is about as much as a poached egg, but without the 350 milligrams of cholesterol. What's more, tofu contains the eight essential amino acids that are necessary for human nutrition and are not produced naturally in the body. Amino acids are very important and play a vital role in rebuilding the cells and tissue of the body. Tofu is also a good source of calcium, iron, magnesium, selenium, folic acid, essential B vitamins, choline, fat-soluble vitamin E and linoleic acid, an essential fatty acid important in the regulation of the body's metabolism.

For health conscious people trying to avoid fatty dairy products, or for those who are lactose intolerant, tofu can be an important source of calcium. Calcium from tofu is nearly as easy for the body to assimilate as calcium from milk. The calcium content of tofu depends on the coagulant used and its firmness. Extra-firm tofu made with the coagulant calcium sulfate or calcium chloride has the highest calcium content.

Several recipes in this book combine the nutrition and health benefits of tofu with other healing foods. For example, a combination of tofu and sweet miso in dips, spreads and salad dressings is easily digested, delicious and nutritious. Just one 4-ounce (115-g) serving of Creamy Dill Dip or Creamy Onion Dip (see variation of Stuffed Endive Leaves, page 152) contains the following percentages of the United States Reference Daily Intake (RDI) of protein, vitamins and minerals:

Protein	25%	Calcium	12%
Thiamine	4%	Iron	16%
Niacin	4%		

The FDA, which sets strict guidelines for nutritional labeling, considers a single serving of food that contains 10 percent of the RDI of protein to be "high" in protein. For vegetarians, tofu-miso dishes can be an important source of protein and essential amino acids. What's more, the miso begins to digest the fats, complex sugars and protein of the tofu before it is eaten, making it even more digestible.

Freeze-Dried Tofu

Freeze-dried tofu is one of the world's most concentrated sources of high quality vegetable protein. Six times as concentrated as regular tofu, freeze-dried tofu has twice the protein of an equal weight of fish, beef or chicken, none of the cholesterol and negligible saturated fat. What's more, with a full complement of essential amino acids, the quality of its protein is comparable to that of meat and dairy foods. Freeze-dried tofu, even more than tofu, is also a concentrated source of iron, calcium and phosphorus. Since freeze-dried tofu is concentrated, it has even more of the medicinal benefits of tofu, such as protection against various forms of degenerative disease.

The Secrets of Tofu's Healing Power

Although tofu has long been highly regarded for its great nutritional value, it has only been in the last few decades that medical science has uncovered the secrets of tofu's incredible healing power. Some scientists believe it is the soybean's ability to protect itself from pests that gives tofu its extraordinary medicinal benefits. During the course of its evolution, the soybean plant evolved biochemicals called plant estrogens, or phytoestrogens, that are repulsive to insects. While these substances keep pests away and have survival value for the soybean, they also inhibit and even cure degenerative diseases in humans. Soybean phytoestrogens, also called isoflavones, have been shown to reduce cholesterol, retard or prevent cancer, reduce osteoporosis, help regulate blood sugar and relieve some of the symptoms of menopause. Since tofu is a concentrated source of soy protein, it has a particularly high concentration of isoflavones.

Cardiovascular Disease. On October 25, 1999, the FDA authorized manufacturers of foods that contain soy protein to state on the label that "25 grams per day of soy protein, as part of a diet low in saturated fat and cholesterol, may reduce the risk of heart disease." In 2000, the Nutritional Committee of the American Heart Association published a major statement in the journal *Circulation* officially recommending the inclusion of 25 grams or more of whole soy protein in the daily diet as a means of promoting heart health. According to a report in the *American Journal of Clinical Nutrition*, when tofu and other soy protein are used to replace animal protein in the daily diet, cholesterol levels are reduced even more. The new, controversial study was not an original clinical exploration of soy protein's effects on cholesterol, but instead was a "meta-analysis," a review of all the studies done to date on the subject.

Population studies in Japan and China have shown that soy protein helps prevent coronary heart disease through the reduction of low density lipoprotein (LDL) levels. A 1995 review of thirty-eight clinical studies in *The New England Journal of Medicine* showed that in thirty-four of the studies there was a reduction of the LDL levels. The levels were reduced by about 13 percent on average.

People with high cholesterol seem to benefit the most from a diet high in soy protein. Isoflavones are the active ingredients in soy protein that are responsible for reducing cholesterol, and tofu has been shown to have over twice the concentration as soymilk. In addition to reducing cholesterol levels, soy protein prevents the oxidation of LDL, which contributes to the blockage of arteries. Soy protein also reduces the risk of blood clots and restores damaged blood vessels.

Cancer. Tofu has also been shown to retard or stop the progress of cancer. Some forms of cancer progress quickly due to a rapid increase in the blood supply going to the tumor. Scientists believe that one of the ways soy foods, such as tofu, prevent and retard the spread of some forms of cancer is by inhibiting the proliferation of blood vessels going to the malignant tissue. Isoflavones are thought to be the active ingredients in tofu and other soy foods that attack the cancer's blood supply.

Several human and animal studies have linked tofu consumption with a reduced risk of several forms of cancer. A major study in Singapore, presented at a medical conference in Brussels in September 1996, revealed that women who eat tofu are at lower risk of developing breast cancer than those who do not. Asian women, who typically eat a diet that includes soy foods such as miso, natto, tamari, shoyu and tofu, have much lower levels of breast cancer than Western women. In Japan, where the average woman eats tofu twice a week, the breast cancer rate is 80 percent less than in the United States.

Other population studies have shown a relationship between tofu and reduced cancer risk. A recent study showed that Americans who make tofu a regular part of their diet have significantly lower rates of colon cancer than those who do not eat soy foods. A Hawaiian study of Japanese men found a direct correlation between consumption of tofu and lower rates of prostate cancer.

According to a 1994 article in *Nutrition and Cancer*, isoflavones in laboratory tissue cultures suppress the growth of a large range of cancer cells. Another study in Japan showed that isoflavones increase the effectiveness of certain cancer drugs.

Reduction of Menopausal Symptoms. Some forms of cancer are associated with hormonal changes in women. It is not surprising that tofu has a beneficial effect on the symptoms associated with menopause and perimenopause, such as hot flashes and sweats. The modern medical approach to relieving the symptoms of menopause has been estrogen hormone replacement therapies, however, these have been linked to certain types of cancers. Research has shown that because they have similar molecular structure to female hormones, the phytoestrogens in tofu and other soy foods reduce menopausal symptoms without the risk of estrogen-linked cancers. Half of all menopausal women in the United States complain of hot flashes, a problem that is so rare in Japan that there is not even a word for it.

Osteoporosis. Hip fractures due to osteoporosis are a major problem among post-menopausal women in the United States. Japanese women have half the rate of hip fractures as American women. Preliminary studies suggest that tofu may help retain bone mass in Japanese women. A study in the *Journal of Nutrition* showed that soy protein is effective in preventing bone loss in animals that cannot produce female hormones. Scientists believe it is the phytoestrogens in tofu that help build healthy bones and may help prevent osteoporosis.

Tofu and other soy products enhance potassium, magnesium and calcium retention, keeping bones strong and dense. On the other hand, soy protein includes low levels of sulfuric amino acids that have negative effects on the body's ability to retain calcium.

Lactose Intolerance. Thirty to fifty million Americans suffer from lactose intolerance—the inability to digest the primary sugar in milk, which is called lactose. Lactose is commonly found in dairy products such as milk, yogurt, ice cream and cheese. The best way to manage lactose intolerance is to reduce or eliminate dairy products from your diet. This may seem like a radical approach for those who love the soothing taste of dairy, however, by using silken tofu you can create delicious creamy desserts that have the mouth-feel and much of the nutritional value of dairy products.

Before the beginning of World War II, most of the tofu made in Japan was produced in small family shops using wood-fired stoves, cast-iron cauldrons and wooden setting boxes, and coagulated with nigari derived from natural sea salt. Although there are some small shops in Japan, China and the United States that still use traditional methods and simple equipment, most of the tofu available today is made in large factories using stainless steel equipment and modern, steam-generated cooking methods.

Making tofu has often been compared to making soft cheese. Like cheese making, tofu involves adding a coagulant to a milky liquid and then separating the solid curds from the liquid whey.

In small traditional shops the tofu making process begins by washing and soaking large, high protein, low oil soybeans for fifteen hours in pure spring water. The quality of the water is critical. Municipal water with chlorine and other impurities will give the tofu an off taste that is unacceptable. One pound (454 g) of dry soybeans makes about 3 to 4 pounds (1360 to 1715 g) of tofu depending on its firmness or final water content.

The soaked beans are drained and crushed in a grinder into a puree called go. The puree is then added to boiling water to extract its rich white soymilk. After being simmered for about 10 minutes the puree is transferred to a straining bag. The bag is hung over a cloth-covered curding barrel, and the soymilk is drained into the barrel. Next the straining bag is placed in a lever, hydraulic or screw press to extrude the remaining soymilk.

The soybean pulp, or okara, that is left in the straining bag is placed in boiling water to extract additional soymilk. Once it comes to a boil, the okara is placed back in the bag and pressed again to extract the remaining soymilk. The byproduct okara is used as filler in burgers and other products, fed to farm animals, or used for compost.

The warm soymilk that has been collected in the curding barrel is now ready to be solidified into tofu by the addition of a coagulant. The traditional Japanese coagulant is nigari, or magnesium chloride, which is extracted from sea salt and makes a light, sweet tofu. Another coagulant commonly used in the United States is calcium sulfate, which makes a more velvety tofu with a higher calcium content. The coagulant is usually dissolved in water and then added to the warm soymilk while it is being stirred. The soymilk is left to sit as the curds begin to form. After about twenty minutes all the curds will have formed, leaving the liquid whey pooling in the curding barrel. Next, a colander is forced into the surface of the curds to help pool the whey, which is ladled out. The curds are then placed in cloth-lined, wood-framed forming boxes. The cloth is folded over the top of the curds and a bamboo pressing mat and wooden pressing lid are set atop the cloth. A 10 to 25-pound (4 ^{1}/$_2$ to 11-kg) weight is placed on the pressing lid for about fifteen minutes to press the remaining whey from the forming tofu. After the tofu has firmed, the weight is taken off and the forming box is turned upside down and placed in cool spring water. The forming box is gently lifted off, leaving the block of tofu submerged in the water. A cutting board is slipped under the tofu, and it is cut into smaller blocks to be packaged.

Silken (*kinugoshi*) tofu is made by a fundamentally different process than that used to make regular tofu. First, a much more concentrated soymilk is used. This is combined with calcium sulfate and poured warm or hot into forming boxes. Whey is not formed and the tofu is not pressed. The resulting pure white solid block is much more delicate than typical tofu and has a smoother texture that is perfect for recipes that require a dairy-like quality. Also, because silken tofu does not form whey, it does not lose any water-soluble nutrients. However, because of its higher water content, it contains less protein.

Before the advent of pasteurization and sterilization tofu was distributed submerged in buckets of water. Modern tofu is usually sold in pasteurized water packs that have a shelf life of about four to six weeks in the refrigerator. Some types of tofu, however, such as silken, are packaged in sterile "aseptic" containers that have a very long shelf life at room temperature.

How Freeze-Dried Tofu Is Made—An Accidental Discovery

Like tofu and many other traditional Japanese food manufacturers, the freeze-dried tofu shops owe their unique processing methods to their Chinese neighbors. According to William Shurtleff, co-author with Akiko Aoyagi of several books on traditional Japanese foods, frozen tofu was probably first made in the cold mountainous regions of northern China about 1,000 to 1,500 years ago. It was found that if tofu was left out in the snow overnight until frozen solid, it underwent a radical transformation. When later placed in warm water, the tofu thawed, leaving a fine-grained, highly absorbent food that had the texture of tender meat.

Freeze-dried tofu makers hang tofu out to dehydrate in the cold, dry air in the high mountains of Japan. Although freeze-drying is considered a modern practice, it has been done in Japan for centuries.

Although Chinese frozen tofu had vast culinary potential, there were two drawbacks. First, it had to remain frozen or, like fresh tofu, it would spoil due to bacterial action. Second, like ice, it was heavy and difficult to transport.

Leave it to the Japanese to make a good thing better. About 1225 CE in a temple on Mount Koya, near Kyoto, a Buddhist monk began drying frozen tofu in a heated shed. This new "dried food" came to be known as *koya dofu*. Because it contained little water, it kept for several months without spoiling. The relentlessly utilitarian Japanese mind, however, was still not satisfied. In the fifteenth century, aggressive warlord Takeda Shingen recognized koya dofu's potential as a military ration. To make the process more mobile, Shingen did away with the heated shed and simply let the frozen tofu dry in the sun for a few weeks. This *kori* (frozen) *dofu*, thus named to distinguish it from the monk's version, was virtually imperishable.

Although there are a few traditional freeze-dried tofu makers high in the mountains of central modern Japan that still naturally freeze tofu on cold winter nights and dry it in the sun, most of this product is now made using electric freezers and dryers.

SHOPPING FOR TOFU

Becasue tofu is made from only water, soybeans and a little coagulant such as nigari or calcium sulfate, the quality of the soybeans and water are critical and determine the quality of the finished product. We strongly recommend buying organic tofu, as this is your assurance that it has been made with the highest quality organic ingredients, contains no genetically modified organisms (GMOs) and has no preservatives. Clearly, the best water for making tofu is spring water, and some manufacturers specify spring water in their ingredient list. Other manufacturers just list water. It is impossible to determine what type of water is being used unless the manufacturer clearly states this information on the package.

Although the coagulant nigari makes a sweeter tofu than calcium sulfate or calcium chloride, tofu made with the latter two contains more calcium. The type of coagulant used will be clearly stated in the ingredient list on the label.

Almost all the tofu sold in natural foods stores is made with organic soybeans, but some of the tofu sold in Asian markets and conventional grocery stores is made with genetically modified soybeans that can have high residues of herbicides. The statement "all natural" on a tofu package most likely means it was not made with organic soybeans. Check the label to see the tofu you buy is made with organic soybeans.

Besides the quality of ingredients, the other important consideration when buying tofu is freshness. Tofu is packaged in three ways: bulk buckets, pasteurized water packs and shelf-stable aseptic packaging. With the exception of shelf-stable aseptic packaged tofu or freeze-dried tofu, all fresh tofu will be found in the refrigerated section. The least expensive and most ecologically friendly way to purchase tofu is from the bulk buckets found in the refrigerated section of some natural foods stores. However, the water the tofu is immersed in should be clear, not milky, and the products should not smell sour. If you question its freshness, find out when it was delivered.

Pasteurized water-packed tofu is the most common packaging and has a considerably longer shelf life than bulk tofu. Check the date on the package to make sure the tofu is fresh. It is best to buy the tofu at least a week or two before the expiration date.

Although some of the tofu packaged in aseptic packages is not made with organic soybeans, the ones that are have an excellent taste and a very long shelf. Once the package is opened, the tofu most be stored covered with water in the refrigerator like other types of packaged tofu. The water should be changed every day, and the tofu should be used within a week.

Freeze-dried tofu, which is sometimes called "snow-dried tofu," is often found in the macrobiotic section of natural foods stores with other shelf-stable goods. You may not be able to find organic freeze-dried tofu, but there is a big difference between brands typically available in natural foods stores and those sold in many Asian food markets. The freeze-dried tofu sold in Asian markets is often made with defoaming agents and additives, such as baking soda and ammonia, to make it softer, less brittle and pristine white. Natural food–quality freeze-dried tofu is made using the finest non-GMO soybeans and processed without the use of additives or defoaming agents. Natural freeze-dried tofu has a beige color and lists only tofu (soybeans, water and nigari) as an ingredient. Dried tofu comes packaged in cellophane envelopes containing several thin, flat, rectangular cakes. Though it stores well for several months, it gradually turns yellow-brown with age, so be sure to buy only light beige-colored dried tofu, and store it in a cool, dry place.

In addition to all of the "heat and serve" tofu products now available, such as baked tofu with different seasonings, as well as tofu-based dips, salad dressings and frozen desserts, there are several varieties of fresh tofu to choose from, and of course freeze-dried tofu. The two main types of fresh tofu are firm, which includes "extra-firm," and soft, or silken. To determine what type of tofu is best suited to the recipe you have in mind, see Cooking with Fresh Tofu below.

COOKING WITH FRESH TOFU

 With its impressive nutritional profile, proven health benefits and incredible versatility, tofu has become indispensable in the whole foods kitchen. Since it has little taste of its own but absorbs flavors well, it is easy to incorporate tofu into a wide variety of tasty main dishes, soups, salad dressings, dips, sauces and desserts. Whether you want to feature tofu in a dish or "sneak" it into a recipe, this culinary chameleon will adapt to your wishes.

When cooking with fresh tofu, the first consideration is whether you need a firm or soft variety. Soft, or silken, tofu has a much higher water content and a smoother texture than firm tofu. It is the perfect choice when you are looking for a creamy texture, such as in salad dressings, sauces and some dips. Health-conscious American cooks commonly use soft tofu as a dairy substitute to make silky-smooth puddings, pie fillings and parfaits, or as a base for creamed soups. All of the above uses involve blending the tofu, which is the easiest way to use this fragile variety. In traditional Japanese cuisine, the sensuous texture of soft tofu cubes adds interest to delicate soups and some popular simmered dishes, such as *yu-dofu* and *nabemono*. When sliced or cubed, care must be taken when cutting the tofu to avoid breaking it. A very sharp knife is essential.

Firm and extra-firm varieties of tofu are the most common types sold in the United States. Extra-firm tofu holds its shape best in stir-fried dishes, stews and other preparations that involve a lot of stirring or mixing. As explained in Preparing Tofu (below), pressing or freezing tofu before use increases its ability to both absorb flavors and hold its shape. Extra-firm tofu is also the best choice for making *age-dofu* (deep-fried tofu). In general, either firm or extra-firm tofu works well in dishes that involve mashing the tofu, such as tacos, sloppy Joes, scrambled tofu, egg-less egg salad, Italian classics that call for "ricotta-like" fillings (see Vegan Lasagne, page 152), vegetable burgers and chili. Both can also be marinated, baked, simmered, barbecued, grilled, broiled or pan-fried with excellent results. Tofu Marsala (page 148) and Tofu Satay (page 150) are two of our favorite ways to enjoy this type of tofu. Although they are a little more involved than many of our everyday recipes, they are a great choice when having dinner guests or a special family meal.

The recipes in this chapter demonstrate a few of the limitless possibilities for using fresh tofu to create beautiful and delicious dishes for your family and friends. If you don't already incorporate tofu into your meals, these recipes and the tips found in Preparing Tofu (below) and Cooking Techniques (opposite) will familiarize you with the possibilities of tofu. Before you know it, you'll find new and interesting ways to use tofu in some of your favorite recipes or come up with entirely new dishes featuring this low-calorie, high protein, healthful soyfood.

Guidelines for Storing Fresh Tofu

- Tofu packaged in water can be stored in the unopened package in your refrigerator. However, if you open the package and do not use it all, or if you purchase bulk tofu, store it in the refrigerator completely submerged in water and change the water daily.

- Fresh tofu has a slightly sweet smell. If it has a sour smell, it is beginning to spoil and should be discarded. The color should be off-white, and the texture should be smooth but never slimy.

- If tofu looks and smells fine, but you question its freshness, before using it in dips or other uncooked recipes, submerge it in a pot of boiling water, reduce the heat, and gently simmer for 2 or 3 minutes. Then transfer the tofu to a cold-water bath and let sit until thoroughly cooled.

Preparing Tofu

To ensure that your tofu recipes have the best possible flavor and texture, follow these basic preparation guidelines.

Drain. Never use the liquid in which tofu is stored. Drain the tofu and discard the liquid.

Cutting. Always use a sharp knife when cutting tofu to avoid squashing it.

Pressing. Some recipes, such as deep-fried tofu, call for pressing the tofu to remove excess water before cooking. In these recipes, start with firm or extra-firm tofu. (Soft or silken tofu has a much higher water content to begin with.) To press it, it is best to cut a block of tofu into slices of even thickness. Spread a clean linen or cotton kitchen towel on a cutting board, arrange the tofu slices on top and cover them with a second cloth. Raise one end of the cutting board a few inches (about 8 cm) to facilitate draining. Pat the tofu gently. Place a baking sheet and a three to five-pound (1.5 to 2.5-kg) weight on top of the tofu and let it stand for at least 10 to 15 minutes and up to an hour if you want it as dry as possible. (In many cases, especially when using extra-firm tofu, simply wrapping the slices in cloth and patting them gently is sufficient.)

Freezing. Freezing tofu changes its texture, making it more chewy and meatlike. Once thawed, frozen tofu absorbs flavors like a sponge. We recommend frozen tofu in stews, chili, and as a substitute for ground meat in various entrees. To freeze, drain and rinse the fresh tofu, evenly slice the block or cut into cubes. Arrange the slices or cubes on a cookie sheet, cover with plastic wrap, and freeze for at least 3 hours. If not using right away, place the slices or cubes in freezer bags and store for up to five months.

Marinating. Marinating firm or extra-firm tofu is an excellent way to give it flavor. Pressing the slices before marinating increases their ability to absorb flavors. If you are in a hurry, start with extra-firm tofu and simply wrap the slices in paper towel and press lightly with your hand to absorb excess water.

The flavor of the marinade will penetrate slices or cubes of tofu in as little as 15 to 30 minutes, so you can prepare the marinade, add the tofu, and set it aside while you prepare the rest of the ingredients. Be sure all surfaces of the tofu are coated with the marinade, and turn the pieces once or twice while marinating. We particularly enjoy tofu marinated in teriyaki sauce or Thai seasonings, but the options are limitless.

Cooking Techniques

Tofu is the most versatile of foods. Try these different cooking techniques to expand your tofu repertoire.

Pan-frying. Pan-frying slices or cubes of firm or extra-firm tofu before adding it to other recipes will help to keep it from breaking apart when stir-fried or simmered. Press tofu slices to remove excess water, then add them to a heated skillet with a little vegetable oil. Cook tofu over medium-high heat until golden brown, then flip and brown the other side. When pan-frying cubes of tofu, stir occasionally to lightly brown all sides. Pan-frying is also a quick and easy way to prepare marinated tofu.

Stir-frying. Always use extra-firm or pressed, firm tofu when stir-frying. Cut into bite-size cubes. In order to prevent the tofu from sticking to the pan, heat the pan before adding the oil, and let the oil become hot before adding the tofu cubes. Stir gently until lightly browned and remove from pan. Stir-fry the rest of the ingredients and add the tofu back to the mixture near the end of cooking along with your favorite seasonings or sauce.

Deep-frying. Deep-fried tofu is a delicious addition to soups, stews and stir-fries. The key to making deep-fried tofu is to thoroughly press the slices to remove as much excess water as possible before frying. This means pressing for a full hour using the method described in Preparing Tofu. Once it is pressed, cut into cubes. Heat at least 1 inch (2.5 cm) of safflower oil to between 350 and 365°F (180 and 185°C) in a wide saucepan. Add several cubes of tofu at once, but do not overcrowd the pot. Deep-fry until golden brown, turning occasionally, then remove all the pieces with a slotted spoon and drain on several thicknesses of paper towel.

Grilling or Broiling. To prepare tofu for grilling or broiling, cut the tofu into ³/₄-inch (2-cm)-thick slices, press them to remove excess water, and marinate for up to 1 hour. Arrange the slices on a rack brushed with oil and grill or broil until the surface becomes firm and lightly crusted. Turn and cook the other side. If the tofu becomes too dry, baste once or twice while cooking.

Simmering. Plain, marinated, pan-fried or deep-fried tofu can be added to soups or stews and simmered. If the tofu has not been precooked, simmer gently to prevent it from breaking apart, and stir only as much as necessary.

Cooking with Freeze-Dried Tofu

With its porous, firm yet tender texture and its mild, unimposing taste, freeze-dried tofu has an amazing ability to absorb the flavors of the foods and seasonings it is cooked with. Unlike fresh tofu, which tends to break apart when sautéed, dried tofu holds its shape even after prolonged cooking. These qualities make it well suited to any cooking method. Appropriately seasoned, it can be used in place of meat or poultry in many culinary styles—from East to West. Lightweight and easy to store and prepare, it is also an ideal camp food.

Freeze-dried tofu must be reconstituted. To reconstitute, soak the cakes in warm water for five minutes, then press them firmly between your hands. Repeatedly dampen and press until the liquid that comes out is no longer milky. Once reconstituted, there are three basic ways of cooking with freeze-dried tofu. First, dried tofu can be diced and added directly to well-seasoned stews, sauces, or other flavorful dishes. The second method is to marinate the diced tofu for thirty minutes. A marinade base of natural soy sauce, mirin, and ginger is perfect when making Asian meals. Soy sauce, white wine, and herbs associated with Western cuisines, such as poultry seasoning or rosemary and bay leaf, impart a flavor suited to Western dishes. The third—and most versatile—method is to simmer the tofu in a well-seasoned broth. It may then be served as is; pan-fried in toasted sesame oil; or diced and added to stews, sautées, grains, sauces and salads.

Coarsely grating dried tofu before reconstituting yields another range of possibilities. Try adding some to stuffings, casseroles and vegetable or grain-based burgers or croquettes.

Tofu Marsala

Wine, mushrooms and herbs give this recipe a rich, satisfying flavor. Dried porcini mushrooms are available in many grocery stores. Round out the meal with rice and a green vegetable or tossed salad.

> ¹/₂ oz (15 g) dried porcini mushrooms
> 1 lb (450 g) extra-firm tofu
> ¹/₃ cup (50 g) unbleached flour

$^1/_4$ teaspoon sea salt
$^1/_8$ teaspoon freshly ground black pepper
$^1/_4$ teaspoon dried thyme leaves
$^1/_4$ teaspoon dried rubbed sage
2 tablespoons extra virgin olive oil
$^1/_2$ onion, diced
2 cloves garlic, minced
4 oz (125 g) fresh button or other small mushrooms, sliced
$^3/_4$ cup (175 ml) Marsala wine
$^3/_4$ cup (175 ml) porcini soaking water
1 teaspoon shoyu (Japanese soy sauce)
1 small bay leaf
1 teaspoon fresh lemon juice
4 tablespoons finely chopped fresh parsley

1. Soak the porcini in 1 cup (235 ml) lukewarm water for 30 minutes. Remove, reserve soaking water and chop mushrooms.

2. While the mushrooms are soaking, cut the block of tofu into 8 equal slices. Place the slices on one half of a clean, dry kitchen towel. Fold the other half over the tofu and gently press to absorb excess moisture.

3. In a shallow bowl, combine the flour, salt, pepper, thyme and sage.

4. Gently roll the tofu slices in the flour mixture to coat all surfaces. Reserve the flour.

5. Heat 1 tablespoon of the olive oil in a large skillet and fry the tofu slices over medium-high heat for 3 to 5 minutes, or until golden brown. Turn and cook the other side until lightly browned. Remove tofu and set aside.

6. Lower the heat to medium, add the remaining 1 tablespoon of olive oil to the pan and sauté the onion and garlic for 1 minute. Then add the porcini, sliced fresh mushrooms and a pinch of salt and pepper and continue sautéing for 2 to 3 minutes.

7. Add 2 tablespoons of the reserved flour and toss to coat vegetables evenly. Sauté 1 minute more to lightly toast the flour.

8. Add the wine and porcini soaking water, 1 teaspoon shoyu, $^1/_8$ teaspoon sea salt, a pinch of black pepper and the bay leaf. Simmer gently, stirring frequently, until the sauce thickens.

9. Stir the lemon juice into the sauce and return the tofu to the pan. Cover and gently simmer for 10 minutes.

10. Add half of the parsley and simmer 1 minute more.

11. Remove the bay leaf and discard. Garnish with the remaining parsley and serve.

SERVES 4

Preparation time: 15 minutes plus 30 minutes soaking time
Cooking time: 30 minutes

Tofu Satay

Enhanced with the flavors of curry and served with a delicious peanut sauce, this is the perfect answer to those who think tofu is bland. At first glance, this recipe may seem complicated, but it is actually quite simple and its rich flavor is a real crowd pleaser.

1 block (14 oz/400 g) extra-firm tofu

Curry Marinade
2 tablespoons unsalted natural peanut butter
2 tablespoons shoyu (Japanese soy sauce)
1 1/2 tablespoons fresh lemon juice
1 1/2 tablespoons fresh coriander (cilantro), chopped
1 tablespoon peanut oil
1 teaspoon honey
1 teaspoon curry powder
1 teaspoon peeled and finely grated fresh ginger
1/8 teaspoon dried red pepper flakes

Peanut Sauce
1 tablespoon peanut oil
2 shallots, minced
2 cloves garlic, minced
1/4 teaspoon dried red pepper flakes
1 teaspoon cumin
3 tablespoons unsalted natural peanut butter
4 tablespoons water
4 tablespoons light coconut milk
1 teaspoon fresh lemon or lime juice
2 teaspoons shoyu (Japanese soy sauce)

1. If using wooden skewers, soak them in water for 1 to 2 hours to prevent them from burning.

2. Cut the tofu crosswise into 3/4-inch (2-cm)-thick slices. Place the slices on one half of a clean, dry kitchen towel, fold the other half over the tofu, and gently press to absorb excess moisture. Cut slices in half vertically and cut in half again horizontally.

3. Combine all the marinade ingredients in a shallow baking dish.

4. Roll tofu pieces in the marinade to cover all surfaces and let sit for 1 hour, turning once or twice.

5. Preheat the broiler or prepare an outdoor grill.

6. To make the peanut sauce, heat the oil in a small skillet over medium-low heat, add the shallots, garlic and red pepper and sauté for 2 minutes, or until shallots are translucent.

7. Add the cumin, then the peanut butter and stir to form a paste.

8. Gradually add the water, stir until creamy, and stir in the coconut milk. Add the lemon juice and shoyu. Place in individual dipping bowls and set aside.

9. Carefully thread one or two pieces of tofu onto each skewer, running the skewer up through the center of the tofu.

10. Place the skewers on a rack over an outdoor grill or in a broiler pan, 3 inches (7.5 cm) from the heat source. Cook for 3 minutes, or until lightly browned, then turn and cook 3 minutes more, or until browned.

11. Serve immediately with Peanut Sauce.

SERVES 4 TO 5

Preparation time: 25 minutes
Cooking time: 10 minutes

Tofu Pesto

Silken tofu contributes a creamy texture along with the benefits of soy to this dairy-free version of a Mediterranean classic. Toss with Italian-style pasta or udon noodles for a simple and tasty dinner. This recipe makes enough pesto to nicely coat four 3-ounce (75-g) servings of pasta or noodles.

4 tablespoons pine nuts or slivered almonds
1 cup (75 g) fresh basil leaves, tightly packed
4 tablespoons finely chopped fresh parsley
1 cup (275 g) soft or silken tofu
3 to 4 tablespoons sweet or mellow white miso
4 tablespoons extra virgin olive oil
$1^1/_2$ tablespoons fresh lemon juice
$^1/_4$ teaspoon freshly ground black pepper
1 large clove garlic, chopped

1. In a dry skillet over medium heat, toast the nuts, stirring constantly, for 5 minutes, or until they are golden brown. Remove from pan to prevent overcooking.

2. Combine the toasted pine nuts with the remaining ingredients in a food processor or blender and process until smooth. Let sit 30 minutes to allow flavors to blend. The pesto will keep in the refrigerator for about 1 week.

MAKES ABOUT 2 CUPS (475 ML)

Preparation time: 5 minutes
Cooking time: 5 minutes

Stuffed Endive Leaves

Minced red bell pepper adds festive color to this simple but elegant appetizer. The tofu spread may be made one or two days in advance.

8 oz (250 g) firm tofu
4 tablespoons sweet or mellow white miso
2 tablespoons brown rice vinegar
2 tablespoons safflower oil
1 clove garlic, minced or pressed
3 tablespoons minced onion
$^1/_2$ cup (50 g) minced red bell pepper
$^1/_2$ cup (60 g) minced celery
16 Belgian endive leaves
16 sprigs watercress

1. Place the tofu, miso, vinegar, oil and garlic in a blender and blend until smooth. If too thick, add a little more oil or water.

2. Remove from the blender and stir in the onion, bell pepper and celery. Let rest, refrigerated, at least 1 hour to allow flavors to heighten. (It is best not to attempt to adjust seasonings before the mixture has rested.)

3. To serve, place a rounded tablespoon on the lower third of each endive leaf. Tuck a sprig of watercress into the spread so it rests on the endive leaf. Place the pieces on a platter in a fan shape, or make another attractive design.

MAKES ABOUT 16 STUFFED LEAVES

Preparation time: 15 minutes plus 1 hour to allow the filling to rest

Variation
Creamy Onion Dip. This delicious dip is excellent with chips or raw vegetables. To make, follow Steps 1 and 2, except eliminate the bell pepper and celery.

Vegan Lasagne

This simple, dairy-free version of one of Italy's and America's favorite pasta dishes is quick and easy to make. Serve it with a salad and garlic toast for a delicious, satisfying meal.

8 lasagna noodles
2 teaspoons extra virgin olive oil
2 cloves garlic, minced
5 to 6 button or other small mushrooms, sliced
Pinch of sea salt
$3^1/_2$ cups (825 ml) spaghetti sauce
$^1/_3$ teaspoon dried oregano or marjoram
$^1/_4$ teaspoon dried thyme leaves
1 recipe Creamy Tofu Filling (see opposite)

1. Bring a large pot of salted water to a rapid boil, and cook the noodles according to package directions. They should be a little underdone (al dente). Drain the noodles, place them in a bowl of cold water and set aside.

2. Heat the oil in a large skillet over medium-low heat. Add the garlic, mushrooms, and salt, and sauté for 2 to 3 minutes, or until the mushrooms begin to soften.

3. Pour in the spaghetti sauce and bring to a simmer. Stir in the oregano and thyme, and simmer for another 2 to 3 minutes.

4. Preheat the oven to 350°F (175°C).

5. When you are ready to assemble the lasagne, drain the noodles. Cover the bottom of a 9 x 13-inch (23 cm x 32-cm) baking dish with a layer of noodles, overlapping them slightly where edges meet. Spread half of the tofu filling evenly over the noodles and top with half of the sauce. Repeat the layers.

6. Bake, uncovered, for 30 to 40 minutes, or until the lasagne is heated through. Remove from the oven and let sit for 10 minutes before serving.

SERVES 6

Preparation time: 20 minutes
Cooking time: 50 minutes

| Creamy Tofu Filling |

Low in calories, nutritious and flavorful, this simple tofu filling is similar to ricotta. It is a satisfying substitute for cheese in dairy-free versions of Italian favorites such as Vegan Lasagne (opposite) and baked ziti.

1 lb (450 g) firm tofu
3 level tablespoons mellow white miso mixed with 2 tablespoons water
2 tablespoons tahini (ground sesame seed paste)
1 clove garlic, finely minced
2 teaspoons fresh lemon juice or brown rice vinegar
3 tablespoons chopped fresh parsley

1. Wrap the tofu in a clean dry towel and gently squeeze to remove any excess water.

2. Crumble the tofu into a medium-sized bowl and mash with a fork or potato masher.

3. Combine the miso and tahini and add it to the tofu. Mix well. Stir in the garlic, lemon juice and parsley.

4. Use this filling immediately, or refrigerate and use within 24 hours.

MAKES ABOUT 2 CUPS (500 G)

Preparation time: 5 minutes

Arame with Dried Tofu and Vegetables

Enhanced with the mild sweetness of mirin, this colorful combination of arame, carrots, sweet corn and parsley is nutritious, delicious and appealing. Dried tofu supplies
concentrated protein and an interesting contrast of texture.

$1^1/_4$ cups (1.76-oz/50 g package) dried arame
4 pieces freeze-dried tofu
2 teaspoons sesame oil (untoasted)
$1^1/_2$ to 2 tablespoons shoyu (Japanese soy sauce) or tamari, or to taste
1 tablespoon mirin
1 carrot, sliced into thin matchsticks
1 cup (150 g) fresh or frozen corn kernels
2 to 3 tablespoons minced fresh parsley

1. Place the arame in a bowl, cover with water and let it soak for just 5 to 10 minutes,
   no longer.

2. Reconstitute the dried tofu by soaking it in lukewarm water for 5 minutes.
   Repeatedly dampen and squeeze excess water from the tofu until the liquid that
   comes out is no longer milky. Dice and set aside.

3. Drain the arame.

4. Heat the oil in a large skillet, add the drained arame, and sauté over medium-high
   heat for 1 to 2 minutes. Add the tofu and enough water to almost cover the arame
   and bring to a boil. Lower the heat, cover the pan and simmer for 15 minutes.

5. Stir in the shoyu and mirin and toss together with the arame and tofu.

6. Place the carrots on top of arame mixture, cover and cook for 5 minutes.

7. Stir in the corn and cook for 5 more minutes. If any liquid remains, cook uncovered over high heat for a few minutes until nearly dry.

8. Sprinkle the parsley on top, cover and steam for 1 minute. Serve hot.

SERVES 6 TO 8

Preparation time: 5 minutes plus 10 minutes soaking time
Cooking time: 30 minutes

Curried Vegetables with Dried Tofu

Full of flavor and color and simple to prepare, this is one of our family's favorites, and it is a good choice when you have unexpected dinner guests. Paired with rice, freeze-dried tofu provides a concentrated source of complete protein. Freeze-dried tofu comes presliced in approximately 1 1/2 x 2 1/2-inch (3.75 x 6-cm) pieces.

> 4 pieces freeze-dried tofu
> 1 tablespoon extra virgin olive oil
> 2 cloves garlic, minced
> 1 onion, chopped
> 2 carrots, cut into bite-size chunks
> 2 potatoes, peeled and diced
> 1 teaspoon sea salt
> 4 teaspoons curry powder
> 2 teaspoons ground cumin
> 4 cups (1 liter) Shiitake Stock (see page 92) or Kombu Stock (see page 176)
> 1 bay leaf
> 2 cups (300 g) small broccoli florets
> 2 teaspoons shoyu (Japanese soy sauce)
> 1 teaspoon mirin (optional)
> 3 tablespoons crushed kuzu starch

1. Reconstitute the dried tofu by soaking it in lukewarm water for 5 minutes. Repeatedly dampen the tofu and squeeze out excess water several times, until the water that comes out is no longer milky. Slice the tofu into small cubes.

2. Heat the oil in a large skillet over medium heat and sauté the garlic and onion for 2 to 3 minutes, or until onion is translucent.

3. Add the carrots and potatoes and sauté 2 to 3 minutes more.

4. Add the salt, curry and cumin and sauté briefly, then add 3 cups (700 ml) of the stock, the bay leaf and dried tofu. Cover and simmer for 20 minutes.

5. Add the broccoli and remaining stock and simmer, covered, for 5 minutes, or until the broccoli is tender-crisp.

6. Stir in the shoyu and mirin.

7. Thoroughly dissolve the kuzu in 3 tablespoons cold water and add it to the mixture while stirring. Continue stirring gently for a minute or two until the sauce thickens, then simmer for 1 minute more.

8. Serve over a bed of rice.

SERVES 4

Preparation time: 15 minutes
Cooking time: 40 minutes

Sesame-Tofu Dressing

This delicious creamy dressing is considerably lower in fat than most French or Italian-style dressings. Try it on Arame Salad (page 178).

> 1 tablespoon sesame seeds
> 5 oz (150 g) silken or firm tofu
> 4 tablespoons safflower oil
> 2 teaspoons toasted sesame oil
> $2^1/_2$ tablespoons brown rice vinegar or apple cider vinegar
> 4 tablespoons water
> 3 tablespoons sweet or mellow miso
> 1 clove garlic, sliced
> 1 tablespoon brown rice malt syrup or mirin

1. In a small dry skillet, toast the sesame seeds over medium heat, stirring constantly, for 1 or 2 minutes or until they are fragrant or begin to pop. Immediately transfer to a small bowl and set aside.

2. Place all of the ingredients except the sesame seeds in a blender. Blend until smooth, transfer to a jar with a lid, and stir in the sesame seeds.

3. Refrigerate before serving. Shake well before using. This dressing will keep in the refrigerator for up to 2 weeks.

MAKES ABOUT $1^2/_3$ CUPS (400 ML)

Preparation time: about 5 minutes

CHAPTER 14

セイタン

SEITAN: THE VEGETARIAN ALTERNATIVE

Seitan, or seasoned wheat gluten, is a highly nutritious, protein-rich food that can be quickly and easily prepared in a variety of interesting ways. Its excellent nutritional profile and total lack of cholesterol, saturated fat and additives are only the beginning. With a delicious flavor and meatlike quality, seitan is instantly familiar and easy to adapt to American recipes. With seitan it is possible to make hundreds of meat-free versions of familiar dishes otherwise denied the vegetarian. It is inexpensive to prepare at home, and is becoming increasingly available in natural foods stores. What's more, it is easy to digest, completely natural and offers the important benefit of satiety, as well as other comforts. With seitan, you can create many delicious foods with a meatlike appearance and a tempting bouquet that triggers memories of hearty flavors and aromas.

Seasoned wheat gluten was traditionally eaten in China, Korea, Japan, Russia, the Middle East and probably other countries that grew wheat. It is also associated with the dietary habits of religious groups such as Buddhists, Mormons and Seventh Day Adventists. *Seitan* is a Japanese word that usually refers to wheat gluten that has been simmered in a broth of soy sauce and kombu. In the West, seitan is often flavored with herbs and spices such as rosemary, bay leaf, ginger and black pepper to give it additional complexity and a flavor profile familiar to the Western palate.

Nutritionally, seitan is a powerhouse. In both quantity and quality, the protein in seitan is similar to that in beef. Sirloin steak and seitan both supply approximately 16 grams of protein per $3^1/_2$-ounce (100-g) serving, or about 25 percent of the United States Department of Agriculture's Reference Daily Intake (RDI). This is twice as much as an equal amount of tofu, and 40 percent more than is supplied by two medium eggs. Although unseasoned seitan is low in the essential amino acid lysine, this is easily offset by cooking the seitan in a broth seasoned with soy sauce, or by combining or serving it with lysine-rich foods such as beans. And while the $3^1/_2$-ounce (100-g) broiled prime sirloin comes with 2.4 grams of saturated fat, 88 milligrams of cholesterol and 185 calories, seitan contains no saturated fat or cholesterol and has only 120 calories per $3^1/_2$-ounce (100-g) serving.

High in protein and essential amino acids, seitan made with whole-wheat flour and cooked in a kombu and soy sauce broth is a good source of some vitamins and minerals. A 4-ounce (115-g) serving of seitan supplies between 6 and 10 percent of the RDI for vitamin C, thiamin, riboflavin, niacin and iron.

Substituting seitan for meat can significantly reduce the risk of heart disease, as well as other health threats. In the United States, a person dies from a heart attack every 65 seconds. According to Pulitzer Prize nominee John Robbins in his best-selling book *Diet for a New America* (H. J. Kramer, 1998), by eliminating meat, dairy products and eggs from the American diet, the risk of heart attack would be reduced by 90 percent! At the same time, the hormones and antibiotics so liberally administered to livestock are avoided and pesticide levels can be reduced by over 50 percent, since meat supplies more than half of the pesticides consumed in the standard American diet, whereas seitan is usually made from organic wheat.

Robbins has also put together a powerful ethical argument in support of vegetarian sources of protein, such as seitan. According to his research, it takes fifty times more fossil fuels to produce a meat-centered diet than a meat-free diet. He points out that 85 percent of topsoil loss in the United States is directly related to livestock raising. Furthermore, five times the population of the United States or 1.5 billion people, could be fed with the grain and soybeans now eaten by the country's livestock, an abominable fact in a world where a child starves to death every two seconds.

In recent years, fish and seafood have been touted as the optimal low-fat, low-cholesterol, high-protein replacements for red meat. More and more reports are cropping up, however, that warn of the dangers of eating fish because many contain heavy metals and other toxins. Seitan is a clean, safe way to get high quality protein.

HOW SEITAN IS MADE

Even today, most seitan is made the traditional way—by kneading a whole-wheat dough to develop the gluten (protein), rinsing the dough to remove the starch (carbohydrates) and bran, thus concentrating the gluten and finally simmering the gluten in a savory broth. Seitan is not difficult to make at home, but the process is labor-intensive and rather messy. Making delicious seitan in a small shop requires a great deal of experience and some simple equipment.

Wheat is preeminent among grains because it is the only one whose endosperm protein interacts to form gluten strong enough to bind together into a tight mass. Gluten is both plastic and elastic—that is, it will change its shape under pressure and tend to reassume its original shape when pressure is removed. It is this elastic and plastic property of wheat gluten that is utilized during the seitan making process.

Seitan makers first place several hundred pounds (approximately 150 kg) of high-gluten whole-wheat flour in the seitan or gluten machine. This is a stainless steel tank with several rotating arms or paddles at the bottom. The machine is turned on and while it is running water is added. Once the flour is mixed with water, the gluten protein begins to spread out into a random network. Water molecules separate and lubricate the long chains of gluten, which begin to stick together to form visible strands. Meanwhile, the wheat bran and starch turn the water into a milky, beige slurry that is carefully discharged from the bottom of the seitan machine. (The liquid is saved and used as animal feed or to make other related foods.) Fresh water is added and drained several times as the constant motion of the paddles keeps concentrating the wheat gluten until it sticks together into a large, rubbery mass at the bottom of the seitan machine. Finally, after a few hours of mixing and several rinsings with fresh water, the concentrated gluten mass is removed from the machine, cut up into small pieces and cooked in a savory broth seasoned with kombu and soy sauce. Seasoned gluten imported from Japan is packed in jars that are placed in a large pressure cooker for a specific time to ensure sterilization and to give them a stable shelf life. Products made in the United States are usually sold frozen or refrigerated.

SHOPPING FOR SEITAN

 The factors that affect the quality of seitan are the choice of ingredients and the subtle aspects of the manufacturing process itself. Because seitan is mostly wheat gluten, the choice of wheat is particularly important. The highest quality seitan is made from only hard winter wheat, which has more protein than soft wheat. The choice of shoyu, which is the main flavor component of seitan, is also very important. Traditional producers use only naturally aged shoyu made from the whole soybean, which imparts a rich flavor and meatlike character to seitan. Finally, the addition of kombu to the cooking broth not only adds important minerals, but also helps give seitan its distinctly meatlike essence.

It is hard to overestimate the importance that the manufacturing process plays in making delicious seitan. Just how much starch and bran remain in the finished product determines not only the texture, but also seitan's capacity to absorb flavors. From years of experience, traditional seitan makers know just the amount of kneading and rinsing whole-wheat flour needs to develop gluten with just the right texture. Raw gluten does not have much flavor, so deciding how much time it must simmer in its savory broth of shoyu and kombu is the last important decision a producer must make. Undercooking will produce a chewy seitan that is weak in flavor. Overcooking will make for a dark, salty seitan that will overpower the flavors of other ingredients in recipes. Only by using the finest ingredients and knowledge gained from experience can wheat be transformed into a truly delicious and satisfying meat substitute.

There are several brands of wheat gluten made from gluten flour and not seasoned with shoyu. These products are usually very chewy and have no depth of flavor. The ingredients in the highest quality seitan are usually organic whole-wheat flour, organic whole soybean shoyu and kombu. There are a number of small producers who supply local stores, as well as several larger companies that make high quality seitan for regional or national distribution. A few brands offer ginger or even barbecue varieties. It is best to shop for seitan in the refrigerated or frozen section of your natural foods store. Imported shelf-stable products are excellent, but very expensive. It is a great convenience to pick up a package of seitan on the way home, then whip up a delicious and wholesome meal in a matter of minutes.

COOKING WITH SEITAN

 Seitan is an exceptional food in its own right, and an ideal meat substitute. With a little experience in preparing seitan dishes, those trying to reduce or eliminate meat will never even miss it. Seitan readily accepts any type of seasoning and is easy to adapt to American recipes. Marinated and cooked in red wine and stock, it makes a succulent French-style bourguignon; ground like chopped meat, it is a great addition to American favorites like chili, meatloaf, sloppy Joes, lasagne, spaghetti sauce, Swedish meatballs, tacos and burgers. Seitan can be breaded and deep-fried or prepared like cutlets; pan-fried and smothered in onions and mushrooms; cooked like pot roast or New England boiled dinner; or added to sandwiches, stews, casseroles, fried rice, kabobs, pot pies, stir-fries and salads. You will intuitively know what to do with this meatlike food, and will quickly be preparing dishes that are pleasantly familiar and enjoyable to guests and family.

| Homemade Seitan |

There is a certain magic in making seitan. I have made it well over a hundred times and haven't lost the sense of wonder that comes when you rinse the dough and, instead of it all dissolving down the drain, you end up holding a special, concentrated food.

Don't be intimidated by the length of the directions—seitan really is quite simple to make, and once you have made it once or twice, you'll be able to quickly prepare enough seitan to create a week's worth of easy and exciting meals.

Here is the basic seitan recipe that I use most frequently, along with a couple of simple variations. Substituting high-gluten flour for a portion of the whole-wheat flour gives a firmer, less spongy texture. This batch size makes enough to feed a family of four twice. After a little experience, you will probably want to double this, but it is a good size batch to start with. If you increase the recipe, remember to adjust the amount of cooking broth accordingly.

> 8 cups (1 kg) whole-wheat bread flour (or substitute unbleached high-gluten
> flour for up to 25 percent of the whole-wheat flour)
> 4 cups (1 liter) cold water

Seitan Seasoning Stock

7 cups (1.75 liters) water
One 6-in (15-cm) strip kombu
$^1/_2$ cup (125 ml) tamari
1 tablespoon finely grated peeled fresh ginger
1 teaspoon dried rosemary (optional)
1 bay leaf

1. In a large bowl, combine the flour and 1 cup (235 ml) of the water with a wooden spoon. Continue adding the water 1 cup at a time to form a sticky but firm dough.

2. Once the flour and water are well mixed, vigorously punch the dough with one closed fist, then the other, about 300 times. Knead the dough by lifting and folding it over on itself several times while punching it. Kneading the dough is easiest if you set the bowl in a sink or other low place so you can use your weight effectively. Thorough kneading develops the gluten and makes the rinsing easy and successful.

3. Cover the dough with cold water and let it sit for at least 30 minutes.

4. Knead the dough slowly and carefully in the water until the water becomes thick and white with starch. Pour off the creamy liquid.

5. Gently cover the dough with water and knead again. Alternate between slightly warm and cold water rinses, kneading each time to extract the cream-colored starch. A large colander will help in draining off the water from the first several kneadings. At first the dough may seem to be falling apart, and the colander will catch any little pieces so you don't lose them down the drain. Continue kneading and rinsing until the rubbery gluten begins to stick together.

6. After about six rinses, only the gluten will remain, and the rinse water will be almost clear. Remaining starch and bran can be rinsed away directly under the tap by pulling the gluten apart and exposing the inside.

7. All that's left now to turn raw gluten into delicious seitan is cooking it in a flavored broth. (The rubbery quality will disappear as soon as the gluten is boiled.) If you do not plan to cook it the same day, store the gluten, covered with water, in a container in the refrigerator. If you place a flat plate on the raw gluten and press it overnight with a light weight, the texture will be more firm after cooking, but it will require slightly longer cooking, because the seasonings will not penetrate as readily. Raw gluten may be refrigerated for at least 3 days or frozen indefinitely.

8. Combine the stock ingredients in a large saucepan and bring to a simmer. Form small handfuls of the gluten into patties by stretching and pulling until fairly thin, or form larger portions into loaves, or pull off balls, and drop them one by one into the simmering stock.

9. Stir occasionally during the first few minutes of cooking to prevent sticking, then, with the lid ajar, very gently simmer for 1 hour for small balls or 90 minutes for larger pieces such as cutlets. I generally cook loaves for at least 2 hours. Rapid boiling will result in a less dense, more airy texture.

10. If time permits, allow the seitan to cool completely in the broth before using. The texture will become firmer as it cools.

11. Seitan will keep for at least 1 week refrigerated in its cooking broth. For longer storage, add more tamari or shoyu to the broth. Seitan can also be frozen without affecting its taste or texture. Seitan should be removed from its broth before freezing.

Note to Cook
Occasionally a batch of flour disintegrates in the washing (Step 5), instead of separating into starch, bran and gluten. In this case, try a different type of whole-wheat flour.

Seasoning Stock Variations

• For an especially rich flavor, omit the ginger, retain the rosemary and bay leaf, and add 2 scrubbed, unpeeled onions, cut into wedges; 1 rib celery, chopped; and 1 scrubbed, unpeeled large beet, finely grated.

• Omit the bay leaf and add 1 teaspoon dried basil and $3/4$ teaspoon dried thyme.

• Omit the ginger and rosemary. Add 1 teaspoon each thyme and sage, and 2 cloves garlic, chopped.

MAKES 41/2 TO 5 CUPS COOKED SEITAN (ABOUT 2 LBS/1 KG)

Preparation time: about 45 minutes plus at least 30 minutes to "rest" the dough
Cooking time: 1 to 2 hours (see Step 9)

Seitan Hot Pot

The ultimate in simplicity, yet wholesome and irresistable, Seitan Hot Pot takes only 15 minutes to prepare and about 20 minutes to cook. It is cooked and served in a large cast-iron or stainless steel skillet.

> 2 cups (475 ml) water or Shiitake Stock (see page 92) or Kombu Stock (see page 176)
> One 4-in (10-cm) piece kombu (optional)
> 2 tablespoons tamari or shoyu (Japanese soy sauce)
> 1 bay leaf
> Pinch of dried rosemary
> $1/2$ large red or yellow onion, cut into 6 wedges
> 3 carrots, cut into bite-size chunks
> $1/4$ head cabbage, cut into 3 to 4 wedges
> 12 button or other small mushrooms, whole
> Several $1/2$-in (1-cm)-thick slices seitan, or 2 cups (about 325 g) bite-size pieces
> Three 1-in (2.5-cm) wedges buttercup squash
> 12 broccoli florets

1. In a large skillet, bring the water, kombu, shoyu and herbs to a boil.

2. Place the onion, carrots, cabbage, mushrooms and seitan in the skillet, arranging them so each variety is separate and colors are balanced. Cover and simmer for 5 minutes.

3. Add the squash and simmer 10 minutes more, or until the vegetables are nearly tender. Add the broccoli and simmer for 5 minutes, or until tender-crisp.

4. Uncover, place the skillet it in the center of the table and serve.

SERVES 3

Preparation time: 15 minutes
Cooking time: 20 to 25 minutes

Seitan Tourtière

Every Thanksgiving my French-Canadian mother made an herbed meat-and-potato stuffing for the turkey. She always prepared extra to make a traditional tourtiére the famed meat pie from Quebec. This was my favorite holiday food and the only meat dish I have ever missed. With seitan, I am able to make this vegetarian version, which is remarkably similar to the original.

2 large potatoes
1 tablespoon vegetable oil, such as canola or safflower
1 onion, diced
4 cups (about 700 g) loosely packed ground seitan (grind in a food grinder, food processor or blender)
2 pinches of sea salt
1 tablespoon Italian seasoning
$1/4$ teaspoon freshly ground white or black pepper
1 recipe Whole-Wheat Pie Crust (see page 106)

1. In a saucepan, bring 6 cups (1.5 liters) water to a boil. Meanwhile, peel the potatoes and cut them into eighths. Add a generous pinch of salt and the potatoes to the boiling water, and cook for 20 to 30 minutes, or until tender.

2. While the potatoes are cooking, heat the oil in a large skillet over medium heat and sauté the onion for 3 minutes, or until translucent.

3. Add the seitan and sauté until lightly browned.

4. When the potatoes are tender, drain and mash them, adding a pinch of salt.

5. Mix the potatoes with the seitan. Add the Italian seasoning and pepper and mix well.

6. Preheat the oven to 425°F (220°C).

7. Line a pie plate with the bottom crust, fill with the seitan mixture and cover with the top crust. Seal and flute edges and make slits in the top to allow steam to escape.

8. Bake at 425° F (220°C) for 10 minutes, then lower the heat to 350°F (175°C) and bake 45 to 50 minutes more.

9. Let cool slightly on a wire rack before slicing and serving.

SERVES 8

Preparation time: 25 to 30 minutes
Cooking time: $1^1/2$ hours

Vegetarian Chili

This tasty vegetarian version of the popular Southwestern dish is a good choice when you are serving guests unaccustomed to meatless cooking. I guarantee they will never know the difference, so don't give away your secret until they've tried it.

1 cup (200 g) dried pinto beans
1 tablespoon extra virgin olive oil
4 cloves garlic, minced
1 onion, diced
1 green bell pepper, deseeded and chopped
2 cups (about 375 g) seitan, minced or coarsely ground
2 teaspoons cumin powder
2 to 3 teaspoons chili powder, or to taste
$^1/_4$ teaspoon freshly ground black pepper
1 teaspoon sea salt
1 bay leaf
4 oz (125 g) tomato paste
1 cup (135 g) fresh or frozen sweet corn kernels (optional)
$^1/_2$ teaspoon ground red pepper (cayenne), or to taste (optional)
1 teaspoon dried oregano
1 to 2 teaspoons paprika (any variety)

1. Soak the beans in 3 cups (700 ml) water for 6 to 8 hours, or bring to a full boil for 2 minutes, remove from heat and let stand for $1^1/_2$ to 2 hours. Drain and discard soaking water.

2. Put the soaked beans in a pot, add 4 cups (1 liter) of water, bring to a boil and simmer until the beans are tender ($1^1/_2$ to 2 hours). Check from time to time and add more water as needed.

3. When beans are nearly tender, heat the oil in a large skillet over medium-low heat and cook the garlic and onion for 3 minutes, stirring frequently, or until the onion is translucent.

4. Add the green pepper and cook 2 to 3 minutes more, stirring frequently.

5. Add the seitan, cumin, chili powder and black pepper and cook a few minutes more.

6. When beans are tender, add the seitan mixture, salt, bay leaf, tomato paste diluted with 4 tablespoons water and, if using, the corn. Add more water if needed. The chili should be thick, but not too dry. Bring to a simmer.

7. Taste the chili and add the cayenne, if desired. Continue simmering for 10 to 15 minutes.

8. Add the oregano and paprika and cook 1 to 2 minutes more. Serve hot.

9. Store leftovers in the refrigerator. The flavor is even better the second day.

SERVES 6

Preparation time: about 25 minutes plus 6 to 8 hours to soak beans
Cooking time: about 2 hours 20 minutes

Seitan Stroganoff with Tofu Sour Cream

Our adaptation of this classic dish is meat-free, dairy-free and delicious. It will have your guests asking how you got the "beef" so tender.

Tofu Sour Cream (Makes 1 cup/235 ml)
8 oz (250 g) soft or silken tofu
2 tablespoons fresh lemon juice
$1/2$ teaspoon sea salt
2 teaspoons mirin

. . . .

3 tablespoons extra virgin olive oil
2 cloves garlic or 2 shallots, minced
2 cups (about 375 g) seitan, cut into bite-size pieces
8 oz (225 g) button or other small mushrooms, sliced
Pinch each of sea salt and of freshly ground white or black pepper
Pinch of dried marjoram
Pinch of dried basil
4 tablespoons white wine
8 oz (225 g) artichoke or spinach noodles (flats, ribbons or shells)
Minced fresh parsley, for garnish

1. Place all the tofu sour cream ingredients in a blender and blend until smooth and creamy. If too thick, add a little soymilk or water. If too sour, add more salt.

2. In a large skillet, heat 1 tablespoon of the oil over medium-low heat and cook the garlic or shallots for 1 to 2 minutes, stirring frequently. Do not brown.

3. Increase the heat to medium. Add the seitan and brown it on both sides. Remove the seitan and set aside.

4. Add another tablespoon of the oil. Sauté the mushrooms with a pinch of salt for 2 to 3 minutes.

5. Add the seitan, pepper, marjarom and basil and toss to mix well.

6. Add the wine and tofu sour cream, heat gently, but do not boil.

7. Meanwhile, cook the noodles in 2 quarts (2 liters) rapidly boiling, salted water until just cooked through but still firm. Drain and, while still dripping wet, toss immediately with the remaining tablespoon of oil.

8. Divide the noodles among 2 or 3 individual bowls, top with the stroganoff, garnish with parsley and serve.

SERVES 2 TO 3

Preparation time: 20 minutes
Cooking time: 20 minutes

Pasta e Fagioli with Seitan

Seitan is a great addition to this traditional Italian pasta and bean stew. Besides lending rich flavor, it adds plenty of protein to enhance that of the beans.

> 1 cup (200 g) dried pinto beans or navy beans
> One 4-in (10-cm) piece kombu (optional)
> 2 teaspoons vegetable oil, such as canola or safflower
> 2 cloves garlic, minced
> 1 onion, thinly sliced
> 1 rib celery, sliced
> 1 carrot, chopped
> 1^1/$_2$ cups (about 250 g) seitan, diced
> ^{1}/$_2$ cup (50 g) dried elbow macaroni
> ^{1}/$_2$ teaspoon sea salt
> 1 bay leaf
> ^{1}/$_2$ teaspoon dried oregano or marjoram
> 2 tablespoons barley or red (rice) miso

1. Soak the beans in water to cover for 3 hours or overnight. Discard the soaking water.

2. Combine the beans with kombu and 4^1/$_2$ cups (1.15 liters) water in a pressure cooker. Boil, uncovered, for 10 minutes. Skim off any foam that rises to the surface. Cover, bring to pressure, lower the heat, and cook for 1 hour. (If pot-boiling rather than pressure-cooking, add more water as needed and simmer for 2 hours, or until beans are completely tender.)

3. Meanwhile, heat the oil in a skillet over medium heat and sauté the garlic and onion for 2 to 3 minutes.

4. Add the celery, carrot and seitan and sauté for 2 to 3 minutes. Reduce the heat to low, cover and cook for 10 minutes. Add a little water if necessary to prevent scorching.

5. Bring 4 cups (1 liter) of water to boil in a saucepan, add a pinch of salt and the elbows. Cook for 5 minutes, or until they just begin to soften. Immediately drain, rinse under cold running water until thoroughly cool, drain again and set aside.

6. When the beans are cooked and the pressure has returned to normal, remove the pressure cooker lid and add the salt, bay leaf, oregano and vegetable-seitan mixture. Simmer for 15 minutes, add the elbows and simmer 5 minutes more. Turn off the heat. Remove the bay leaf and discard.

7. Dissolve miso in 2 tablespoons water, add to pot, stir, cover and let sit briefly before serving.

SERVES 4

Preparation time: 25 minutes
Cooking time: about 2 hours plus 3 hours or more to soak beans

海
草

SEA VEGETABLES: UNDERWATER HARVEST

Harvesting plants from the sea may be the wave of the future, but many varieties of sea vegetables have been enjoyed since before the development of agriculture. Archaeological evidence suggests that Japanese cultures have been consuming sea vegetables for more than 10,000 years. In ancient Chinese cultures, sea vegetables were a noted delicacy, suitable especially for honored guests and royalty. Properly prepared, high-quality sea vegetables are delicious and provide a concentrated source of nutrition.

In addition to their impressive nutritional profile, Neptune's jewels offer other health benefits. For centuries, Asian medicine has recognized that sea vegetables contribute to general well-being. Over the last few decades, medical researchers have discovered that including sea vegetables in one's diet reduces the risk of some diseases and helps the body eliminate dangerous toxins. In fact, surveys reveal that people, such as the Japanese, who regularly include sea vegetables in their diet tend to live longer, healthier lives.

Sea vegetables are virtually fat-free, low in calories and rich in essential minerals, vitamins, protein and important trace elements that are often lacking in land vegetables due to soil demineralization. "Sea vegetables contain more minerals than any other kind of food," claim Doctors Seibin and Teruko Arasaki, authors of *Vegetables from the Sea* (Japan Publications, 1981). Analysis has shown that a wide range of minerals account for 7 to 38 percent of their dry weight. All of the elements essential to health—including calcium, sodium, magnesium, potassium, iodine, iron and zinc—are present in sea vegetables in sufficient amounts. Of the wide variety of minerals present, calcium, iron and iodine are of particular importance to people eating a dairy-free, grain-based vegetarian, vegan or macrobiotic diet. For example, $1/4$ cup (4 tablespoons) of cooked hijiki contains over half the calcium found in a cup (250 ml) of milk and more iron than in an egg. Although iodine is, by nature, volatile and somewhat difficult to obtain, sea vegetables contain complex natural sugars that stabilize their iodine, making them excellent sources of this essential mineral.

Edible plants from the sea also contain important vitamins, including vitamin A (in the form of beta-carotene), vitamins B1, B2, B6, niacin, vitamin C, pantothenic acid and folic acid. Analysis has found measurable amounts of vitamin B-12, which never occurs in land vegetables.

A study published in the *American Journal of Clinical Nutrition* suggests that vegetarian nursing mothers with low vitamin B-12 levels get an acceptable source of this nutrient by consuming sea vegetables that are naturally high in B-12. According to research, the relatively high vitamin B-12 content of some sea vegetables is thought to reflect a high level of vitamin B-12–producing microorganisms in these plants.

For those watching their weight, sea vegetables are the perfect food. Their carbohydrates pass through the digestive system as complex fiber, cleansing the intestines while adding no calories to the diet.

Medicine from the Sea

Besides their nutritional abundance, sea vegetables offer numerous health benefits. Asian medicine has long recognized that sea vegetables contribute to general well-being, and especially to the health of the endocrine and nervous systems, while helping the body eliminate dangerous toxins from environmental pollution.

For thousands of years, herbalists and pharmacologists around the world have tested and experimented with medicinal plants. Many modern medicines are either derived from plant extracts or are synthetic copies of substances originally derived from plants. Although there is a long tradition of using sea vegetables as medicine in Japan and China, modern medicine usually regards these remedies as mere folklore.

More recent medicinal treatments using sea vegetables, seawater and mud from the ocean—such as thalassotherapy and algotherapy—are primarily external applications rather than internal medicines. Advocates of these therapies claim reduced or cured symptoms of hypertension, chronic rheumatism, gout, neuralgia, asthma, eczema and even hemorrhoids.

Current interest in the medicinal value of sea vegetables began in 1927, when Professor S. Kondo, of Tohoku University in Sendai, Japan, discovered that Japanese people living in regions where large amounts of sea vegetables were eaten regularly enjoyed a particularly long lifespan. For example, on Oki Island in the Shimane Prefecture, where people eat an abundance of sea vegetables, there is the longest life expectancy in the nation. Before World War II, it was not uncommon to see Oki women who were seventy years old and older diving in the sea for abalone and red algae.

Since Kondo's fieldwork, scientists have learned that sea vegetables, in addition to being very nutritious, have antibiotic and antitumor properties. Sea vegetables have also been found to reduce blood pressure and serum cholesterol. As a result of this research, a few new medicines have been developed from sea vegetable extracts.

Cancer. Diets high in sea vegetables have been associated with a lower risk for both colon and rectal cancers. During a study undertaken in Saitama Prefecture, seven hundred people were closely monitored for their daily food intake. Researchers found that the more sea vegetables an individual ate, the less likely he or she was to develop colon and rectal cancer.

Sea vegetables are also believed to inhibit breast cancer. In Japan, laboratory tests showed that adding sea vegetables to the diet had a significant inhibitory effect on mammary tumor development. The onset of tumors was delayed and the tumors were smaller.

A Japanese animal study found evidence that consumption of sea vegetables inhibited the growth of implanted sarcoma tumors by 89 to 95 percent. According to researchers, more than half of the animals studied experienced complete regression. The report also showed promising results with leukemia.

Although medical researchers cannot point to any particular substance in sea vegetables that accounts for their impressive anticancer properties, Jane Teas, Ph.D., affiliated with the Harvard School of Public Health, suggests lignans may play an important hormonal role. Lignans become phytoestrogens in the body and can have an influence on estrogen levels, particularly in postmenopausal women. Thus, they may have therapeutic and preventive roles in cancers where estrogen levels have an important influence. Lignans are also credited with reducing the blood supply to fast growing tumors, thus decreasing their ability to metastasize to other parts of the body, and can even have a positive influence on menopausal symptoms such as hot flashes. Another substance, fucoidan, a water-soluble carbohydrate that is concentrated in sea vegetables, appears to have a powerful inhibitory effect on cancer cells and reduces inflammation due to tissue damage.

The high levels of iodine and selenium found in brown sea vegetables, such as wakame and kombu, can also shrink breast tumors. Scientists believe that iodine and selenium combine with certain fatty acids to inhibit the growth of some cancers.

Thyroid Hormones. Sea vegetables are nature's richest source of iodine, an important component of the thyroid hormones thyroxine and triiodothyronine. These hormones help regulate metabolism in every cell of the body, so iodine deficiency can have a devastating effect on your health. Because of modern dietary changes and extensive food processing, it is estimated that 200 million people worldwide suffer from thyroid problems, such as goiter. Of these all but 4 percent are thought to be due to iodine deficiency. The American Thyroid Association cautions against consuming too much iodine, so use in moderation. If you are already taking thyroid medication, talk to your doctor before eating large amounts of sea vegetables.

Cardiovascular Disease. Folic acid, which is abundant in sea vegetables, plays an important role in the prevention and cure of cardiovascular disease by breaking down dangerous chemicals, such as homocysteine, that are produced during normal metabolism. Homocysteine can directly damage blood vessel walls, thus increasing the risk of stroke and heart attack. As a result of scientific research, a few new medicines have been developed from this underwater harvest, such as laminin, which is used to reduce blood pressure.

What's more, animal studies presented by a group of Japanese scientists at the September 2006, American Chemical Society's annual meeting in San Francisco showed that the brown pigment in the sea vegetable wakame, a type of kelp, stimulated the animals' livers to release omega-3 fatty acids, which reduce the cholesterol that contributes to arteriosclerosis (the thickening and hardening of the artery walls).

A Powerful Toxin Cleanser. The most important discovery about sea vegetables for modern living, however, is their ability to cleanse the body of toxins. This powerful cleansing action has been linked to a substance called alginic acid, a large chain carbohydrate that is abundant in those sea vegetables classified as brown algae, including kombu, hijiki, arame and wakame. Scientific researchers, including a team led by Dr. Yukio Tanaka, Ph.D., at McGill University, have demonstrated that alginic acid binds with any heavy metals found in the intestines, rendering them indigestible and causing them to be eliminated from the body. So, any heavy metals, such as barium, cadmium, lead, mercury, zinc and even radioactive strontium that may be present in the intestines will not be absorbed by the body when alginic acid is present.

Doctors Seibin and Teruko Arasaki, two Japanese scientists cited above, also report this cleansing property of alginic acid in *Vegetables from the Sea*. They conclude, "Heavy metals taken into the human body are rendered insoluble by alginic acid in the intestines and cannot, therefore, be absorbed into body tissues."

What's more, Dr. Tanaka discovered that the alginic acid in sea vegetables actually helps bind and draw out any similar toxins that are already stored in our bodies, thus "lowering the body's burden."

Brown algae's natural affinity for binding with toxic heavy metals may soon be exploited by industry. Research conducted over the last decade has shown that treating heavy metal-bearing industrial effluents with brown algae is an effective and economical way to detoxify industrial waste. The process, called "biomass bioabsorption," is particularly effective for lead and cadmium.

Antimicrobial Properties. A study done in the early 1960s seems to confirm the traditional belief that sea vegetables have an antibacterial effect in the intestines. Moreover, in the test tube, seaweed extract was shown to be an effective antibiotic drug against common food poisoning bacteria. Sea vegetables have even been shown to inhibit the growth of herpes virus in test tubes.

Stress Reliever. A diet rich in sea vegetables can help relieve the stress and anxiety caused by today's fast-paced, high-pressure culture. Because they are high in pantothenic acid, sea vegetables support the adrenal glands, which become depleted during times of prolonged stress, leading to feelings of fear, chronic fatigue and reduced resistance to allergies and infections. Magnesium and riboflavin are two additional substances found in sea vegetables that reduce stress and promote relaxation.

Other Health Benefits of Sea Vegetables. Researchers led by Kazuo Miyashita, Ph.D., of Hokkaido University, in northern Japan, recently investigated the dietary benefits of wakame, the sea vegetable commonly served in miso soup. They found that fucoxanthin, the pigment in brown sea vegetables, promoted a 10 percent reduction in abdominal fat in some rodents. Scientists pointed out that the studies were on animals and need to be repeated using human subjects, but there is hope that the increased metabolism caused by the brown pigment may be effective in the worldwide fight against obesity.

CORNUCOPIA FROM THE SEA

 The nutritional value of sea vegetables is due in part to the ideal growing conditions of the world's oceans. Living in a marine environment, sea vegetables have ready access to the abundance of nutrients found in the ocean. The gentle wave action of the underwater currents delivers nutrients to sea vegetables and carries away the plants' waste. As a result, sea vegetables concentrate minerals and other nutrients at levels that are rarely found in land plants.

Although biologists classify sea vegetables as plants, the only important characteristic they share with typical land plants is the ability to make food (sugar) from sunlight, carbon dioxide and water. Both sea and land plants use a light-activated catalytic chemical reaction to accomplish this. In green sea vegetables, like land plants, the catalyst is the green pigment chlorophyll. In red and brown sea vegetables, other pigments, such as phycoerythrin, phycocyanin and fucoxanthin, predominate.

One way scientists classify sea vegetables is by their pigment or color. Most of the popular edible sea vegetables, such as wakame, kombu, arame and hijiki, are classified as brown sea vegetables (algae), while nori, the most widely used sea vegetable, falls under the classification of red sea vegetables. Scientists believe that the different colored pigments allow sea vegetables to make food in the ocean depths, where light intensity and wave lengths are different from those found at the surface.

Beyond the ability to make food, sea vegetables bear little resemblance to land plants. Since they have no true leaves, stems or roots, and as they reproduce by a primitive method that does not utilize flowers or seeds, sea vegetables are structurally more like mushrooms and other fungi. From a chef's point of view, the simple structure of sea vegetables is an asset. Without woody roots and stems, there is much more to eat.

Kombu

In the cold seas off Hokkaido, Japan's northernmost island, a brown algae known as kombu, or kelp, grows in a dense underwater forest. Swaying with the rhythm of the sea, individual fronds reach up from the ocean floor sometimes to a height of thirty feet (9 m) or more.

Of the many different grades of kombu gathered from Japan's oceans, the kombu from the Hidaka region is prized above all others. By late summer, the kombu is ready to harvest. Floating on the water in small skiffs, men and women cut the kombu free using razor-sharp knives that are attached to long bamboo poles. As the kombu floats to the surface, it is gathered with wooden rakes and placed in the boats. Once back on land, the kombu is laid out to dry slowly and naturally in the sun.

The quality of Hidaka kombu is evident from its broad flat blade, and its deep, even color when soaked and reconstituted. The white minerals found on the kombu's dried surface contain the prized natural glutamic salts that help make kombu a supreme flavoring agent. These minerals should not be washed off. Simply wipe the kombu with a damp cloth before use.

Hijiki

It has been said that the thick, black, lustrous hair of the Japanese is partly due to their regular diet of hijiki, a brown sea algae. Indeed, this black cylindrical sea vegetable resembles hair as it grows on the ocean floor. Research has shown that minerals are important to healthy hair growth, and hijiki has an incredible 34 grams of minerals per every 100 grams. In fact, there is more calcium in hijiki than that contained in an equal weight of cow's milk. So, there is probably some truth to this Japanese old wives' tale.

Boshu hijiki, which is harvested along the Boshu peninsula on the east coast of Japan's main island, is Japan's premium hijiki. The mild climate of Boshu is ideal for this sea vegetable, which flourishes along the rocky tide line.

This vegetable from the sea is harvested in the early spring, just as it reaches its peak of flavor. When the lowest tides expose the shallows, the hijiki is cut and brought into the shop for processing. After it is washed, the entire plant is steamed for nine hours in its own juices. At this point, the plant has softened considerably, and its color has changed from light brown to black. Left overnight to cool, it is then thoroughly air-dried before being packaged.

The traditional process used by the natural foods suppliers differs from the methods that are typically used to prepare commercial hijiki. In the commercial process, hijiki is boiled in water for long periods, resulting in mineral loss. Furthermore, during the drying process, many of the tiny seedlike hijiki buds get detached from their stems, and collect like a harvest of black grain at the bottom of the drying tank. Whereas many producers sell these separately, traditional processors often mix the nutritious buds back in with the stems, believing that it is important to be able to consume the entire plant, not just one part of it. Hijiki that contains both stems and buds of the plant is known as whole hijiki.

Arame

Like hijiki, arame is a brown algae, but it grows in deeper waters and has a much milder taste. The highest quality arame is gathered off the Ise peninsula, the site of one of Japan's most famous shrines.

In late summer, local fishermen wade out to gather the young, tender plants at low tide, or dive into shallow waters and cut the arame from its holdfast (the plant's rootlike structure). The plants are then finely shredded and processed in a manner similar to that of hijiki.

Nori

Japanese nori is a sea vegetable that has been dried and pressed into thin sheets. Versatile and easy to prepare, nori is rich in protein and in vitamins A, B and C; it is also abundant in a wide range of minerals, most notably calcium and iron. The Japanese consume almost nine billion sheets of nori per year. Nori is also quickly gaining worldwide popularity, due partly to the proliferation of sushi bars that offer various combinations of rice and vegetables or fish wrapped in nori.

After being harvested from the sea, nori is placed in bamboo frames to slowly dry. The process is similar to making fine rice paper.

Along the northeast coast of Japan, in the Sendai region, are the pine-covered islands of scenic Matsushima. This pristine, cold-water coastline is a seemingly endless series of quiet coves and sheltered shallows—the perfect place to grow nori seaweed.

Although originally gathered wild, nori has been cultivated by the Japanese for more than three hundred years. Nets made of woven rope are suspended between long bamboo poles that are set deep into the gentle bays. During the cold months of winter, the nori slowly grows until it covers the entire net. The nets are positioned so they remain above the water level during low tide in order for the growing nori to get maximum sunlight, yet receive a regular washing below the water level during high tide. In January and February, this fragile, red sea vegetable is gathered from the water and brought ashore. There the nori is washed, first in seawater, then in fresh water; it is finally placed in bamboo frames to dry slowly and carefully, a process much like the making of fine paper.

Like many foods in Japan, nori is available in numerous grades. Sendai Select ranks in the top 1 percent of all Japanese nori. Its fine, even texture and translucent, deep-green color are indications of its high quality. Lesser grades of nori are a dull, purplish-black and lack Sendai nori's vibrant luster. When nori quality is important, such as when making fine sushi, Sendai nori is often the choice.

Wakame

The artificial cultivation of *wakame*, a brown algae related to kombu, is a growing industry in Japan. A technical understanding of wakame's complex life cycle has enabled businessmen to grow young wakame in tanks and then transplant them to the ocean floor once they are mature enough to fend for themselves. The mature plants are then harvested by machine and dried with hot air.

Although rare, some wild wakame is still harvested in Japan. The remote fishing villages on the Sanriku Coast of northeastern Japan are renowned for superb seafood and wild wakame. The cold Pacific waters are clean and clear, providing the perfect environment for wakame. The wild wakame from Sanriku has a vitality and depth of flavor that is unequaled by cultivated varieties. There is no fishy flavor, and the fronds are particularly tender and tasty.

Around Sanriku, the wakame harvest takes place in early spring, from February until the end of March. As the plants reach maximum size and before their leaves start to harden, the local fishermen go out in small boats and cut the seaweed by hand, using long, razor-sharp sickles to cut the holdfasts (their rootlike structure). The wakame is brought back to land, briefly washed, then hung up to dry in the sun for several days until it is completely crisp and dry.

Kanten

Known as agar-agar in the West, *kanten* is an ancient vegetable gelatin traditionally made by freezing and drying extracts of various red sea vegetables. Kanten's natural jelling ability, mild flavor and total lack of calories have made it a favorite with health-conscious cooks around the world. Kanten comes prepackaged in bars and flakes.

Today, almost all kanten is made by a modern process that involves the use of sulfuric acid to dissolve the starches, and chemical bleaches and dyes to neutralize the color and flavor. However, a few small producers, such as the Mizoguchi family, in the mountains of Nagano, in central Japan, still use the traditional labor-intensive method.

The natural snow-dried method begins on the coast, where certain red sea vegetables of the Gelidium genus are harvested in the fall and sun-dried. The dried sea vegetables are bundled and taken up to the Mizoguchi shop to be made into kanten during the cold winter months.

Beginning in December, the sea vegetables are placed in a large cauldron with water and allowed to cook down for several hours. The resulting gel is allowed to cool. It is then cut into blocks, arranged on bamboo trays, and set outside on snow-covered rice paddies. Moisture in the gelatin freezes each night then thaws during the day. In about ten days, all the moisture is gone and the light, flaky bars of pure kanten remain. The crisp, porous, feather-light bars are then shaved into fine flakes and packaged.

SHOPPING FOR SEA VEGETABLES

Like land vegetables, the quality of sea vegetables can vary. In Japan, most sea vegetables are supplied in bulk by brokers or middlemen in large quantities. Bulk sea vegetables are packaged under various Asian and natural foods labels for export and domestic use. Some sea vegetables are artificially cultivated, and others are picked from or grown in polluted waters. The highest quality sea vegetables are picked wild from clean waters at just the right time. Most of the natural foods brands of sea vegetables are bought from small, traditional suppliers who have been harvesting wild sea vegetables as a way of life for decades.

When shopping for sea vegetables it is important to read labels carefully and closely inspect the condition of the product before purchase. Most high quality suppliers proudly describe the process of collecting and processing their products on the package. Sea vegetables should not be broken into small pieces in the package.

It is particularly important to purchase only naturally made kanten. Today, almost all kanten found in Asian markets is made by a modern process that involves the use of sulfuric acid and chemical bleaches and dyes. Natural kanten has a beige color and lists only sea vegetables on its label.

COOKING WITH KOMBU

Kombu can be used to create delicious clear soups and cooling molded salads, as well as hearty stews and bean dishes. In most recipes kombu need not be soaked before use. When soaking is called for, merely soak the kombu until it softens and opens up. The nutritious soaking water can be used in the recipe, or reserved and used at a later time in soups or stews.

Kombu's most common and important use is in the preparation of *dashi*, Japan's multipurpose stock for soups, stews and sauces. Dashi appears simple, but it is integral to Japanese cooking, since it is the first step in many traditional dishes. The flavor and quality of the stock help determine the taste of the finished dish.

Kombu is also good when sliced and used in soups, stews and vegetable and bean dishes. When cooking beans, the addition of kombu is particularly recommended, because it helps soften the beans, reduces cooking time and makes them easier to digest. The Japanese commonly use kombu to enhance the flavor of the brine or mash that is used to marinate various types of pickles. Sometimes, the kombu itself is one of the ingredients to be pickled. Kombu can also be cooked in a seasoned broth, wrapped around pieces of burdock or other vegetables and then served as an appetizer.

ALL-PURPOSE KOMBU SEASONING

A nutritious seasoning can be made by roasting kombu and then grinding it to a powder. First, cut the kombu into small pieces and place in an unoiled skillet over medium heat. Stir the kombu pieces constantly until they become very crisp. Transfer the roasted kombu pieces into a *suribachi* (Japanese grinding bowl) or mortar and grind the kombu into a fine powder. Add this powder as a seasoning to soups, or sprinkle it over grains and vegetable dishes before serving.

Kombu Stock (Dashi)

This subtle, flavor-enhancing stock can be made in a very short time using only kombu and water. Two delicious variations on this basic stock—Kombu-Shiitake Stock and Kombu-Bonito Stock—give you endless possibilities for using this healthful flavor base in a variety of soups, sauces, stews and other dishes.

> One 6-in (15-cm) piece dried kombu
> 6 cups (1.5 liters) water

1. Combine the kombu and water in a large saucepan and let soak for 15 to 20 minutes.

2. Bring the stock just to a simmer over medium heat. Gently simmer for 2 to 3 minutes, then remove kombu and reserve for another use.

3. If not using the stock immediately, store it in a covered container in the refrigerator for up to 5 days, or freeze for up to 6 months.

MAKES 6 CUPS (1.5 LITERS)

Preparation time: 2 minutes
Cooking time: 5 minutes, plus 15 to 20 minutes soaking time

Variations

Kombu-Shiitake Stock. This combination makes an especially good stock. Kombu and shiitake offer rich flavor as well as potent health benefits. To prepare Kombu-Shiitake Stock, simply add 4 or 5 dried shiitake mushrooms along with the kombu in Step 1. In Step 2, after removing the kombu, simmer the stock and mushrooms over medium-low heat for about 15 more minutes. Remove the mushrooms and reserve for another use.

Kombu-Bonito Stock. The addition of bonito flakes results in a mild fish-flavored stock that is especially appropriate as a base for fish soups, hearty vegetable soups and Japanese noodle broths. To prepare Kombu-Bonito Stock, after removing the kombu in Step 2, remove the saucepan from the heat, and add 4 tablespoons bonito flakes. Let sit for 1 to 2 minutes, then strain through a fine strainer, pressing any liquid from the flakes with the back of a spoon. Discard the flakes.

4-Hour Daikon Pickles

The crunchy texture and stimulating flavor of these quick pickles piques the appetite and adds interest to simple, whole grain-centered meals.

> One 2-in (5-cm) section kombu
> 1 small daikon, peeled and cut into thin matchsticks
> 1 large carrot, scrubbed and cut into thin matchsticks
> $^1/_2$ cup (125 ml) brown rice vinegar
> 2 tablespoons shoyu (Japanese soy sauce)
> 4 tablespoons mirin or 1 tablespoon honey
> 2 tablespoons water
> 1 small, dried Japanese chile (about $1^1/_2$ in/4 cm long), seeded and cut into slivers, or $^1/_8$ to $^1/_4$ teaspoon dried red pepper flakes

1. Soak the kombu in lukewarm water for 5 to 10 minutes, until it completely opens up. Cut in half lengthwise and slice crosswise into slivers. Combine the kombu, daikon and carrot in a nonmetallic bowl.

2 In a small saucepan, combine the rice vinegar, shoyu, mirin or honey, water and chile slivers and bring to a boil for just 1 minute. Immediately pour over the vegetables in the bowl, mix well and cover the bowl with a cotton towel to keep heat in but allow steam to escape. Mix occasionally.

3. The pickles are ready to eat in about 4 hours. Refrigerate leftovers in a covered container along with the pickling liquid. They will keep for about a month.

MAKES 3 TO 4 CUPS (700 ML TO 1 LITER)

Preparation time: 10 minutes plus 4 hours to pickle

Cooking time: 2 minutes

COOKING WITH HIJIKI AND ARAME

 When properly cooked and presented, hijiki is very attractive. Its shimmering black color adds vivid contrast and beauty to any meal. When planning a meal that includes hijiki, try to use foods with colors that create an attractive counterpoint to the blackness of the hijiki. Carrots, winter squash and pumpkin offer deep orange colors, while lightly steamed broccoli and watercress provide bright green tones. Cold hijiki salad topped with a creamy white tofu dressing and a sprinkle of finely minced green onion or parsley presents an appealing contrast of colors and is particularly enticing on a hot summer day. Although hijiki and arame are prepared in similar ways, there are a few important differences. Hijiki is thicker, somewhat coarser, and has a stronger ocean flavor. Arame's considerably milder aroma and taste make it a good choice for anyone just beginning to use sea vegetables.

Both should be rinsed quickly but carefully to remove foreign matter such as sand and shells, then soaked in water to cover. However, because of the difference in their textures, hijiki should be soaked for 10 minutes, while the more delicate arame needs only 5 minutes. Longer soaking draws out important nutrients and waterlogs these vegetables, making them less able to absorb the flavor of seasonings used in the recipe.

If you use the soaking water in cooking, pour it carefully so as not to disturb any sand or shells that may have sunk to the bottom. Keep back a small amount in the bowl and then discard it. Using the soaking water results in a somewhat stronger flavor and decreases the need for added salt or shoyu. In the recipes that follow, fresh water was used, so if you choose to use soaking water, cut the amount of shoyu in half and add more only if needed.

Take into consideration that soaking increases the dried volume of arame and hijiki by about three times. For general preparation, squeeze out excess water after soaking and sauté the sea vegetable in a little oil for a few minutes. Add soaking water or fresh water to almost cover and simmer until the vegetable is tender and most of the liquid is absorbed (about 35 minutes for hijiki and 25 minutes for arame). Finally, season the tender vegetables with shoyu and mirin, and cook a few minutes more. Both hijiki and arame are delicious when sautéed with sweet vegetables such as carrots, slow-cooked onions, winter squash, lotus root, shiitake mushrooms and corn. Hijiki and arame are also delicious when served with deep-fried fresh tofu or when sautéed with dried tofu (see Arame with Dried Tofu and Vegetables, page 154). A little chopped hijiki or arame can be combined with cooked rice, millet or barley. Hijiki and arame are good additions to salads, especially when topped with a tofu dressing.

Although the following recipes specify hijiki or arame, if you wish to substitute one for the other, simply make the previously mentioned adjustments in soaking and cooking time.

Arame Salad

A dollop of cooked arame makes a nutritious and exotic addition to tossed salads, or it can stand on its own, with just a bed of lettuce and a creamy, white tofu dressing sprinkled with parsley to contrast the almost black sea vegetable.

> 1 cup (15 g) dried arame
> 5 cups (1.25 liters) water
> 1 tablespoon shoyu (Japanese soy sauce)
> 1 teaspoon mirin (optional)
> Several lettuce leaves
> 1 to 2 tablespoons Sesame-Tofu Dressing (see page 156)
> Minced fresh parsley, for garnish

1. Soak the arame in lukewarm water for 5 minutes, or until tender. Drain the arame, rinse, and drain again.

2. Bring the water, shoyu and mirin, if using, to a boil, add the arame and simmer for 20 minutes. Drain and let cool to room temperature, or chill slightly.

3. On a serving plate, make a bed for the arame with the lettuce leaves. Set the arame on top, sprinkle with the Sesame-Tofu Dressing and garnish with the parsley.

> SERVES 4
>
> *Preparation time:* 5 minutes plus time to cool the cooked arame
> *Cooking time:* 25 minutes

Marinated Hijiki-Sesame Salad

Here's a delicious marinated sea vegetable salad that we like to process in small batches in a hot water bath, so we'll have some on hand to add interest and concentrated nutrition to simple meals. This recipe makes enough for two 12-ounce (350 ml) jars. Use glass preserving jars with metal screw bands and new lids. If you prefer to make more, simply double or triple the recipe.

> 1 oz (25 g) hijiki
> 1 carrot, thinly sliced

$^1/_2$ cup (50 g) turnips, diced into bite-size pieces

2 teaspoons sesame seeds

1 small onion, sliced

6 tablespoons brown rice vinegar

6 tablespoons shoyu (Japanese soy sauce)

$1^1/_2$ tablespoons mirin

$1^1/_2$ teaspoons toasted sesame oil

2 pinches of sea salt

$^2/_3$ cup (175 ml) water

1. To reconstitute the hijiki, soak in lukewarm water for 10 minutes, or until softened. Rinse, drain and cook in boiling water for 1 minute. Transfer to a bowl of ice cold water. When cool, drain and set aside.

2. Cook the carrots in boiling water for 20 seconds. Cool immediately, drain and set aside.

3. Cook the turnips for 10 seconds, cool immediately, drain and set aside.

4. In a small dry skillet, lightly toast the sesame seeds over medium heat for 1 to 2 minutes, or until they are fragrant or begin to pop. Remove from pan and set aside.

5. Combine the hijiki, carrots, turnip, onion and sesame seeds well and pack the mixture into the 12-ounce preserving jars to within $^1/_2$ inch (1.3 cm) of the top.

6. Combine the vinegar, shoyu, mirin, sesame oil, salt and water in a small saucepan. Heat the liquid until it reaches 180°F (80°C). Do not boil. Pour the hot brine mixture over the vegetables to cover. Screw caps on.

7. In a tall pot, bring enough water to a boil to cover the jars. With tongs, lower the jars into the boiling water. Keep them in the boiling water for 10 minutes. Remove the jars, check lids and tighten if necessary. Let cool. Store until ready to use. They will keep for up to a year.

MAKES TWO 12-OUNCE (350 ML) JARS

Preparation time: about 20 minutes

Cooking time: 15 minutes

COOKING WITH WAKAME

 The taste and texture of different varieties of wakame vary considerably. If you have been put off by the strong ocean flavor and relatively tough texture of one brand, look for a wild variety. You may be surprised at how mild and delicious wakame can be. Dried wakame is reconstituted by soaking in water for 10 to 15 minutes. Once soaked, remove the wakame, squeeze out the excess moisture, cut away any tough ribs, and slice the fronds. Wakame is especially good in soups and salads. It can also be added to stews and vegetable or bean dishes. Wakame is tender and should not be cooked for more than a few minutes.

Miso Soup with Wakame

This is an energizing way to start the day, and our favorite way to enjoy wakame. Feel free to vary the vegetables according what you have on hand.

> 6 cups (1.5 liters) Kombu Stock (see page 176) or Kombu-Shiitake Stock (see page 176)
> 1 potato, peeled and diced
> 1 carrot, thinly sliced on the diagonal
> One 6-in (15-cm) section wakame
> 2 green onions (scallions), thinly sliced on the diagonal
> 3 to 4 tablespoons red (rice) or barley miso

1. In a saucepan, bring the stock to a simmer over medium heat. Add the potato and simmer for 5 minutes.

2. Add the carrots and simmer for 10 to 15 minutes, or until tender.

3. Meanwhile, soak the wakame in cold or tepid water for 10 minutes. Cut away any tough ribs and slice the fronds into 1-inch (2.5-cm) pieces.

4. When the carrots are tender, add wakame to the soup, and simmer for 1 minute.

5. Add the green onions and simmer another minute. Remove from the heat.

6. Dissolve the miso in some of the broth, then return to the saucepan. Allow to steep briefly before serving.

> SERVES 4
>
> *Preparation time:* 10 minutes
> *Cooking time:* 25 to 30 minutes

Wakame-Cucumber Salad

A Japanese friend taught me this nutritious, low-calorie salad, which we find especially refreshing on hot days.

> 1 cucumber, peeled if waxed
> $^1/_2$ teaspoon sea salt
> 2 cups (475 ml) water, plus more for soaking wakame
> $^1/_2$ cup (10 g) dried wakame
> 2 tablespoons brown rice vinegar
> 2 teaspoons mirin

2 teaspoons shoyu (Japanese soy sauce)

1 teaspoon water

Boston lettuce leaves to make a bed for the salads

1 small red radish, very thinly sliced, for garnish (optional)

About 2 tablespoons clover sprouts, for garnish (optional)

1. Thinly slice the cucumber, sprinkle with the salt and toss. Gently squeeze the cucumber in your hand and set aside.

2. Soak the wakame in tepid water to cover for 10 minutes, or until soft.

3. Bring the 2 cups (475 ml) of water to a boil in a small saucepan, drop in the soaked wakame for about 10 seconds, then immediately remove and plunge it into cold water to brighten and set the color. Remove any tough ribs and chop the wakame into ³/₄-inch (2-cm) pieces. Wrap it in a clean towel to remove excess moisture.

4. Gently squeeze the sliced cucumbers once again to remove excess liquid. Place them in a bowl with the wakame.

5. Combine the vinegar, mirin, shoyu and water in a small bowl. Pour this dressing over the vegetables and toss.

6. Arrange the dressed cucumber and wakame on a bed of Boston lettuce. Garnish with the radish slices and a light sprinkling of sprouts, if desired.

SERVES 3

Preparation time: 10 minutes plus 10 minutes soaking time

Cooking time: 1 minute

COOKING WITH NORI

Except for sushi nori, which comes already toasted, nori should be lightly toasted just before using by briefly passing the unfolded sheet over a gas flame or electric burner. The nori is ready when the color changes to a more brilliant green and it becomes crisp and fragrant.

Nori is most commonly used to wrap around rice balls, which are probably the most common and popular addition to Japanese lunch boxes and picnic baskets. Nori is also used to wrap other foods, such as nori-maki sushi. When cut into 2-inch (5-cm) strips, nori is delicious wrapped around mouthfuls of warm rice dabbed with *umeboshi* paste. Crumbled or cut into slivers, nori can be used to garnish soups, vegetables and grain or noodle dishes.

Recently nori has become popular as a party food in a variation of nori-maki called *te-maki*. Te-maki literally means "wrapping by hand." A quarter sheet of toasted nori is topped with a little sushi rice along with an assortment of foods such as raw tuna, avocado or raw vegetables. Condiments such as umeboshi or wasabi may be added, then the nori "package" is rolled into a funnel or cone shape. Te-maki adds an exotic flair to parties, especially when served with hot sake.

Another variety of nori, called *ao nori*, or green nori, is sold in flake form. Ao nori is used as a garnish or as a seasoning in fried rice. This type of nori is the richest in iron and protein.

Noodle Rolls

Noodle rolls require a delicate hand but are not difficult to make. When patiently and skillfully prepared, the reward is a beautiful, elegant and tasty main dish. For variety, add other ingredients with the noodles to fill the rolls. Strips of fried tempeh or seitan, sauerkraut, blanched scallion greens, radish sprouts, and toasted and ground sesame seeds are excellent filling choices.

8 oz (250 g) dried thin (ito) soba or whole-wheat somen noodles
4 sheets nori
2 teaspoons wasabi powder (Japanese horseradish)

Dipping Sauce
1¹/₂ tablespoons shoyu (Japanese soy sauce)
1¹/₂ tablespoons water or Vegetable Stock (see opposite)
1¹/₂ teaspoons mirin (optional)

1. Cook the noodles according to the directions on the package. Rinse under cold running water or in a cold water bath until cool enough to handle, then drain thoroughly. Once drained, neatly arrange the noodles on a clean, dry towel. Spread them out in even lines from left to right.

2. Toast the nori (or use pretoasted sushi nori). Place one sheet of nori, toasted side down, on a sushi mat, small towel or counter. Lay one quarter of the noodles side by side across the nori. There should be ¹/₂ inch (1.25 cm) of uncovered nori at the bottom and 1¹/₂ inches (3.75 cm) at the top. Roll up nori as firmly as possible. Let the roll rest on its seam.

3. Repeat with remaining sheets of nori and noodles.

4. Using a sharp knife, and cleaning the blade after each cut, carefully slice rolls in half, then cut each half into 3 equal pieces.

5. Combine the shoyu, water or stock and mirin in a small bowl and mix well. Place in small individual saucers.

6. Add one drop of water at a time to the wasabi and mix until it forms a thick paste.

7. To serve, place noodle roll pieces, cut side up, on a platter along with the mound of wasabi paste. You may also add wasabi to individual bowls of dipping sauce. Wasabi is strong-flavored, so begin by adding a small amount to the sauce, then add more depending on individual taste.

SERVES 4

Preparation time: 25 minutes
Cooking time: 10 minutes

Vegetable Stock

Leftover vegetable trimmings and peelings, such as onion skins, wilted greens, tops of leeks and scallions, carrot and celery ends, mushroom stems and wakame "ribs," can all be used to produce a good vegetable stock. Basically, avoid using members of the cabbage family, such as broccoli and cauliflower, and don't use peels that have been waxed or scraps that are spoiled. Trimmings from organic vegetables are recommended. Store the peelings and other trimmings in a container or plastic bag, and refrigerate until you have about a quart (4 cups/750 g). Keep in mind that most trimmings are highly perishable and should be used within a few days.

4 cups (750 g) vegetable trimmings
8 cups (2 liters) water
$^1/_2$ teaspoon sea salt
Bay leaf (optional)
2 sprigs fresh parsley (optional)
A pinch each of 2 to 3 flavorful dried herbs of your choice, such as rosemary, thyme, chervil, tarragon, majoram or oregano (optional)

1. Place all of the ingredients in a soup pot and bring to a boil over medium heat. Reduce the heat to medium-low and simmer, covered, about 20 minutes. Strain the stock into another pot or large bowl.

2. Use immediately or refrigerate in a covered container for up to 5 days. Vegetable stock can also be frozen for up to 6 months.

Note to Cook

When there are no trimmings on hand, you can still make a good stock using whole vegetables. For a basic recipe that yields 6 cups (1.5 liters), use 1 onion that has been cut into wedges; 1 or 2 chopped carrots, 1 chopped celery rib, a few sprigs of fresh parsley and a bay leaf. Don't peel the vegetables. Just scrub them well and cut off the root and stem ends. Place the ingredients in a soup pot with 6 cups (1.5 liters), water, and follow the directions above.

MAKES ABOUT 8 CUPS (2 LITERS)

Preparation time: 5 minutes
Cooking time: 25 minutes

Stuffed Nori Cones

Also called *te-maki*, these cones make an attractive snack, party food or meal starter. Thanks to Peter and Montse Bradford, authors of *Cooking with Sea Vegetables* (Healing Arts Press, 1986), for sharing this festive recipe.

    2 sheets toasted nori
    1 cup (200 g) cooked brown rice
    $^1/_2$ cup (25 g) chopped watercress
    1 small carrot, grated
    4 tablespoons toasted sesame seeds
    1 tablespoon fresh lemon juice
    1 tablespoon natural prepared mustard
    1 tablespoon umeboshi vinegar
    Watercress sprigs, for garnish

1. With scissors, cut each nori sheet in half lengthwise, then cut both pieces in half crosswise to make four quarters. Set aside.

2. Place all remaining ingredients in a bowl and mix together well.

3. Taking one piece of nori at a time, carefully fold into a cone shape. A drop of water rubbed on the edge will help the overlapping sides stick together.

4. Just before serving, fill each cone with the mix, decorating the top of each with a sprig of watercress.

5. Arrange filled cones neatly on a tray and serve.

MAKES 8 CONES

Preparation time: 20 to 25 minutes

COOKING WITH KANTEN

Light and refreshingly cool, kanten dishes are especially popular in the summer. In any season, kanten can be used with vegetables and stock to make aspics; as a substitute for pectin in jams, jellies and cranberry sauce; and in desserts such as puddings and pie fillings. Even without refrigeration, kanten sets quickly as it cools and seals in the natural flavor and sweetness of any fruits and vegetables used.

According to Peter and Montse Bradford, authors of *Cooking with Sea Vegetables* (Healing Arts Press, 1986), the jelling ability of natural kanten varies according to the acidity or alkalinity of the food with which it is used. Acidic foods may require more kanten than alkaline foods. Testing the recipe is recommended. This can be done by simply taking a spoonful of the heated mixture and allowing it to rapidly set on a cool surface. If the mixture does not set in a few minutes, add a little more kanten to the pot and simmer a few more minutes.

Kanten comes in flakes and bars. The flakes are very convenient and easy to use. Brief soaking is called for in some recipes, but it is not required. Simply sprinkle the measured amount over the liquid before heating and proceed as instructed in the recipe.

If using kanten bars, tear them into several pieces and soak them in water for 30 to 60 minutes. Remove the kanten, squeeze out any excess water and place in a saucepan along with the liquid called for in the recipe. The liquid should be cold or at room temperature. Bring to a simmer over medium heat without stirring. Once the liquid begins to simmer, stir occasionally until the kanten dissolves (about two to three minutes).

In any recipe, flakes can be substituted for bars and vice versa. The jelling strength of one bar of kanten is equal to two slightly rounded tablespoons of flakes.

| Plum Sorbet |

This is a simple and pretty dessert. Although plums are not used in frozen desserts as often as peaches, berries and citrus fruit, they make an especially creamy sorbet.

6 soft, ripe, flavorful plums (12 to 16 oz/350 to 450 g)
$^1/_3$ cup (75 ml) water
$1^1/_2$ teaspoons kanten flakes
$^2/_3$ to $^3/_4$ cup (150 to 175 ml) brown rice malt syrup or $^1/_4$ to $^1/_3$ cup
    (50 to 75 ml) honey, or to taste
1 teaspoon fresh lemon juice

1. Halve and pit the plums. Combine them with the water in a stainless steel, glass or enamel-coated saucepan and set over medium heat. Bring to a simmer, cover, and cook gently over medium-low heat, stirring occasionally, for 10 to 15 minutes, or until tender. Remove from the heat.

2. With a slotted spoon transfer the plums, including skins, to a blender or food processor.

3. Sprinkle the kanten flakes over the remaining cooking liquid and gently simmer for 2 to 3 minutes, stirring occasionally.

4. Add the liquid to the plums, and purée until smooth.

5. While plums are still hot, mix in the sweetener and lemon juice and mix well. Pour the mixture into a baking pan, casserole dish or undivided ice tray and cover with foil or plastic wrap. Freeze until solid, at least 6 hours.

6. Scoop out and eat as is or, for a creamier texture, blend it again at least 1 hour and up to 1 day before serving. To blend, scrape the frozen mixture with a fork until it resembles finely crushed ice. Purée half the sorbet at a time in chilled bowl of blender or food processor until light and smooth but not thawed. Place the blended sorbet in a pint container, cover, and freeze for 1 to 3 hours, or until firm.

MAKES 1 PINT (425 G)

Preparation time: 10 to 20 minutes plus at least 6 hours to freeze
Cooking time: 20 minutes

Raspberry-Peach Kanten

Kanten makes an especially good summer dessert since it is light and cooling and requires little time or heat to prepare. This combination of fruits makes a colorful and tasty "Jell-O," but feel free to substitute other juices and fruits. Or, eliminate the fresh fruit and simply gel your favorite fruit juice.

> 1 quart (1 liter) peach juice
> 5 level tablespoons kanten flakes
> 2 level tablespoons crushed kuzu starch
> 2 teaspoons fresh lemon juice
> $1^1/_2$ cups (200 g) fresh red raspberries

1. Pour the juice into a saucepan and sprinkle with the kanten. Let sit 5 minutes.

2. Bring the juice to a simmer over medium heat without stirring. Once it begins to simmer, gently stir if necessary to dissolve the kanten.

3. Dissolve the kuzu in 2 tablespoons water and add it to the mixture while stirring. Continue stirring until the juice returns to a simmer and thickens slightly. Simmer for 2 minutes and remove from the heat.

4. Add the lemon juice and pour the hot juice over the berries in a casserole dish or mold. Refrigerate or set in a cool place, uncovered. The kanten will be firm in 1 to 2 hours. (If you want the kanten to set more quickly, pour the mixture into shallow individual serving bowls and refrigerate.)

SERVES 8

Preparation time: 5 minutes plus 5 minutes soaking time
Cooking time: about 8 minutes

MIRIN: SWEET RICE WINE

If you have not yet discovered authentic mirin (sweet rice wine), you are in for a treat. An exquisite, versatile seasoning, mirin has the unique ability to coax out and accentuate the flavors from bland or light-tasting foods. Known as one of the three essential tastes of traditional Japanese cuisine, mirin's mild sweetness balances many dishes and tones down strong flavors.

Mirin had its birth more than five hundred years ago as a thick, sweet drink. According to ancient Japanese texts, around the twelfth century, the Japanese began mixing cooked sweet glutinous rice with sake (rice wine) to enjoy as a festive drink. However, due to its high yeast and natural sugar content, the mirinlike liquid spoiled easily. In an effort to prolong shelf life, brewers in the warm southern islands began distilling the sweet rice beverage in the sixteenth century. The clear alcoholic concentrate that resulted, called *shochu* (literally, "fiery spirits"), was about 80 proof and tasted somewhat like vodka. Over the next few centuries, breweries in Japan's central region experimented by adding natural enzymes and sweet glutinous rice to the shochu. The mixture underwent long aging and purification, after which the thick, sweet liqueur was bottled, becoming one of Japan's most exclusive and expensive alcoholic beverages. Later, as its seasoning virtues were discovered, mirin became a dominant flavor in the traditional art of *kaiseki*, Japan's highest form of cooking.

Traditional mirin is a delicious and healthy substitute for refined sugar in many savory dishes. Mirin has some of the sweet characteristics of sugar, but it is nutritionally more complex, like rice syrup. Unlike white sugar, mirin does not shock the body's blood sugar regulating mechanism. Also, in contrast to sugar, mirin delivers more than just empty calories. One of mirin's complex sugars, known as oligosaccharide, helps maintain a beneficial bacterial population in the intestines. This so-called probiotic effect is important in the prevention of colon cancer and other diseases of the digestive system.

Like several other fermented foods, the alcohol in mirin acts as a preservative and has a beneficial effect on metabolism. In fact, mirin is sometimes added to the finest tamari as a preservative. Various components in the koji (cultured rice) used to make mirin are broken down by enzymes during fermentation and blend well with tamari's amino acids to create a delicious, complex flavor. Although mirin contains more alcohol than most wines, it seems to have less of a tranquillizing effect. In fact, during Japan's samurai period it was considered an energy drink.

Mirin's complex double fermentation process enhances its nutritional value. The fermenting microorganisms produce B vitamins such as B1, B2 and B6. Japanese researchers report that authentic mirin has four times more antioxidants than less expensive mirin substitutes that are not traditionally aged, such as sugar-sweetened rice wine. There is also some evidence that cooking with mirin can help vegetables retain important phytochemicals.

TRADITIONAL MIRIN PRODUCTION—A WAY OF LIFE

By the 1940s, production of mirin was a thriving industry with over two hundred producers. However, the processing of mirin did not survive the rice shortages of World War II or the post-war 76 percent liquor tax. As reported in the *Asahi Shinbun*, Japan's leading daily news-paper, by 1959 only one small shop in Japan was using the traditional methods of mirin brewing. Recently, however, a handful of small companies have begun the production of authentic mirin using the labor-intensive fermentation methods that are steeped in the history and culture of preindustrial Japan. More than a process, the ancient art represents a way of life that, like authentic mirin, is rare in the modern world.

At traditional mirin shops, the year-long cycle begins in the fall with the making of koji, the thousand-year-old ubiquitous catalyst that starts the fermentation of many important foods such as sake, rice vinegar, miso, shoyu and tamari. The making of koji begins with brown rice that is polished to remove the oily outer bran (preventing an off-taste) and then soaked in spring water overnight. The following morning, the rice is steamed and then cooled until it is warm to the touch. Next, *Aspergillus* mold spores are sprinkled over the rice and mixed in carefully so that each rice grain comes in contact with a microscopic spore. Finally, the warm inoculated rice is hurriedly carried to a uniquely constructed room called the *muro*. This traditional koji incubation room has three-foot (90-cm)-thick cedar-lined walls that are insulated with rice hulls to retain heat.

Through the night, in the warm, humid condition of the muro, the spores of the starter culture germinate and send enzyme-laden filaments into the individual grains of rice. These filaments digest complex carbohydrates, transforming them into sweet sugars.

By morning, the mound of rice is fused together into a dense, damp mass. Using their hands and wooden shovels, mirin producers work through the morning breaking up the huge mound of rice into individual grains. They work in temperatures over 100°F (38°C) with 100 percent humidity. While visitors cannot stand the stifling air of the muro for more than a few minutes, traditional mirin makers, after decades of acclimatization, work at a relaxed pace, stopping briefly to gossip or to wipe the perspiration from their faces. After lunch, the rice is placed in dozens of wooden trays and left to ferment for a second night.

At the Sumiya Bunjiro Shoten in Hekinan, sweet rice is steamed and cooled in the preparation of mirin, Japan's sweet rice wine seasoning. Traditionally crafted mirin is rare in modern Japan.

Through the second night, as he has done since childhood, the mirin brewmaster visits the muro often to check the developing koji and to regulate the muro temperature by opening or closing the windows, which are located in the ceiling. Even after decades of making koji, one traditional producer said, "It's a world of mystery, which is better left to intuition than to modern technology." Early the next morning, workers enter the warm, misty muro to taste the fluffy-white, glistening koji. The best handmade koji is sweet and soft. When the koji is finished, the next phase of mirin making is ready to begin.

Although most mirin manufacturers, past and present, buy inexpensive shochu that has been distilled from molasses, a few families still prepare their own from handmade koji, premium rice and spring water. These ingredients are mixed together and stirred each day for about a month. The resulting alcoholic mash, called *sake moromi*, is placed into cotton sacks, pressed, filtered and distilled into clear rice shochu. This completes the first phase of authentic mirin processing.

Next, sweet glutinous rice is soaked in water and steamed. Stripped to the waist, the mirin maker mounts a platform beside the rice steamer. Here he begins the back-breaking, hours-long task of shoveling the cooked sweet rice onto a cooling table. Before the day is over, some producers will repeat this process two more times, shoveling a total of three or four tons of rice. The cooked sweet rice is then added to the shochu along with more koji. This second mash, called mirin moromi, is placed in 1,000-gallon (3,785-liter) enamel vats that are insulated with rice-straw mats. With the exception of an occasional stirring, the mirin moromi is left to ferment for about three months. Gradually, the koji enzymes break down the complex carbohydrates and protein of the glutinous rice into sweet simple sugars and amino acids that blend with the shochu to form a delicious alcoholic rice pudding that, unfortunately, only traditional mirin manufacturers ever get to sample.

Standing over the huge vats, the brewmaster sniffs the sweet rising vapors to judge the progress of the developing mash. A quick taste confirms what his nose has already discovered: It's time to pump the mash into cotton sacks and press out its sweet essence. (The remaining flavorful pressed moromi is used to make delicious mirin pickles.) Finally, this sweet essence (immature mirin) is returned to the enamel vats and left to age for about 200 days. During the hot days of the long Japanese summer, the subtle color and flavor of the mirin develops further. In the fall, mirin makers eagerly sample their golden harvest and confirm that their old recipe yields mirin that is as delicious as ever. The mature mirin is then filtered through cotton and bottled, unpasteurized, for shipment to customers in Japan and, more recently, in the West.

SHOPPING FOR MIRIN

 Although there are now about ninety mirin producers in Japan, only a few use the simple ingredients sweet rice, koji and shochu, and the traditional process just described. Some manufacturers buy inexpensive molasses shochu and use koji made by automated machines, then they add sweet rice or cornstarch to make a quicker, less expensive mirin, which is rarely aged more than a few months. Other mirins usually sold in Asian food markets are actually synthetic blends of syrup, glucose, corn syrup, ethyl alcohol, amino acids and salt. This type of mirin has no depth of flavor and can serve only as a sugar substitute in some types of cooking. There is also a related product sold in some natural foods stores that is made without sweet rice and has salt added to it. Although this product is often called mirin, it is known as ajinohaha. Ajinohaha cannot be legally sold as mirin in Japan; however, if you cannot find authentic mirin, it is the best substitute.

Authentic mirin contains rice, sweet rice and water, and it has no additives or preservatives—surprisingly simple ingredients for such a complex, delicious and versatile food. The best place to find authentic mirin is in natural foods stores.

Mirin is indispensable in Japanese cooking. In fact, mirin, shoyu and dashi (kombu stock) are known as the three essential tastes of old Japan. The traditional sweetening agent long before the arrival of white sugar, mirin is still commonly used in Japan to provide a balance for salty seasonings and to enhance the flavor of vinegared dishes. With a little experience you can use mirin in a variety of ways to enhance Western-style cooking as well. It is excellent in marinades, vinaigrettes, both sweet and savory sauces, noodle broths, simmered vegetable or fish dishes, with sautéed vegetables, fried noodles and in dips for tempura or sushi. Mirin's mild sweetness rounds out the flavor of many dishes, providing a satisfying, balanced taste.

Cooking Techniques

The following are tips for using mirin in both Asian and Western cooking styles.

Sautéeing and Stir-Frying. Mirin adds depth of flavor to sautéed and stir-fried vegetables, fish and noodle dishes, enhancing and rounding out the flavors while contributing to the richness of the dish. Its high natural sugar content means it can burn easily, so it is often best to add toward the end of cooking.

Simmering. Mirin is used to flavor many simmered and poached dishes including fish, shiitake mushrooms, reconstituted dried tofu and deep-fried tofu. When simmering foods, use 1 tablespoon of mirin and 1 tablespoon of shoyu per 1 cup (235 ml) of water or stock.

Suggested Uses

Here are some typical ways in which mirin is used to enhance the flavor of foods.

In Dipping Sauces. Tempura and other deep-fried Japanese foods, such as mochi, are almost always dipped in a sauce that includes mirin and shoyu (soy sauce).

In Marinades. Sake or other wines act as tenderizers and are generally preferred for marinating fish. Mirin, on the other hand, makes food firmer and helps maintain the food's texture and shape. Mirin marinade is best used with such tender foods as tofu. Occasionally mirin is added in small amounts to fresh fish in order to help tone down a strong taste and aroma.

In Noodle Broths. Mirin is the "secret" ingredient that lends a characteristic flavor to Japanese noodle broths and dips. Without mirin, these dishes tend to be flat. (See Japanese Noodles in Broth, page 193).

In Sauces and Gravies. A tablespoon of mirin will transform a ho-hum sauce into a rich, gourmet's delight.

In Sushi. Before sugar became cheap and widely available, mirin was used along with salt and rice vinegar to season sushi rice. Mirin makes the rice soft yet firm and gives the grain a desirable glossy appearance. For 3 cups (575 g) of uncooked rice, use $^1/_3$ cup (75 ml) of brown rice vinegar, 1 teaspoon of sea salt and 2 tablespoons of mirin.

Cook the rice, let it cool somewhat, and "cut" the vinegar mixture into the cooked rice with the side of a bamboo rice paddle or wooden spoon. Do not stir it in, or the rice will become gummy.

In Desserts. Mirin is not just for savory dishes. It is a delicious addition to poached fruits, fruit cakes, tea cakes and glazes for cakes and muffins.

Teriyaki Tempeh with Soba and Steamed Vegetables

This is a delicious way to get the benefits of tempeh. Simple to make and full of flavor and nutrition, it is a complete meal that can be ready to eat in just over a half hour. The teriyaki sauce in this recipe can also be used to make an ultra easy tofu dish— simply marinate slices of firm tofu in the sauce, pan-fry the tofu and add the sauce to the skillet during the last minute of cooking.

Teriyaki Sauce
3 tablespoons shoyu (Japanese soy sauce)
3 tablespoons mirin
1 tablespoon brown rice vinegar
. . . .
1 tablespoon peanut or grapeseed oil
2 teaspoons peeled and minced fresh ginger
2 teaspoons minced garlic
$1/4$ teaspoon dried red pepper flakes (optional)
4 oz (125 g) tempeh
8 oz (250 g) dried soba (buckwheat) noodles
12 to 15 asparagus spears
1 carrot, cut into thin matchsticks
$1/2$ red onion, cut crosswise into $3/8$-in (1-cm)-thick half rings
2 teaspoons toasted sesame oil
2 green onions (scallions), sliced

1. Combine the teriyaki sauce ingredients in a small bowl.

2. In a large skillet or wok with a lid, heat the peanut oil and sauté the ginger, garlic and the red pepper flakes, if using, over medium heat for 1 minute.

3. Cut the tempeh in half, then cut each piece in half by thickness and dice into bite-size pieces. Add the tempeh to the skillet and sauté for 5 minutes.

4. Add half of the teriyaki sauce to the skillet, reduce the heat to low, cover, and gently simmer for 10 minutes, stirring occasionally.

5. Bring 8 to 10 cups (2 to 2.5 liters) of water to a boil in a large saucepan. Add the soba noodles, and cook until tender but firm. Immediately drain noodles and rinse them briefly under cold running water or in a cold-water bath. Drain and set aside.

6. Discard the tough ends of the asparagus and cut the tender spears in half crosswise. Place the asparagus, carrot and onion in a steamer basket, set over boiling water, cover and steam for 5 minutes, or until the vegetables are just tender. Remove the vegetables and set aside.

7. Add the remaining teriyaki sauce and the toasted sesame oil to the tempeh, bring to a simmer, then add the vegetables and toss well. Add the soba and toss gently until heated through.

8. Garnish with green onion and serve immediately.

SERVES 2 TO 3

Preparation time: 15 minutes
Cooking time: 30 to 35 minutes

Japanese Noodles in Broth

This popular, satisfying dish takes little time to prepare. Simply served with a garnish of green onion, Japanese Noodles in Broth makes a filling lunch or can be served as the soup course in a heartier meal. You can top the noodles with a colorful assortment of steamed, simmered or deep-fried vegetables, fish, tofu, mochi or seitan for a complete dinner. Udon or soba noodles are recommended.

8 oz (225 g) dried udon or soba (buckwheat) noodles
3 cups (700 ml) Kombu-Shiitake Stock (see page 176) or Kombu-Bonito
   Stock (see page 176)
$1/8$ teaspoon sea salt
2 tablespoons shoyu (Japanese soy sauce)
$1^1/2$ tablespoons mirin
1 to 2 teaspoons fresh ginger juice (finely grate fresh ginger and squeeze to
   extract juice)
Finely minced green onion (scallion), for garnish

1. Bring 8 to 10 cups (2 to 2.5 liters) water to a boil in a large saucepan, add the noodles and cook until tender but still firm. Drain, rinse briefly under cold running water, drain well and set aside.

2. In the saucepan, combine the stock, salt, shoyu and mirin. Simmer for 1 minute. Remove from the heat and add the ginger juice.

3. To serve, divide noodles between two deep individual serving bowls and ladle hot broth over noodles to almost cover. Garnish with minced green onion or topping of choice.

SERVES 2

Preparation time: 5 minutes
Cooking time: 15 to 20 minutes

Glazed Acorn Squash

A perfect side dish for a holiday meal, this golden-colored treat can also be enjoyed any day of the week. For a satisfying meal, try serving it with a hearty grain, such as wild rice, and a tofu, tempeh or seafood dish.

1 small acorn squash, quartered, seeded, peeled and cut crosswise into $3/8$-in (1-cm)-wide slices
$1/2$ cup (125 ml) water
4 tablespoons mirin
$1/2$ cinnamon stick
3 or 4 whole cloves
Pinch of sea salt

1. Combine all ingredients in a large saucepan and bring to a boil. Lower the heat and gently simmer, covered, for 15 to 20 minutes, or until squash is tender. With a slotted spoon, immediately transfer squash to a warmed serving dish and keep warm in a 170°F (75°C) oven.

2. Strain the cooking liquid and return it to the saucepan. Boil down the liquid rapidly to half its volume—you should have about 3 tablespoons. Check frequently to avoid burning.

3. Pour glaze over squash and serve.

SERVES 4

Preparation time: 5 minutes
Cooking time: 25 minutes

Mediterranean Sea Bass

Simple and delicious, this is one of our favorite seafood recipes. Mirin is the perfect addition, as it deglazes the pan after the fish is cooked and adds a sweetness that balances the acidity of the tomatoes, eliminating the need for added sugar. Grouper fillets can be used in place of sea bass, if desired.

$1^1/2$ tablespoons extra virgin olive oil
4 skinless sea bass fillets, about 5 oz (150 g) each and $1^1/4$ in (3 cm) thick
Sea salt and freshly ground black pepper
2 tablespoons mirin
1 tablespoon minced garlic
1 tablespoon capers
One 15-oz (425-g) can diced tomatoes with Italian herbs (do not drain)
2 tablespoons finely chopped fresh parsley, preferably flat-leaf
2 tablespoons finely chopped fresh basil

1. Heat the oil in a large skillet over medium-high heat. Sprinkle the fillets with salt and pepper, add them to the pan, cover and cook for 5 minutes. Turn the fillets over, cover once again and cook 5 minutes more. Transfer the fish to a heatproof plate and place in a warm oven (lowest setting) while you prepare the sauce.

2. Add the mirin to the skillet along with the garlic and capers and cook over medium heat for 1 minute.

3. Add the tomatoes and their juice and partially mash them with a potato masher or fork. Add a pinch of salt and pepper and cook rapidly over medium-high heat, uncovered, for about 5 minutes to reduce excess liquid. Add the herbs and cook 1 to 2 minutes more, or until the mixture is reduced to a sauce consistency.

4. Place the fish fillets on individual serving plates, top with the tomato sauce, and serve.

SERVES 4

Preparation time: 10 minutes
Cooking time: 20 minutes

Cider-Poached Pears

This simple dessert provides a warm, sweet ending to fall or winter meals.

3 ripe but firm pears, halved and cored
2 to 2^1/$_2$ cups (500 to 600 ml) apple cider or juice
1 teaspoon cider-spice mixture or 1 cinnamon stick and several whole cloves
Pinch of sea salt
1 tablespoon mirin
1 tablespoon crushed kuzu starch
Walnuts or pecans, toasted and chopped, for garnish (optional)

1. Arrange the pear halves in a single layer in the bottom of a saucepan.

2. Pour the juice or cider over the pears. The liquid should almost cover the pears. Add the spices and salt. Simmer, covered, for 15 minutes, or until the pears are tender.

3. Remove the pears with a slotted spoon, drain and place in small individual bowls.

4. Strain the liquid, then return it to the pan. Boil the liquid down until you have about 1 cup (235 ml). Stir in the mirin.

5. Thoroughly dissolve the kuzu in 1 tablespoon cold water and add it to the hot liquid while stirring briskly. Continue stirring over medium-low heat until the kuzu thickens and becomes translucent. Simmer for 1 minute more.

6. Immediately ladle the hot sauce over pears. If desired, add a sprinkle of toasted nuts.

SERVES 6

Preparation time: 10 minutes
Cooking time: about 25 minutes

Spiked Apricot Glaze

Spiked with mirin, this apricot glaze is delicious spread on cakes, steamed puddings, muffins or sweet buns, or between the layers of a yellow cake.

$^2/_3$ cup (175 ml) apricot preserves
1 tablespoon mirin
1 teaspoon fresh lemon juice
1 tablespoon water
$^1/_2$ teaspoon grated lemon or orange zest

1. Combine all the ingredients in a small saucepan and cook for about 5 minutes over low heat, stirring frequently. The glaze will become thin, then thicken somewhat as it reduces.

2. Let cool slightly before glazing, but don't cool completely or it will be too thick to easily spread.

MAKES ABOUT $^2/_3$ CUP (175 ML)

Cooking time: 5 minutes
Preparation time: 5 minutes

舞
茸

MAITAKE: THE KING OF MUSHROOMS

Mushrooms have been treasured for centuries for preserving health, curing disease and maintaining vitality. Maitake (*Grifola frondosa*), also known as Hen-of-the-Woods, is considered the king of mushrooms, because not only are the mushrooms a scientifically proven potent medicinal food, they are also a prized culinary delicacy. Deep in the forests of ancient Japan, wild maitake often grew to be 100 pounds (45 kg). In Japanese, *maitake* literally means "dancing mushroom." Some say this is because people who found this prized mushroom began dancing with joy. Others attribute its name to the way the fruit bodies of the mushroom overlap each other, giving the appearance of dancing butterflies. Maitake was considered so precious and rare in ancient Japan that it was literally worth its weight in silver. However, with modern cultivation methods, both dry and fresh maitake are now available at reasonable prices in natural foods stores and Asian markets around the world.

Nutritionally, maitake is low in calories and carbohydrates and loaded with 25 to 27 percent protein. It is an excellent of source essential amino acids and contains up to 14 percent B-glucans—the mushroom's most active medicinal ingredient. Maitake is a source of some fiber, and it is rich in a number of important vitamins and minerals including B vitamins, niacin, vitamins C and D, magnesium, calcium, iron, potassium, selenium and zinc.

Maitake is considered an adaptogen, which means that it helps the body adapt to stress and normalize body function. In Japanese herbal medicine, maitake has been used as a treatment for a variety of conditions and as a tonic to strengthen the body and improve overall health.

In traditional Chinese medicine, maitake is said to be the most cleansing of the medicinal mushrooms, targeting the liver and lungs. Most health professionals agree that if the liver function can be improved, overall health will benefit, because the liver is one of the largest organs and performs innumerable functions, including detoxification of internally and externally produced poisons.

In the last several decades, scientists working in laboratories around the world have confirmed maitake's powerful medicinal benefits, particularly with regard to degenerative disease. In the East maitake extracts are being formulated and approved for use in treating certain types of cancer, while in the West maitake's popularity as a culinary delight and potent medicine is rapidly growing.

Cancer and HIV/AIDS

In an article published in *The Townsend Letter for Doctors*, Dr. Anthony J. Cichoke, MA, D.C., said that scientific studies show that maitake is the most potent immunostimulant of all the mushrooms. The most medicinally effective way to take maitake is to use the D-fraction, a standardized extract of the active consitituent 1.6 beta-glucan, developed by Hiroki Namba, Ph.D., of Kobe Pharmaceutical University. Dr. Namba discovered that 90 percent of mice injected with cancer cells and then fed maitake D-fraction did not have any evidence of metastasis of cancer cells. In another study on humans, Dr. Namba reported that "tumor regression or significant symptom improvement was observed in 11 of 15 breast cancer patients, 12 out of 18 lung cancer patients, and 7 of 15 liver cancer patients." Even when tumor regression was not observed, most of the patients taking maitake claimed improvement of overall symptoms one way or another. When maitake D-fraction was administered in conjunction with chemotherapy, the responses improved by 12 percent to as much as 28 percent. Also, the various side effects of chemotherapy, such as hair loss and nausea, were greatly reduced among about 90 percent of the patients studied. Reduction of pain was also reported from 83 percent of cancer cases studied.

In the past twenty years, medical researchers in several countries have been studying the antitumor activity of many types of mushrooms. Most medicinal mushrooms, such as reishi, shiitake and maitake, share a common property of enhancing immune function by stimulating cell-mediated immunity. Simply put, they can, for example, stimulate the immune system's T-cells, which travel the bloodstream seeking and destroying cancer cells.

The chemical structure of maitake's medicinally active polysaccharide compound, beta 1.6 glucan, is different from the beta-glucans found in other medicinal mushrooms. It is recognized by researchers as a very effective agent for stimulating cellular immune responses. Activity of natural killer cells and cytotoxic T-cells is increased up to three times by oral consumption of maitake. An increase in the production of interleukin-l, which activates T-cell and superoxide anions, which damage tumor cells, has also been demonstrated by the consumption of maitake.

Although most of the human and animal maitake cancer studies have been done in Japan and China, in 1998 the United States Food and Drug Administration (FDA) approved an Investigation of New Drug (IND) application to conduct phase II clinical trials using maitake extract on advanced breast and prostrate cancer patients. The study is examining the immune activity effects of maitake extract on tumor size, clinical symptoms and quality of life.

Maitake's anticancer properties are impressive; however, it is its anti-HIV effect that is the source of this mushroom's greatest renown. Studies have found that maitake improves the helper T-cell count of those with HIV. Researchers at the National Cancer Institute (NCI) said that maitake extract is as powerful as the AIDS drug AZT, but without its toxic side effects. In tissue culture studies, D-fraction was found to enhance the activity of other immune cells as well as T-lymphocytes. Another study reported that maitake extract prevented HIV infected helper T-cells from being destroyed by as much as 96 percent in tissue culture!

Cholesterol Reduction and Weight Loss

Like shiitake, maitake may be effective in lowering cholesterol and helping the body eliminate excess fat. Data suggest that maitake has the ability to alter lipid metabolism by inhibiting the formation of fat deposits, the accumulation of liver lipids and the elevation of lipids in the blood.

Recent animal research in Japan found that high doses of maitake fed to rats on a high cholesterol diet significantly altered their fat metabolism, resulting in a much higher rate of cholesterol excretion than that of control rats on the same diet, but without maitake. In just four weeks, the maitake-fed rats excreted 300 percent more cholesterol than the control group. The maitake-fed rats also had much lower body weight, body fat and serum cholesterol than the control animals.

Taking the clue from animal studies, a Tokyo clinic tested the effects of maitake on thirty overweight patients. Without making other changes in their diet, Masamori Yokota, M.D. gave patients both dried and powdered maitake (equivalent to 200 grams of fresh maitake) daily for two months. Yokota reported that maitake is more effective than any other regimen he has ever tested. During the relatively short time of the experiment, all of his patients lost weight and got nearly halfway to their optimal weight. Weight loss ranged between 11 pounds and 26 pounds (5 to 12 kg); the average person lost 11 to 13 pounds (5 to 6 kg) in just two months!

Aging

Medical researcher Harry G. Preuss, M.D, is a strong believer and advocate of metabolic syndrome, which claims that the chronic disorders that are common in the aging population, such as hypertension, diabetes, obesity and arteriosclerosis, are all associated, at least in part, with disturbances in glucose/insulin metabolism. He believes that the findings in his initial study indicate that maitake D-fraction would favorably influence the glucose/insulin system and help prevent the onset of age-related chronic disorders.

Other Medicinal Benefits of Maitake

In an effort to increase public awareness of the benefits of maitake, maitake interests in the United States have funded a study at Georgetown University. Dr. Preuss, the principal investigator, announced his preliminary findings at the October 1998 meeting of the American College of Nutrition, held in Albuquerque, New Mexico. Using rats with symptoms of high blood pressure and diabetes, Preuss demonstrated that oral doses of maitake extract had an antihypertensive effect and a positive effect on insulin metabolism. What's more, blood glucose levels in diabetic mice decreased by 50 percent in less than two weeks after consumption of maitake-enriched feed. It has also been reported that maitake acts as a laxative and promotes hair growth. No wonder maitake is called "the dancing mushroom."

HOW MAITAKE ARE CULTIVATED

All maitake are not the same. Although wild maitake still exist deep in some forests, almost all the maitake used for food and medicine are cultivated. Like other medicinal and culinary plants, the quality of maitake depends on growing conditions and genetic constitution. Through the years scientists have learned that this mushroom produces the most potent medicinal effects and has the best flavor when the highest quality of spores are used for cultivation under ideal growing conditions.

Most of the dry and fresh maitake available in natural foods stores come from Yukiguni Maitake Inc., in Nigata Prefecture, Japan's largest producer of high quality maitake and maitake products. At their state-of-the-art facilities, Yukiguni produces over 200,000 pounds (90,900 kg) of high quality maitake a day!

The key to Yukiguni's success is their exclusive, high-tech cultivation process. Using only spores selected for their favorable genetic qualities, Yukiguni's technical staff inoculates sterile organic growing media consisting of sawdust, bran, water and micronutrients. Sprouting takes place in a controlled environment where each mushroom is grown separately to ensure the ideal conditions. No agricultural chemicals of any kind are used, and independent laboratory analysis shows that Yukiguni maitake do not have any detectable amounts of lead, arsenic or mercury.

SHOPPING FOR MAITAKE

The highest quality Japanese shiitake are grown outdoors in a semi-wild environment. Yet maitake, due to their delicate nature and stringent growing requirements, must be grown under laboratory conditions. Most of the maitake sold in natural foods stores in the United States comes from the Yukiguni company, which has high standards and a very good reputation.

Dried maitake from the Yukiguni company will say "Product of Japan" on the label. There are also a few Chinese brands of maitake available. When shopping for dried maitake, look for large pieces and packages without a lot of fragments and dust. When good quality maitake are reconstituted, the fronds should be thick and fleshy.

Fresh maitake are difficult to find, but if you can find fresh, well-formed mushrooms that are thick and light in color, it is well worth the search. They are truly delicious! Fresh maitake should be dry and never slimy or waterlogged. The mushrooms should have a clean, earthy smell. Beware of fresh maitake in sealed packages, because it can be difficult to tell if they are really fresh until you get home and open the package.

COOKING WITH MAITAKE

Maitake is a new and exciting ingredient in the Western culinary world. In addition to its powerful health benefits, maitake has a distinctive aroma and woodsy flavor that makes it a prized gourmet mushroom. Its flavor has been described by various food writers as "meaty" and "delicately nutty." Although fresh maitake is a rare find in the United States, high-quality dried maitake is becoming more widely available in natural foods stores and some supermarkets. Slow drying concentrates the rich taste and medicinal qualities of this versatile mushroom for year-round use.

To reconstitute dried maitake, simply soak the mushrooms in water for about 40 minutes. Chop the maitake to use along with the soaking water to make superb soups or sauces, or add the mushrooms to stir-fries, fried rice or noodles, side dishes or casseroles. Maitake maintains its delicious taste and satisfying texture extremely well when cooked.

Maitake is a welcome addition to any type of cuisine. With all that is now known about the immune-enhancing qualities of this choice mushroom, we recommend making it a regular part of your diet. It can be substituted for other mushrooms in many recipes with excellent results. If you are not familiar with maitake, try some of the following recipes. You will soon be using these offerings as a springboard for your own creativity.

Stir-Fried Tempeh, Maitake and Vegetables

Served over a bed of rice, this makes a nutritious and delicious complete meal that takes little time to cook. Tempeh, a traditional fermented soyfood from Indonesia, offers a concentrated source of protein and the benefits of soy. Combined with maitake's powerful medicinal qualities and a variety of colorful vegetables, this dish is just what the naturopath ordered.

If substituting tofu for tempeh, choose firm or extra-firm varieties and press the tofu before marinating (see Preparing Tofu, page 146). Marinating time can be reduced to as little as 30 minutes if using tofu.

8 oz (250 g) tempeh
$^1/_2$ cup (10 g) dried maitake mushrooms
5 cups (300 g) broccoli florets
2 tablespoons peanut oil
1 dried Japanese chile, seeded and minced, or $^1/_4$ teaspoon dried red pepper
   flakes (optional)
3 teaspoons minced garlic
1 onion, cut in half lengthwise and thinly sliced into half moons
1 rib celery, thinly sliced on the diagonal
8 button mushrooms, quartered
$^1/_2$ red bell pepper, deseeded and sliced into thin strips
Pinch of sea salt and freshly ground black pepper

Marinade
3 tablespoons shoyu (Japanese soy sauce)
3 tablespoons mirin
1 tablespoon fresh lemon juice or brown rice vinegar
1 teaspoon toasted sesame oil
1 tablespoon arrowroot or 2 teaspoons crushed kuzu starch

1. Cut the tempeh in half, then cut each piece in half by thickness and dice into bite-size pieces. Arrange the pieces in a single layer in a baking dish.

2. Thoroughly combine the marinade ingredients in a small bowl and pour them over the tempeh. Marinate the tempeh for 1 hour or up to 24 hours, turning occasionally.

3. Soak the maitake in 1 cup (235 ml) lukewarm water for 30 to 60 minutes to reconstitute, then gently squeeze out excess water, coarsely chop, and set aside. Reserve the soaking water.

4. Steam the broccoli florets for 3 minutes, or until bright green and tender-crisp. Remove from the steamer and set aside.

5. In a large wok or skillet, heat 1 tablespoon of the peanut oil over medium-high heat and stir-fry the chile, if using, and $1^1/_2$ teaspoons of the garlic for 10 to 15 seconds. Add the onion and stir-fry for 1 to 2 minutes.

6. Add the maitake, celery, button mushrooms and bell pepper along with a pinch of salt and pepper. Stir-fry for 2 minutes more and remove from the pan.

7. Drain the tempeh, reserving the marinade. Heat the remaining 1 tablespoon of peanut oil in the wok over medium-high heat, add the rest of the garlic and stir-fry for 10 seconds. Add the tempeh and stir-fry for 2 minutes, then add the reserved marinade and $1/3$ cup (75 ml) of the maitake soaking water while stirring. Continue stirring until the sauce simmers and thickens. Lower the heat and gently simmer for 5 minutes. If the sauce becomes too thick, add a little more of the maitake soaking water.

8. Return the stir-fried vegetables to the pan along with the broccoli and toss another minute. Serve hot over rice.

SERVES 4

Preparation time: 20 to 25 minutes plus 1 hour marinating time
Cooking time: 15 to 20 minutes

Szechuan Soup

Perfect when you're looking for a zesty, light, but warming soup. Kuzu-thickened soups hold their heat well. The addition of a little fiery chili oil will have you wondering who turned up the thermostat.

$1/2$ cup (10 g) dried maitake mushrooms
$3/4$ teaspoon sea salt
1 carrot, cut into thin matchsticks
2 cups (150 g) chopped, loosely packed bok choy or Chinese (napa) cabbage
8 oz (250 g) tofu, cut into $1/2$-in (1-cm) cubes
1 tablespoon tamari or shoyu (Japanese soy sauce)
$1/2$ tablespoon mirin
3 tablespoons crushed kuzu starch
$1/4$ teaspoon chili-flavored sesame oil
1 or 2 green onions (scallions), thinly sliced on the diagonal, for garnish

1. In a saucepan soak the maitake in 5 cups of water for 30 to 40 minutes, then gently squeeze out excess water and coarsely chop.

2. Return the maitake to the soaking water, bring to a boil, add the salt and gently simmer, covered, for 10 minutes.

3. Add the carrots, greens, tofu, tamari and mirin and gently simmer 5 minutes more. Remove from the heat.

4. Dissolve the kuzu in 3 tablespoons of cold water and add it to the soup while stirring briskly. Return the pot to the heat and continue stirring until the soup simmers and thickens.

5. Remove from the heat, sprinkle with the hot and spicy sesame oil and stir.

6. Serve hot with a garnish of sliced green onion.

SERVES 4

Preparation time: 10 minutes plus 30 minutes soaking time
Cooking time: 25 minutes

Maitake Barley Stew

Rice or barley stew seasoned with miso or *umeboshi* is the Japanese mother's cure-all. Maitake adds its healing and rejuvenating qualities to make an even more powerful dish. Enjoy this creamy, soothing stew anytime during the colder months, especially when you feel weak or out of balance. Make plenty—this dish tastes even better a day or two after it is made.

1 cup (200 g) barley
1 cup (15 g) dried maitake mushrooms
4 quarts (3.5 liters) water
One 6-in (15-cm) piece kombu (optional)
2 teaspoons sea salt
1 bay leaf (optional)
$^1/_2$ teaspoon dried oregano (optional)
1 onion, diced
1 leek, white part only, slit lengthwise to center, rinsed well to remove dirt
  then sliced
2 large carrots, cut in half lengthwise and thinly sliced into half moons
1 rib celery, thinly sliced
$1^1/_2$ cups (150 g) fresh peas
2 to 3 tablespoons brown rice miso or barley miso, or to taste
Minced fresh parsley or thinly sliced green onion (scallion), for garnish

1. Rinse and drain the barley 2 or 3 times, or until the rinse water runs clear. Place the barley in a large soup pot along with the maitake, water and, if desired, the kombu. Use a small plate or bowl to keep the mushrooms submerged. Set aside to soak for 30 minutes.

2. Remove and chop maitake, and return to the pot. Bring the soup to a boil over medium-high heat, and add the salt and bay leaf, if using. Remove the kombu and reserve it for another use. Reduce the heat and simmer, with the lid ajar, for 45 minutes, or until barley is tender. (Cook longer for a creamier texture.)

3. Add the oregano, if using, onion, leek, carrots and celery and simmer for 10 minutes.

4. Stir in the peas and simmer 10 minutes more. Remove from the heat.

5. Dilute the miso in a little water and add it to the stew. Remove the bay leaf and discard.

6. Serve hot, garnished with the parsley or green onion.

SERVES 6

Preparation time: 20 minutes plus 30 minutes soaking time
Cooking time: 1 hour 20 minutes

Somen with Maitake and Spinach

This has become one of our favorite main courses. It is so easy it's practically a convenience food, yet it's still delicious, satisfying and healthy.

$^3/_4$ cup (12 g) dried maitake mushrooms
4 tablespoons extra virgin olive oil
Pinch of sea salt
3 cloves garlic, minced
2 teaspoons shoyu (Japanese soy sauce)
8 oz (250 g) dried somen noodles or angel hair pasta
2 bunches green onions (scallions), trimmed and sliced into $^1/_4$-in (6-mm) pieces
1 lb (450 g) fresh spinach leaves, rinsed, stemmed and coarsely chopped
1 tablespoon balsamic vinegar
Herb seasoning salt or sea salt, to taste

1. Soak the maitake in $1^1/_2$ cups (375 ml) tepid water for 30 to 40 minutes, then gently squeeze out excess water and coarsely chop. Save the soaking water in a container in the refrigerator for an instant stock for soups or sauces. It should be used within 1 week.

2. In a large saucepan bring 2 quarts (2 liters) water to a boil.

3. Put 2 tablespoons of the olive oil and a pinch of sea salt in a large serving bowl and set aside.

4. While the water is coming to a boil, heat the remaining 2 tablespoons olive oil in a skillet, add the garlic, and sauté over medium heat for 15 to 30 seconds.

5. Add the soaked maitake and cook for 2 minutes, then add 1 teaspoon of the shoyu, toss, and cook 1 to 2 minutes more.

6. When the water comes to a full boil, add the noodles and stir to prevent them from sticking together. If using angel hair, add a teaspoon of salt to the water. Cook the noodles for 4 to 5 minutes, or until just tender, checking frequently to be sure you do not overcook the pasta. (See page 130 for tips on cooking noodles.)

7. While the noodles are cooking, add the green onions to the maitake, sauté briefly, then cover and cook for 2 minutes.

8. Add the spinach, sauté for 30 seconds, then toss in the remaining teaspoon of shoyu, cover and cook for 1 minute.

9. Drizzle the balsamic vinegar over the vegetables, toss and cook another minute. Add the herb seasoning salt or sea salt to taste, if desired.

10. When the noodles are done, drain them in a colander and quickly transfer them to the bowl with the olive oil and salt. Toss well, then add the mushroom mixture, toss again and serve immediately.

SERVES 2 TO 3

Preparation time: 15 minutes plus 30 to 40 minutes soaking time
Cooking time: 10 minutes

Miso Soup with Maitake

This simple soup is a delicious way to give your immune system a boost. Substitute other vegetables, if desired, and cook until tender.

$^1/_3$ cup (5 g) dried maitake mushrooms
$1^3/_4$ oz (50 g) daikon, peeled and cut into thin matchsticks (about $^1/_2$ cup)
2 cups (100 g) baby spinach leaves
3 tablespoons brown rice miso or barley miso
1 or 2 green onions (scallions), thinly sliced on the diagonal, for garnish

1. In a small saucepan, soak the maitake in 5 cups (1.25 liters) water for at least 30 minutes. Remove the maitake, gently squeeze out excess water, and coarsely chop. Return the maitake to the saucepan.

2. Bring to a simmer, add the daikon, and gently cook, covered, for 15 minutes.

3. Add the spinach and simmer 1 minute more. Remove from the heat.

4. Ladle a little hot stock into a small bowl, add the miso and stir until it dissolves. Then add the dissolved miso to the soup.

5. Serve with a garnish of sliced green onions.

SERVES 4

Preparation time: 5 minutes plus 30 minutes soaking time
Cooking time: 25 minutes

CHAPTER 18

JAPANESE TEA: A HEALTHY TONIC

Originally a medicinal beverage brought to Japan from ancient China by Buddhist monks, tea (*cha*) was both rare and expensive on the Japanese islands for many centuries. The first tea seeds were planted in Japan during China's T'ang dynasty (618–907 CE), and cultivation of the plants was associated with temple life and religious activity.

Today, more than a thousand years later, tea has become Japan's national beverage. From the Zen Buddhist tea ceremony, *chanoyu*, to the daily three o'clock tea break, *o-cha*, drinking tea is a Japanese institution.

Both stimulating and relaxing, Japanese teas such as tangy *sencha*, smoky *hojicha* and earthy *kukicha* refresh the palate and heighten the pleasure of eating all types of food. Although all Japanese teas come from the evergreen shrub *Camellia sinensis*, unique processing produces teas with different tastes, colors and physiological effects. While hojicha and kukicha complement a grain-based and mostly vegetarian diet, the typical Japanese fish-based diet is well balanced with sencha, or green tea. Like many herbal brews, such as black cohosh and chamomile, Japanese tea has legendary health benefits, many now scientifically proven.

The art of Japanese tea preparation and presentation involves being mindful of water temperature, steeping time and serving traditions. If the water is hotter than required, the delicate taste of green tea might be lost; steeping too long can produce teas that are dark and bitter. The Japanese traditionally serve sencha in small delicate teacups; hojicha and kukicha are generally poured into larger, handle-less mugs. Tea is never served with sugar or milk—if sweetness is desired, a little rice syrup can be added.

Kukicha is the easiest Japanese tea to brew. Unlike other varieties, which are never boiled, kukicha is simmered to extract the full flavor from its twigs. Simply add 3 level tablespoons of kukicha to 1 quart (1 liter) of water, bring to a boil and simmer gently for 3 to 5 minutes. Pour the tea through a strainer into the cups and return the twigs to the pot. The twigs can be used once again, but a few fresh twigs may need to be added for full-bodied flavor. If you are using kukicha tea bags, steep one tea bag in one cup of hot water for 3 to 5 minutes. Serve hot or chilled with lemon, if you prefer. For a refreshing summer drink, combine chilled kukicha with an equal quantity of apple juice.

Hojicha, bancha and sencha are closely related and are brewed in the same way. Because sencha contains more caffeine, however, it is served in smaller quantities. A large teapot is useful if you are serving more than two people. Never boil water for tea in an aluminum teakettle or steep tea in plastic or aluminum. Warm the teapot by filling it with hot water. Pour the water out and add 1 level tablespoon of tea for each cup of water you will be boiling. In another pot, bring cold, pure water to a full boil, then immediately remove it from the heat. Let the water sit a minute before pouring it over the tea leaves or tea bag in the warmed pot. For the best flavor and most infusion, brew green tea in water with a temperature of 160 to 170°F (71 to 76°C). Allow the tea to steep for only 1 to 2 minutes, or it will become bitter. If you are using bulk tea, strain it as it is poured into the cups. Alternate pouring a little tea into each cup, until the pot is completely drained. This pouring method will ensure each person's tea to be about the same strength. The leaves may be reused once or twice. For sencha, bancha and hojicha, fresh leaves should not be added to used ones—discard spent leaves, rinse the pot and begin fresh. Unlike sencha and bancha, which become bitter when cooled, hojicha makes a delicious and refreshing cool summer beverage.

Sencha, bancha, hojicha and kukicha are available in good-quality tea bags and loose in bulk. However, if stored improperly, these teas can become stale quickly. Buy no more than a one-month supply at a time, and keep it stored in an airtight container in a cool, dry place.

Green tea with its sweet aroma and clean, fresh taste is savored for its palate-pleasing flavor. Yet, it is also revered, more than any other daily beverage, as a powerful medicine. In fact, green tea has such a remarkable ability to regulate the body's physiological functions that medical researchers often refer to it as a "functional food."

Caffeine

Although caffeine has received bad press in the West, it might have been this very quality in tea, which instantly invigorates the body, that attracted early religious leaders and physicians. Scientists have identified caffeine as one of a potent group of drugs called methylxanthines, found in over sixty plant species. By blocking the natural tranquilizer adenosine, caffeine stimulates the brain and in turn heightens intellectual activity. The highest quality Japanese green tea, which is picked from tender spring leaves high in caffeine, has less caffeine than coffee, and its high tannin and vitamin C content are believed to moderate the stimulating effect. This synergistic quality of vitamin C and tannin with caffeine may explain why Zen monks use green tea during long meditations to stay alert but calm.

A Tonic for What Ails You

Caffeine aside, recent research has found that drinking green tea may not only help to prevent heart disease and strokes, but also may reduce the risk of many types of cancer, regulate blood sugar, lower blood pressure, boost the immune system, increase bone density, help prevent arthritis, facilitate weight loss, help prevent ulcers, slow the aging process, increase fertility, and fight colds and flu.

Many of the broad health benefits of green tea are derived from its rich supply of plant chemicals called polyphenols, one of nature's most powerful antioxidants. Of the polyphenols, epigallocatechin gallate (EGCG) is the most powerful; a University of Kansas study found that it is one hundred times more effective than vitamin C and twenty-five times more potent than vitamin E in blocking the cell mutations that cause cancer. A study conducted by the USDA's Human Nutrition Research Center on Aging found that one cup (250 ml) of brewed green tea contains about the same amount of antioxidants as one serving of some important vegetables. Lester A. Mitscher, Ph.D., former chair of the Department of Medicinal Chemistry at the University of Kansas and author of *The Green Tea Book* (Avery, 1997), recommends that people consume the equivalent of at least four cups (960 ml) of green tea per day to provide 300 to 400 milligrams of beneficial polyphenols.

Antioxidants reduce the formation of free radicals, which play a key role in the development of degenerative diseases and premature aging. Fermented black teas lose much of their health promoting properties during processing. Research at Rutgers University has confirmed that green tea has six times the antioxidant capability of black fermented teas.

Cancer. Green tea's amazing ability to fight cancer is well documented in human and animal studies. Researchers have proposed that drinking as few as four cups of green tea a day may significantly reduce the risk of many forms of cancer. A 1989 study of people living in Japan's tea growing regions, published in the *Japanese Journal of Nutrition*, reported a significantly lower death rate from all types of cancer and from gastrointestinal cancers in particular, as compared to the general population. A study at the Chinese Academy of Preventive Medicine in Beijing showed a reduced risk of oral cancer for people who drank green tea for six months. A report in the *European Journal of Cancer Prevention* found that 69 percent of women with precancerous cervical lesions had a decrease or complete remission when green tea extract was taken orally and applied locally to the cervix. Moreover, studies of mice with various types of cancer or that were exposed to cancer-causing agents report markedly reduced incidence of cancer when green tea extract was added to their diets. It has also been documented that drinking green tea increases the survival rate of cancer patients after conventional treatments such as surgery, radiation and chemotherapy.

Although scientists are not certain why green tea is such a potent anticancer agent, many researchers believe that the damage to chromosomal DNA that usually precedes the onset of cancer is prevented by a high concentration of polyphenols. Polyphenols are antioxidants that help the body neutralize dangerous free radicals that can destroy the normal hereditary makeup of healthy cells, turning them into rapidly growing cancers.

Recently research, conducted at the University of Rochester and published in *Chemical Research in Toxicology*, discovered that chemicals in green tea related to flavonoids shut down a key molecule that can play a significant role in the development of cancer.

Researchers at the University of Murcia in Spain and the John Innes Centre in Norwich, England, reported that EGCG in green tea prevents cancer cells from growing by binding to a specific enzyme in cancer cells that makes DNA. It was shown for the first time that EGCG, which is present in green tea at relatively high concentrations, inhibits the same cancer-promoting enzyme that is targeted by toxic anticancer drugs used in conventional cancer therapy.

Another way in which green tea prevents cancer is by inhibiting the activation of carcinogens. Studies published in the *European Journal of Cancer Prevention* and the *Journal of Cellular Biochemistry* suggest that green tea actually detoxifies carcinogens as they enter the body, which may explain why smokers who drink green tea are much less likely to develop lung cancer than smokers who do not. In fact, a study in Japan that compared the cancer-causing agents in the blood of smokers who drink large amounts of green tea (10 small Japanese-size cups or 5 to $7^1/_2$ cups $1^1/_4$ to $1^3/_4$ liters a day) with the blood of non-smokers found no significant difference!

Cardiovascular Disease. According to the *American Journal of Clinical Nutrition*, green tea also protects against cardiovascular disease. The journal published a report in 1999 that found that flavonoids, components of the yellow pigment found in green tea, and catechins reduced the formation of LDL (bad) cholesterol that accumulates in blood vessels. A recent study published in the journal *Circulation* found that drinking more than two cups (500 ml) of tea a day decreased death following a heart attack by 44 percent.

Epidemiologist Shinichi Kuriyama M.D., Ph.D., from the Tohoku University School of Medicine, headed a study that looked at more than 40,000 adults and compared those who drank less than one cup of tea a day to those who drank three to five cups a day. For women who drank five or more cups of green tea daily, there was a 31 percent lower risk of death from heart disease. For men, the risk was reduced by 22 percent. For both sexes the biggest decrease was in the rate of death due to stroke.

Research has shown that the reduced risk of fatal heart attack is associated with green tea's high flavonoid concentration. Green tea's powerful ability to reduce cholesterol has also been demonstrated in numerous studies of animals on a high fat diet. However, not all cholesterol is bad; in fact, it plays a very important structural role in the healthy functioning of the body. Some health professionals even warn against the dangers of "low cholesterol." Amazingly, green tea helps the body maintain a healthy cholesterol balance. In a series of experiments reported in the *Proceedings of the Third International Symposium on Tea Science*, scientists discovered that the cholesterol level of animals fed a diet that was not high in fats was unaffected by green tea extract. They concluded that green tea acts only to limit the excessive rise in blood cholesterol.

Blood Pressure. High blood pressure places a serious burden on the circulatory system and contributes to arteriosclerosis, stroke, heart disease and kidney disease. Green tea lovers will be happy to learn their beverage of choice is one of the world's most effective treatments for high blood pressure. Research has shown that drinking two cups of green tea a day can reduce the risk of high blood pressure by 50 percent. The risk can be reduced even more for those with risk factors for high blood pressure, such as high sodium intake.

Blood Sugar. A landmark study done over sixty years ago at Kyoto University uncovered a remarkable relationship between blood sugar and green tea consumption. When hospitalized diabetic patients participated in the tea ceremony (*chanoyu*), their blood sugar dropped. Unfortunately, this important report was ignored due to the outbreak of World War II. Several Japanese studies have demonstrated that various components of green tea can lower blood sugar in mice that have a form of hereditary diabetes. In light of the old Kyoto study and more recent laboratory research, green tea may be an effective aid in controlling our blood sugar.

Premature Aging. It is good to age gracefully, but not prematurely. Although oxygen is necessary for life, it can also combine with molecules in the body to form free radicals, which scientists now believe are a major cause of premature aging. One way to slow the aging process is to prevent the production and accumulation of active oxygen in the body by consuming lots of antioxidants such as vitamins E and C. Research has found that the higher the concentration of antioxidants in the bodies of animals, the longer they live. As was noted above, the antioxidants in green tea are many times more powerful than those in vitamins E and C.

You do not have to drink green tea to benefit from its antiaging quality. The *Archives of Dermatology* reported that experimental studies suggest that just rubbing green tea on the skin can tone the face and help prevent some skin disorders. By bathing the skin in antioxidants, green tea may be able to stop free radicals from destroying healthy skin cells. This may explain why cosmetics and skincare products made with the addition of green tea extracts are flooding the health and beauty aid market. However, before using green tea as a sunscreen you may want to consult your health professional.

Fertility. If you are so inclined, green tea may even help you get pregnant. In a study conducted at Kaiser Permanente Medical Care Program of Northern California, in Oakland, researchers discovered that women who drank more than one half cup (125 ml) of green tea every day doubled their odds of conceiving. When tested, other caffeinated beverages did not yield similar results.

Other Health Benefits of Green Tea

Much of the traditional folklore associated with Japanese green tea has been confirmed by modern medical research. In the past, pregnant women were often told to drink green tea. It is now known that it contains zinc, which is important during pregnancy. Although pregnant Japanese women have been consuming large amounts of green tea for centuries there is concern among some physicians that green tea's EGCG blocks the enzyme necessary for folic acid to be utilized in the cells. Inadequate intake of folic acid has been linked to an increased risk of giving birth to an infant with neural tube defects. However, according to well known holistic health advocate Andrew Weil, "I know of no studies suggesting that you shouldn't continue to drink green tea while you're trying to conceive or during pregnancy."

According to another study, because of tea's natural tannins and fluorides, a cup of tea a day for children can cut the number of reported cavities in half. Green tea is a boon to oral hygiene for several reasons; it interrupts the formation of plaque, kills the cariogenic bacteria that cause tooth decay and is a great tasting treatment for morning bad breath.

Tannin, an astringent responsible for green tea's bitter taste, is thought to help the body discharge toxins due to pollution and to accelerate the metabolism of fats, which can aid in weight reduction. In fact, a study published in the *American Journal of Clinical Nutrition* found that those who drank green tea experienced a significant increase in calorie burning, a measure of metabolism. Tea's ability to reduce body fat was confirmed in animal studies and does not seem to be related to caffeine levels.

Some tea historians believe that tea was first used over two thousand years ago as a means to purify contaminated drinking water. Modern research has confirmed that the catechins in green tea are powerful sterilizing agents that destroy many of the bacteria that cause food poisoning while having no negative effect on the beneficial bacteria in the intestines. Moreover, a Japanese report in 1989 concluded that green tea is even effective against the microorganism that causes cholera. What's more, components of green tea have been found to have an inhibitory effect on the influenza and AIDS viruses in laboratory tests.

Japanese researchers report that flavonoids may prevent the formation of some forms of cataracts. It may also control the agglutination of blood platelets, which indicates that it may be effective in preventing blood clots and strokes.

If you are not already convinced that green tea is one of the world's healthiest beverages, there is more to this incredible story. If your habitual caffeine jolt comes in the form of unhealthy carbonated sodas or coffee house lattes, switching to green tea many even save you some money!

Health Benefits of Twig Tea

Although there has been little, if any, research into the health benefits of drinking kukicha, or twig tea, traditional folklore suggests that this beverage has a soothing, beneficial effect on digestion, blood quality and the mind. Several healing tonics made from combinations of kukicha, soy sauce and umeboshi or ume extract have many medicinal uses, ranging from alkalinizing the blood to relieving hangovers. Chemical analysis of the kukicha twigs reveals that the tea may be a good source of calcium, iron, and vitamins A and C and, because it has very little caffeine, a small amount—such as one-quarter to one-half cup (50 to 125 ml) a day—is safe for children and infants to drink.

TRADITIONAL REMEDIES MADE FROM TWIG TEA

Combining twig tea, or kukicha, with other medicinal foods such as shoyu and umeboshi makes several folk medicines for specific medical conditions. *Note:* we do not recommend these teas as a substitute for professional medical advice. If you have any of the conditions listed below, check with your personal health care provider before using the suggestions offered here.

Ume-Sho-Ban. One natural foods company offers a prepared *Umesho* concentrate that can be added to tea. However, if you wish to prepare your own, follow these simple instructions. Crush the meat of one umeboshi and add 1/2 teaspoon shoyu. Add boiling kukicha tea (1/2 to 1 cup / 125 to 250 ml, according to individual taste). You may also add several drops of ginger juice. Stir well and drink. For children, it should be prepared without the ginger and with less shoyu.

This drink can be useful for the following conditions:
• headache caused by excessive consumption of foods high in sugar or oil
• stomach trouble (nausea, lack of appetite)
• fatigue
• anemia, weak blood and weak circulation

Sho-Ban or Soy-Bancha. Put 1 or 2 teaspoons of shoyu in a cup. Add hot kukicha tea to fill the cup. This tonic is known to activate the circulation, and it will have a strengthening and refreshing effect on healthy people. If you add a little grated ginger to this drink, it is particularly effective in cases of flatulence or stomach trouble such as nausea. Take 1 to 2 cups a day until relief is obtained, but do not continue for more than 3 to 4 days in a row.

This drink can be useful for the following conditions:
• stomach troubles (in particular stomach acidity and indigestion)
• menstrual cramps
• flatulence
• rheumatism

For more than eight hundred years Japan's finest teas have been grown around the town of Uji, which is located on the old road between the ancient capitals of Nara and Kyoto, about 230 miles (370 km) southwest of Tokyo. Birthplace of both Japanese green tea and the tea ceremony, Uji, with its rich, slightly acidic soil, is ideal for growing tea. Early morning mist from the Uji River moistens the leaves of the plants and shields them from the sun, and the volcanic soil is well drained by the sloping terrain. Following the natural contours of the valleys and surrounding hills, Uji's landscape is patched with three and four-acre (about 1.5 hectares) tea fields. Straight rows of smooth, tightly trimmed bushes look more like ornamental hedges than individual tea plants.

Off the main road, on a hill overlooking Uji, the manicured look of the plantations below gives way to fields of lumpy, irregular rows of tea plants—the remote, centuries-old tea plantations of the Nagata organic tea co-operative, producers of most of the organic Japanese sencha, hojicha and kukicha teas sold in the world's natural foods stores. Following the principles of an agricultural method known as nature farming, the Nagata organic tea co-op, a group of associated tea growers, has been a curiosity to their tea-farming neighbors. Most tea farmers spray their plants with chemicals fifteen to twenty times a year, but the Nagata co-op members have rejected chemical agriculture completely. They do not use animal manures, chemical fertilizers, herbicides or pesticides; they replenish the nutrients in their topsoil with vegetable-quality compost only. Nature farming stresses the importance of building soil vitality by maintaining a semi-wild natural environment. Plants are not overly protected or pampered but are allowed to fend for themselves with the help of a strong, balanced topsoil.

Co-op chief Aijiro Nagata insists that it is not necessary to prune tea bushes uniformly. Each bush, he says, should be allowed to grow according to its own pattern. Although he harvests a little less tea than similar-size farms that use chemical methods, his plants have far less mold and blight. Also, the co-op tea plants usually produce tea leaves for twice as long a period of time as plants that have been chemically treated. Chemically treated tea plants generally burn themselves out in about twenty years, but the Nagata co-op plants commonly produce for forty years, some for as long as one hundred.

In early spring, Uji farmers cover their tender tea leaves with dark netting or slotted bamboo screens to protect them from the afternoon sun. These first spring leaves are processed into *gyokuro* (jewel dew), Japan's rarest, most expensive tea. Steamed, dried and ground to a fine powder, these early leaves become *matcha*, the jade green tea of the ancient tea ceremony.

Later in the spring, the co-op growers process their most prized leaves into sencha, the high-quality green tea offered to house guests and served at fine Japanese restaurants. Sencha goes especially well with sushi and sashimi (raw fish), as it is said to aid in the digestion of fish oil and protein.

To make sencha, the freshly picked tender leaves are immediately steamed for a minute or so. Steaming softens the leaves and turns them a delicate emerald green color. (The steaming process prevents the tea from fermenting and turning dark. This distinguishes Japanese tea from partially fermented oolong and fully fermented black English teas.) Once steamed, the leaves are rolled into thin curls, dried slowly in ovens, cooled and immediately packed to seal in their fresh taste and aroma. Slightly bittersweet sencha, more than any other tea, has the fresh taste of just-picked leaves.

The Nagata growers continue to pick sencha throughout the spring. By late June or July the leaves are too large and coarse to qualify as sencha and are processed into hojicha. These leaves are steamed, mixed with black volcanic sand, and roasted in revolving ovens. The sand, later removed, helps the leaves roast slowly and evenly. Roasting further neutralizes the leaves' already weak astringent and stimulating qualities (tea leaves lose caffeine strength as they grow), so both children and adults can drink Hojicha at any time of day. Hojicha is one of the Nagata group's most popular teas.

Usually coarse summer leaves are not roasted, but are processed like sencha and sold as lower-quality green tea called bancha. This is the mild, yellow-green tea served in many Japanese and Chinese restaurants around the world. Within the American natural foods world, however, bancha has quite a different meaning. It has become associated with a popular tea made from roasted twigs and very coarse leaves. Often referred to as kukicha, roasted twig tea is little known in modern Japan.

In the areas of Japan where it is known, kukicha has been stigmatized as a poor man's drink, because, like brown rice, it brings back memories of the days of deprivation during and after World War II. Macrobiotics founder George Ohsawa introduced kukicha to the West forty years ago. Since it contains only one-tenth the caffeine of sencha and because it is the most alkalinizing Japanese tea, Ohsawa considered it to be the most balanced beverage. Indeed, kukicha is an excellent complement to the grain-based, mostly vegetarian diet he advocated.

Nagata growers keep the caffeine level in kukicha as low as possible by selecting only older twigs and harvesting them in fall and winter when caffeine is naturally lowest. Twigs are steamed, dried and stored in paper bags for two to three years in order to develop the best flavor. After aging, twigs are cut and graded to size. Each grade is then roasted separately at different temperatures and lengths of time to ensure uniformity. Finally, the twigs are blended and packaged. The Nagata co-op formula for just the right ratio of twig size and age is a carefully guarded company secret.

SHOPPING FOR GREEN TEA

 All green teas are not the same. Indian and Chinese green teas are usually oven-dried rather than steamed. Oven-drying can cause oxidation of important vitamins, minerals and flavor components, which can alter the taste as well as the medicinal and nutritional qualities of delicate green teas. Recent chemical analysis has revealed that because Japanese green teas are steamed immediately after they are picked, most of their oxidative enzymes are destroyed. Consequently, they retain their green color, natural vitamins and high concentration of polyphenols. Moreover, the amino acid content, which determines the depth of flavor in green teas, is much higher in Japanese teas. When shopping for teas look for the words "Product of Japan" on the label. Also, because conventional tea is grown using lots of agrochemicals, look for 100 percent organic products.

Green tea is such a delicious and healthy plant, why not use it in cooking? Although cooking with green tea is not an important Japanese tradition, in China it has been used in cooking for as long as the Chinese have been drinking it. There are a few good cookbooks that are devoted entirely to cooking with green tea. One of our favorites is *Cooking with Green Tea* (Avery, 2000), by Ying Chang Compestine, a native of the People's Republic of China.

In both Asian cooking and Western-style fare, green tea is a vibrant, innovative and versatile ingredient. Also, the sweet yet astringent taste of green tea adds a subtle flavor to dishes that cannot be easily duplicated with any other ingredient. This is particularly true in mild soups where the unique qualities of green tea can be more easily experienced.

For those who want to use as much green tea as possible, adding it to food can greatly increase one's daily intake. Green tea is most commonly used in cooking as a concentrated liquid or a dry, herblike seasoning.

GREEN TEA BASICS

When using green tea as a cooking liquid, follow the simple directions for Concentrated Green Tea (below). This makes a concentrated green liquid with a powerful flavor that is excellent in sauces, salad dressings and soups. Any leftover infused tea can be stored in the refrigerator for later use.

When using tea leaves dry as an herblike seasoning, you may use bulk leaves or the ground tea in tea bags. If you're using tea bags, cut open the tea bags and remove the contents, discarding the empty tea bags. Two tea bags contain about ¹⁄₂ tablespoon of loose tea. The tea is gently heated in oil in a saucepan, skillet or wok until the tea releases its fragrance.

Concentrated Green Tea

The most common way to include this medicinal Japanese food in cooking is by adding a concentrated brewed green tea as a stock in sauces and soups.

2 to 4 green tea bags
1 cup (235 ml) boiling water

1. Place the tea bags in a pot. Immediately pour the boiling water over the tea bags and let them steep for 2 to 3 minutes. Remove the tea bags.

2. Leftover brewed tea can be stored in the refrigerator for about 1 week.

MAKES 1 CUP (235 ML)

Preparation time: 1 minute plus steeping time

Green Tea–Miso Soup

This hardy medicinal soup combines three of the world's healthiest foods: green tea, shiitake, and soybeans (tofu and miso). Loaded with antioxidants, isoflavones and a plethora of nutrients, this miso soup is a traditional power breakfast.

1 teaspoon vegetable oil, such as canola or safflower oil
1 onion, thinly sliced into half moons
Pinch of sea salt
5 cups (1.25 liters) Concentrated Green Tea (see opposite)
4 dried shiitake mushrooms
1 carrot, thinly sliced
5 oz (150 g) fresh tofu, cut into $1/2$-in (1 cm) cubes
2 cups (100 g) watercress or baby spinach, sliced into $1^1/2$-in (4-cm) lengths
3 to 4 tablespoons miso, or to taste
1 to 2 green onions (scallions), very thinly sliced on the diagonal, for garnish

1. In a saucepan, heat the oil over medium heat, add the onion and salt, and sauté for 3 minutes, or until the onion becomes translucent.

2. Add the brewed tea and dried shiitake and bring to a boil. Lower the heat and simmer, covered, for 20 minutes. Remove the shiitake mushrooms and cut off and discard the stems. Thinly slice the caps and return them to the pot.

3. Add the carrots and simmer for about 8 minutes.

4. Add the tofu and simmer for 2 minutes, then add the watercress and simmer 1 minute more. Remove from the heat.

5. Ladle a little hot stock into a small bowl, add the miso and stir until it dissolves. Add the dissolved miso to the soup.

6. Serve with a garnish of sliced green onion.

SERVES 3 TO 4

Preparation time: 10 minutes
Cooking time: 35 to 40 minutes

Green Tea–Basil Sauce

This attractive, creamy sauce is easy to prepare and can be used in several ways. If used without thickening, it makes an excellent salad dressing and dipping sauce for raw foods. Adding a little thickener transforms it into a delicious sauce for tofu, white fish and grains.

$^1/_2$ cup (125 ml) Concentrated Green Tea (see page 216)
2 tablespoons sweet or mellow miso
1 to 2 tablespoons brown rice syrup, or to taste
2 tablespoons brown rice vinegar
2 tablespoons toasted sesame oil
$^1/_2$ cup (35 g) fresh basil leaves, chopped
2 cloves garlic, minced
$^1/_4$ teaspoon freshly ground white pepper
2 teaspoons crushed kuzu starch or 1 tablespoon arrowroot

1. Combine all the ingredients except the kuzu or arrowroot in a blender and process until smooth. It is now ready to use as salad dressing or as a dipping sauce for raw foods.

2. To make a sauce for cooked foods place the green tea–basil mixture in a saucepan. Add 1 tablespoon of kozu or arrowroot, bring to a simmer, and stir constantly until thick. Continue to simmer gently for 1 minute.

MAKES ABOUT 1 CUP (235 ML)

Preparation time: 10 minutes
Cooking time: 5 minutes

Green Tea–Fried Rice with Mushrooms and Ginger

Delicious and satisfying, this dish is my favorite way to use leftover cooked rice. The fresh ginger is a perfect complement to the aromatic tea leaves.

$1^1/_2$ tablespoons toasted sesame oil
1 tablespoon loose green tea (approximately 4 tea bags)
4 fresh shiitake mushroom caps or other variety of mushroom, rinsed and sliced
1 carrot, cut into thin matchsticks
Scant pinch of sea salt
1 tablespoon mirin
4 green onions (scallions), sliced into $^1/_2$-in (1.3-cm) lengths
2 teaspoons shoyu (Japanese soy sauce)
$^3/_4$-in (2-cm) section fresh ginger, peeled and minced
2 cups (400 g) cooked brown or white rice

1. Heat the oil in a skillet over medium heat. Add the tea and gently heat for 15 seconds, or until the tea releases its fragrance.

2. Add the mushrooms, then the carrot and toss in the salt. Add the mirin and cook for 1 minute.

3. Add the green onions and cook for 3 to 5 minutes. The carrots should still be a little crunchy, but not raw tasting.

4. Lower the heat and stir in 1 teaspoon of the shoyu and the ginger. Add the rice, breaking up clumps with the side of a wooden spoon. Sprinkle the remaining 1 teaspoon of shoyu over the rice. Mix thoroughly, cover and cook 1 to 2 minutes more.

SERVES 2

Preparation time: 10 minutes
Cooking time: 10 minutes

Cha Soba with Sesame Vinaigrette

Cha (green tea) soba is made by adding green tea powder to a blend of buckwheat and wheat flour when making the noodle dough. The result is a delicate noodle with a light green color and distinctive, aromatic flavor that is especially delicious served chilled in salads and in the traditional Japanese dish that we simply call Summer Soba (page 134). This simple yet satisfying dish is perfect when you are in a hurry. For a complete meal, it goes very well with grilled seafood and steamed greens.

4 tablespoons sesame seeds
8 oz (225 g) dried cha soba noodles
$1^1/_2$ tablespoons brown rice vinegar
1 tablespoon shoyu (Japanese soy sauce)
2 teaspoons toasted sesame oil
4 tablespoons very thinly sliced green onions (scallions)

1. Toast the sesame seeds in a dry skillet over medium-high heat for 1 to 2 minutes, or until they become fragrant. Immediately pour them into a small bowl to prevent them from scorching.

2. In a large saucepan, bring 8 cups (2 liters) of water to a rolling boil and add the noodles. To prevent them from sticking together, stir until the water returns to a boil. Cook for 5 to 6 minutes, or until just tender. Immediately drain the noodles and plunge them into a cold water bath. Set aside.

3. In the bowl you will use to serve the noodles, whisk together the vinegar, shoyu and oil.

4. Drain the noodles well, then add them to the serving bowl with the vinaigrette. Add the green onions and toss.

5. Add the toasted sesame seeds and toss again. If time allows, let the noodles sit for about 20 minutes to heighten the flavors.

SERVES 4 AS A SIDE DISH

Preparation time: 10 minutes
Cooking time: 15 minutes

ACKNOWLEDGMENTS

This book would not have been written or even imagined without the efforts of hundreds of natural foods pioneers who created the interest and markets for high quality Japanese natural foods. Jan and I are particularly indebted to the early Zen and macrobiotic movements that created the opportunity for companies such as Erewhon, Eden, Oak Feed, Essene, Westbrae, Natural Import Company, Tree of Life, Great Eastern Sun, Granum, Clearspring, Natural Lifestyles, Gold Mine, Edwards & Sons and others to begin importing and distributing traditional Japanese foods. Without the great efforts of these companies and people, these foods would never have become so popular and well known in the West. In this regard we would like to acknowledge the outstanding achievements of Michio and Aveline Kushi, the founders of Erewhon and the leaders of the international macrobiotic movement. We want to recognize the significant influence of Bill Shurtleff and Akiko Aoyagi who began introducing foods from Japan to the West over thirty years ago. Their books about miso, tofu and kudzu have been an inspiration to us.

We would especially like to thank Takamichi and Itsuko Onozaki and family for sharing their home and centuries-old knowledge of Japanese miso craftsmanship. Their adventurous yet traditional spirit as well as their example and teachings has had a profound impact on our lives since our meeting in 1979. We also want to thank Akiyoshi Kazama, founder of Mitoku Company, in Tokyo, Japan's largest exporter of traditionally crafted Japanese foods, for maintaining the highest quality standards and for introducing us to Mr. Onozaki. We would also like to express our appreciation to Yuko Okada, one of the founders of Muso Company in Osaka, Japan, international supplier of excellent traditional Japanese foods.

This book would not have been written if it were not for our opportunity to be part of the conception, founding and building of the American Miso Company in Rutherfordton, North Carolina. Natural foods businessman and macrobiotic advocate Sandy Pukel, of Miami, Florida, spearheaded the project of making miso in the United States. Jan and I are grateful for the profound influence he has had on our personal lives. We also want to give special thanks and appreciation to Barry Evans, who has been successful in keeping American Miso Company and Great Eastern Sun going for over twenty-five years. These two companies continue to have an impact on the distribution and availability of quality Japanese foods in the United States and Canada.

Some of the information we have gathered was provided by Mitoku Company and their staff and suppliers. We are particularly indebted to Christopher Dawson, who is now the CEO of Clearspring, in London, and who spent many years at Mitoku. Christopher gave us with a great deal of information about the history and craft of making traditional Japanese foods. We are also very grateful to Tomoko Katagiri, of Mitoku, who has translated Japanese texts and contacted Japanese food experts on our behalf.

Jan and I are also grateful for the culinary expertise of award-winning chef John Belleme, Jr., Chef-Partner of Gotham City Restaurant in Delray Beach, Florida. He was a great source of creative ideas for blending Japanese and Western ingredients in delicious and unique recipes.

I would personally like to thank my long-time friend Lyle Lansdell for sharing with me her passion for natural foods almost forty years ago. Lyle was my first cooking teacher and her love of food had a profoundly positive impact on my life. I am grateful for the help and encouragement of my friend Bill Grier who spent many hours editing my early attempts at food writing. Another person I would like to thank is Jim Mijanovich, M. D., my friend and spiritual mentor, whose patience is second only to Mother Theresa's.

We would like to thank all those on the staff of Tuttle Publishing Company, especially Edward Walters, Publishing Director, and Holly Jennings, our editor, for her patience, encouragement and editorial expertise. Finally, thanks to our agent Bob Silverstein for his support of this project.

We are very fortunate that all of the traditional Japanese foods included in this book are now available in most natural foods stores and food co-ops, and, increasingly, in conventional grocery stores in the United States, Canada and Europe. In the United States, if your local natural foods store does not have some of these foods, ask them to order them for you from United Natural Foods Inc., the wholesale distributor that delivers to just about every natural foods store in the United States. In addition to United Natural Foods, Inc., many of the suppliers listed below sell directly to retailers. In some cases high-quality Japanese foods can be found in Asian markets in the West, but again, read labels carefully.

If you are having trouble finding a Japanese food at the brick-and-mortar stores near you, try the mail order companies listed below. They are excellent sources for the products discussed in this book. Please call one or more and request a catalog. Some of these companies offer online shopping.

Choice Organic Teas/Granum, Inc.
2414 SW Andover St.
Bldg. C-100
Seattle, WA 98106
Phone: 206-525-0051
Fax: 206-523-9750
Web: www.choiceorganics.com

Clearspring Ltd.
19A Acton Park Estate
London, W3 7QE
United Kingdom
Phone: +44-20-8749-1781
Fax: +44-20-8811-8893
Web: www.clearspring.co.uk

Discount Natural Foods
14 Londonderry Turnpike #10
Hooksett, NH 03106
Phone: 888-392-9237
Fax: 603-232-1356
Web: www.discountnaturalfoods.com

Eden Foods Inc.
701 Tecumseh Road
Clinton, MI 49236
Phone: 888-424-3336
Fax: 517-456-7854
Web: www.edenfoods.com

Gold Mine Natural Foods
7805 Arjons Drive
San Diego, CA 92126
Phone: 800-475-3663
Fax: 858-695-0811
Web: www.goldminenaturalfoods.com

Great Eastern Sun
92 McIntosh Road
Asheville, NC 28806
Phone: 800-334-5809
Web: www.great-eastern-sun.com

The Kushi Store
P.O. Box 500
Becket, MA 01223-0500
Phone: 800-645-8744
Fax: 413-623-2315
Web: www.kushistore.com

Natural Import Company
9 Reed Street Suite A
Biltmore Village, NC 28803
Phone: 800-324-1878
Fax: 828-277-8892
Web: www.naturalimport.com

Natural Lifestyle Mail-Order Market
16 Lookout Drive
Asheville, NC 28804-3330
Phone: 800-752-2775
Fax: 828-253-7537
Web: www.natural-lifestyle.com

Amazake (rice milk). A sweetener or refreshing drink made from cooked sweet rice and koji starter that has fermented into a thick liquid. Also spelled *amasake*.

Arame. A mild-tasting sea vegetable that is similar to hijiki. Arame is a brown algae that grows in deep waters. Rich in iron, calcium and other minerals, arame is often cooked with sweet root vegetables and served as a side dish.

Aspergillus. A genus of molds used to inoculate beans and grains to make koji, *Aspergillus* is the starter for many Japanese fermented foods.

Azuki beans. Small, dark red beans. Especially good when cooked with kombu and winter squash. Also spelled *adzuki* or *aduki*.

Bancha tea. Japan's coarse summer tea leaves that are sold as lower-quality green tea.

Bifun noodles. Light, transparent noodles made from rice flour and potato starch.

Burdock. A hardy plant that grows wild and is cultivated throughout the United States, as well as in Japan. The long, dark burdock root is delicious in soups, stews and vegetable dishes. It is highly valued in macrobiotic diets for its strengthening qualities. Burdock's Japanese name is *gobo*.

Cha. The Japanese word for tea.

Cha-no-yu. The Zen Buddhist tea ceremony.

Daikon. A long, white radish. Daikon helps dissolve stagnant fat deposits that have accumulated in the body. Freshly grated raw daikon is especially helpful in the digestion of oily foods.

Dashi. An all-purpose broth usually made with kombu and flavored with dried shiitake or bonito flakes.

Eritadenine. A substance found in shiitake that lowers blood cholesterol.

Fu. A dried wheat-gluten product. Available in thin sheets or thick round cakes, fu is a satisfying high-protein food used in soups, stews and vegetable dishes.

Gyokuro. Japan's rarest, most expensive tea, Gyokuro is made from the tender first tea leaves of spring.

Hijiki. A dark brown sea vegetable that turns black when dried, hijiki has a spaghetti-like consistency. It is stronger tasting than arame and is very high in calcium, iron and protein. Also spelled *hiziki*.

Hojicha tea. A Japanese tea made from roasted coarse leaves and stems.

Japanese chile (togarashi). Small, hot, red Japanese chile available in supermarkets and Asian food stores. It is most often sold in whole dried form or as dried flakes.

Kaiseki. A traditional Japanese meal consisting of a series of small, seasonal dishes, each resembling an appetizer both in size and beauty of presentation. Natural, hand-crafted serving ware is carefully chosen to complement the season, the food and the food's arrangement. Like the tea ceremony, kaiseki was initially a formal, highly refined, spiritual discipline marked by the Zen ideals of simplicity, harmony and restraint.

Koji. Grains or beans inoculated with *Aspergillus* mold and used as a starter for most Japanese fermented foods, including miso, tamari, shoyu, amazake, mirin and rice vinegar.

Kombu. A wide, thick, dark green sea vegetable that is rich in minerals. Kombu is often cooked with beans and vegetables. A single piece may be used two or three times to flavor a soup stock.

Kori dofu. Tofu that has been dehydrated by a natural freezing and drying process. Also called snow-dried tofu.

Koya dofu. A form of snow-dried tofu that has been dehydrated in a heated shed.

Kukicha tea. A Japanese tea made from roasted tea twigs and stems.

Kuro-su. The Japanese name for brown rice vinegar. Kuro-su is valued for its high concentration of essential amino acids, medicinal qualities and mellow taste.

Kuzu. A white starch made from the root of the wild kuzu plant. In the United States, the plant densely populates the southern states, where it is known as kudzu. Kuzu root powder is used in making soups, sauces, desserts and medicinal beverages.

Matcha. The jade green powdered tea used in the Japanese tea ceremony.

Mirin. Sweet rice wine traditionally made by a complex distillation and double-fermentation process. Used in cooking as a high-quality sweetener and seasoning.

Miso. A protein-rich, fermented bean paste made from soybeans, usually with the addition of barley or brown or white rice. Miso is used in soup stocks and as a seasoning.

Mizu ame (sweet water). *See* Rice malt syrup.

Mochi. A heavy rice cake or dumpling made from cooked, pounded sweet rice. Mochi is especially good for lactating mothers, as it promotes the production of breast milk. Mochi can be made at home or purchased ready-made.

Moromi. The thick slurry of fermenting koji and other ingredients that forms during the brewing process of soy sauce, sake and mirin.

Mugwort. A mineral-rich herb that is dried and used as a medicinal tea. Dried, ground mugwort is also added to mochi and soba noodles.

Muro. A uniquely constructed room used to incubate koji.

Nigari. The traditional Japanese tofu coagulant, nigari is extracted from dehydrated sea water.

Nori. Thin sheets of dried sea vegetable. Nori is often roasted over a flame until its color turns from black or purple to green. It is used as a garnish, wrapped around rice balls or other foods, or cooked with tamari as a condiment. It is rich in vitamin B-1, B-2, C and D.

Nori-maki. Vinegared rice that is rolled with vegetables, fish or pickles, then wrapped in nori, and sliced into rounds. The most healthful sushi is made with brown rice and other natural ingredients.

O-cha. The Japanese word for tea, o-cha is also used to designate a tea break.

O-hagi. Mochi that has been formed into small flat cakes or balls, then coated with pureed azuki beans or chestnuts, roasted and ground nuts or sesame seeds, or soybean flour.

Okeyasan. Name for Japanese carpenters who specialize in making and repairing traditional wooden vats and barrels..

O-toso. A medicinal drink made by infusing a combination of herbs in mirin. O-toso is traditionally drunk on New Year's Day.

Rice malt syrup. A natural, high-quality sweetener made from malted barley or koji, rice and water.

Sake. Fermented rice wine made from koji and rice. Sake is usually served warm in small cups but can be served at room temperature or chilled. Also used as a seasoning in Asian cooking.

Sashimi. Raw, slivered fish, usually served with a dip made of shoyu and wasabi.

Sencha. High quality Japanese green tea made from young, tender leaves.

Shiitake. Cultivated medicinal mushrooms grown on hardwood logs or enriched sawdust.

Shochu. A concentrated distilled alcoholic drink.

Shoyu. Fermented soy sauce made with cultured wheat and soybeans, water and sea salt.

Soba. Noodles made from buckwheat flour or a combination of buckwheat and wheat flour. Some varieties contain other ingredients such as dried mugwort powder, mountain yam flour or powdered green tea.

Somen. Very thin Japanese wheat noodles.

Suribachi. A special serrated, glazed clay bowl. Used with a pestle called a *surikogi*, the suribachi is used for grinding and pureeing foods. An essential item in the macrobiotic kitchen, the suribachi can be used in a variety of ways to make condiments, spreads, dressings, baby foods, nut butters and medicinal preparations.

Tahini. A nut butter that is obtained by grinding white sesame seeds until smooth and creamy. It is used like sesame butter.

Tamari. A wheat-free fermented soy sauce made with cultured soybeans, water and sea salt.

Tempura. A method of cooking in which vegetables, fish or seafood are coated with batter and deep-fried in vegetable oil. Tempura is often served with soup, rice or noodles, and pickles.

Te-uchi udon and soba. Handmade Japanese noodles.

Tofu. Soybean curd made from soybeans and nigari. Used in soups, vegetable dishes, dressings, etc., tofu is high in protein, low in fat, and cholesterol-free. *See* also Kori-dofu.

Udon. Japanese noodles made from wheat, whole wheat or whole wheat and unbleached flour.

Umeboshi. Tart, salty Japanese pickled plums, which stimulate the appetite and digestion, and aid in maintaining an alkaline blood quality. Shiso leaves impart a reddish color and natural flavoring to the plums during pickling. Umeboshi can be used whole or in the form of paste.

Wakame. A long, thin brown sea vegetable used in a variety of dishes. High in protein, iron and manganese, wakame has a sweet taste and a delicate texture. It is especially good in miso soup.

Wasabi. A light green Japanese root that has been dried, powdered and made into a paste. It is traditionally used as a seasoning in sushi, sashimi and in dipping sauces. Wasabi is very hot with a taste reminiscent of horseradish.